Environmental and Property Protection in Europe

Europa Law Publishing, Groningen 2016

Environmental and Property Protection in Europe

Edited by Gerd Winter

The Avosetta Series (12)

Proceedings of the Avosetta Group of European Environmental Lawyers

Europa Law Publishing is a publishing company specializing in European Union law, international trade law, public international law, environmental law and comparative national law.
For further information please contact Europa Law Publishing via email: info@europalawpublishing.com or visit our website at: www.europalawpublishing.com.

Typeset in Scala and Scala Sans, Graphic design by G2K Designers, Groningen/Amsterdam

NUR 828
ISBN 978-90-8952-167-5 (paper)
ISBN 978-90-8952-168-2 (ebook)

The Avosetta Series publishes texts that present innovative discourse on European Environmental Law.

Authors

Alexandra Aragão, PhD in Public Environmental Law, is Professor of Environmental Law at the Faculty of Law of the University of Coimbra, and vice director of the Portuguese Review on urban, planning and environmental law. She is member of research groups in the field of environmental law, nature conservation, international law and sociology of law. Her recent publications include: Transboundary nature conservation. Are there no boundaries within the Natura 2000 network? (Born, C-H co-editor, [2014] *The Habitats Directive in its EU Environmental Context: European Nature's best hope?* London: Routledge-Earthscan); Red Ecológica y Servicios de los Ecosistemas (González Ríos, I. (coordinator) [2015] *Estudios jurídicos hispano-lusos de los servicios en red (energía, telecomunicaciones y transportes) y su incidencia en los espacios naturales protegidos.* Madrid: Dykinson); Les intérêts diffus, instruments pour la justice et la démocratie environnementale (Camproux-Duffrène, M. P. and Sohnle, Jochen (director), [forthcoming] *La représentation de la Nature devant le juge: Approches comparative et prospective.* Strasburg: Université de Strasbourg/SFDE). See further https://apps.uc.pt/mypage/faculty/aaragao/pt/publicacoes_internacionais.

Gyula Bándi, DSc. is a Jean Monnet Professor of EU Environmental Law, Director of the Jean Monnet Centre of Excellence and also of the Doctoral School of the Pázmány Péter Catholi University, Faculty of Law in Budapest. He has also been active in various form of environmental practice – as a private lawyer or as the President of the National Environmental Council in the period of 2014-16. His three recent publications are: Környezetjog (Environmental Law), Hungarian book, Szent István Társulat, Budapest, 2014; Bándi Gyula, Szabó Marcel, Szalai Ákos: Sustainability, Law and Public Choice, Groningen: Europa Law Publishing, 2014; Bándi Gyula (ed.): Environmental Democracy and Law, Groningen: Europa Law Publishing, 2014. See further publications under: https://jak.ppke.hu/en/teaching/faculty-members-and-researchers/bandi-gyula-32ef4.

Mariusz Baran, Dr. iur., Legal Counsel, is a researcher in the Department of Environmental Law at the Jagiellonian University in Krakow. He is author of scientific papers in the field of European Union law and environmental law, scholar of the National Science Centre in Krakow and winner of the national award for the best doctoral dissertation in the field of legal sciences. His recent publications include: 'Application of European Union Law on an ex office basis by the national courts', Warsaw 2014; 'Transformations in the legal system of forms of the public administration acclivities', (in :) R. Hauser, Z. Niewiadomski, A. Wróbel (eds.) The System of Administrative Law, Vol. 3 'Europeanisation of Administrative Law', Warsaw 2014 and 'The provisions of EU environmental law and the reconstruction of the pattern legality of administrative decisions on matters of environmental protection (selected issues)', Wrocław 2015. For further information see: http://www.law.uj.edu.pl/~kpos/site/pliki/wykaz_publikacji_MB.pdf.

Mery Ciacci holds a PhD in International and European Law from the European University Institute (Florence, Italy) and is research assistant at the University of Siena (Italy). She also serves as legal adviser for the Italian Ministry of Environment, Land and Sea. Her main research areas encompass International and EU Environmental Law, Biodiversity Law, Sustainable Development, Cultural Heritage Law, Cultural Diversity, and EU external relations law. Her most recent research project explores the link between culture, environment and development, and this interaction with international and EU law. She has published in these fields. She is also a member of the Environmental Legal Team (ELT – www.elt.unisi.it), a University-based research and consultancy team of lawyers based at the University of Siena. Previously, she has served as legal and policy adviser for the Italian National Commission for UNESCO (Rome) and the BRESCE (UNESCO Regional Office in Europe, Venice).

Ole Kristian Fauchald is Professor at the Faculty of Law, University of Oslo and Research Professor at the Fridtjof Nansen Institute. His fields of research are international investment law, international and domestic environmental law, and international trade law. Currently, he is coordinating research on investment tribunals at PluriCourts – Centre of Excellence on The Legitimate Roles of the Judiciary in the Global Order. His recent publications include: World Peace through World Trade? The Role of Dispute Settlement in the WTO, in C.M. Bailliet and K.M. Larsen (eds.) Promoting Peace through International Law, Oxford: OUP, 2015, pp. 189–206; Fauchald, Gulbrandsen and Zachrisson: Internationalization of Protected Areas in Norway and Sweden: Examining Pathways of Influence in Similar Countries, in International Journal of Biodiversity Science, Ecosystem Services and Management, 10:3 (2014), pp. 240–252; and Regulating Environmental Impacts of Mining in Norway, in Nordic Environmental Law Journal, 1/2014 s. 53–65. For further publications, see http://www.jus.uio.no/ior/english/people/aca/olefa/publications.html.

Matthieu Galey is a Doctor in Public Law. His PhD thesis is entitled: 'The Legal Forms of Environmental Protection in English Law: Property, Public Power and Environment in a Common Law Context'. After working as a litigation lawyer for the French ministry of overseas territories, he has been admitted to the bar of Paris. He teaches comparative land law at the University of Paris-Est Créteil as well as constitutional and administrative law at the University of Cergy-Pontoise. His publications include : 'Genèse de l'Etat et droit des sols: l'empreinte de la dynamique institutionnelle sur la formalisation juridique de la propriété', *Revue Internationale de Droit Comparé,* septembre 2004 ; 'La typologie des systèmes de propriété de C.R. Noyes: un outil d'évaluation contextualisée des régimes de propriété commune, privée et publique', in C. Eberhard (dir.), *Law, Land Use and the Environment: Afro-Indian Dialogues,* Institut Français de Pondichéry, 2007; 'Gestion patrimoniale et éthique de surintendance (*stewardship*): Parentés, complémentarités, inadéquations' in C. Eberhard (dir.), *Traduire nos responsabilités planétaires, recomposer nos paysages juridiques*, Bruylant, 2008.

Jakub Hanák, PhD, is Assistant Professor of Environmental and Land Law at the Masaryk university in Brno. His recent publications include eg. 'Experts and expert's opinion in expropriation procedure. Acta iuridica olomucensia, 2014, vol. 9, No 5, p. 67-76.' See further (http://www.muni.cz/people/108169/publications).

Barbara Iwańska, an Associate Professor of Legal Sciences, specialized in Environmental Protection Law, is a researcher in the Department of Environmental Law at the Jagiellonian University in Krakow. She authored or co-authored scientific papers in the field of environmental law, public administrative law and medical law. She is a member of the Scientific Council of the Tatra National Park and the Avosetta Group. Her recent publications include: 'The Europeanisation of Environmental Law (Selected issues)' (in:) R. Hauser, Z. Niewiadomski, A. Wróbel (eds.), The System of Administrative Law, Vol. 3 'Europeanisation of Administrative Law', Warsaw 2014, pp. 709-741; The Protection of Biodiversity and Ecological Connectivity in Poland, (in): Toward the Protection of Biodiversity and Ecological Connectivity in Multi-Layered Systems, M. Alberton (ed.), Nomos Publishing, 2013, Baden Baden, Germany, pp. 127-166. For further information see: http://www.law.uj.edu.pl/~kpos/site/pliki/BI-spis_publikacji.pdf

Jan H. Jans is Professor of Administrative Law and Vice-Dean at the Law Faculty of the University of Groningen. He has published widely on Public Law, Constitutional Law, Environmental Law, European Law, European Public Law. His book 'European Environmental Law' – now in its 4th edition – is generally regarded as one of the leading publications on European environmental law. He is also Deputy Judge of the District Court Noord Nederland and member of the Netherlands Commission for Environmental Assessment.

Ilona Jancarova, doc. JUDr., Ph.D., is Associate Professor at the Masaryk University in Brno, Czech Republic. She is the head of the Department of Environmental Law and she is also acting as a legal advisor in the field of environmental law and land law. As a member of the Legislative and Appellate Commmissions of the Czech minister of the environment she participates in drafting of environmental acts and she is involved in decision-making procedures as the consultant. Her recent publications include: Jančářová, Ilona. Komparace vybraných aspektů správního a soudního trestání. Acta Universitatis Carolinae, Iuridica, Praha: Univerzita Karlova v Praze, 2015, roč. 2015, č. 1, s. 57-72; Jančářová, Ilona. Current Trends in the Czech Environmental Liability System. In Damohorský, M., Stejskal, V.: Environmental Law in the Czech Republic and EU – Ten years after. 1. vyd. Beroun: Nakladatelství Eva Rozkotová, 2014. s. 9-17, 9 s. The Czech Society for Environmental Law; Jančářová, Ilona, Milan Pekárek, Ivana

Průchová, Lenka Bahýľová a Vojtěch Vomáčka. Odpovědnost v právu životního prostředí – současný stav a perspektivy. 1. vyd. Brno: Masarykova univerzita, 2013. 345 s. Spisy Právnické fakulty MU č. 461 (řada teoretická). See further http://is.muni.cz/osoba/1514#publikace.

Rajko Knez, Dr. iur., is full Professor at the Faculty of Law University of Maribor, primarily covering *European Union Law* (the internal market and EU system of legal remedies), and *Environmental Protection Law.* He accomplished education in Slovenia and additional educations at the University in Graz (Austria), the University of Amsterdam (The Netherlands), the Faculty of Law in Bonn (Germany), at the attorney's offices in Washington and Richmond (USA), at the Court of Justice of the EU in Luxemburg (Luxemburg). He also acts as visiting professor at faculties of law in Vienna-Juridikum (A), Graz (A), Zagreb (CRO). Currently he holds UM Jean Monnet Centre of Excellence (Environmental law). His publication list is available here: http://izumbib.izum.si/bibliografije/Y20150721070647-14452.html.

Luc Lavrysen, Ph.D, LL.M, is Professor of Environmental Law and Director of the Centre for Environmental and Energy Law of Ghent University, Belgium. He is a judge in the Belgian Constitutional Court in Brussels and President of the EU Forum of Judges for the Environment. His recent publications include 'Justice Constitutionnelle et Natura 2000' in Natura 2000 et le juge : situation en Belgique et dans l'Union Européenne/ Natura 2000 and the Judge : Situation in Belgium and in the European Union (Brussels Bruylant – Groupe Larcier, 2014)and 'Constitutional Review of European Environmental Law' in National Courts and EU Environmental Law(Groningen, Europa Law Publishing, 2013). See further: https://www.ugent.be/re/epir/en/researchgroups/public-law/department/environmental-law/llavrysen.htm.

Žaneta Mikosa, LLM, PhD Scholar/Research Fellow in the Faculty of Law of the Copenhagen University and lecturer of EU Environmental Law in the Riga Graduate School of Law. Since 2000 she was working as legal adviser and later Parliamentary secretary in the Ministry of Environmental Protection and Regional Development in Latvia. During the Latvian Presidency of the EU Council she was the main responsible person for the Presidency issues being as deputy state secretary in the Ministry (2014 /2015). See further in web: http://www.rgsl.edu.lv/en/inside-rgsl/who/faculty/?i=156.

Massimiliano Montini is Associate Professor of European Union Law at the University of Siena (Italy). He teaches EU Law and Sustainable Development Law. His main research areas cover International and EU Environmental Law, Climate Change and Sustainable Development Law, Energy Law. He has widely published in these areas. He is Founder and Director of the Environmental Legal Team (ELT – www.elt.unisi.it), a University-based research and consultancy team of lawyers based at the University of Siena. Moreover, he is Co-Director of the R4S (Regulation for Sustainability – www.r4s.unisi.it), an Interdisciplinary Research Group of the University of Siena.

Lana Ofak, Ph.D., is an Assistant Professor at the Faculty of Law, University of Zagreb, Croatia where she teaches Administrative Law, Administrative Procedural Law and Environmental Law. She has been involved as a lecturer in training programs in the field of environmental law for lawyers, judges, journalists, civil servants in municipal governments and members of the environmental non-governmental organizations from Croatia and the neighbouring countries. For the list of her publications see: http://www.pravo.unizg.hr/en/lana.ofak.

Annalies Outhuijse, LLM, is, as of October 2015, a PhD fellow at the Department of Administrative Law at the University of Groningen. Under the supervision of Prof Dr J.H. Jans and Prof Dr H.H.B. Vedder, her PhD research focuses on the functioning of dispute settlement procedures and the public enforcement of competition law in the Netherlands. Next to her undergraduate and LLM studies, she was a research and teaching assistant at the same department since April 2012. Both in collaboration with Prof Dr J.H. Jans and independently she has carried out multiple studies and published articles amongst others on the subject of Dutch competition law. The topics of her research included the relationship between the decisions taken by the Netherlands competition authority and the recommendations of its advisory committee, the appraisal of these decisions by the court of first instance and the differences between judgments of the administrative and civil courts in competition law cases. Ms Outhuijse taught tutorials in the second year LLB course 'Administrative law'. This course, for international students, discusses which effect European Union rules have on the administrative law systems of the EU Member States. In 2015 she completed her study years with an LLM in Dutch Law specialisation Constitutional and Administrative Law (*summa cum laude*) and the LLM Research Master (*cum laude*).

Peter Pagh, Dr. iur., is Professor of EU Environmental Law at the University of Copenhagen. He is chief editor of the Danish Legal Magazine on Environmental Case Law and has published more than 300 articles on environmental law in Danish and international legal magazines. His recent publications include the books 'Real estate – regulation and purchasing' (Danish title: Fast ejendom – regulering og køb, 2013), 'Succession in liability regarding polluted sites' (Danish title: Ansvarssuccession ved forurenende ejendomme, 2014) and an article on the Air Frame Directive commenting case C-404/13 and the united cases C-401-403/12 P (TfM 2015.56). See further: https://curis.ku.dk:8015/admin/workspace/personal/family/publication/filter/personal/ (website referring to publication list).

Eloise Scotford, Dr. iur.,is Senior Lecturer in Environmental Law at The Dickson Poon School of Law, King's College London. She researches in all areas of environmental law, focusing currently on climate change law, access to environmental information, waste law and the legal roles of environmental principles. She has co-authored a leading UK environment law textbook with Professor Liz Fisher and Dr Bettina Lange – *Environmental Law: Text, Cases and Materials* (OUP 2013) – and has also done work with the UK government on reforming UK environmental legislation (see E Scotford & J Robinson, 'UK Environmental Legislation and its Administration in 2013: Achievement, Challenges and Prospects' (2013) Journal of Environmental Law 389). See further www.kcl.ac.uk/law/people/academic/escotford.aspx.

Agustin Garcia-Ureta, LL.M (Exeter), Ph.D (Exeter) is Professor of Administrative Law at the university of the Basque Country, Bilbao. His recent publications include 'Directive 2014/52 on the assessment of environmental effects of projects: new words or more stringent obligations?' (2015) *Environmental Liability* 239-255; 'Instruments for sites active management of Natura 2000: balancing between stakeholders and nature conservation?' in Hubert-Born, C., *The Habitats Directive After 20 Years: European Nature's Best Hope?* (Routledge, 2015) 71-92 (with Lazkano. I.); and 'The Role of Law in Protecting Wilderness in Spain', in Bastmeijer, K., (ed.), *The Role of International, European and National Law in Protecting Wilderness in Europe*, Cambridge University Press, (forthcoming). See further www.ehu.es/garcia-ureta.

Vojtech Vomacka, Ph.D., is an Assistant of Judge at the Supreme Administrative Court of the Czech Republic and assistant professor in the field of Environmental Law and Policy at Masaryk University. Recently, he joined the Czech Judicial Academy as a lecturer. He focuses on environmental impact assessment, animal protection and common market.

Bernhard Wegener, Dr. iur., M.A. (Bruges), is Professor of Public and European Law at the university of Erlangen-Nuremberg. His recent publications include 'Europäische Querschnittpolitiken', Enzyklopädie Europarecht Bd. 8 (ed.) 2014; 'Aktuelle Fragen der Umweltinformationsfreiheit', NVwZ 2015, 609 ff.; 'Die Aarhus-Konvention in der Rechtsprechung des EuGH', EurUP 2014, 226 ff. See further http://www.oer2.jura.uni-erlangen.de/lehrstuhlinhaber/index.shtml.

Gerd Winter, Dr. iur., Dr. iur. h.c. (Luzern), Lic. rer. soc., is professor of public law and the sociology of law at the university of Bremen. He in 1995 founded the Forschungsstelle für Europäisches Umweltrecht (FEU) and has since been its director or co-director. He has consulted on administrative and environmental law development i.a. in Georgia. His recent publications include (ed. with E. Chege Kamau and P.-T. Stoll) Research and Development on Genetic Resources. Public Domain Approaches in Implementing the Nagoya Protocol, Routlege

2015; Ecological proportionality: an emerging principle of law for nature?, in: Voigt, Christina (ed.), Rule of Law for Nature. Cambridge University Press 2013: 111 – 129. See further http://www-user.uni-bremen.de/~gwinter/veroeffchronol.html.

PART I

Property and Environmental Protection

An Overview

Gerd Winter

1. General Reflections on Private Property*

Some general reflections may be appropriate when considering the role of private property in a sectoral area such as the utilization of natural resources. They deal with the basic reasons for why private property should be guaranteed at all, the political source constituting private property, the institutional level on which property is protected, and the method and benefit of comparing concepts of property.

1.1 Reasons for a Property Guarantee

The major reasons justifying private property have comprehensively been treated by John Locke. For Locke the appropriation of an asset such as a piece of land is legitimate if meant to secure the life of an individual (need-based approach). In addition, those objects that have been created by the work of an individual are legitimately his/her own (labour-based approach). While need and labour appear as excluding possessions beyond need and acquired other than by labour Locke acknowledges that possessions may be acquired by paying money as well as by letting employees do the work.[1] This means that the investment of capital and hired labour is a third ground to legitimise private property.[2]

In a functional perspective private property has been grounded on that it indirectly contributes to society's general welfare. Egoistic aims, it is supposed, serve collective goals.[3]

While these grounds are based on an individualist concept of society commons theory like K. Marx'[4] and E. Ostrom's[5] contest the indirect benefits of private property and rather expect welfare to be reached by common property or strict regulation.

These different framings are not purely academic but have played a role in deciding concrete questions. For instance, the question if there is private prop-

* I am grateful to Eloise Scotford for her helpful comments to an earlier draft.

1 J. Locke, Two treatises of government, ed. by P. Laslett, Cambridge Univ. Press 2nd ed. 1967, Second Treatise ch. 124.

2 C. B. Macpherson, The political theory of possessive individualism. Hobbes to Locke, Clarendon Press 1964.

3 B. Mandeville, The fable of the bees, or private vices public benefits (1714); A. Smith, An inquiry into the nature and causes of the wealth of nations (1775), Book 1 Ch. 1. Hardin, G., The tragedy of the Commons, Science, New Series, Vol. 162, No. 3859 (Dec. 13, 1968), pp. 1243-1248. A variant of this approach is system's theory which conceives the property guarantee as stabilizing the autonomous functioning of the economic subsystem. See N. Luhmann, Grundrechte als Institution, Duncker & Humblot, Berlin 1965, pp. 127 et seq.

4 K. Marx, Capital. A Critique of Political Economy (1867) vol. 1 ch. 24 (available at https://www.marxists.org/archive/marx/works/download/pdf/Capital-Volume-I.pdf).

5 E. Ostrom, Governing the commons : the evolution of institutions for collective action, 22. print. Cambridge Univ. Press, 2008.

erty in a social right or – in the environmental context – in environmental subsidies and permits might be dependent on whether the labour theory of property is applied (then, there cannot be property because the subsidy is a public gift) or whether the functional theory is favoured (then there can be a right as long as the activity induced by the subsidy is beneficial for society). Likewise, the labour and functional theory may react differently to the question whether the business of a craftsman deserves more property protection than that of a multinational enterprise. When it comes to pollution of *de facto* commons such as air and water there is of course a difference between individualist and commons theory the latter pleading in favour of stringent public regulation[6] and even of framing such commons as public property.[7]

In view of environmental concerns a more general perspective on property may need to be taken. While property has traditionally been conceived as a structure of relations between human beings the growing scarcity and fragility of natural resources suggest to more fundamentally build nature concerns into property concepts, and that into both the individual and the collective variant. Property may have to be construed not as a thing *'proprius'* (own) or *'Eigen-tum'* entailing free and exclusive rights to use, destroy and dispose the asset, but rather as a 'lease' or *'Leihe'* (*mutuum*) from nature allowing to harvest its yield within margins of reproduction and obliging to preserve it for subsequent users.

1.2 Institutions Determining Property Concepts

Who determines the scope and content of private property would be another general question. Is private property a fundamental 'pre-state' institution of natural law, is it the outcome of societal discourses and subsequent political decisions, or is it emerging from reasoned weighing of private and public interests? In the first case the concept is 'given' and only to be reconstructed by the polity and the courts, in the second it is a 'decision' of the polity and its changing majorities, and in the third it is professional legal reasoning by the courts. The concept of natural right was proclaimed in the French revolution and codified in Art. 544 Code Civil, although its 'absolute' character has much been adjusted to public interests by subsequent regulation and court jurisprudence.[8] The polity approach has been advocated by the German Federal Constitutional Court (BVerfG). The court frames it as a power of the legislator to determine the content and limits of the property guarantee (*Inhalts- und Schrankenbestimmung des Eigentums*). The legislator is however not absolutely free but must ensure that the possession of private property is an option in social life. This is called the guarantee of property as an institu-

6 It should be noted that even Hardin in his famous article (above fn. 3) pleaded in favour of stringent regulation insofar as common goods 'cannot be fenced.'

7 See on related concepts of the different European states M. Montini/ M. Ciacci, Ch. Common Goods.

8 U. Mattei, Basic Principles of Property Law. A Comparative Legal and Economic Introduction, Greenwood Press 2000, pp. 13-18.

tion (*Institutsgarantie*).[9] The concept appears to have been followed by the Polish Constitutional Court.[10] The legal reasoning approach is characteristic in the common law countries where the courts basically weigh up individual and public interests according to their own discretion (to be sure being bound by stare decisis and good reason).[11] The court based approach is also reflected in the conceptions of the Court of Justice of the European Union (CJEU) and the European Court of Human Rights (ECtHR), which advocate the balancing of property positions and public interests.[12] Often they refer to wide discretionary powers of the government, thus building a bridge to the polity concept.

1.3 Multilevel Property Protection

A third general problem is the role of property protection in a multilevel perspective. The property guarantee can be framed on the level of normal law, such as by the courts in common law systems. In an increasing number of countries it has however been established on the hierarchically superior level of constitutional law. In addition, property has been enshrined in international conventions such as the European Convention of Human Rights (ECHR) which is accepted as directly applicable and of supreme value by some contracting states. We must therefore be clear about the level of law when we analyse property issues, and in particular, when compensation claims for governmental encroachments on property are considered: When the normal law is examined the question can be whether a legal system has a general (judge made) rule of compensation for governmental interventions, or if such rules may only be found in existing statutory legal acts. In contrast, if constitutional law is examined one would inquire if the constitutional guarantee must be understood as setting aside a law refusing compensation where it should provide for that, and even creating a right of compensation in such situation contra legem. As the wardens of the higher levels are higher level (constitutional and international) courts the realm of the polity is confined, unless the courts themselves grant the legislator a broad margin of discretion.

9 See G. Winter, Ch. Germany, sec. G.

10 See B. Iwanska/ M. Baran, Chapter Poland, sec. G.

11 See E. Scotford, Chapter UK. It can be argued, though, that the extensive regulation of private land in a modern administrative state amounts to a form of common law property, which is partly determined by the land use policies of the government of the day. See E. Scotford and R. Walsh, The Symbiosis of Property and English Environmental Law – Property Rights in a Public Law Context' (2013) 76(6) MLR 1010.

12 See further J. H. Jans/ A. Outhuijse, Chapter CJEU, sec. D. 1 and B. Wegener, Chapter ECtHR, sec. C. 1. a).

1.4 Comparing Property Protection

Why should we present and compare different regimes of property in relation to environmental protection? First of all, it of course is of interest for lawyers practicing in the transnational sphere to know the specific brand of the national or international system within which he or she is acting. More importantly, however, national and international courts mutually observe each other's legal principles in order to learn when construing their own. This has been most obvious (and was recognized by treaty law[13]) in the bottom-up way taken by the CJEU when establishing basic rights at the level of primary law. But such mutual learning is also happening in the horizontal dimension between national courts as well as in the vertical dimension – top down – between the CJEU and the ECtHR on the one side and national courts on the other. By these tokens a European *ius commune* might evolve.

In this perspective a summary report should not list all details of the legal systems. Rather, only significant differences and convergences shall be highlighted. In doing this a functional perspective should be applied: Rather than only comparing structures functions should be identified and examined as to how different legal constructs fulfil the functions. In this way it can (and will often) be the case that two very diverging constructs are nevertheless functionally equivalent. For instance, while indirect expropriation may be classified as one subcategory of expropriation in one legal system, it may be regarded as a separate category in the another, both of them however having the same effect, namely to trigger compensation.

A workable structure of analysis would be to distinguish between the scope of property, the intensity of protection, different kinds of interventions, and the respective preconditions and consequences attached to these interventions. It must however be kept in mind that the four steps of analysis are closely interrelated. For instance, the scope of property is intricately linked to the obligation to compensate an encroachment. The broader the scope the more restrictive the preconditions of compensation must be expected to be, and vice versa. For instance, if market opportunities are included in the scope of property , one can expect that only in extreme cases of full loss of market access an (indirect) expropriation will be acknowledged as given.

2. Private Property, Public Property, Common Good

Private property is a basic category of liberal societies. The individual is construed as proprietor of assets entailing the exclusive right to use, pledge, trade and dispose them. Even in liberal states the state (including central, regional and local authorities) can also own private property such as land, buildings and various equipment. It is then – as a *fiscus*, as it is called in

[13] Art. 6 sec. 2 TEU of 1992; Art. 6 sec. 3 TEU of 2007.

some jurisdictions – subject to private and public law like any other proprietor.[14] In addition, however, special rights and duties may be imposed to the extent the assets provide a public service or must specially be protected in the public interest. This is the case for exploitable goods such as minerals, for public infrastructure like roads, and – increasingly – for life sustaining natural resources such as forests and waters.

Some legal systems, such as the Italian and the Hungarian, have established the category of public property for this purpose. This category entails prerogatives and duties of management and preservation in the public interest.[15] With regard to natural resources some jurisdictions have created specific legal constructs such as 'national asset', 'common heritage', 'common good', etc. that also indicate and entail special duties of management and protection.[16]

3. Private Property in Private and Public Law

Private property is of importance both in private and public law. In private law the object of property normally is real things, immovable and movable. While also other assets may be framed as exclusive rights, such as a personality right or a patent right, prompting economists to also call them property rights, they are commonly not classified as property in private law. This is due to the diverging contractual and non-contractual rights and duties attached to the different categories of exclusive rights.

The rights and duties attached to private property may vary depending on whether the actor encroaching on the property is a private person or an administrative body. Civil law systems construe rights and duties between the owner of private property and administrative bodies as special remedies of administrative law, while common law systems, still based on Dicey's denial of differences between private and administrative actors, apply the same remedies in both relationships.[17] For instance, the rules on contract, nuisance, torts etc. apply indistinctly in common law systems, while in civil law systems a special form of administrative contract, injunction in case of encroachment, liability for unlawful and even for lawful administrative action, and tort liability for administrative negligence have emerged. However, the systems somewhat converge because when administrative bodies are involved common law does acknowledge special concerns while, vice versa, civil law does partially apply general principles of private law. Thus, in functional terms, both systems subject administrative bodies to some special regime that on the one hand concedes certain preroga-

[14] See, for instance, Z. Mikosa, Ch. Latvia, sec. J, on the applicability of environmental law to the municipal waste disposal site.

[15] M. Montini, Ch. Italy, sec. D.G. Bandi, Ch. Hungary sec. E, citing Art. 38 of the Fundamental Law.

[16] See for a cross-country analysis M., Montini/ M. Ciacci, Ch. Common Goods.

[17] For an in-depth and critical analysis of the common law approach see C. Harlow, R. Rawlings, Law and Administration, Cambridge University Press 2006, pp. 7-9, 39-45.

tives required in the public interest and on the other hand erects barriers controlling public power.

4. Constitutionalising Private Property

The protective content of property in public law is in liberal societies taken so seriously that it is framed as a property guarantee of constitutional importance. In common law systems, that guarantee is construed as an interpretive principle underlying rights of the proprietor in relation to the government, including, notably, the presumption of compensation in case of expropriation. In most civil law systems, the property guarantee was established as part of the written constitution. This means in many countries that it has a higher status than ordinary law nullifying the latter in cases of breach. Those countries, like the Netherlands, which do not recognize the higher status of the property guarantee have accepted it by dint of the European Convention of Human Rights.[18] In addition, it has to be noted that the right to property as developed by the CJEU and codified in Art. 17 ChFR is binding on the Member States insofar as they implement EU law.[19] This obligation has somewhat confined the scope of Art. 345 TFEU which reserves the property guarantee to the discretion of the Member States. One concrete problem arising from this tension is what authority actually determines the regulatory encroachment on a citizen's property and is thus liable to pay compensation if the pertinent preconditions are given: the EU by its regulation or directive, or the Member State by its implementing measures.[20]

5. The Objects of Property

The scope of objects of property is in most reported legal system broader in public law than in private law. While private law property is commonly confined to material things[21], public law property usually extends to more assets such as an existent contractual or tort liability claim, a concession based on administrative law, a vested interest in using a public good, a right to

18 See J. H. Jans/ A. Outhuijse, Ch. The Netherlands, sec. A. .On the case law of the European Court of Human Rights (ECtHR) see the analysis of B. Wegener, Ch. ECtHR.

19 See analysis of case law by J. H. Jans/ A. Outhuijse, Ch. CJEU, sec. A and C.

20 See J. Jans/ A. Outhuijse, Ch. CJEU, sec. C. For an in-depth analysis focussing on nature protection law, see A. Garcia Ureta, Ch. Nature Protection. Court cases related to the EU emissions trading directive and its compatibility with the property guarantee are reported by L. Lavrysen, Ch. Belgium, sec. L, and G. Winter, Ch. Germany, sec. L.

21 See however for intangible objects as property object in France M. Galey, Ch. France, sec. A,; in Croatia L. Ofak, Ch. Croatia, sec. A, in Latvia Z. Mikosa, Ch. Latvia, sec. A, and in Norway O. Fauchald, Ch. Norway, sec. A.

a pension payment, etc.[22] The reason for this difference of scope might be that the state has broader powers and means to intervene than a private person, so that a more comprehensive concept of property is needed. Another reason could be that the doctrinal sophistication of interrelations between asset owners and encroachers is more advanced in private than in public law.

Looking at property in natural resources it must be noted that many of them are not subject to property at all. The atmosphere, the air, the outer space, the sea, the wind, radio waves, the genetic resources, wild animals, for instance, are not owned by anybody. They have been considered to be *res nullius*.[23] While this remains a precise category if viewed from the legal construct of property, the increasing exploration and exploitation of those resources have prompted legal systems to embed *res nullius naturae* in a conglomerate of powers and duties of management and preservation in the public interest which have been labelled as common good, commons, heritage, patrimony, *domanialité publique, öffentliche Sache*, etc.[24] Confusingly, these notions can also reach into private and public property and make them bound to public interests.

Natural resources other than *res nullius* are subject to property. Many of them can be private property and are as such subject to environmental protection regulation. A major object of private property is land.[25] According to all reported legal systems land property includes plants, the soil, and the underground. Wild animals are a free good until appropriation by the hunter. Differences exist as to the extension to minerals and other underground resources: In rare cases the minerals and groundwater belong to the landowner.[26] Often a horizontal layer is drawn with resources above belonging to the landowner and below to the state, regions, municipalities or society as a whole.[27] Other systems draw the line resource-wise allocating some resources (such as gravel and sand) to the land owner and others (such as metals, oil and coal) to the public sphere.[28] The air column above a real estate is rather conceived as a free good, although a layer close to the ground may be considered to belonging to the land.

---

22 See L. Lavrysen, Ch. Belgium, citing ECtHR (Depalle v France) of 29 March 2010, Appl. No 34044/02, no. 62. See further B. Wegener, Ch. ECtHR, sec. C.

23 For Belgium see L. Lavrysen, Ch. Belgium, sec. A/B. If deer is kept in closed preserves it may be considered property of the breeder, see for Czechia I. Jancarova, J. Hanak, V. Vomacka, Ch. Czechia, sec.A, citing a constitutional court judgement..

24 See e.g. I. Jancarova, J. Hanak, V. Vomacka, Ch. Czechia, sec.A.; M. Galey, Ch. France, sec. D.

25 The former socialist countries in Europe have all given up their earlier policy that land should in principle belong to the state or sub-state collectives. See the country reports on Czechia, Hungary, Poland and Latvia.

26 This is the case in Latvia. The landowner must however obtain a permit of exploitation under certain circumstances. See Z. Mikosa, Ch. Latvia, sec B.

27 See for the French example M. Galey, Ch. France, sec. B.

28 See for an elaborate system in Norway see O. Fauchald, Ch. Norway, sec. A.

6. Property as Opponent and as Defender of Environmental Protection

The most common way to look at private property in relation to environmental protection is to see both as opposing each other, such as, for instance, if a farmer is asked to reduce the application of agrochemicals for reasons of protection of groundwater and biodiversity, or if the operator of an industrial installation is commanded to reduce the emission of air polluting substances. This common conflict will be the focus of the remainder of this report. It should however be noted that private property may not only be an opponent to but also a defender of environmental protection.[29] For instance, the owner of land in the vicinity of a dangerous installation may claim more protection against noxious emissions, by filing action under private law against the polluter or action under administrative law against the supervisory authority.[30] If the pollution is caused by public infrastructure, the land owner may bring a nuisance action against the responsible administrative body.[31] The same can be done by a private trust or NGO that buys land in order to protect its biodiversity.[32]

To put it shortly, in the first setting the conflict is between property used for economic purposes and environmental protection, while in the second setting it is the conflict between property used/ asking for environmental protection and economic activities (be it of private parties or the state).

The picture becomes more complicated if conflicts between different environmental goods are included in the analysis. Thus, a farmer producing biomass as a renewable energy source may conflict with regulation protecting biodiversity.

Table 1 summarizes the three constellations of conflict between property use and regulatory aims.

---

29 These uses of property are dealt with in Rajko Knez, Ch. Property in defense of environmental protection. See also the comparative analysis of B. Pozzo, Property rights in the defense of nature, in: B. Pozzo (ed.) Property and environment, Stämpfli Publ. 2007, pp. 3-61. For the related case law of the ECtHR see B. Wegener, Ch. ECtHR, sec. C.2. As J. H. Jans/ A. Outhuijse, Ch. CJEU, sec. D. 2. note, jurisdiction of the CJEU is still scarce in this regard.

30 For an example of the variety of remedies available in defense of environmental protection see I. Jancarova, J. Hanak, V. Vomacka, Ch. Czechia, sec.C.

31 This would be the normal nuisance action in common law systems, while civil law systems have special remedies under administrative law such as the French action for 'dommage de travaux publics', see M. Galey, Ch. France, sec. I.

32 For examples in that regard see M. Galey, Ch. France, sec C., and G. Winter, Ch. Germany, sec. C.

Table 1: Conflicts between property and regulation

regulatory aims ↓ / property use →	economic	environment
economic	[e.g. competition law]	industrial property vs pollution regulation (classical case)
environment	houseowner vs industry	biomass vs biodiversity (new case)

7. The Scope of Private Property in Relation to Environmental Protection

Environmental protection measures often encroach upon private business. This raises the question if business is considered a private property. The answer is: not in every respect. All reported legal systems including also EU law and the ECHR exclude from the protected scope mere market opportunities. For instance, the sales quantity of a product that due to costly and price driving environmental regulation may have decreased is not protected as property. Differences exist as to whether the entirety of a business amounts to property. A legal system may tend to only recognize the real substratum of the business, such as the land, buildings and machinery, as property[33], while other systems may include the business know how and good will.[34] In the context of ICSID arbitration the functional equivalent of property is the investment. It is remarkable how easily property protection concepts have been transferred to investment. The scope of protected assets has even been extended to market opportunities.[35]

Permits allowing the emission of polluting substances are as such not considered as property by any of the reported legal systems, nor by the EU and ECHR jurisprudence.[36] This does not exclude that legitimate expectations are protected. For instance, a lawful permit cannot be withdrawn without compensation, except if the holder has disregarded conditions attached to the permit. Even if the permit is unlawful its removal is excluded or must be compensated if the holder *bona fide* trusted in its legality.[37] In fact, the ECtHR has sometimes

33 See for Germany G. Winter, Ch. Germany, sec. A.

34 Thus the ECtHR jurisdiction, see B. Wegener, Ch. ECtHR, sec. A.

35 See further O. Fauchald, Ch. Arbitration, sec. 2.

36 As an example see I. Jancarova, J. Hanak, V. Vomacka, Ch. Czechia, sec.B.

37 For details see the provisions of the Administrative Procedure Acts of several reported countries on the withdrawal and revocation of lawful and unlawful administrative acts, as, for instance, the Latvian (Z.

considered legitimate expectations as a property right *per se*[38], but this is rarely found in domestic law.[39] A permit can however be part of a real property if it was put into practice e.g. through the construction and operation of the authorized factory. Then the authorization is protected together with the real asset. For instance, when operators of cement producing installations were by EU based MS legislation forced to obtain and surrender CO2 emission allowances, they argued that their IPPC permit embraced the right to emit CO2 and that the removal of this right was an expropriation. The German Federal Administrative Court (BVerwG) however rejected this allegation arguing that the IPPC permit was part of the entire business ('*Gewerbebetrieb*') including the installation and its operation, and that its modification did not expropriate the business but rather regulated its use.[40]

Other than simple permits concessions to exploit natural resources are in many legal systems considered as property.[41] This may be the case because a concession is issued on the ground that the project may have negative environmental impacts which are accepted in view of its benefits.

Subsidies for economic or environmental purposes are commonly not regarded as property. They are rather considered as governmental gifts, a perception that can be explained by the labour theory of property.[42] Other forms of legal protection are however available to protect statutory entitlements, even if they fall short of constituting property in a legal sense. A recurrent example is the cutting back or withdrawal of guaranteed feed-in tariffs for electricity from renewable sources. First of all, the general rules of administrative law apply. In particular, based on the principle of legitimate expectations, the grant of a subsidy may only be revoked and the money reclaimed if the grant was unlawful, or if the recipient breached the conditions of subsidy use. Further, if the time period for recurrent subsidy payments was defined and the recipient set up an undertaking legitimately trusting in the perseverance of the scheme, the subsidy cannot easily be terminated.[43] This situation is even considered as a property position in some legal systems, such as Czechia.[44] However, that posi-

Mikosa, Ch. Latvia, sec. I).

38 ECtHR (Pine Valley Developments Ltd v Ireland) of 29 November 1991 (Appl. no 12742/87). See for a related judgement of the Croatian Constitutional Court L. Ofak, Ch. Croatia, sec. C fn. 7.

39 For an example see I. Jankarova, J. Hanak, V. Vomacka, Ch. Czechia, sec. B.

40 BVerwGE 124, 47 et seq. (127); similar the Belgian Constitutional Court in its judgement case n° 92/2006, 7 June 2006 (nv Cockerill Sambre and sa Arcelor), cited by L. Lavrysen, Ch. Belgium, sec. L fn. 49.

41 See, e.g., for France M. Galey, Ch. France, sec. B; for Norway O. Fauchald, Ch. Norway, sec. A citing a related Supreme Court case.

42 Based on the personality theory subsidies for small family based business would qualify as property.

43 See Scotford, Ch. UK, sec. C, citing R (Bancoult) v Secretary of State for Foreign and Commonwealth Affairs [2009] 1 AC 453.

44 I. Jancarova, J. Hanak, V. Vomacka, Ch. Czechia, sec.A. To some extent also Denmark, see P. Pagh, Ch. Denmark, sec. D. In contrast, the freedom of policy change without compensation duty is stressed by French courts, see M. Galey, Ch. France, sec. E.

tion can nevertheless be restricted and possibly removed, as will be discussed in section 10 below.

Traditional and consolidated uses of possessions or vested rights are in some states considered as property.[45] For instance, the establishment of protected areas may be regarded as indirect expropriation of property if encroaching on long practiced agricultural uses.[46]

8. Self-Binding Obligations as Property Content

Even if an asset falls in the scope of property in a particular legal system, the owner may nevertheless not be guaranteed to enjoy its fullest use. The scope and nature of property protection also varies within and across legal cultures. Qualifications on the use of property are sometimes expressed in the relevant provision of the constitution. For instance, Art. 14 para 2 of the German Constitution says: 'Property obliges. Its use should also serve public welfare.'[47] Similarly Art. 48 para 2 of the Croation constitution formulates: 'Ownership shall imply obligations. Holders of the right of ownership and its users shall contribute to the general welfare.'[48] Art. 66 of the Portuguese Constitution specifies these obligations in relation to the environment: 'Everyone has the right to a healthy and ecologically balanced human living environment and the duty to defend it'.[49] This constitutes a self-restriction of the proprietor. Within the margin of that self-restriction, legal and governmental regulation is not even categorized as a genuine restriction of an established right but rather as a reiteration of what the proprietor is constitutionally expected to do by herself.

In addition, basic obligations of property holders are sometimes laid down in laws called basic or organic, which set a framework for further legislation and executive regulation. An example is the Portuguese 'Law on the public policy for soils, setting the framework for land use planning and urbanism' that lays down citizens' duties such as 'to use the territory and the natural resources in a sustainable and rational way, to respect the environment, cultural heritage and landscape, to use correctly the public domain goods, public infrastructures, urban services, equipment, green spaces or other spaces for collective use; and to refrain from performing any acts or from developing any activities which pose a danger to them.'[50] One can interpret these basic obligations to shape or construct property in land, rather than to restrict it.

---

45 See e.g. A. Garcia Ureta, Ch. Spain, sec. G.

46 See further sec. 10.3 below.

47 Remarkably the provision does not say „property is bound' but „binds' which means that there is not only a duty to tolerate governmental interventions but an active duty to use one's property for societal purposes.

48 L. Ofak, Ch. Croatia, sec. G.

49 Emphasis added. See further A. Aragao, Ch. Portugal, sec. B.

50 A. Aragao, Ch. Portugal, sec. D.

Courts have also contributed to develop basic principles of property self-obligation. For instance, the German Federal Court of Justice (BGH) has in relation to uses for agricultural and development purposes proposed the concept of 'situational binding'. If the situation of the real estate is characterised by the presence of valuable biodiversity, the land is 'bound' not to be used for more profitable uses. Such use potential does not form part of the property and must not be compensated in case of protective environmental regulation.[51] Generalising this approach one may argue that natural cycles demand a 'contribution' from those who make use of them so that there is no property used purely for industrialised agriculture, in other words for farming methods that take the land for nothing but as a tool for maximal yield.[52] However, that principle of adaptation to natural cycles should not be overdrawn in order to prevent counterproductive effects such as if farmers willfully hinder the growing of valuable nature in order to prevent stricter nature protection.[53]

A special problem of proprietors' bondage is liability for environmental damage on his/her own land. In many legal systems a principle applies stipulating that the landowner is liable for cleaning up his/her polluted land.[54] The principle stems from general police power law where it is assumed that he who governs an asset is responsible for its safety. It has become problematic in cases where the damage is large and the landowner did not cause it. Many legal systems still apply this principle, at least as a secondary resort if the actual polluter is not available anymore.[55] Some however discharge the innocuous landowner and put the burden on the public budget.[56]

9. Regulation of Property Uses

Beyond constitutional and framework legal principles, property owners' use of property can be restricted by state regulation. There is a vast practice of regulation of property uses that does not entail compensation. Such 'normal' regulation is also called police power in some jurisdictions[57], a term that is somewhat misleading because the concept of police power emerged in

[51] BGHZ 60, 124 (134). For a similar argument see the Portuguese Supreme Administrative Court, cases 996/06 of 20 June 2013 and 412/10 of 28 September 2010, viz A Aragao, Ch. Portugal, sec. B fn 4..

[52] G. Winter, Property rights and nature conservation, in: Ch.-H. Born e.a. (eds.) The Habitats Directive in its EU environmental law context, Oxon: Routledge 2015, 215-228, at 224.

[53] See for the example of payments for damage caused by wild animals Z. Mikosa, Ch. Latvia, sec. E, citing a Constitutional Court case on damage to a fish farm from herons.

[54] See answers to question J in the national reports.

[55] See e.g. for Italy M. Montini, Ch. Italy, sec. J; for Norway O. Fauchald, Ch. Norway, sec. J, citing a Supreme Court case on the extension of the proprietor's liability to its mother company.

[56] Thus, for instance, Denmark, see P. Pagh, Ch. Denmark, sec. E., citing a Supreme Court judgment on the clean-up of an oil-polluted site.

[57] The term is also used in the context of transnational arbitration, see O. Fauchald, Ch. Arbitration.

times when state intervention was to be restricted to cases of danger for public safety, i.e. cases where the predicted damage is large and imminent or highly probable. Modern regulation, at least that of environmental protection, must however also allow for precautionary measures, i.e. measures in situations where the damage is medium or creeping and the probability is low or uncertain.

Many states and the EU as well the ECHR require that regulatory interventions into property positions must be based on a parliamentary law, pursue a public interest, and respect the principle of proportionality.[58] There are variations to this principle. Some legal systems, mostly those with directly elected presidents like the French, acknowledge a genuine power of the executive to make rules in policy fields that are not reserved for parliamentary legislation.[59] By contrast, other countries, mostly parliamentary democracies stipulate that whenever the executive regulates a matter in a way encroaching on basic rights, it must have a legal basis (reservation of law, *Gesetzesvorbehalt*). Some constitutions, such as the German, even require that the law must lay down the content, purpose and scope of the delegation and decide on the essential issues at stake.[60]

The courts, when assessing the executive's power in regulating property rights, often concede that the legislator and the regulator enjoy a broad margin of political discretion in determining the public interest and applying the principle of proportionality.[61] This is sometimes motivated by a general culture of judicial self-restraint in political matters such as in UK law, or by a reluctance of courts to tamper with scientific and technical issues, or by acknowledging the democratic legitimation of the legislator, including also its delegation of powers to the executive.

---

58 For the EU see Art. 52 paragraph 1 which reads: 'Any limitation on the exercise of the rights and freedoms recognised by this Charter must be provided for by law and respect the essence of those rights and freedoms. Subject to the principle of proportionality, limitations may be made only if they are necessary and genuinely meet objectives of general interest recognised by the Union or the need to protect the rights and freedoms of others.' For the ECHR see B. Wegener, Ch. ECtHR, sec. C. 1 b).

59 Art. 37 of the French Constitution. However, according to Art. 34 paragraph 3 the determination of the fundamental principles of environmental preservation and of property belong to the realm of laws and must thus be based on a parliamentary law. The governmental powers are thus restricted in these realms.

60 Art. 80 *Grundgesetz* and case law of the BVerfG such as in BVerfG 49, 89 (127). These requirements have been taken up for inclusion in Art. 290 para 2 TFEU which reads: 'The objectives, content, scope and duration of the delegation of power shall be explicitly defined in the legislative acts. The essential elements of an area shall be reserved for the legislative act and accordingly shall not be the subject of a delegation of power.' It must however be kept in mind that there are still areas of EU law-making for which the Council and thus the executive is the legislator. In the environmental sector this concerns provisions primarily of a fiscal nature and measures affecting quantitative water management, land-use and energy sources and supply (Art. 192 paragraph 2).

61 See for the ECtHR case law B. Wegener, Ch. ECtHR, sec. C. 1. For a national example see P. Pagh, Ch. Denmark, sec. C.

Jurisdictions vary as to the diversity of sectoral environmental laws and regulations specifying the environmental protection goals and instruments.[62]

In several legal systems the environmental protection interest legitimizing the regulation of property use is framed as a constitutional obligation. This can be in the form of a human right to environmental protection[63], or of an 'objective' obligation of the state[64] which may constitute the environment/ natural resources as a common good, patrimony, public trust, or else.[65]

It should also be kept in mind that, as suggested in Section 6 above, the legislative and regulatory measures affecting private property may partly be considered not as intervention into predetermined property positions but as expression and concretization of the social bonds that are intrinsic to the very notion of property.

10. The Taking of Property

The taking of property is a form of property-related regulation that, for its interventionist weightiness, is subjected to additional requirements. 'Taking' is the core of what has traditionally been called expropriation. An analysis must distinguish between the definition or characterization of takings and the preconditions and effects they must respect/provide in order to be legally acceptable.

10.1 Characterization of Taking

The characteristic of a taking is that a property position is taken away from the owner. A clear case is the complete removal from the property holder of civil law property (eg in land), of a right under the law of obligations, of a concession and of a right to subsidy (if regarded as property). Less clear but also regarded as a taking is the compulsory establishment of a servitude or other real obligation.

Legal systems diverge or are undecided if the taking must include the transfer of the property position to a beneficiary, be it a public authority or a third person acting in the public interest. If a transfer is not required, the dissolution of a right also qualifies as a taking. The German BVerfG, following its narrow construction of taking, tends to advocate the first position, thus broadening the

---

62 See for an example of high specificity and diversity B. Iwanska/ M. Baran, Ch. Poland sec. A.

63 See for a strong example G. Bandi, Ch. Hungary sec. A, citing Arts. 18 and 70/D of the Hungarian Constitution. Most importantly, a subjective right to environmental protection (albeit of the individual, not the public at large) was also developed by the ECtHR, see B. Wegener, Ch. ECtHR, sec. B and D.

64 Such as in Art. 37 ChFR. J. Jans, Ch. CJEU, sec. B, critically characterises the environmental protection obligation to be weaker than the tight to property.

65 See further the cross-country report of M. Montini, Ch. Common Goods.

discretionary powers of the legislature to determine the content and limits of the property guarantee.[66]

Legal systems also diverge as to whether property owned by public bodies are also protected by the constitutional taking's guarantee. Some treat them just as private owners, others conceive basic rights including the property guarantee as rights of citizens against the state, not of state bodies against other state bodies.[67]

10.2 Preconditions and Effects of Lawful Taking

If a measure qualifies as a taking (or expropriation in the narrow sense), it must respect certain preconditions in order to be lawful. If the preconditions are not met, the measure is unlawful. Appropriate judicial review may be available for applications to annul the relevant individual or regulatory or even legislative act. If in the course of unlawful expropriation damage has been caused, compensation can be claimed based on pertinent general rules on compensation for unlawful governmental action.[68]

The preconditions of a lawful taking of property are similar in all reported jurisdictions. They include that the taking must be made by individual act based on a law, it must serve a public interest, and compensation must be provided. Some jurisdictions, such as the German[69], also accept expropriations self-executed by a legal act.

Legal systems diverge as to whether the public interest may be framed in general terms or must be specified by law, and if the public interest must be qualified or can reflect any political priority. Some countries have adopted a cross-sectoral expropriation law in which the allowable reasons for expropriation are specified.[70] In other countries, expropriation powers are spread over various sectoral laws such as construction laws, nature protection laws, etc.[71] Concerning the qualification of the public interest some jurisdictions stipulate that the

---

66 G. Winter, Ch. Germany, sec. F. Likewise the jurisdiction of the Belgian Constitutional Court, L. Lavrysen, Ch. Belgium, sec. E.

67 See for the first variant L. Lavrysen, Ch. Belgium, sec. E.

68 See chapters of the national reports sec. I.

69 G. Winter, Ch. Germany sec. F.

70 See e.g. J. Ofak, Ch. Croatia, sec. F. The Croatian Expropriation Act, for instance, lists certain infrastructure projects, constructions for public uses and minerals exploitation as grounds for expropriation, but not environmental protection. Contrastingly the expropriation laws of Czechia and Hungary do allow expropriation for environmental protection objectives, see I. Jankarova, J. Hanak, V. Vomacka, ch. Czechia sec. F, and G. Bandi, Ch. Hungary, sec. F.

71 See e.g. B. Iwanska, M. Baran, Ch. Poland, sec. F, citing as an example the Polish Real Property Management Act..

same must be imperative and overriding[72], which may have to be established by an analysis of the costs and benefits of the project requiring expropriation.[73]

As for the degree of compensation, some legal systems provide full compensation, for instance the market value of the expropriated asset, while others provide some flexibility taking into account the intensity of protection and the importance of the public interest.

11. Onerous Restrictions of Property Uses (Indirect Expropriation, Conditioned Content Determination)

11.1 Categorizing Use Restrictions

The taking of property is commonly distinguished from restrictions of property uses, which are often allowable forms of regulation, as discussed in section 8 above. However, most legal orders acknowledge that some restrictions on use can be so harsh that they equal the full taking of property. This is sometimes called 'de facto expropriation', but I believe inappropriately so, because in the normal case the de facto restrictions do have a basis in legal acts. Neither is 'regulatory expropriation' a better characterization because also the taking of property can be based on regulation. 'Indirect expropriation' better points to the fact that the direct regulation of uses indirectly challenges the substance of the property right at issue.

Some jurisdictions categorize indirect expropriation as a subcategory of expropriation besides direct expropriation (or taking).[74] This causes a problem if the constitution provides full compensation for expropriation because in that case also indirect expropriation must be compensated in full. The other option – to categorize it as a separate rule – allows for more flexibility, or, more particularly, a weighing up of the severity of impact and the amount of compensation. It appears that this second form of legal control is found in the majority of reported states.

In Germany, a different approach to restrictions with compensation has been developed based on the above-mentioned theory of legislative determination of the content and limits of property ('content determination'). Traditionally, the German civil courts had adopted the concept of indirect expropriation, although differingly calling it 'expropriating encroachment' (*enteignender Eingriff*). The concept was called reversion theory (*Umschlagtheorie*), indicating that at some point of increasing encroachment, the normal regulation reverses into a to-be-

[72] See BVerfG concerning the construction of a cable car connecting a city with a nearby mountain for touristic reasons. The court denied the overriding character of this public interest.

[73] See for the French déclaration d'utilité publique M. Galey, Ch. France, sec. E, and for the Italian dichiarazione di public utilità M. Montini, Ch. Italy, sec. F.

[74] ECtHR appl. 12033/86 (Fredin), no. 42.

compensated regulation. The BVerfG[75] rejected this approach drawing a clear line between expropriation in the narrow sense of taking and 'content determination' as the remainder of the regulatory realm. It thus advocates a dualist approach, not the triple approach of normal regulation, direct and indirect expropriation. The major reason for rejecting the reversion theory was its implication that the courts interfere with the realm of the legislator by subjecting its policy to compensation claims. It should be the legislator who decides whether burdens caused by a political measure should be compensated or not.

The BVerfG nevertheless posits that the legislator is not without constitutional limits when exerting its discretion, the major yardstick being the proportionality principle. Most importantly in the present context, a regulation may disrupt a property position so gravely that the proportionality principle requires compensation. Such a proposition is similar to that within the concept of indirect expropriation; it was therefore labelled as 'content determination stipulating compensation' (*entschädigungspflichtige Inhaltsbestimmung*). The BVerfG concept is somewhat more flexible because monetary compensation is only one variant of command of proportionality others being alternative means mitigating or alleviating the burden.[76] I submit that both, 'indirect expropriation' and 'content determination stipulating compensation' should be put together under the notion of onerous restriction of property.

11.2 Characterization

As with direct expropriation, the characterization of a measure as an onerous use restriction should be distinguished from the preconditions and effects it must respect/provide. The characterization should discriminate into two directions: direct expropriation on the one side and normal use restrictions on the other. In distinction from direct expropriation, indirect expropriation is, as already said, concerned with use restrictions rather than the removal of property. In distinction from normal use restrictions indirect expropriation presupposes that certain criteria are fulfilled. These criteria are very diverse and controversial. Three criteria are outstanding: gravity of impact, sacrifice for the common good, and importance of the public interest. Table 2 is an attempt to compare the three categories of encroachment on private property.

75 BVerfGE 58, 300 et seq.

76 See BVerfGE 100, 226 (245) concerning a case of monument conservation where the court said that the authorities need to test various possibilities of alleviating the burden of the proprietor.

Table 2: Categories, qualification and preconditions of regulation of property

categories	qualification	preconditions/effects
normal regulation	restriction of property uses	legal basis, proportionality, public interest
taking (= expropriation in the narrow sense)	removal of property	legal basis, high public interest requiring expropriation, full compensation
onerous use restriction (= indirect expropriation, content determination)	grave/unequal/unbalanced restriction of property uses	legal basis, public interest, proportionality, variable compensation

II.2.1 Gravity of Impact

One criterion advocated by many jurisdictions is the gravity of impact of the use restriction. If the use of the property (considering the scope and intensity of protection) becomes utterly unprofitable the core precondition of indirect expropriation is fulfilled. The wording describing this threshold differs in various jurisdictions, including, for instance, deprivation of all usefulness of the property asset,[77] loss of control or use of the investment[78], etc. Of course, there is leeway of the courts to assess the facts of the case, whether the impact actually is so harsh as alleged, etc. In the Netherlands, for instance, the courts have until now never accepted claims for compensation for reasons of serious restrictions of property use.[79] The ECtHR too advocates a very narrow concept of compensable property uses. In Pine Valley[80] a construction permission for industrial and office development was issued but later nullified for breach of land-use planning provisions. The court found that while this is interference with possessions, it is neither direct nor de facto expropriation given the fact that the proprietor is still able to use the property for agricultural purposes or sell it, even if at a lower price.

77 E. Scotford, Ch. UK, sec. F.

78 O. Fauchald, Ch. Norway, sec. F.

79 J. Jans, A. Outhuijse, Ch. The Netherlands, sec. D.

80 See Pine Valley (application no. 12742/87) where the ECtHR says: 'There was no formal expropriation of the property in question, neither, in the Court's view, can it be said that there was a de facto deprivation. The impugned measure was basically designed to ensure that the land was used in conformity with the relevant planning laws and title remained vested in Healy Holdings, whose powers to take decisions concerning the property were unaffected. Again, the land was not left without any meaningful alternative use, for it could have been farmed or leased. Finally, although the value of the site was substantially reduced, it was not rendered worthless, as is evidenced by the fact that it was subsequently sold in the open market.' See further B. Wegener, Ch. ECtHR.

11.2.2 Sacrifice for the Public Benefit

Another criterion refers to unequal treatment of the burdened property holders. The idea is that one group of proprietors is taken out of the general public and made to serve the public's interest. The group is asked to bring a special sacrifice for society, this being a reason for compensation.[81] Sometimes, this criterion is somewhat formalized by pointing to whether the measure is general, i.e. equal for anyone, or specific, i.e. burdening only a few.[82]

The use of the sacrifice concept does not imply that in the relevant cases the principle of equal treatment is breached. The measure itself is considered to be justifiable, only the compensation is possibly due.

11.2.2 Weighing up the Gravity of Impact and the Public Interest

A regulation rendering the property unprofitable or requesting a sacrifice for the public interest is readily subject to compensation in some jurisdictions. In others the encroachment does not by itself trigger compensation but may be legitimated by an overriding public interest such as, in particular, environmental protection.

While the ECtHR and CJEU jurisdiction[83] as well as many national courts[84] have applied such balancing test in many judgments, transnational investment arbitration has struggled with the problem for some time. While earlier panel decisions were exclusively based on the gravity criterion, called sole effects doctrine, more recent ones have complemented this by weighing the impact up with the public interest pursued by the regulation.[85] This concept is called police power doctrine. It appears that the combination of both: onus and public interest, is the better solution. One might even add the equality criterion to the test allowing sacrifices of property interests if the public interest pursued is particularly important.[86]

The possibility to disregard an encroachment for overriding reasons of public interests have in the recent past of budget cuts played a major role in relation to the restriction or even dissolution of rights to governmental subsidies.[87] In the

81 See notably the Netherlands where this is called the *égalité*-principle (J. Jans, A. Outhuijse, The Netherlands, sec. C).

82 P. Pagh, Ch. Denmark, sec. A 1.

83 See analysis of B. Wegener, Ch. ECtHR, sec. C. 1 a) and of J. H. Jans/ A. Outhuijse, Ch. CJEU, sec. D. 1.

84 See, e.g., See P. Pagh, Ch. Denmark, sec. A 1.

85 See further O. Fauchald, Ch. Arbitration, sec. 4.

86 I appears that the Dutch Circular on Damage Compensation can be read in these terms. Cf. J. Jans, Ch., A. Outhuijse, Ch. The Netherlands, sec. B and C.

87 R. Knez, Ch. Slovenia, sec. 7 and B. Iwanska, M. Baran, Ch. Poland, sec. 4.3., citing related recent judgments.

environmental policy realm this has affected subsidies for nature protection[88] and for the production of renewable energy.[89]

II.2.3 Sectoral Legislation and Case Law

Legal systems are not always clear about the precise quality of the criteria for onerous use restrictions. Some just posit a rule of compensation that can readily be applied. Others posit such rule as a higher level constitutional requirement that is addressed to the legislator rather than being operational.

Given the elusiveness of abstract criteria for onerous and thus compensatable restrictions of property use it is of course helpful if the legislator itself decides when compensation shall be due, and to what extent. Many legal systems do take such decisions in a large variety of sectoral laws.[90] The courts that may be invoked in the process of application of the laws may then reinterpret them in the light of constitutionally or otherwise principled constructions, or even hold them unconstitutional.

One example of sectoral legislation and judicial reconstruction is land use and nature protection. As mentioned earlier some jurisdictions follow a principle of 'situational binding' of the land. A principle of protecting vested and profitable practices is often applied in addition, which means, for instance, that a farmer who has exploited her land in profitable ways, say mowing the grass twice a year, may claim compensation if nature protection measures only allow one mowing, thus significantly reducing her income. If however the farmer has not exploited an area that later became a valuable habitat of birds she cannot claim compensation because the area is 'bound' by its nature. This is even the case where governmental restrictions of land use is increased over time to protect the valuable habitat.[91]

Land-use for the construction of buildings also poses problems of accommodating conflicts between property use and regulation in the public interest. The major criterion applied by jurisdictions is the protection of vested interests as weighed against the importance of the public interest. For instance, if a proprietor lawfully built a house and is by new land-use planning or technical requirements ordered to remove it, hindered to extend it or asked to renovate it at significant costs, this may trigger compensation or at least the granting of a generous

[88] See, for instance, Z. Mikosa, Ch. Latvia, sec.E, citing a judgment of the Latvian constitutional court on cutting back compensation payments for damage caused by protected species.

[89] See R. Knez, Ch. Slovenia, sec. H and I. Jankarova, J. Hanak, V. Vomacka, Ch. Czechia, sec. E.

[90] See, for instance, B. Iwanska, M. Baran, Ch. Poland, sec. 1; G. Bandi, Ch. Hungary, sec. G.; P. Pagh, Ch. Denmark, sec. A 2.

[91] See E. Scotford, Ch. UK, sec. G. See also J. Jans/ A. Outhuijse, The Netherlands, sec. B citing the Dutch Supreme Court on the introduction of pig quota for pig rearing undertakings.

grace period.[92] If however the land was not yet developed, hardly any jurisdiction recognizes a *ius aedificandi* as an intrinsic element of land property.[93]

Industrial activities may serve as a third example. EU and national regulation has rather strict rules even for already built and operated installations, stipulating that the operator must keep up with technological development empowering administrative oversight to take appropriate measures such as the modification of permit conditions orders to install better technology.[94] The basic idea here is that certain installations are intrinsically risky for human health and the environment so that the authorization and subsequent investment are not regarded as a fixed property position but rather as a privilege that is held open for new regulatory requirements. For this reason no compensation can be claimed.

II.3 Preconditions and Effects

As any regulation encroaching on private property onerous restrictions must be based on a parliamentary law, pursue a public interest and comply with the principle of proportionality. It would be logical to also require that compensation is provided by the empowering law. This would imply that if no compensation is foreseen the law is unconstitutional and the restrictive measure void. If a damage has already been caused state liability for unlawful action would apply. Alternatively, if a law fails to provide compensation the courts may complement the law accordingly.[95]

If compensation is due most legal systems allow for some flexibility in adjusting the amount of payment to the character of the encroachment and the public interest pursued by the regulation. When there is a legitimate public interest which is not important enough to fully justify the encroachment on property it may nevertheless be considered as a reason to reduce the amount of compensation.

92 See e.g. for Germany G. Winter, Ch. Germany, sec. G. Compensation may even then be legally excluded in certain zones of high public interest, see e.g. for Latvia Z. Mikosa, Ch. Latvia, sec. G, citing a Supreme Administratice Court case that puts this into question.

93 For the sophisticated example of Portugal see A. Aragao, Ch. Portugal, sec. E.

94 See e.g. the Spanish construction of installations as continuous installations ('tracto continuo'), A. Garcia Ureta, Ch. Spain, sec. G. For an elaborate example of the powers of the supervisory authority see Z. Mikosa, Ch. Latvia, sec. C.

95 In Germany the latter has been the solution practiced by the civil courts while the BVerfG appears to follow the former construction. See G. Winter, Ch. Germany, sec. C and I.

12. Dissolution of Property Positions Through Fundamental Policy Change

When a fundamental change of governmental policy requires that property positions must be dissolved, it would be very costly and thus an obstacle for innovative politics if compensation had to be paid. Some jurisdictions have tackled this problem and sought to find an answer in order to allow transformation of industrial and social practices on imperative social grounds.

One case decided in several jurisdictions concerns the removal of gravel and other minerals in view of groundwater and nature protection. Minerals on or close to the surface have traditionally been attached to land-ownership. The protection of groundwater and other concerns have led states to detach the exploitation right from the property, dissolve the right and establish a regime of prior authorization. Where the exploitation had already been subject to a permit regime and a permit had been obtained without time limits set, the old permits were dissolved and a new, more precautionary authorization regime introduced. The German BVerfG approved such fundamental reorientation construing it as a dissolution of rights that is not expropriation but a kind of determination of property content. It however stipulates that a time period must be granted to the addressee allowing her to gradually reorientate her business.[96]

This doctrinal construction is possible if one assumes that expropriation is conditioned on the transfer of property. Alternatively, if expropriation is construed to in principle also cover the dissolution of property rights, compensation can still be avoided if the original property position is more closely examined. It can be argued that the property position weakens by itself in times of basic change of social needs and political priorities so that at the time of the taking of the legal decision the constitutional legal protection is about to whither away considering also that a time period is granted for the adaptation to the new circumstances. The jurisprudence of the ECtHR can be read to have adopted this very solution. In *Fredin* where gravel exploitation was at stake the court points to the fact of a longer process of policy change arguing that the proprietor could not trust anymore in the perseverance of her permit.[97] *Jahn* can be read in similar terms. During the occupation of the later German Democratic Republic (GDR) by the Soviet Union land of noblemen who were considered to have collaborated with the Nazi regime were expropriated. The land was redistributed to individual farmers. Their offspring could only inherit the land if the heir continued the farming. In the last few years of the GDR the heritance right was extended to the heirs who did not continue operation. Two years later, after reunification, this right was again taken away as part of a comprehensive complex approach to land property questions of the GDR. The ECtHR ruled that

---

96 G. Winter, Ch. Germany, sec. H, citing BVerfG 58, 300 (351). See also the Croatian Constitutional Court on the necessity to grant phasing out time in J. Ofak, Ch. Croatia, sec. H.

97 ECtHR appl. 12033/86, no 42.

the inheritance right of the non-farming heirs was a right indeed but an uncertain one given the situation of ongoing fundamental policy change.[98]

When finding the correct doctrinal construction one should not lose sight of the more fundamental context. At stake is the ability of societies and their elected government to find and implement answers to new problems. Property cannot stand as a pillar if there is a historical landslide of law.[99] It must fall down, or, in other words, it should not make legal change so costly that the change cannot be realized. In the past when slavery was abandoned many states just forbade it, whilst others, in great injustice, made the slaves pay for their liberation. The same controversy took place in the times of liberation of dependent farmers from the bounds to their feudal lords. Land reform in socialist countries was one more historical move, which after the dissolution of the Soviet Union and Warsaw Treaty made succeeding states to largely acknowledge that historical fact.[100]

It may well be that we live in a time where the overexploitation of natural resources once more necessitates a fundamental and uncompensatable dissolution of many kinds of property rights. The stepping out of nuclear power is a case in point. The phasing out of nuclear power by some countries including Germany leads to a confronting property question: where the phasing out of nuclear power stations is motivated by reasons of energy policy change rather than of proven risks of the individual plant, would that be an expropriation according to a narrow construction of property and thus trigger huge compensation payments? Alternatively, would it be regarded as a case of fundamental change that is organized as a systematic phasing out not entailing compensation?[101] This example is no longer a hypothetical case and it shows the importance of environmental lawyers and lawyers generally revisiting their conceptions and protections of property rights in an era of radical industrial transformation on environmental grounds.

---

98 ECtHR, appl. 46720/99.

99 Phrase taken from the 19th century socialist politician and lawyer Ferdinand Lassalle. Cf. G. Winter, Über Pflöcke im wandernden Rechtsboden. Die Eigentumskonzeption des Bundesverfassungsgerichts und Ferdinand Lassalles Theorie erworbener Rechte, Kritische Justiz 1986: 459 – 470.

100 See G. Brunner, Verfassungsrechtlicher Eigentumsschutz und Restitution enteigneten Vermögens in Osteuropa, in: G. Manssen, B. Banaszak, Wandel der Eigentumsordnung in Mittel- und Osteuropa, A. Spitz Verlag, Berlin 1998. 29-68.

101 See G. Winter, The Rise and Fall of Nuclear Energy Use in Germany: Processes, Explanations and the Role of Law, in: 25: 1 JEL (2013), 95 – 124. While the German phasing out of nuclear power is pending at the German BVerfG, interestingly the like Belgian phasing out has not been challenged at Belgian courts. See L. Lavrysen, Ch. Belgium, sec. G.

PART II

Jurisprudence of the European Court of Human Rights, Court of Justice of the European Union and Courts of Transnational Arbitration

Property and Environmental Protection in the Jurisprudence of the European Court of Human Rights

Bernhard Wegener

A. Historical Development

The protection of property and the protection of the environment were both not initial elements of the European Convention on Human Rights. Both were missing in the 1950 text of the Convention.

Environmental protection still had to be invented in the 1970's. Even today the Convention – as many other fundamental guarantees on human rights – does not enshrine any right to a healthy environment. It has been left to the European Court of Human Rights to develop case-law establishing that some of the rights guaranteed in the Convention may be undermined and infringed by the existence of harm to the environment and exposure to environmental risks.

With property, it was quite another story: in the preliminary negotiations on the Convention it was generally agreed to insert a right to property into the text. However, no agreement was reached concerning the content of the right in time. Therefore the Convention was adopted in 1950 without such guarantee. It was only two years later that the right to property was laid down in Protocol No. 1, which was signed on 20th March 1952.[1] Except of the right to property, the Convention is nearly totally without further guarantees of economics and social fundamental rights.[2]

B. Importance of Environmental Protection in the Court's Case-Law

In a number of cases the European Court of Human Rights has stressed the importance of the protection of the environment.[3] In the absence of a specific provision dealing with environmental protection, the Court emphasised that the effective enjoyment of such explicitly guaranteed rights as the

---

[1] See Article 1 of Protocol No. 1 to the European Convention on Human Rights:
'Every natural or legal person is entitled to the peaceful enjoyment of his possession. No one shall be deprived of his possessions except in the public interest and subject to the conditions provided for by law and by the general principles of international law.
The preceding provisions shall not, however, in any way impair the right of a State to enforce such laws as it deems necessary to control the use of property in accordance with the general interest or to secure the payment of taxes or other contributions or penalties.'
The additional protocol was ratified in Germany in 1957. As to the history of the Convention and the Protocol No. 1 cf *Robertson*, Human Rights in Europe (1977) pp 5 et seq; *Grabenwarter*, European Convention on Human Rights (2014), p 366.

[2] *Frowein* in: MacDonald/Matscher/Petzold (eds), The European System for the Protection of Human Rights (1993), p 515.

[3] See, among many others: Taşkin and Others v. Turkey, 46117/99, 29 January 2004; Moreno Gómez v. Spain, 4143/02, 16 November 2004; Fadeyeva v. Russia, 55723/00, 9 June 2005. See also: Manual on human rights and the environment, Council of Europe Publishing, 2nd edition, 2012; European Court of Human Rights, Press Unit, Environment and the European Convention on Human Rights, 2015.

right to life[4] and the right to respect for private and family life[5] depends on a sound, quiet and healthy environment conducive to well-being.

According to the established case-law of the Court, the right to life in Art. 2 ECHR and the right to respect for private and family life in Art. 8 ECHR not only protect against direct actions but also create a positive obligation of the State to safeguard the lives and well-being of those within its jurisdiction. Public authorities have to take appropriate measures of protection even when those rights are threatened by third party activities. This obligation to protect also applies to environmental risks. So far, the Court has applied Art. 2 and Art. 8 ECHR rather cautiously and in a rather limited number of cases.[6] Positive obligations to protect arise in the context of dangerous activities such as nuclear tests[7] or the operation of chemical factories or waste-disposal sites. Art. 8 ECHR can be violated by the failure of the authorities to resettle a family living in a severely polluted area and to design or apply effective measures to reduce industrial pollution.[8]

Generally, the Court gives States a wide margin of appreciation when determining the necessary protection measures.[9] This margin may be narrow enough to establish an infringement of the human rights in question in cases of gross negligence and when specifically harmful or dangerous activities are

4 Art. 2 ECHR:
'1. Everyone's right to life shall be protected by law. No one shall be deprived of his life intentionally save in the execution of a sentence of a court following his conviction of a crime for which this penalty is provided by law.
2. Deprivation of life shall not be regarded as inflicted in contravention of this article when it results from the use of force which is no more than absolutely necessary:
in defence of any person from unlawful violence;
in order to effect a lawful arrest or to prevent the escape of a person lawfully detained;
in action lawfully taken for the purpose of quelling a riot or insurrection.'

5 Art. 8 ECHR:
'1. Everyone has the right to respect for his private and family life, his home and his correspondence.
2. There shall be no interference by a public authority with the exercise of this right except such as is in accordance with the law and is necessary in a democratic society in the interests of national security, public safety or the economic well-being of the country, for the prevention of disorder or crime, for the protection of health or morals, or for the protection of the rights and freedoms of others.'

6 See L.C.B. v. United Kingdom, 23413/94, 9 June 1998, para. 36; Paul and Audrey Edwards v. United Kingdom, 46477/99, 14 March 2002, para. 54; Öneryildiz v. Turkey, 48939/99, 30 November 2004, para. 71.

7 L.C.B. v. United Kingdom, 23413/94, 9 June 1998, para. 36.

8 Fadeyeva v. Russia, 55723/00, 9 June 2005.

9 See Budayeva a.o. v.Russia, 15339/02, 21166/02, 20058/02, 11673/02 and 15343/02, 22 March 2008, para. 128.

concerned or when the risks to life or property have been foreseeable.[10] More limited obligations to protect may also arise in the event of natural disasters.[11]

C. Property and the Environment

Under Art. 1 Protocol No. 1 ECHR, individuals are entitled to the peaceful enjoyment of their possessions, including protection from unlawful deprivation of property.

The term 'possessions' in Art. 1 Protocol No. 1 ECHR has an autonomous meaning which is not limited to the ownership of physical goods and is independent from the formal classification in domestic law. Other rights and interests constituting assets can also be regarded as 'property rights', and thus as 'possessions' for the purpose of the Convention. The Protocol expresses a broad international legal concept of property implying all 'acquired' rights that constitute assets.[12] Consequently the material scope contains the protection of acquired property, the business relationships which a company has formed in the past and which have an influence on the value of business (goodwill) and claims under Public Law. Furthermore, the property right also covers intellectual property rights. Notwithstanding that the regulation does not explicitly refer to the right of succession, the Court deems the owner´s right to dispose of his assets as he chooses.[13] It always needs to be examined whether the circumstances of the case, considered as a whole, confer on the applicant a title to a substantive interest protected by Art. 1 Protocol No. 1 ECHR. Moreover, the personal scope of Art. 1 Protocol No. 1 ECHR comprises both, individuals and explicitly legal persons.[14]

Analysing the jurisprudence, two categories can be distinguished: One with an adversary and one with a complementary relationship of environmental protection and property. The first is characterised by the competition of individual property rights with the public interest. The Court approves or denounces restrictions brought to the applicants' property rights to protect the environment. On the other hand owners invoke property rights to strengthen environmental cases.

---

10 Öneryildiz v. Turkey, 48939/99, 30 November 2004, para. 73; L.C.B. v. United Kingdom, 23413/94, 9 June 1998, para. 37-41.

11 Budayeva a.o. v.Russia, 15339/02, 21166/02, 20058/02, 11673/02 and 15343/02, 22 March 2008.

12 *Wegener*, in: Ehlers (ed), European Fundamental Rights and Freedom (2007), p 132; *Grabenwarter*, European Convention on Human Rights (2014), p 367.

13 Marckx v Belgium, 6833/74, 13 June 1979.

14 *Grabenwarter*, European Convention on Human Rights (2014), p 367; *Wegener*, in: Ehlers (ed), European Fundamental Rights and Freedom (2007), p 133.

1. Depriving or Restricting Property to Protect the Environment

Art. 1 Protocol No. 1 ECHR recognises that public authorities are entitled to regulate and restrict the use of property in accordance with the general interest.[15] In this context the Court has found that the environment is an increasingly important consideration and can therefore legitimize a deprivation or a restriction of the use of property.

a) Deprivation

Art. 1 Protocol No. 1 ECHR allows the deprivation of possessions in the 'public interest and subject to the conditions provided for by law and by the general principles of international law.' Considering the importance of environmental protection, the Court accepts that applicants can be legally deprived of their property 'in the public interest', namely to protect public health and the environment.[16] The Court follows a broad understanding of the environment as to its meaning and scope.[17] It generally accepts environmental purposes as a legitimate goal and leaves the state a great degree of deference, especially in complex planning issues. A deprivation of property that intends to protect the environment pursues a legitimate aim. Due to the 'immediate familiarity' of the national authorities with the local situation or with the 'respective social needs', the court acknowledges that they have a broad discretion to determine the general public interest in question.[18] In assessing the fairness of the balance between the individual and the public interest the Court recognises that the national authorities are generally in a better position than the Court to judge how to weigh the various interests at stake. Generally speaking, the Court checks whether:

- the deprivation is in accordance with internal law and not arbitrary,
- a legitimate purpose for the limitation of the applicant's rights is pursued,
- a fair balance is struck between the competing public and owner interests.

A typical application of this test by the Court may be observed in Fredin v. Sweden.[19] The applicant exploited a gravel pit that was situated on his own land. The Swedish authorities did not renew the permit, based on the Swedish Nature Conservation Act. The permit had to be renewed every ten years. The applicant was thus aware of the possibility that such a renewal would not take place. The authorities had to take into consideration the protection of the environment.

15 Fredin v. Sweden, 12033/86, 18 February 1991, para. 41.

16 Lazaridi v Greece, 31282/04, 13 July 2006, para. 34.

17 *Nükhet Yilmaz Turgut*, The European Court Of Human Rights And The Right To The Environment, Ankara Law Review, Vol. 4 No 1, Summer 2007, pp. 1-24, 10.

18 Wiesinger v. Austria, 11796/85, 30 October 1991, para. 76, with reference to Fredin v. Sweden, 12033/86, 18 February 1991 (1991) 13 EHRR 784.

19 Fredin v. Sweden, 12033/86, 18 February 1991.

As the applicant had also received a 3 year and eleven month period for closing down the pit, the measure was considered not disproportionate. The Court denied a breach of Art. 1 Protocol No. 1 ECHR.

A large number of other cases[20] concern conflicts between property owners and the urban planning efforts of public authorities. In *Pine Valley Ltd and others v. Ireland*[21] one applicant had bought land for construction. The authorities withdrew a permission to construct because a local zoning plan which was implemented to preserve a so-called 'green belt' indicated that no construction should take place. Local authorities were opposed to granting a derogation. The Court held that the legislation served the general interest and the protection of the environment. Moreover, the applicant was a company which knew of the existing legislation and was thus aware of the risks arising from the complex legal framework concerning its premises. In *Kapsalis and Nima-Kapsali v. Greece,*[22] a case which also concerned the withdrawal of a permission, the Court held that in fields such as urban planning and environmental protection, the assessment of the national authorities should prevail unless it is manifestly unreasonable.[23] The applicants bought land for the construction of a house, while the planning legislation which were to fix the stretches where construction was allowed, was still in elaboration. They obtained a permit for construction. However, when the planning legislation was final, the permit was withdrawn. The Court found that in areas of urban planning or environmental protection, the authorities had a margin of discretion. The applicants had not taken due care, when buying the land. In the actual case, the withdrawal of the planning permission had been validated by the Greek Administrative High Court following a thorough examination of all aspects of the problem and there was no indication that its decision had been either arbitrary or unforeseeable. On the contrary, two other building permissions on land situated in the same area as the applicants' own site had already been annulled by the Greek courts prior to the annulment of the applicants' own permission. Moreover, the decision to allow building in the zone where the applicants' property was situated had not been finalised when they had purchased it. The authorities could not be held responsible for the applicants' negligence in verifying the status of the land which they were buying. Therefore again, the Court held that considering the aim of protection of the environment, the withdrawal of the planning permission was not disproportionate and dismissed the complaint as being manifestly ill-founded.

Another classical case showing the wide margin of appreciation of public planning authorities is *Hamer v. Belgium.*[24] The applicants' parents had built, in

---

[20] See also: Chapman v. United Kingdom, 27238/95, 18 January 2001.

[21] Pine Valley Ltd and others v. Ireland, 12742/87, 29 November 1991.

[22] Kapsalis and Nima-Kapsali v. Greece, 20937/03, 23 September 2004.

[23] Kapsalis and Nima-Kapsali v. Greece, 20937/03, 23 September 2004, para. 3, 'law' part. See also: Brosset-Triboulet and Others v. France, 34078/02, 29 March 2010, para. 87; Depalle v. France, 34044/02, 29 March 2010, para. 84.

[24] Hamer v. Belgium, 21861/03, 27 November 2007.

1967, a holiday house in a forest area, without permission. In 1994, the police found that some trees had been cut on the property and discovered the absence of a permit. The applicant was ordered to restore the site to its original state. The Court found that the measure was justified. The environment was an asset whose protection was of concern to society and to public authorities. Economic considerations and even the right to property should not be given precedence over the protection of the environment. The measure was also considered proportionate, though the house had existed since more than thirty years, and the authorities knew or should have known of this fact.

Very similarly, in *Depalle v. France*[25] the applicant had built a house on the seashore in an area of maritime public property. The permit to build had been given half a century ago, but only for a temporary construction. No property right had ever been recognized by the French authorities. The applicant was asked to restore the site at his cost, without compensation. The Court weighed the general interest – free access to the shore, protection of the environment – against the interests of the applicant. It did not accept that the time element pleaded in favour of the applicant. It saw a growing need to protect coastal areas and their use by the public, and to ensure compliance with planning regulations. Thus, the fact that no compensation was paid, was not considered disproportionate.

Infringements of planning laws can not only result in the deprivation of the land in question. In *Valico v. Italy*[26] the applicant, a company, had received a construction permit, but did not respect it and was imposed a fine. The Court again found that the respect of planning law was a legitimate objective to protect the landscape. Even though the amount of the penalty was considerable,[27] it was not disproportionate, as the demolition of the building was not requested.

Art. 1 Protocol No. 1 ECHR does not contain an explicit provision on the necessity of compensation. The conditions provided by the general rules of public international law to which the Article refers, contain a compensation duty only for those national measures which concern the property of foreign nationals.[28] Nevertheless, the Court has held that a deprivation of property without payment of an amount reasonably related to its value will generally constitute a disproportionate interference, and that a total lack of compensation can be considered justifiable under Art. 1 Protocol No. 1 ECHR only in exceptional circumstances.[29] Under those circumstances and if the expropriation was legal

---

25 Depalle v. France, 34044/02, 29 March 2010.

26 Valico v. Italy, 70074/01, 21 March 2006.

27 Under the terms of the applicable italian law, anyone erecting a building in a manner that is wholly non-compliant (*totale difformità*) with the authorisations granted by the competent regional authorities is liable to a fine equal to 100% of the value of the unlawfully erected building. On the basis of an expert report, the extraordinary committee of the Municipality imposed a fine of approximately 1,385,260 EUR.

28 *Wegener*, in: Ehlers (ed), European Fundamental Rights and Freedom (2007), p 144.

29 *Von Danwitz* in: Von Danwitz/Depenheuer/Engel (eds), Bericht zur Lage des Eigentums (2002), p 256.

and not arbitrary, the dearth of compensation alone does not cause an unreasonable expropriation.[30] It is further necessary to determine whether the complainant had to bear a disproportionate or excessive burden.[31] In some 'environmental' cases, the Court concluded that due to a lack of compensation the applicants have been victims of an unlawful expropriation[32] or a violation of Art. 14 ECHR (equal treatment), taken together with Art. 1 Protocol No. 1 ECHR.[33]

In the case of *Papastavrou and others v. Greece*,[34] the 25 applicants are Greek nationals who are involved in a long-standing dispute with the State over ownership of land in Omorphokklisia, Galatsi, which is part of a wider area called the Veïkou Estate that was expropriated between 1923 and 1941. On 10 October 1994 the prefect of Athens decided that an area of the Veïkou Estate should be reforested. The applicants challenged that decision before the Council of State, claiming that the land earmarked for reforestation included their plot of land and that reforestation would deprive them of their property rights over it. Their appeal was dismissed on the ground that the prefect's decision had merely confirmed an earlier decision made by the Minister for Agriculture in 1934. However, in 1999 the Athens Forest Inspection concluded that only part of the area concerned had been forest in the past and could therefore be reforested. The applicants alleged a violation of Art. 1 Protocol No. 1 ECHR in that their property had effectively been expropriated without their being paid any compensation. According to the decision of the Court it was not for itself to settle the issue of ownership of the disputed land, but for the purposes of the proceedings before the Court the applicants could be regarded as the owners of the land in issue or at least as having an interest in it that attracted the protection of Art. 1 Protocol No. 1 ECHR. In the Court's view, the authorities were wrong to have ordered the reforestation measure without first assessing how the situation had evolved since 1934. In dismissing the applicants' appeal on the sole ground that the prefect's decision had merely confirmed an earlier decision, the Council of State had failed to protect the property owners' rights adequately, especially as there was no possibility of obtaining compensation under Greek law. A reasonable balance had not therefore been struck between the public interest and the requirements of the protection of the applicants' rights. The Court held unanimously that there had been a violation of Art. 1 Protocol No. 1 ECHR and that the question of just satisfaction was not ready for decision.

In the case of *Turgut a.o v. Turkey*,[35] the applicant claimed his family had owned property consisting of a piece of land for more than fifty years. The

[30] Jahn and Others v Germany, 46720/99, 30 May 2005, para 83.

[31] *Wegener*, in: Ehlers (ed), European Fundamental Rights and Freedom (2007), p 144.

[32] Papastavrou and others v Greece, 46372/99, 10 April 2003, see also N.A. and Others v.Turkey, 37451/97, 11 October 2005; Yildirir v. Turkey, 21482/03, 24 November 2009.

[33] Pine Valley Ltd v Ireland, 12742/87, 29 November 1991.

[34] Papastavrou and others v. Greece, 46372/99, 10 April 2003 (see also Katsoulis a.o. v. Greece, 66742/01, 8 July 2004).

[35] Turgut a.o v. Turkey, 1411/03, 8 July 2008.

authorities annulled his title to the land on the constitutional principle of the inalienability of ownership of State forests. His title was therefore considered to be without legal value and no compensation was paid. Buildings have since been erected on the disputed land. The Court found the purpose of the expropriation justifiable in order to protect nature and forests. However, the lack of compensation was not proportionate.

In the case of *Z.A.N.T.E. – Marathonisi A.E. v. Greece*,[36] which concerned the compensation in connection with a dispute relating to a small islet which the applicant company had purchased, the Court again pointed to the wide margin of appreciation that States were granted when implementing spatial planning policies and held that the interference with the applicant company's right to its property satisfied the requirement of being in the general interest. The case is of special environmental interest, because it concerned an island which is a reproduction site for *caretta-caretta* turtles and therefore specially protected as a natural reserve. Nevertheless, the Court rejected the authorities' argument that it was impossible for the prohibition of building on the disputed land to infringe the right to protection of property as construction on the land in question was, at all events and by its very nature or 'destination', impossible. The Court inferred from this that the authorities had applied an irrefutable presumption which took no account of the distinctive features of each piece of land not covered by an urban zone and found that a lack of compensation would give rise to a violation of Art. 1 Protocol No. 1 ECHR. The Court also took into consideration that the authorities had not established a coherent protection programme. On the contrary, they had not prohibited other uses of the island which had been polluted by a great number of tourists visiting its beaches. Under these circumstances, the Court considered the reasoning of the authorities too general and vague.

A legally designated compensation can mitigate the hardship of an expropriation to such an extent that the measures are altogether proportional.[37] Where a compensation regime is established by the state, the Court's power of review is limited to ascertaining whether the choice of compensation terms falls outside the State's wide margin of appreciation in this domain.[38] However, the Court strictly controls the amount and the general appropriation of the compensation for expropriation.

b) Restrictions of use

Art. 1 (2) Protocol No. 1 ECHR stipulates that it 'shall not, however, in any way impair the right of a State to enforce such laws as it deems necessary to control the use of property in accordance with the general interest or to secure the payment of taxes or other contributions or penalties.' A 'control of the use of

36 Z.A.N.T.E. – Marathonisi A.E. v. Greece, 14216/03, 6 December 2007, para. 50-52.

37 The former king of Greece and others v Greece, 25701/94, 23 November 2000, 33 EHRR 516.

38 James a.o. v. the United Kingdom, 8793/79, 21 February 1986, para. 45.

property' can be any measure to command or forbid the use of property.[39] Such measures must have at least some 'substance' in order to constitute a potential violation of the right of property.[40] The requirements which have to be fulfilled for justifying the encroachment on the right to property by restricting the use of property are similar to those applying in cases of deprivation of possessions. The criterion of a legal basis and the principle of proportionality apply equally.[41] However, generally speaking the Court gives Member States an even larger margin of discretion or appreciation concerning restrictions of the use of property. Such restrictions must generally not be compensated. This broad margin of discretion concerning restrictions and (non)compensation is even broader when the Member States measures intend the protection of the environment. Conversely, a legally designated compensation can mitigate the hardship of a restriction on use to such an extent that the measures are altogether proportional.[42] So far, the Court has declared no general national environmental protection measure restricting the use of the environment to be violating Art. 1 Protocol 1 ECHR.

2. Property Protecting the Environment

Art. 1 Protocol 1 ECHR, in principle, does not guarantee the right to continue to enjoy those possessions in a pleasant environment. Therefore, in the case of *Kyrtatos v. Greece*,[43] the applicant unsuccessfully claimed that urban development had led to the destruction of a swamp adjacent to their property and that the area around their home had lost its scenic beauty. The Court held that 'neither Article 8 nor any other articles of the Convention are specifically designed to protect general protection of the environment as such'. The Convention on Human Rights meant to protect individual human rights rather than the general interest and the needs of the community taken as a whole. In accordance with this line of argument, property owners have so far been regularly unsuccessful trying to establish a violation of their property rights in the case of negative environmental impacts such as noise or the destruction of scenic beauty caused by private or state activities.

A common feature of the decisions is the question of whether the nuisances in question affected the market value of the property. In *Powell and Rayner v. United Kingdom*,[44] the applicants lived in the vicinity of Heathrow airport. They complained of excessive noise. The Court rejected their claims and stated that the operating of the airport was necessary for the economic well-being of the United Kingdom. The property of the applicants had not lost value and therefore

[39] *Grabenwarter*, European Convention on Human Rights (2014), p. 372.

[40] As to the notion and the requirements for the regulation of use, see *Hartwig* (1999) RabelsZ 63, p 569.

[41] Gasus Dosier- und Fördertechnik GmbH v NED, 15375/89, 23 February 1995, para. 62.

[42] The former king of Greece and others v Greece, 25701/94, 23 November 2000, 33 EHRR 516.

[43] Kyrtatos v. Greece, 41666/98, 22 May 2003.

[44] Powell and Rayner v. United Kingdom, 9310/81, 21 February 1990.

the Court saw no violation of Art. 8 ECHR or Art. 1 Protocol No. 1 ECHR. In the very similar judgments, *Hatton v. United Kingdom*[45] and *Flamenbaum a.o. v. France*,[46] the Court rejected complaints against excessive noise levels at airports. The Court referred to an economic interest in maintaining the night flights or the extension of a runway and to the fact that house prices had not dropped.

Only in exceptional cases, the right of property could also be invoked in order to establish a failure of the state to protect individuals against natural disaster. In the case of *Budayeva a.o. v. Russia*,[47] exceptionally heavy rainfalls caused a mudslide which destroyed the applicant's house. The Court, however, held that the obligation of the authorities with regard to property rights was limited to 'what is reasonable in the circumstances'. The authorities had a wide margin of appreciation in deciding what measures to take in order to protect private property. Insofar, the Court differentiated between natural disasters and man-made catastrophes: 'natural disasters, which are as such beyond human control, do not call for the same extent of State involvement. Accordingly, its positive obligations as regards the protection of property from weather hazards do not extend necessarily as far as in the sphere of dangerous activities of a man-made nature.'[48] Interestingly enough, the Court also differentiated between the positive obligations under Art. 2 ECHR and those under Art. 1 Protocol No. 1 ECHR: 'While the fundamental importance of the right to life requires that the scope of the positive obligations under Article 2 includes a duty to do everything within the authorities' power in the sphere of disaster relief for the protection of that right, the obligation to protect the right to the peaceful enjoyment of possessions, which is not absolute, cannot extend further than what is reasonable in the circumstances. Accordingly, the authorities enjoy a wider margin of appreciation in deciding what measures to take in order to protect individuals' possessions from weather hazards than in deciding on the measures needed to protect lives.'[49] Although there was some sort of negligence on the side of public authorities, this was only a factor which aggravated the natural disaster; it was not the only cause of the damage. As a result, the Court saw no violation of private property.

Nevertheless, the right of property can be invoked under certain circumstances in order to protect ones property against environmental degradations caused by the state or by third parties. The Court has repeatedly noted that certain activities which could affect the environment adversely could seriously reduce the value of a property to the extent of even making it impossible to sell it, thus amounting to a partial expropriation, or limiting its use creating a situ-

45 Hatton v. United Kingdom, 36022/97, 8 July 2003.

46 Flamenbaum a.o. v. France, 3675/04 and 23264/04, 13 December 2012.

47 Budayeva a.o. v.Russia, 15339/02, 21166/02, 20058/02, 11673/02 and 15343/02, 22 March 2008.

48 Budayeva a.o. v.Russia, 15339/02, 21166/02, 20058/02, 11673/02 and 15343/02, 22 March 2008, para. 174.

49 Budayeva a.o. v.Russia, 15339/02, 21166/02, 20058/02, 11673/02 and 15343/02, 22 March 2008, para. 175.

ation of de facto expropriation.[50] This is true for exceptionally dramatic cases: in the case of *Öneryildiz v. Turkey*,[51] the applicant had built a house on a municipal rubbish tip, without permission. Also other houses had been built there. An explosion occurred, killing 39 persons, among them nine members of the applicant's family. Two years before the accident, an expert opinion had drawn the attention of the municipality on the risk of a methane explosion; yet, the authorities had not done anything. The Court found that there was gross negligence on the side of the authorities. Since they had tolerated the applicant's house for several years, the applicant was entitled to claim protection of his property, though he had constructed illegally. Waste management was a public responsibility, and therefore, Turkey was breaching its obligations under property law.

Art. 1 Protocol No. 1 ECHR has also been invoked successfully against potentially environmentally relevant limitations of the right of property in cases concerning ethical questions. A number of judgments on hunt cases indicate that an adjustment payment is generally inappropriate to compensate owners obliged to allow hunting on their premises against their ethical convictions. *Herrmann v. Germany*,[52] concerned a landowner's complaint about being forced to accept hunting on his land, even though he is morally opposed to hunting. The Court expressed misgivings of principle about the argument that strongly-held personal convictions could be traded against annual compensation for the restrictions on the use of the property (the amount of which being above all very limited at hand). In the earlier case of *Chassagnou a.o. v. France*,[53] the Court had contented itself with the lack of compensation for the exception to the principles that ownership means the right to enjoy and dispose of things in the most absolute manner, and that no one may hunt on land belonging to another without the owner's consent. Then, in Schneider v. Luxembourg,[54] it became apparent that the financial compensation could not reasonably be balanced with regard to the ethical convictions of an opponent of hunting. The jurisprudence slightly tightened the requirements of a fair balance between protection of the right of property and the requirements of the general interest.

D. The Parallel Jurisdiction Concerning Art. 8 ECHR

The environmental protection via property rights under Art. 1 Protocol No. 1 ECHR has a parallel in the jurisdiction of the Court concerning the protection of private life under Art. 8 ECHR. In Kania v. Poland,[55] for example, the applicants complained of excessive noise levels. The Court found that 'there is no right in the Convention to a clean and quiet environment, but that

[50] Taşkın and Others v. Turkey, 46117/99, 29 January 2004, 'law' part (available in French only).

[51] Öneryildiz v. Turkey, 48939/99, 30 November 2004.

[52] Herrmann v. Germany, 9300/07, 26 June 2012; see also Chabauty v. France, 57412/08, 4 October 2012;

[53] Chassagnou a.o. v. France, 25088/94 28331/95 28443/95, 29 April 1999.

[54] Schneider v. Luxembourg, 2113/04, 10 July 2007.

[55] Kania v. Poland, 59444/00, 21 July 2009.

where an individual is directly and seriously affected by noise or other pollution, an issue may arise under Article 8'. In the case in question, however, the noise levels were considered not to be excessive, all the more, as they ended due to the closure of the plant in question. The similarities to cases such as Powell and *Rayner, Hatton* and *Flamenbaum*[56] are obvious.

The same parallel approach can be observed in other cases. In the famous case *Lopez Ostra v. Spain*,[57] for instance, the applicant complained of noise and fumes from a waste treatment plant, installed at 12m from her home. She suffered the pollution for more than three years; finally she and her family moved elsewhere. The Court considered the nuisance serious enough to constitute a breach of Art. 8 ECHR. Due only to the fact, that the applicants were not the owners of their home, the case was decided under Art. 8 ECHR and not under Art. 1 Protocol No. 1 ECHR.

E. Some Preliminary Conclusions

The case-law of the European Court of Human Rights on property and the protection of the environment is still developing. The Court has established some general lines of argument, which it uses again and again to outline its general understanding of the relationship of property and environmental protection. Nevertheless, some fundamental questions and concepts still show only limited signs of consolidation.

Environmental protection is generally considered to be in the public interest. Public measures intended to promote the protection of the environment can therefore limit the use of property. This is especially true in the case of environmental protection legislation that defines the scope and the content of property and limits its use. So far, the Court has not considered any general Member State legislation aiming at the protection of the environment to be violating Art. 1 Protocol No. 1 ECHR.

The Court has applied its general concept of the Member States margin of appreciation also in cases concerning limitations of the use of property. Where environmental protection is at stake, this margin of appreciation seems to be even broader.

Some uncertainties still exist concerning the question of compensation. Although limitations of the use of property generally do not necessarily require any compensation, the jurisdiction is somewhat more obscure in cases concerning classical or de facto deprivations. Here, the Court so far mainly had to decide in cases concerning the application of Member State planning law. While in many cases of – mainly illegal – construction, the Court again stressed the Member States wide margin of appreciation, in others, Member States actions to refuse or withdraw land-use permits or to order the abolishment of construc-

56 Above sec. C. 2.

57 Lopez Ostra v. Spain, 16798/90, 9 December 1994.

tions or the restoration of natural sites have been considered to be violating the right of property. Especially the question whether a certain national measure called for compensation has been treated differently in different but substantially similar cases. At this point, the jurisdiction of the Court shows some arbitrary elements and seems to be hardly predictable.

The right to property can also serve as an instrument to protect the environment against the degrading effects of actions of the State or of private parties. The Court, however, limits the respective obligations of the State to refrain from action or to protect against actions by third parties. It again accepts a wide margin of appreciation of the public authorities. According to the Court, Art. 1 Protocol No. 1 ECHR cannot be regarded as a right to enjoy ones possession in an unaltered and pleasant environment. In cases concerning the right of property, applicants must show that the market value of their possessions has dropped. Property in this respect is therefore still mainly regarded as an economic right only.

Property and Environmental Protection in the Jurisprudence of the Court of Justice of the European Union

Jan H. Jans & Annalies Outhuijse

A. Introduction[1]

For European environmental lawyers the provisions in the treaty on environmental protection (Articles 191-193 TFEU) are quite familiar. The literature on the role and meaning of the environmental objectives and principles and their legal status is abundant.[2] However, with respect to the role of property, property rights and their influence on European environmental law and policy matters are quite different. In the current treaty the following provision (Article 345 TFEU) on 'property' can be found: 'The Treaties shall in no way prejudice the rules in Member States governing the system of property ownership.' The origin of this provision goes back to the founding EEC Treaty, which contained a similar provision. Regulating property ownership is therefore primarily a matter for the Member States.[3] In view of this provision it must be acknowledged that the Member States are, in principle, free to regulate property ownership for reasons of environmental protection.

However, it is also clear that the EU institutions, in view of the explicit competences attributed to them in the Articles 191-193 TFEU, are entitled to take necessary measures in order to protect the environment. Accordingly, the measures taken may very well restrict the use of property in the Member States.

It goes without saying that measures taken with the objective to protect the environment may restrict persons in the use of their property. Occurring both when the measures are taken by the EU itself or by the Members States, when implementing EU policies or taking measures on their own accord. The main objective of this paper is to discuss some of the tensions between property rights and environmental protection.

B. The Legal Status of the Right to Property in EU Law

Well before the entry into force of the Charter, the Court of Justice of the European Union (hereinafter: CJEU) had already acknowledged that 'the right to property' is to be regarded as a 'general principle' of EU law. The origin of this right to property can be traced back to the *Hauer* case.[4]

Ms Hauer was refused permission to use her plot of land for wine-growing purposes on account of the unsuitability of the soil. In this landmark case the

---

[1] This paper builds on previous publications of the first author, in particular J.H. Jans & H.H.B. Vedder, *European Environmental Law*, Groningen: European Law Publishing 2012.

[2] J.H. Jans & H.H.B. Vedder, *European Environmental law*, Groningen: European Law Publishing 2012, at 32 et seq.

[3] Cf. the 'old' law, e.g., Case C-483/99 *Commission v. France* [2002] ECR I-4781, ECLI:EU:C:2002:327, para. 44, making it clear that although property ownership is a matter for the Member States, this provision does not provide a carte blanche to the Member State to disregard their obligations under the E(E)C Treaty.

[4] Case C-44/79 *Hauer* [1979] ECR 3727, ECLI:EU:C:1979:290.

Court affirmed that fundamental rights, including the right to property, form an integral part of the Community legal order. With respect to the right to property the CJEU explicitly referred to Article 1 of Protocol 1 to the ECHR. However, while the right to property forms part of the general principles of Community law, the Court argued that it is not an absolute right and must be viewed in relation to its social function.[5] As a consequence the EU itself and the Member States have the possibility to regulate the use of property in accordance with the general interest; and CJEU case law shows that they both have a large amount of discretion in doing so. With respect to the right to property the CJEU only rarely comes to the conclusion that reasons of general interest do not justify a restriction to the right to property.[6] In the words of the CJEU:

> 'that the right to property is not absolute but must be considered in relation to its function in society. Consequently, its exercise may be restricted, provided that the restrictions in fact correspond to objectives of public interest pursued by the Community and do not constitute, in relation to the objective pursued, a disproportionate and intolerable interference, impairing the very substance of the right guaranteed.'[7]

Of course, and as we are all aware, this case law has evolved and is now been codified in Article 6(3) TEU:

> 'Fundamental rights, as guaranteed by the European Convention for the Protection of Human Rights and Fundamental Freedoms and as they result from the constitutional traditions common to the Member States, shall constitute general principles of the Union's law.'

The entry into force of the *Charter of fundamental rights of the European Union* has strengthened the protection of fundamental rights in the EU. The provisions of the Charter are binding upon to the Union institutions, bodies, offices and agencies, and upon the Member States 'when they are implementing Union law' (Article 51(1) Charter). With respect to the concept of 'property' the Charter contains the following provision in Article 17:

> 'Everyone has the right to own, use, dispose of and bequeath his or her lawfully acquired possessions. No one may be deprived of his or her possessions, except in the public interest and in the cases and under the conditions provided for by law, subject to fair compensation being paid in good time for their loss. The use of property may be regulated by law in so far as is necessary for the general interest.'

---

5 *Inter alia* Case C-44/79 *Hauer* [1979] ECR 3727, ECLI:EU:C:1979:290; Case C-280/93 *Germany v Council* [1994] ECR I-4973, ECLI:EU:C:1994:367; Case C-5/88 *Wachauf* [1989] ECR 2609, ECLI:EU:C:1989:321.

6 Case C-5/88 *Wachauf* [1989] ECR 2609, ECLI:EU:C:1989:321.

7 Case T-138/07 *Schindler Holding Ltd v. Commission* [2011] ECR II-04819, ECLI:EU:T:2011:362, para. 189.

With respect to possible limitations to the rights mentioned in the Charter Article 52(1) provides:

> 'Any limitation on the exercise of the rights and freedoms recognised by this Charter must be provided for by law and respect the essence of those rights and freedoms. Subject to the principle of proportionality, limitations may be made only if they are necessary and genuinely meet objectives of general interest recognised by the Union or the need to protect the rights and freedoms of others.'

This provision makes it perfectly clear that environmental concerns are legitimate reasons to restrict the right to property. Since the ruling of the CJEU in the *ADBHU* case,[8] from the early 1980's, 'environmental protection' must be regarded as such an official objective of the EU.

Another relevant provision of the Charter to be taken into account in this respect is Article 52(3). It states:

> 'In so far as this Charter contains rights which correspond to rights guaranteed by the Convention for the Protection of Human Rights and Fundamental Freedoms, the meaning and scope of those rights shall be the same as those laid down by the said Convention. This provision shall not prevent Union law providing more extensive protection.'

The explanatory notes for ex Article 52(7) of the Charter[9] explicitly state that Article 17 of the Charter is based on Article 1 of the Protocol to the ECHR. The relevance of this is that with respect to the interpretation of Article 17 of the Charter, the ECHR is leading. Article 17 Charter guarantees at least the same level of protection for the right to property as Article 1 Protocol 1 ECHR.[10] The explanatory notes state in this respect: 'the meaning and scope of the right [the right to property of Article 17, authors] are the same as those of the right guaranteed by the ECHR and the limitations may not exceed those provided for there.' In other words: Article 17 Charter has imported Article 1 Protocol 1 ECHR and the case law of the ECtHR relating to that provision into the EU legal order.

However, to have a more comprehensive picture of the legal status of the right to property vis-à-vis environmental protection, we also have to address the question on whether there is a similar guarantee in the Charter for 'environmental protection'. Regrettably, this is not the case. With respect to 'environmental protection' Article 37 of the Charter contains a text similar, but not identical, to Article 11 TFEU:

---

8 Case 240/83 *ADBHU* [1985] ECR 531, ECLI:EU:C:1985:59.

9 See Explanations relating to the Charter of fundamental rights, OJ 2007 C 303/17.

10 We refer in particular to the observations of B. Wegener in chapter II.1. of this book.

> 'A high level of environmental protection and the improvement of the quality of the environment must be integrated into the policies of the Union and ensured in accordance with the principle of sustainable development.'

Most importantly this provision, known as the 'integration-principle' is not formulated as 'a right'. In view of Article 51(1) of the Charter 'rights' must be 'protected' whilst 'principles' must be observed and their application thereof promoted. Also in view of the fact that the ECHR does not contain a dedicated[11] explicit fundamental right to environmental protection, one has to come to the conclusion that in the EU the right to property has the status of a fundamental right, whilst this is not the case with respect to environmental protection.

Taking into account the above points, we come to the following conclusions. In EU law the 'right to property' has the legal status of a 'fundamental right'. Yet for 'environmental protection', despite being an official objective of the EU, there seems to be no 'right to environmental protection' that has fundamental legal status. Having said that, even the fundamental rights, the right to property included, do not have an absolute character.[12] The right to property can be restricted if it is necessary for reasons of general interests. Environmental protection is such an interest. However, it seems that in the balancing of the right to property and the need for environmental protection, the right to property is in the driver's seat and environmental protection is more *defensive* than *offensive*. In this respect we mean the following: Restricting the right to property for reasons of environmental protection is, as such, not a problem, but its status as a fundamental right requires that the very essence of that right must be protected. The lack of 'fundamental status' of environmental protection means that in balancing the right to property and the need for environmental protection, the latter seems to be weaker.

C. Who is Responsible For What?

According to the Charter, in particular Article 51, the provisions of the Charter are addressed to the EU institutions and 'to the Member States only when they are implementing Union law'. In interpreting this provision the CJEU has build upon its older pre-Charter fundamental rights case law. In *Åkerberg*[13] the Court ruled:

[11] Of course the authors are aware of the case law of the European Court of Human Rights on the importance of in particular Article 2 (protection of life), Articles 6 and 13 (access to justice), Article 8 (privacy), Article 10 (freedom of expression) for environmental protection.

[12] F.M.J. den Houdijker, *Afweging van grondrechten in een veellagig rechtssysteem*, Nijmegen: Wolf Legal Publishers 2012, at 472.

[13] Case C-617/10 *Åkerberg* [2013] ECR I-0000, ECLI:EU:C:2013:280.

'19 The Court's settled case-law indeed states, in essence, that the fundamental rights guaranteed in the legal order of the European Union are applicable in all situations governed by European Union law, but not outside such situations. In this respect the Court has already observed that it has no power to examine the compatibility with the Charter of national legislation lying outside the scope of European Union law. On the other hand, if such legislation falls within the scope of European Union law, the Court, when requested to give a preliminary ruling, must provide all the guidance as to interpretation needed in order for the national court to determine whether that legislation is compatible with the fundamental rights, the observance of which the Court ensures (see inter alia, to this effect, Case C-260/89 ERT [1991] I-2925, paragraph 42; Case C-299/95 Kremzow [1997] ECR I-2629, paragraph 15; Case C-309/96 Annibaldi [2007] ECR I-7493, paragraph 13; Case C-94/00 Roquette Frères [2002] ECR I-9011, paragraph 25; Case C-349/07 Sopropé [2008] ECR I-10369, paragraph 34; Case C-256/11 Dereci and Others [2011] ECR I-11315, paragraph 72; and Case C-27/11 Vinkov [2012] ECR, paragraph 58).

20 That definition of the field of application of the fundamental rights of the European Union is borne out by the explanations relating to Article 51 of the Charter, which, in accordance with the third subparagraph of Article 6(1) TEU and Article 52(7) of the Charter, have to be taken into consideration for the purpose of interpreting it (see, to this effect, Case C-279/09 DEB [2010] ECR I-13849, paragraph 32). According to those explanations, 'the requirement to respect fundamental rights defined in the context of the Union is only binding on the Member States when they act in the scope of Union law'.

21 Since the fundamental rights guaranteed by the Charter must therefore be complied with where national legislation falls within the scope of European Union law, situations cannot exist which are covered in that way by European Union law without those fundamental rights being applicable. The applicability of European Union law entails applicability of the fundamental rights guaranteed by the Charter.

22 Where, on the other hand, a legal situation does not come within the scope of European Union law, the Court does not have jurisdiction to rule on it and any provisions of the Charter relied upon cannot, of themselves, form the basis for such jurisdiction (see, to this effect, the order in Case C-466/11 Currà and Others [2012] ECR, paragraph 26).'

Whether someone can rely on Article 17 of the Charter, the right to property, as a shield against environmental regulation depends on the question if the legal situation falls within or outside the scope of European law.

An example in the case law of the CJEU of a national measure falling outside the scope of European Union law is the *Annibaldi* case. If there is no link at all with European environmental law one cannot rely on the Charter or any other EU fundamental rights as was made clear in the *Annibaldi* case.[14] In this case the Court ruled that as the law stands at present, regional legislation, which

[14] Case C-309/96 *Annibaldi* [1997] ECR I-7493, ECLI:EU:C:1997:631.

establishes a nature and archaeological park in order to protect and enhance the value of the environment and the cultural heritage of the area concerned, applies to a situation which does not fall within the scope of Community law. The case concerned the authorities' refusal to grant Annibaldi permission to plant an orchard of 3 hectares within the perimeter of a regional park. Annibaldi argued that such a refusal without financial compensation violated his right to property. Although this case was ruled upon prior to the entry into force of the Charter, the line of argument can be held applicable to the Charter as well.

Another recent judgment of the CJEU with an environmental context concerning the Charter is the *Siragusa* case of 6 March 2014.[15] Mr Siragusa owned property in a landscape conservation area. He made alterations to that property without first obtaining landscape compatibility clearance as required by Italian law and then applied to the Comune di Trabia (Municipality of Trabia) for retrospective planning permission for those alterations. According to Italian law, the owner of a property in protected landscape conservation area may not destroy it or alter it in such a way as to impair the features of the landscape, and must apply for 'landscape compatibility clearance' before carrying out any alterations. If he carries out alterations without applying for clearance, the authority may, however, authorise those alterations retrospectively if the work carried out is compatible with the features which are under protection. However, the Italian public authority, the *Soprintendenza* adopted an order requiring Mr Siragusa to restore the site to its former state by dismantling, within 120 days, all work which had been carried out illegally. The order was made on the grounds that the work in question was not eligible for certification as compatible with the landscape conservation rules. Mr Siragusa brought an action contesting that order before the local administrative court, the Tribunale amministrativo regionale per la Sicilia. This court wondered whether Article 17 of the Charter, the right to property, precluded legislation like the contested Italian legislation. The CJEU decided that it had no jurisdiction to answer the question referred by the Tribunale amministrativo regionale per la Sicilia as the Italian court failed to establish, by demonstrating a sufficient connection, that the disputed Italian legislation falls within the scope of EU law or implements that law.

The judgments in *Annibaldi* and *Siragusa* are clear examples of cases where the connection of national environmental law with European law were absent or too remote to trigger the application of Article 17 of the Charter.

At the other side of the spectrum we can find cases where the Member States have implemented EU environmental measures and that individuals have opposed these national measures by relying on the right to property. One of the oldest cases in this respect is the *Standley* case, which is also interesting due the ruling of the CJEU.[16] In the *Standley* case, the Court considered the

[15] Case C-206/13 *Siragusa* [2014] ECR I-0000, ECLI:EU:C:2014:126. See also the blog from Xavier Lewis: http://eulitigationblog.com/2014/03/13/case-c-20613-siragusa-the-scope-of-the-charter-of-fundamental-rights-preliminary-references-and-national-law/comment-page-1/.

[16] Case C-293/97 *Standley* [1999] ECR I-2603, ECLI:EU:C:1999:215.

Nitrates Directive. It was argued that this directive gave rise to disproportionate obligations on the part of farmers, so that it offended against the principle of proportionality and their fundamental rights to property. They argued in particular that the right to property was infringed by imposing on farmers the entire responsibility for, and economic burden of, reducing nitrate concentrations in the waters concerned when others are the major or substantial causes of those concentrations. The Court was not impressed. After a careful study of the Nitrates Directive, it came to the conclusion:

> 'As regards infringement of the right to property, the Court has consistently held that, while the right to property forms part of the general principles of Community law, it is not an absolute right and must be viewed in relation to its social function. Consequently, its exercise may be restricted, provided that those restrictions in fact correspond to objectives of general interest pursued by the Community and do not constitute a disproportionate and intolerable interference, impairing the very substance of the rights guaranteed (Case 44/79 Hauer v Land Rheinland-Pfalz [1979] ECR 3727, paragraph 23, Case 265/87 Schräder v Hauptzollamt Gronau [1989] ECR 2237, paragraph 15, and Case C-280/93 Germany v Council [1994]ECR I-4973, paragraph 78).'

It is true that the action programmes which are provided for in Article 5 of the Directive and are to contain the mandatory measures referred to in Annex III impose certain conditions on the spreading of fertiliser and livestock manure, so that those programmes are liable to restrict the exercise by the farmers concerned of the right to property.

However, the system laid down in Article 5 reflects requirements relating to the protection of public health, and thus pursues an objective of general interest without the substance of the right to property being impaired.'

Finally, the Court came to the conclusion that the directive contains 'flexible provisions' enabling the Member States to avoid any disproportionate restrictions on the right to property. This case shows that where an EU environmental measure leaves Member States a certain degree of discretion when implementing it, it is the responsibility of the Member States that the right to property is observed and for the national courts to review the legality of the measures taken.[17] Also, one cannot challenge the validity of the EU measure in such a case by relying on the fundamental right to property.

This same approach can be found in the *Ferdinand Stefan* case. In this case Mr Stefan, having problems with the implementing Austrian legislation, challenged the validity of Directive 2003/4/EC on environmental information. According to Mr Stefan the directive violated Article 47(2) of the Charter (right to an effective remedy). The CJEU reiterated that under Article 51(1) of the Charter, the fundamental rights guaranteed therein must be respected where national legislation comes within the scope of EU law and that Member States

[17] Building upon previous case law like the *Wachauf* case: C-5/88.

are required to respect Article 47(2) of the Charter when they implement Directive 2003/4. Subsequently, it argued that a provision of secondary EU law must, so far as possible, be given an interpretation which renders that provision consistent with the Treaties and the general principles of EU law, including the right to an effective remedy. In other words: EU directives must be assumed to be in line with the Charter and its fundamental rights. Therefore it is the Member States who must use their margin of appreciation, conferred on them by the directive, 'in a manner which is consistent with the requirements flowing from that article of the Charter'.

The final case to discuss which illustrates the important role the Member States and their court's play in ensuring the right to property, within the EU legal order, is the *Sahlstedt* case.[18] Private landowners challenged the decision of the Commission, taken under the Habitats Directive, adopting the list of sites of Community importance for the Boreal biogeographical region as their property was included in the list. The landowners argued that this decision had a significant effect, both legally and factually, on their property rights. The Court of First Instance ruled however that they were not directly concerned, as required by Article 263 TFEU:

> 'it cannot be held that the contested decision – which designates, as sites of Community importance, areas of Finland in which the applicants own land – produces, by itself, effects on the applicants' legal situation. The contested decision contains no provision as regards the system of protection of sites of Community importance, such as conservation measures or authorisation procedures to be followed. Thus, it affects neither the rights or obligations of the landowners nor the exercise of those rights. Contrary to the applicants' argument, the inclusion of those sites in the list of sites of Community importance imposes no obligation whatsoever on economic operators or private persons. Article 4(4) of the habitats directive states that once a site of Community importance has been adopted by the Commission, the Member State concerned is to designate that site as a 'special area of conservation' within six years at most.
>
> In that regard, Article 6(1) of the habitats directive states that the Member States are to establish the necessary conservation measures for special areas of conservation, the aim being to meet the ecological requirements of the natural habitat types and species present on the sites.'

In sum, the CFI ruled that the Finnish landowners are not directly affected by the decision of the Commission, but by the national measures implementing that decision. It is remarkable, that in appeal, the CJEU did not mention 'direct concern' at all, but declared the landowners inadmissible because they were not individually concerned by the Commission decision. The CJEU ruled that since the contested decision was not adopted in light of the specific situation of the landowners, it could not be regarded as a group of individual deci-

18 Case C-362/06 *Sahlstedt* [2009] ECR I-2903, ECLI:EU:C:2009:243.

sions addressed to each landowner and that the appellants are not individually concerned by the decision. Therefore they had no standing in an action for annulment ex Article 263 TFEU. The landowners were advised to bring their case before their national court. If necessary that national court could ask the CJEU, in the context of a preliminary ruling, to rule on the validity of the decision of the Commission.

Both the *Standley* and the *Sahlstedt* case show the important role Member States have to play to ensure that the right to property is protected. *Standley* shows that the Member States must ensure substantive protection; while *Sahlstedt* shows the role Member States play in offering legal protection.

D. Balancing the Right to Property and Environmental Protection Requirements in the Case Law of the CJEU

The right to property can be used either to 'shield' against environmental regulation or as a 'sword' to trigger environmental protection. If we look at the case law of the CJEU of the EU it is quite clear that most of the cases concern using property rights as a shield. This might not surprise us in view of the legal status of the right to property as a fundamental right. Wegener made it quite clear in his contribution to this book that Article 1 Protocol 1 ECHR does not guarantee the right to enjoy ones possessions in a pleasant environment.[19] In the European Union the legal situation is similar.

Wegener's contribution also shows us that the right to property of Article 1 Protocol 1 ECHR can be triggered to combat environmental degradation when this degradation creates a situation of *de facto* expropriation.[20] Although there is no case of the CJEU to support this, our argument is that in EU law a similar legal situation exists. Measures falling within the scope of EU law causing environmental degradation to such an extent that it amounts to a *de facto* expropriation, must be deemed to be unlawful in EU law as well.

1. The Right to Property as 'Shield' to Environmental Regulation

Above we already mentioned that, in EU law, the right to property is not an absolute right and must be viewed in relation to its social function. The right to property may be restricted for environmental reasons, provided that those restrictions are not disproportionate and intolerable, and do not impair the very substance of the right to property.

[19] B. Wegener, Chapter II.1., referring to the judgment of the ECtHR in *Kyrtatos v. Greece*, Judgment of 22 May 2003, Application 41666/98.

[20] Referring to case ECtHR, *Taşkin and Others v. Turkey*, Judgement of 10 November 2004, Application 46117/99.

There are a couple of cases that illustrate the above point. In the *ERG* case the CJEU made it clear that it may be justified to make the right of the operators to use their land subject to the condition that they implement the necessary environmental remedial measures, in order to oblige them actually to take those measures.[21] The measure has to be 'justified by the objective of preventing a deterioration of the environmental situation' or, 'pursuant to the precautionary principle, by the objective of preventing the occurrence or resurgence of further environmental damage to that land'.[22] However, the measures may not exceed the limits of what is appropriate and necessary in order to attain the objectives legitimately pursued by the legislation in question.[23]

Križan concerned the construction of a landfill by Ekologická Skládka on the grounds of former brickworks in the Slovak city Pezinok. The environmental inspection granted an integrated permit for the construction and operation of the landfill.[24] Some residents of Pezinok, including Joseph Križan, objected and appealed the decision, requesting annulment of the permit. Ekologická Skládka invoked its property rights from Article 17 Charter. In appeal, the Supreme Court suspended the operation of the integrated permit and annulled the permit because the competent authorities did not observe the rules for public participation and with regard to the environmental assessment did not carry out enough research on the environmental impact of the construction of the landfill. After the Constitutional Court set aside the decision and referred the case back, the Supreme Court asked the CJEU for a preliminary ruling concerning whether Article 17 Charter was violated by the annulment of the permit on the grounds of breach of Article 15a of Directive 96/61 and Article 9(2) and (4) of the Aarhus Convention. After stating the general rule that a property right is not an absolute right, the Court held that the protection of the environment is one of the objectives of general interest and is therefore capable of justifying a restriction on the use of the right to property. In addition, the Court examined whether the restriction was proportionate and the Court ruled that 'it is sufficient to state that Directive 96/61 operates a balance between the requirements of that right [the right to property of Article 17 Charter, authors] and the requirements linked to protection of the environment'. The Court held that a decision of a national court, taken in the context of national proceedings implementing the obligations resulting from Article 15a of Directive 96/61 and from Article 9(2) and (4) of the Aarhus Convention, which annuls a permit granted in infringement of the provisions of that directive is not capable, in itself, of constituting an unjustified interference with the developer's right to property enshrined in Article 17 of the Charter. This case shows that it is possible to rely on the right to property for the annulment of a permit and that the ownership interests and community interests are weighed on an abstract level.

---

21 Case C-379/08 en C-380/08 *ERG* [2010] ECR I-2007, ECLI:EU:C:2010:127, para. 80.

22 *ERG*, para. 85.

23 *ERG*, para. 86.

24 Case C-416/10 *Križan* [2013] ECR I-0000, ECLI:EU:C:2013:8.

2. The Right to Property as a 'Sword'

Above we argued that in EU law only occasionally the right to property is invoked as a sword to trigger environmental protection. Most of these cases deal with state liability for failing to implement EU directives by the Member States. A recent case in this respect is the *Juta Leth* case.[25] In this case Ms Leth argued that the Member State (Austria) is liable to pay damages for the decrease in value of her property. This decrease was the result of an extension of an airport runway in violation with EIA Directive 85/337/EEC. The CJEU accepted that exposure to noise resulting from a project covered by the EIA Directive has significant effects on individuals, in the sense that a home affected by that noise is rendered less capable of fulfilling its function and the individuals' environment, quality of life and, potentially, health are affected, a decrease in the pecuniary value of that house may indeed be a direct economic consequence of such effects on the environment. However, this does not necessarily mean that Ms Leth had to be compensated as the failure to carry out the assessment prescribed by the directive, does not, in principle, by itself constitute the reason for the decrease in the value of a property. In other words, even with an environmental assessment carried out the runway extension could have been approved. The fundamental question: does EU law contain a rule to enjoy one's possession in an environmentally sound manner, and if so, does the violation of such a rule trigger financial compensation, was not addressed at all.

E. Restricting the Right to Property With or Without Compensation?

The previous section showed that the right to property can be regulated and restricted for reasons of environmental protection. A separate question, at least to a certain extent, is whether there is, or can be, a legal duty in EU law to compensate the financial loss for those individuals who are confronted with restrictions to their property.

Let us start by saying that if the damage is the direct result of an intervention by the European legislator, the European legislator might provide for financial compensation. Outside environmental law we can find some examples in particular in the area of agricultural policy and law.[26] There is also case law of the CJEU, e.g. the *Wachauf* case, where restrictions to the right to property were

[25] Case C-420/11 *Leth* [2013] ECR I-0000, ECLI:EU:C:2013:166.

[26] See for example Commission Regulation (EC) No 349/2005 of 28 February 2005 laying down rules on the Community financing of emergency measures and of the campaign to combat certain animal diseases under Council Decision 90/424/EEC, OJ 2005, L 55/12. See also Council Directive 2000/29/EC of 8 May 2000 on protective measures against the introduction into the Community of organisms harmful to plants or plant products and against their spread within the Community, OJ 2000, L 169/1. Cf. M.K.G. Tjepkema, *Nadeelcompensatie op basis van het égalitébeginsel*, Deventer: Kluwer 2010, at 852.

deemed to be illegal, particular in view of the fact that no compensation was offered.[27]

Another question is whether EU law provides for a remedy to compensate for lawful actions. Many Member States know of a rule saying that the state, under very specific circumstances, has a duty to compensate financial loss even if the measures taken to restrict the right to property for the general interest are lawful.[28] These remedies are mainly based on concepts like 'excessive burden', *égalité devant les charges public*, etc. Of course, the EU treaties do not contain a remedy for lawful measures. Article 340 TFEU and the duty to compensate only deals with unlawful measures by the EU institutions. So with respect to any duties for the Member States, it suffices to say that state liability according to the *Francovich*-doctrine also only refers to infringements of EU law by the Member States.

In light of this a specific EU-based remedy to compensate for financial loss due to lawful restrictions to the right to property, seems to be far-fetched. Although earlier case law[29] of the CJEU seemed not to exclude this possibility completely, in its landmark case *FIAMM*, the CJEU denied the existence in EU law of such a specific remedy.[30] However, the Court did open a backdoor to such a remedy by stating that an EU 'legislative measure whose application leads to restrictions of the right to property and the freedom to pursue a trade or profession that impair the very substance of those rights in a disproportionate and intolerable manner, perhaps precisely because no provision has been made for compensation calculated to avoid or remedy that impairment, could give rise to non-contractual liability' on the part of the EU. In other words, a lawful measure can become unlawful if no compensation is offered.

If the EU measure itself offers no compensation, the question arises whether the Member States are required to offer compensation. The case law of the CJEU shows that the Member States enjoy a large amount of discretion in this respect.[31] The case *Booker Aquaculture* concerned the outbreak of a fish disease and the fish that had to be destroyed as a result of a European directive to combat fish disease.[32] The fish owners relied on their property right. The Court was faced with the question whether the State was obliged to compensate the loss of the fish owner as a result of the Directive. First, the Court ruled that the directive contained no provisions on compensation. The Court stated that although the Member States were empowered to adopt rules for compensation, they were not required to do so on the basis of European law. The destruction of

27 Case C-5/88 *Wachauf* [1989] ECR 2609, ECLI:EU:C:1989:321; Den Houdijker 2012, at 478-479.

28 Cf. the comparative legal research undertaken by the CJEU in the *FIAMM* case, discussed below.

29 Case T-184/95 *Dorsch Consult* [1998] ECR II-667, ECLI:EU:T:1998:74; Case T-196/99 *Area Cova* [2001] ECR II-3597, ECLI:EU:T:2001:281.

30 Case C-120/06 P and C-121/06 P *FIAMM* [2008] ECR I-6513, ECLI:EU:C:2008:476.

31 Cf. also the *Wachauf* case.

32 Case C-20/00 and C-64/00 *Booker Aquaculture* [2003] ECR I-7411, ECLI:EU:C:2003:397; Den Houdijker 2012, at 485-488.

the fish could not in any event be regarded as a 'disproportionate and intolerable interference impairing the very substance of the right to property.[33] The Court emphasized that the act served the public interest and that the fish owners could expect that a fish disease may break out at any moment and cause them loss. According to the Court such risk is inherent to the business of raising and selling livestock and is the consequence of a natural occurrence. Finally, apart from the fact that it was not a disproportionate and intolerable infringement of the right to property, the Court held that the Member States can nevertheless compensate if they want to.

F. Conclusion

All of the above leads us to the following final observations. Firstly, we have demonstrated that the legal status in EU law of the 'right to property' and the 'right to environmental protection' are quite different. The right to property enjoys the legal status of being a 'fundamental right'. This is reflected in the case law of the CJEU when balancing property and environmental rights. Property rights are mainly used to shield against environmental regulation, rather than as a sword to demand environmental protection.

Secondly, it is argued that with respect to the interpretation of the 'right to property', the ECHR is leading. Article 17 of the Charter mirrors Article 1 Protocol 1 ECHR and follows its interpretation.

Thirdly, it is argued that in order to comply with Article 17 of the Charter Member States have an important role to play. The case law of the CJEU seems to suggest that Member States, when implementing EU environmental measures, must use their discretion in such a manner that the property right guarantee of Article 17 Charter is ensured; either by offering substantive protection or providing financial compensation in the case of *de facto* expropriation.

[33] *Booker Aquaculture*, paras. 79-85, 91 and 92.

The ECJ Jurisprudence on Nature Protection and Ownership Rights

Agustin Garcia- Ureta

A. Introduction*

Much has been written in the last years on the protection of sites and species in EU law.[1] The attention has mainly been focused on the designation of protected areas, the scope of prohibitions and exemptions set forth in the corresponding directives and the overall development of biodiversity policy in the EU. However, not much thought has arguably been devoted to the impact of such prohibitions on property rights bearing in mind the current trend to resort to market mechanisms, e.g., biodiversity banking, as available tools to provide (it is claimed) more efficient protection to habitats and species and in general to ecosystems services. This contribution does not pretend to elaborate on this matter or on the more general issue of property rights and the environment,[2] but on the impact (if any) of existing EU biodiversity protection pillars on ownership rights. As examined in the ensuing paragraphs, the Wild Birds and Habitats directives (WDB and HD)[3] contain limited references to such rights, this matter apparently being left to the Member States. The TFEU proclaims that '*in no way* prejudice(s) the rules in Member States governing the system of property ownership'[4] reinforcing the view that the link between on the one hand sites and species protection and on the other hand property rights does not pertain to EU law. By contrast, the protection of property rights is conceived as a legitimate justification to exempt the application of the prohibitions set out in the Directives.[5] However, it could be argued that an analysis of some of

* The author wishes to thank Gerd Winter and Nicolas de Sadeleer for their comments on a previous draft. Any errors are the author's alone.

1 See among others, de Sadeleer, N., 'The Birds, Habitats, and Environmental Liability Directives to the Rescue of Wildlife under Threat', in *The Yearbook of European Environmental Law*, vol. 7 (Oxford University Press, 2007), 36-75; de Sadeleer, N., 'EC Law and Biodiversity', in Macrory, R. (Ed.), *Reflections on 30 years of EU environmental law* (Europa Law Publishing, 2006), 351-369; de Sadeleer, N., y Born, C., *Droit international et communautaire de la biodiversité* (Dalloz, 2004); García-Ureta, A., *Derecho Europeo de la Biodiversidad* (Iustel, 2010); García-Ureta, A., (coord.), *La Directiva de Hábitats de la Unión Europea: balance de 20 años* (Thomson-Aranzadi, 2012); Krämer, L., *EC Environmental Law* (seventh edition, Sweet & Maxwell), 181-205; Krämer, L., 'Monitoring the Application of the Birds and the Habitats Directives', (2013) *Journal for European environmental & planning law* 209-232; Verschuuren, J., 'Effectiveness of Nature Protection Legislation in the EU and the US: The Birds and Habitats Directives and the Endangered Species Act', (2003) *Yearbook of European Environmental Law* 305-328; Wils, W.P. J., (1994) *Journal of Environmental Law* 219-242.

2 See Tegner Anker, H., and Basse, E., *Land use and nature protection* (DJØF Publishing, 2000); Cole, D.H., *Pollution & Property* (Cambridge University Press, 2002); Pâques, M., 'Proprieté et zonage écologique, compensation et indemnisation' in CEDRE, *Le zonage écologique* (Bruylant, 2002), 241-294; Rogers, C., 'Nature's place? Property rights, property rules and environmental stewardship', (2009) *Cambridge Law Journal* 550-574.

3 Directive 2010/147; Directive 92/43.

4 Article 345 TFEU, emphasis added.

5 Article 9(1)(a) (third indent) WDB; in express terms, Article 16(1)(b) HD.

the relevant provisions of both directives in the light of ownership rights is still missing.[6] The above mentioned directives require the implementation of *positive* provisions regulating the exercise of ownership rights, these not just being affected as a result of a set of prohibitions. Admittedly, one basic field, i.e., the management of designated sites, is devoid of substance in the directives[7] but, as argued below, both directives do limit property rights and restrict the manner in which they may be carried out. Private and public owners do not remain free to adopt the type of land use they wish. It is for the Member States to close the gap between the prohibitions and limitations set forth in the directives and the free use of ownership rights be they agricultural, urban, aerial, forestall, fishing or recreational. This contribution aims to examine some basic features of EU biodiversity protection from the angle of such rights. For the attainment of this purpose four main matters are analysed: (1) the role of ownership rights in the WBD and HD; (2) compensation measures in environmental assessment procedures as required by the HD; (3) declassification of sites; and (4) the status of species.

B. Natura 2000 and Ownership Rights

1. Introductory Remarks

The WBD and HD neither expropriate private property rights nor in principle impose a *de facto* expropriation.[8] EU law does not prohibit the carrying out of activities in protected areas. However, that does not mean that they may be freely executed. The prohibitions set forth in the WBD and HD are motivated by the protection of habitats and species but they do not pretend to directly regulate ownership rights. A different matter is whether activitics likely to affect protected areas are to avoid their deterioration or be subject to environmental assessment. Nevertheless, as examined below, Member States may prohibit such activities. In addition, management of special conservation areas (SCAs) and special protection areas for birds (SPAs), does not include rules on how to regulate activities and property rights, this matter being left to the Member States. Even though the WBD includes a reference to a 'common heritage',[9] EU law does not provide guidance as to the legal categorization of species and habitats and their link with property rights. The fact that species are labelled as priority species in the HD or that bird species cannot be hunted during certain periods of the year, as set out in the WBD, casts doubts on their

6 See, however, Winter, G., 'Property rights and nature conservation', in Born, C-H., *The Habitats Directive in its EU Environmental Law Context* (Routlegde, 2015), 215-228.

7 Garcia-Ureta, A., and Lazkano Brotons, I., 'Instruments for sites active management of Natura 2000: balancing between stakeholders and nature conservation?' in Born, *supra* note 6, 71-92.

8 Winter, *supra* note 6, at 221.

9 Fourth recital to the preamble.

specific status from the angle of ownership rights or on whether properties hosting them could no longer be regarded as (entirely) 'private'.[10]

As mentioned above, the EU Treaties have since 1958 contained an unconditional clause according to which they '*in no way* prejudice the rules in Member States governing the system of property ownership'.[11] Article 345 TFEU may represent an obstacle to European integration, given that it leaves out from the EU an important element of the economic constitutions of the Member States. As far as biodiversity protection is concerned, it also leads to disparate approaches as to how to reconcile this objective with ownership rights. Member States remain competent to develop and specify the rules concerning property ownership in the light of Article 1 of Protocol 1 and Article 17 EUCFR.[12] The treaties do not establish a transfer of the competence on property rights to the EU or on the status of certain goods, e.g., public domain. In other words, the regulation of property rights is first and foremost a national competence. In addition, the EU has not adopted any detailed legislation regarding expropriation[13] (save Article 17 EUCFR), and it cannot be concluded that there is a general principle in EU law requiring compensation to be paid in all circumstances, e.g., by the destruction of specimens bred in aquaculture facilities.[14] In this sense, Directive 2004/35 indicates that without prejudice to relevant national legislation, it does not give private parties a right of compensation as a consequence of environmental damage or of an imminent threat of such damage.[15]

It has been submitted that the expression 'system of property ownership' contained in Article 345 TFUE refers not to the civil rules concerning property relationships but to 'the ideal body of rules of every kind, deriving from both private and public law which allow a person vested with such ownership to exercise decisive influence on the definition and implementation of all or some of its economic objectives'. This position, based on a historical and teleological viewpoint,[16] sheds some light on matters concerning Article 345 TFUE. First, EU law may certainly affect property rights by adopting rules within its sphere

[10] This issue is examined below.

[11] Article 345 TFUE, emphasis added.

[12] See, among others, Lasagabaster Herrarte, I., 'Protección de la propiedad', in Lasagabaster Herrarte, I., (dir.), *Convenio Europeo de Derechos Humanos* (Thomson, 2015, forthcoming); Riza Çoban, A., *Protection of Property Rights within the European Convention on Human Rights* (Ashgate, 2004); Grgić, A., Mataga, Z., Longar, M., and Vilfan, A., *The right to property under the European Convention on Human Rights. A guide to the implementation of the European Convention on Human Rights and its protocols* (Council of Europe, 2007); van Dijk, P., van Hoof, F., van Rijn, Zawaak, L., (eds.), *Theory and Practice of the European Convention on Human Rights* (Intersentia, 2006), 863-893.

[13] Case C-309/96, Annibaldi v. Sindaco del Comune di Guidonia y Presidente Regione Lazio, para. 23.

[14] Joined cases C-20/00 y C-64/00, Booker Aquaculture Ltd, y Hydro Seafood GSP Ltd v. The Scottish Ministers, para. 85.

[15] Article 3(3).

[16] See the conclusions of Advocate General Jarabo-Colomer in case C-583/99, *Commission v. Portugal*, paras. 49-52.

of competences, e.g., agriculture, fisheries, intellectual property, or environmental policy. However, the Treaties do not allow the EU to adopt general rules on property rights. As advocate general Jarabo-Colomer noted in this respect, the civil rules concerning property relationships appear to be '*wholly alien* to the purposes of the Treaties'.[17] It is for this reason that EU biodiversity law refrains from setting out specific rules on the conduct of ownership rights. Although Article 345 TFEU respects Member States' competences to regulate the system of property ownership, including restrictions that may be imposed on the grounds of public interest, this is permissible as long as such rules do not fall within the scope of application of EU law, e.g., the freedoms protected by the Treaties or fundamental rights (including property ownership).

2. The Role of 'Economic' Requirements in the WBD and HD

The WBD and HD include a parallel provision when referring to so-called 'economic requirements'. According to the former directive, 'Member States shall take the requisite measures to maintain the population of [all species of naturally occurring birds in the wild state in the European territory of the Member States] at a level which corresponds in particular to ecological, scientific and cultural requirements, while *taking account of* economic and recreational requirements, or to adapt the population of these species to that level'.[18] In a similar fashion, the HD declares that measures taken pursuant to this Directive shall be designed to maintain or restore, at favourable conservation status, natural habitats and species of wild fauna and flora of Community interest and that *they shall take account of* economic, social and cultural requirements and regional and local characteristics.[19] Neither the WBD nor the HD defines the term 'economic requirements'. In principle both directives conceive such notion in a negative fashion as opposed to the environmental objectives underpinning them. It is for this reason that the ECJ has repeatedly held that economic requirements do not constitute an 'autonomous derogation' from the general system of protection set out in the directives because they have already been taken into consideration by the EU legislature when drafting them.[20]

The preamble to the HD declares that the maintenance of biodiversity 'may in certain cases require *the maintenance, or indeed the encouragement*, of human activities'.[21] Accordingly, the Directive does not prohibit the carrying out of activities in protected areas, e.g., agriculture or forestry.[22] The ECJ has held that even

[17] Advocate General Jarabo-Colomer, *supra* note 16, paras. 54 and 56, emphasis added.

[18] Article 2 WBD, emphasis added.

[19] Article 2(2) and (3) HD, emphasis added.

[20] Case C-44/95, The Queen v. Secretary of State for the Environment, ex parte: Royal Society for the Protection of Birds, para. 25.

[21] Second recital to the preamble, emphasis added.

[22] See COM(2001) 162 final, Communication from the Commission to the Council and the European Parliament – Biodiversity Action Plan for Agriculture.

if the conversion of a natural fluvial ecosystem 'into a *largely man-made* fluvial and lacustrine ecosystem were to have a negative impact on the integrity of sites which are part of the Natura 2000 network, it does not necessarily follow that consent may not be given to the project which causes that conversion'.[23] According to the ECJ, compensation measures to be adopted under Article 6(4) HD have to be interpreted in the light of Article 11 TEU (sustainable development). This reasoning arguably undermines the duty to go beyond mere restoration of habitats and species and ultimately weakens the presumption in favour of biodiversity conservation that pervades the WDB and HD. The Commission has declared that some Natura 2000 sites may be unexploited nature reserves, 'but most sites will be in areas where significant human activities have always existed and helped to create or maintain habitats. For this reason the designation of Natura 2000 sites *is not intended to block economic activity in and around* the affected land'. On the contrary, according to the Commission, the emphasis will be 'on encouraging a level of economic activity that will be sustainable and compatible with the conservation requirements of the habitats and species for which the sites have been designated. In its opinion, this is best achieved within the framework of management planning, the success of which will frequently depend upon the full involvement and support of landowners and users'.[24]

However, Member States' regulations must necessarily be subordinated to the objectives of the HD. Therefore, they may control, or as the case may be, curtail ownership rights to guarantee such objectives. In this sense, the EU Economic and Social Committee has correctly indicated that 'whilst tapping the regional economic development potential of Natura 2000 sites would be desirable (since it is becoming clear that nature conservation may also actually bring economic benefits), this aspect is, however, *not necessarily relevant* to the issue of species conservation'.[25] The previous quote from the Commission indicating that most sites are in areas where significant human activities have always existed raises the question as to whether EU biodiversity laws demand the encouragement of intact or untouched areas in the Member States and not merely maintaining the *status quo* of existing areas.[26] Admittedly, due to the territorial features of continental Europe, i.e., densely populated areas within relatively small countries, it may be difficult (but not impossible) to exclude any activities from Natura 2000 sites (or from certain sections of those sites). Likewise,

[23] Case C-43/10, Nomarchiaki Aftodioikisi Aitoloakarnanias v. Ypourgos Perivallontos, para. 135, emphasis added.

[24] Communication from the Commission to the Council and the European Parliament – Biodiversity Action Plan for the Conservation of Natural Resources (COM/2001/0162 final), para. 23, emphasis added.

[25] Opinion of the European Economic and Social Committee on the Communication from the Commission to the Council and the European Parliament: Financing Natura 2000 (COM(2004) 431 final, para. 3.17, emphasis added.

[26] See Bastmeijer, K., (ed.), The Role of International, European and National Law in Protecting Wilderness in Europe (Cambridge University Press, 2015, forthcoming).

resettling people away from those sites may be complicated as it would require important amounts of funding to compensate for the loss of property rights. However, construction works, e.g., dams, requiring displacement of citizens have not been uncommon,[27] as guaranteeing water supply is an objective that may require such measures.[28] The question would be why biodiversity protection does not enjoy a similar position even if achieveing a favourable conservation status may certainly demand abandonment of territories.[29]

3. Restrictions on the Carrying out of Activities in ECJ Case Law

The ECJ has been asked to examine the compatibility of activities affecting protected sites (also Natura 2000 sites) with ownership rights. In broad terms, the ECJ held in *Cascina*, a case related to the declassification of a Natura 2000 site owing to the extension of an airport and the increase of environmental degradation, that as long as the quality of the site in question met the requirements for its classification, such restrictions of the right to property were, 'as a rule', justified by the objective of protecting the environment laid down in the HD.[30] The ECJ used the expression 'as a rule' since it would be necessary to verify each kind of restriction to determine whether it may warrant the payment of compensation. Other cases submitted before the ECJ did not fall within the scope of EU law and no interpretation of Article 17 EUCFR and of the requirements (if any) imposed by the WBD and HD on ownership rights was provided. The relationship between measures to limit available activities and agriculture was raised in *Annibaldi*.[31] The case concerned the refusal to grant permission to plant an orchard of 3 hectares within the perimeter of a regional park. National law imposed a number of prohibitions on certain activities within the perimeter of the park which, in exceptional cases, were subject to certain derogations relating to the pursuit of the objectives of the park. The person affected by the refusal argued that the law carried out an expropriation without compensation and was also contrary to the provisions of the Treaty on the common organization of the agricultural markets which excluded any discrimi-

---

27 For instance, Riaños, Itoiz and Yesa dams in Northern Spain.

28 See for instance the case of La Breña II dam in Southern Spain and Commission's opinion under Article 6(4) of the Habitats Directive: http://ec.europa.eu/environment/nature/natura2000/management/docs/art6/labrena_en.pdf.

29 For instance, Spanish law indicates that in a national park there can exist neither lands capable of town-planning transformation nor urbanized lands. However, this provision applies to future national parks since the existing ones host such lands; see Garcia-Ureta, A., 'The Role of Law in Protecting Wilderness in Spain', in Bastmeijer, *supra* note 26.

30 Case C-301/12, *Cascina Tre Pini Ss v. Ministero dell'Ambiente e della Tutela del Territorio e del Mare, Regione Lombardia, Presidenza del Consiglio dei Ministri, Consorzio Parco Lombardo della Valle del Ticino, Comune di Somma Lombardo*, para. 29.

31 Case C-309/96, *Annibaldi v. Sindaco del Comune di Guidonia and Presidente Regione Lazio*.

nation between producers or consumers. Not surprisingly the ECJ held that the establishment of a common organization did not have the effect of exempting agricultural producers from any national provisions intended to attain objectives 'other than those covered by the common organization'. There was nothing in the case to suggest that the national law was intended to implement a provision of EU law either in the sphere of agriculture or the environment or culture. The absence of EU competence on ownership rights was also a key matter in the ECJ ruling. According to the Court, given the absence of specific EU rules on expropriation and the fact that the measures relating to the common organization of the agricultural markets had no effect on systems of agricultural property ownership, it followed from Article 222 of the Treaty (as it was then, now Article 345 TFEU) that the law concerned an area which fell within the purview of the Member States.[32]

In later judgments the ECJ has maintained a similar position, insofar as the subject-matter of the cases was unrelated to EU law. *Siragusa v. Regione Sicilia – Soprintendenza Beni Culturali e Ambientali di Palermo* concerned an order requiring a site to be restored to its former state and its compatibility with Article 17 EUCFR. The site was located in a landscape conservation area. According to the national law, the owner of a property which was protected by law could not destroy it or alter it in such a way as to impair the features of the landscape which were under protection. Hence, he had to apply for landscape compatibility clearance before carrying out any alterations. The authority could authorise those alterations retrospectively if the work carried out was compatible with the features under protection. The plaintiff in the main proceedings had made alterations to his property without first obtaining landscape compatibility clearance but the competent authority declared that the works were not eligible for permission. The ECJ concluded that the objectives pursued by EU legislation were not the same as those pursued by national law, even though the landscape was one of the factors to be taken into consideration in assessing the impact of a project on the environment in accordance with environmental impact assessment rules and among the factors to be taken into consideration as part of the environmental information referred to in the Aarhus Convention.[33] By reference to *Annibaldi*, the ECJ reiterated that national legislation capable of indirectly affecting the operation of a common organisation of the agricultural markets could not in itself constitute a sufficient connection between that legislation and EU law. In conclusion, there was nothing to suggest that the provisions of national law at issue fell within the scope of EU law, this assumption being reinforced by the fact that the national law did not implement EU law.[34]

A more elaborated position on admissible restrictions to carry out certain activities in Natura 2000 sites and the compatibility of *prima facie* contradicting

[32] Case C-309/96, *supra* note 31, para. 23.

[33] Case C-206/13, *Siragusa v. Regione Sicilia – Soprintendenza Beni Culturali e Ambientali di Palermo*, para. 28.

[34] Case C-206/13, *supra* note 33, para. 35.

objectives can be found in *Azienda Agro-Zootecnica Franchini Sarl, Eolica di Altamura Srl v. Regione Puglia*. The central issue was the congruence of a ban on the installation of wind turbines not intended for home consumption with the provisions of WBD and HD. According to the ECJ, the system of protection afforded by the directives to sites forming part of the Natura 2000 network did not prohibit all human activity within those sites but 'simply' made authorisation of such activity conditional upon a prior assessment of the environmental impact of the project concerned. The effect of national law was that any plan or project for a new wind power plant was automatically refused, without any requirement for an assessment of the environmental impact of the individual plan or project on the particular site. In the light of the foregoing, it was clear that such legislation established a system for protecting Natura 2000 sites which was 'more stringent' than that established by the HD and WBD.[35]

Therefore, it was necessary to determine whether, and if so under what conditions, EU law permitted Member States to introduce stricter national protective measures than those laid down by those directives. In this particular respect, the ECJ observed that EU rules did not seek to effect complete harmonisation in the area of the environment and that Article 14 WBD indicated that Member States could introduce stricter protective measures than those provided for under that directive. Admittedly, there was no parallel provision in the HD. However, the lack of an express rule did not represent an insurmountable obstacle for the ECJ in so far as it observed that the HD had been adopted on the basis of Articles 192-193 TFEU that provided that Member States could adopt more stringent protective measures. To the extent that a measure of domestic law pursued the same objectives as the directive, Article 193 TFEU made provision for and authorised the minimum requirements laid down by that directive to be exceeded, in accordance with the conditions set by that Article.[36]

The judgment in *Azienda Agro-Zootecnica* confirms that the HD allows the carrying out of activities in Natura 2000 sites thus in principle respecting ownership rights ('the system of protection afforded by the Habitats and Birds Directives to sites forming part of the Natura 2000 network does not prohibit *all human activity* within those sites').[37] However, Member States are entitled to overcome the minimum standard set forth in the Directive and prohibit activities that, in their view, could collide with conservation objectives. In this sense, the ECJ held in *Azienda Agro-Zootecnica* that the essential purpose of national and regional legislation at issue in the main proceedings was the conservation of the areas forming part of the Natura 2000 network, and in particular the protection of the habitats of wild birds against the dangers which wind turbines could represent for them.[38]

---

35 Case C-2/10, *Azienda Agro-Zootecnica Franchini sarl and Eolica di Altamura Srl v. Regione Puglia*, para. 46.

36 Case C-2/10, *supra* note 35, para. 52.

37 Case C-2/10, *supra* note 35, para. 40, emphasis added.

38 See Sergio A., Lambertucci, S.A., Shepard, E., and Wilson, R., 'Human-wildlife conflicts in a crowded airspace', (2015) 348 *Science* 502-504.

> '[L]egislation such as that at issue in the main proceedings which, with a view to protecting wild bird populations inhabiting protected areas forming part of the Natura 2000 network, *imposes an absolute prohibition* on the construction of new wind turbines in those areas, pursues *the same objectives* as the Habitats Directive. To the extent that it provides for a stricter system of protection than that established by Article 6 of that directive, it therefore constitutes a more stringent protective measure within the meaning of Article 193 TFEU'.[39]

Arguably, the above passage contains two different statements. On the one hand, it holds that an 'absolute prohibition' is part of the objectives of the Directive. In other words, the ECJ would have accepted that, under reasonable justifications, Member States were entitled to prohibit activities altogether, not just those expressly mentioned in respect of species mentioned in Annex IV or wild birds including those whose presence requires the declaration of SPAs (Annex I WBD). The second statement holds that a general prohibition aligned with the objectives of the Directive is a more stringent measure and should be viewed in the light of Article 193 TFEU.

Nevertheless, the analysis of the compatibility of a general prohibition was not limited to the objectives of the HD. In effect, the ECJ examined a second dimension that was related to 'the other provisions' of the TFUE, in particular those relating to energy. The plaintiffs in the main proceedings argued that the objective of developing new and renewable energies (Article 194(1) TFUE), as set out in EU policy should take precedence over the goals of environmental protection pursued by the HD and WBD. This argument was weak in the light of the TFUE as EU energy policy must take into account the need to preserve and improve the environment.[40] In addition, the ECJ observed that the general prohibition did not entirely rule out the installation of wind turbines in Natura 2000 sites. A measure only prohibiting the location of new wind turbines not intended for self-consumption on those sites, with the possibility of exemption for wind turbines intended for self-consumption with a capacity not exceeding 20 kW, was not, in view of 'its limited scope', liable to jeopardise the EU objective of developing new and renewable forms of energy.[41] However, the ECJ judgment raises some questions. First, whether a limited prohibition of wind turbines beyond a given threshold could actually jeopardize an EU energy objective. In other words, whether the ECJ properly employed comparable terms, i.e., a limited prohibition in certain territorial areas in a Member State *versus* a policy objective applicable to the EU as whole. Conversely, the ECJ did not consider whether an accumulation of wind turbines intended for self-consumption could eventually jeopardise Natura 2000 objectives. It assumed that below the threshold set out by national law the wind turbines were acceptable in terms of biodiversity protection.

39 Case C-2/10, *supra* note 35, para. 57, emphasis added.

40 Article 194(1) TFEU; see case C-213/96, *Outokumpu Oy*, para. 33.

41 Case C-2/10, *supra* note 35, para. 57.

4. Compensation Measures and Property Rights in Environmental Assessments under the Habitats Directive

The HD requires the carrying out of environmental assessments in the case of plans or projects likely to affect Natura 2000 sites.[42] It is not the purpose of this contribution to examine this mechanism in detail but the effects derived from compensation measures, as required by Article 6(4) HD, on ownership rights. It should first be observed that projects not subject to environmental assessment still fall within the duty to avoid deterioration enshrined in Article 6(2) HD. Secondly, there are no references in that provision concerning the possible location of compensatory measures, or the types of properties that may host such measures, these issues being left to the Member States. According to the Commission's guidelines,[43] the local conditions necessary to reinstate the ecological assets at stake are to be found as close as possible to the area affected by the plan or project. Therefore, the carrying out of compensation measures within or nearby the Natura 2000 site concerned in a location showing suitable conditions for the measures to be successful seems 'the most preferred option'.[44] However, the Commission has also acknowledged that this is not always possible. It is for this reason that three possibilities have been suggested: (a) compensation within the Natura 2000 site provided the necessary elements to ensure ecological coherence and network functionality exist within the site; (b) compensation outside the Natura 2000 site concerned, but within a common topographical or landscape unit, provided the same contribution to the ecological structure and/or network function is feasible; (c) compensation outside the Natura 2000 site, in a different topographical or landscape unit.[45] The HD (and the Commission) seems to assume that the execution of such compensatory measures can always be possible. Leaving aside the question of transferable credits,[46] developers may encounter difficulties in carrying out

[42] Article 6(3). See Krämer, L.,'The European Commission's Opinions under Article 6(4) of the Habitats Directive' (2009) *Journal of Environmental Law* 59-85; García-Ureta, A., 'Habitats Directive and Environmental Assessment of Plans and Projects', (2007) *Journal for European environmental & planning law* 84-96; McGillivray, D., 'Compensating biodiversity loss: the EU Commission's approach to compensation under Article 6 of the Habitats Directive', (2012) *Journal of Environmental Law* 417-450; de Sadeleer, N., 'The Appropriate Impact Assessment and Authorisation Requirements of Plans and Projects likely to have Significant Impacts on Natura 2000 Sites', (2013) *ELNI Law Journal* 7-22; Aragão, A., and van Rijswick, H., 'Compensation in the European Union: Natura 2000 and Water Law', (2014) *Utrecht Law Review* 155-160.

[43] Guidance document on Article 6(4) of the 'Habitats Directive' 92/43/EEC (hereinafter Guidance document); http://ec.europa.eu/environment/nature/natura2000/management/docs/art6/guidance_art6_4_en.pdf.

[44] Guidance document, *supra* note 43, at 18.

[45] Ibid.

[46] According to the Commission, '[t]he option of habitat banking as compensatory measure under Article 6(4) is of very limited value due to the tight criteria mentioned in relation to the need for compensation

compensatory measures, especially when they involve the creation of new areas, unless they hold other available lands or conclude agreements with third parties owing such lands. But what would happen if such third parties refuse to sell their land or to allow the execution of compensatory measures on their terrains? Member States laws could certainly impose such obligation but it would surely require the payment of compensation. Should the competent authorities in the Member States carry out the corresponding purchases or expropriations (also at the developer's expense)? Should public lands host compensation measures in those cases? More acute difficulties may be encountered if expropriations are to be performed outside the competence of a particular authority or the implementation of compensation measures are to take place in a third Member State because of the transboundary character of the habitats or species concerned. These issues should be resolved by the Member States in so far as EU law does not provide any guidance thus undermining the transfrontier dimension of Natura 2000. However, it should be noted that EU law does not accept as justification for the breach of the duty to compensate the existence of internal difficulties, e.g., the opposition of landowners likely to be affected by those measures. The (strangely) limited number of opinions delivered by the Commission under Article 6(4) has not tackled the relationship between ownership rights and the execution of compensation measures by assuming that the measures submitted by the Member States (and accepted by the Commission) could be carried out in spite of certain difficulties on the side of ownership rights.

5. Declassification of Sites and Ownership Rights

An arguably clear-cut vision of ownership rights versus Natura 2000 sites emerged in a case related to the declassification of a Natura 2000 site. As seen above, in *Cascina* the ECJ had to examine whether it was possible to declassify a site owing to the extension of an airport and the increase in environmental degradation. According to the ECJ, the obligation on the Member States to propose to the Commission the declassification of a site on the list of sites which had become '*irretrievably* unsuitable' to achieve the objectives of the HD, was 'all the greater' when that site included land belonging to an owner whose exercise of his ownership right was restricted as a result of that listing, when it was no longer warranted for the site to remain subject to the provisions of the directive. As long as the quality of the site in question met the requirements for its classification, such restrictions of the right to property were, 'as a rule', justified by the objective of protecting the environment laid down in that directive. However, where those qualities 'definitively disappeared', continuing to restrict the use of that site could be an infringement of the right to property.[47]

to ensure the protection of the coherence of the network': Guidance document, *supra* note 43, at 14.

47 As elsewhere in the judgment, the ECJ coincided with the findings of the advocate general, who had said that the determining factor was the fundamental right to property. In her opinion, it was incompatible with an interpretation and application of Article 4(1) (fourth sentence) of the HD in accordance with

The questions whether the HD allows a declassification of SCIs and how the ECJ employed a rather disputable reasoning in *Cascina* is a matter that exceeds the purposes of this contribution. It suffices now to address the relationship between the declassification of sites and ownership rights as the ECJ ruling reflects an underlying contradiction with its position concerning actions for annulment (Article 263 TFUE) against the classification of SCIs carried out by the Commission. In the light of consistent but restrictive standing criteria, the ECJ has held that the Commission's classification decision is *vis-à-vis* any person concerned 'of general application inasmuch as it applies to all economic operators who, in whatever capacity, carry on or are likely to carry on activities in the areas concerned which could jeopardise the conservation objectives of the Habitats Directive'.[48] The fact that it is possible to determine more or less precisely the number, or even the identity, of the persons to whom a measure applies by no means implies that that decision must be regarded as being of individual concern to those persons where it is established that that application takes effect by virtue of an objective legal or factual situation defined by the measure in question. In conclusion, as the ECJ held in *Sahlstedt*, the classification decision is of concern to appellants only in so far as they have rights in the lands covered by some of the SCIs adopted by the Commission, that is to say, 'by virtue of an objective legal or factual situation defined by the measure in question and not in accordance with criteria specific to the category of landowners'. In other words, the contested decision is not adopted in the light of the specific situation of the landowners. Hence, it cannot be regarded as a group of individual decisions addressed to each landowner.[49]

The ECJ ruling in *Cascina* contradicts the previous (and disputable) case law as it is now acknowledged that the classification of SCIs does in effect affect ownership rights. This inconsistency was also perceived by the Advocate General in *Sahlstedt*. In his opinion, the Commission's decision classifying SCIs did in itself have direct consequences on the legal situation of the landowners, even in the absence of any conservation measures adopted by the Member State concerned. According to the Advocate General, the decision was neither a 'declaratory act' nor merely an intermediate measure, because it laid down definitively the Commission's position with regard to the sites SCIs.[50] In addition, the Commission's decision also constituted a measure having adverse effects. By classifying as SCIs the areas of land in which the landowners had rights, the decision deprived the landowners of the right to use that land as they wished. The consequence of the decision was to encumber their rights with new restrictions which were not in existence at the time when they acquired those rights and which make them more difficult to exercise. As a result of the

fundamental rights for the consideration of a reasoned application by owners for a proposal for the reclassification of SCIs to be left to the discretion of the competent authorities.

48 Case C-362/06 P, *Sahlstedt v. Commission*, para. 28.

49 Case C-362/06 P, *supra* note 48, paras. 30-33.

50 Advocate General Bot, in case C-362/06 P, *supra* note 48, para. 68.

decision, the landowners could no longer use or sell their lands without account being taken of the fact that they were classified as sites of Community importance. The measures to be adopted by the Member States to comply with the HD constituted further restrictions on the exercise of the right to property and were directly linked to the classification of the landowners' property as SCIs.[51] Although the case law derived from *Sahlstedt* was arguably held to deter an avalanche of challenges against decisions approving the corresponding lists of SCIs in the Member States,[52] the ruling in *Cascina* could be regarded as an unacquainted recognition that those decisions do in fact affect third parties' rights, paving the way to further challenges. In fact, the classification of a protected site on property rights may admit different degrees depending on the stages of that procedure, i.e., formal designation *versus* the adoption of management rules (as required by Article 6(1)) that could lead to a *de facto* expropriation.[53]

6. Habitats, Species and Ownership Rights

a) The status of species in EU law

EU law does not regulate the status of species in terms of property ownership. Species are protected due to scientific criteria (e.g., degree of vulnerability). The WBD and HD follow a different approach in this particular respect. The first Directive enshrines three layers of protection. The first layer protects 'all' species of naturally occurring birds in the wild state in the European territory of the Member States to which the Treaty applies.[54] The second layer concerns hunting provisions.[55] Only the birds included into Annex II (a) and (b) can be subject to hunting. This also means that only legally hunted birds can be commercialized (sale, transport for sale, keeping for sale and the offering for sale).[56] The third layer encompasses bird species that deserve special conservation measures concerning their habitat in order to ensure their survival and reproduction in their area of distribution.[57] Even though the HD sets out

[51] The Spanish Supreme Court has held a similar doctrine according to which the list of sites drawn up by the Autonomous Communities is not something innocuous, something that does not produce legal effects. It is not a mere neutral proposal, but an administrative act that enables and obliges the Autonomous Community to adopt 'adequate protective measures' for the sites included in such lists, which may perhaps affect certain elements of ownership rights; Spanish Supreme Court Judgment of 11 May 2009, appeal 2965/2007.

[52] See Case T-136/04, Freiherr von Cramer-Klett-Rechtlerverband Pfronten v. Commission; Case T-80/05, Bavendam v. Commission; case T-100/05, Compagnie d'entreprises CFE SA v. Commission; T-117/05, Rodenbröker v. Commission; Case T-122/05, Benkö v. Commission; Case T-322/06, Espinosa Labella v. Commission; Case T-323/06, Fresyga S.A. v. Commission; Case T-345/06, Complejo Agrícola v Commission; Case T- 366/06, Calebus v Commission.

[53] On this matter see Winter, *supra* note 6, at 220-223.

[54] See, however, case C-202/94, Criminal proceedings against Godefridus van der Feesten, para. 12.

[55] Article 7 WBD.

[56] Article 6(1) WBD.

[57] Article 4 and Annex I WBD.

hunting, picking, collecting, cutting, uprooting and trade prohibitions, it does not protect 'all' European species or habitats albeit the CBD requires both the EU and the Member States to protect 'biodiversity' which is a much broader notion. The Directive enlists a series of priority habitats and species that require the designation of special areas of conservation. In addition, certain species are under a system of strict protection.[58] By contrast, Member States may take measures to ensure that the taking in the wild of specimens of species of wild fauna and flora listed in Annex V as well as their exploitation is compatible with their being maintained at a favourable conservation status. In other words, these latter species are in principle subject to exploitation.

The provisions and annexes to the WBD and HD are not conceived in patrimonial terms, nor are birds, habitats and other species categorized as public domain. It may be debatable whether the two directives demand the adoption of particular rules to classify them as special ownership rights owing to their EU categorization as 'common heritage'. As indicated before, EU Law has refrained from setting out ownership rules in respect of protected species. Its main concern is their protection. Nevertheless, this statement should be nuanced in various ways. First, birds and specially protected species may not be killed or captured (the latter including the taking of eggs, even empty ones).[59] Likewise, they may not be deliberately disturbed. These prohibitions do necessarily affect property rights. Species have traditionally been regarded as property that may be acquired by occupancy.[60] Hunting (or capture) prohibitions impose clear cut obstacles for the acquisition of such species even if they are located in private properties. Unlike birds or other animal species, protected plants do not move freely but they cannot be exploited by owners of lands hosting them, including public lands.[61] Therefore, as in the case of animals, a private owner or a public authority, e.g., a scientific body requires an exemption under the limited number of justifications set forth in both directives to overcome any of the prohibitions protecting the species.[62] Therefore, it could be concluded that in those cases ownership rights are mainly restricted to aesthetic enjoyment of such species, e.g., bird watching or plant contemplating. The question whether such prohibitions amount to deprivation of ownership rights would basically be for the Member States to examine in the light of Article 1 of Protocol 1.

The prohibition on disturbing species also provides a different perspective on the reach of the WBD and HD when analysed from the angle of ownership rights. Both Directives forbid the deliberate disturbance of protected species particularly during the period of breeding, rearing, hibernation and migration.[63]

---

58 Article 12 HD.

59 Article 5 WBD.

60 E.g., Article 610 of the Spanish Civil Code.

61 Likewise, Directive 2004/35 protects habitats and species regardless of property titles.

62 Article 9 WDB; Article 12 HD.

63 Article 5(d) WBD. Article 4(4) refers to protection areas requiring the Member States to take appropriate steps to avoid any disturbances affecting the birds, in so far as these would be significant having

Compliance with this prohibition may well entail the proscription to carry out any operations which are usually within the core content of property ownership, e.g., access to certain lands, grazing fields, let alone circulate with vehicles in private properties as long as there may be a danger of disturbance.[64] Neither the WDB nor the HD expressly requires the adoption of measures to restrict access to properties to comply with the said prohibitions but this would be the natural outcome derived from the directives. In fact, it is somewhat remarkable that the HD requires the Member States to adopt regulations regarding access to certain properties but only in respect of species enumerated in Annex V (the exploitation of which is in principle allowed).[65] Be that as it may, it should be noted that the WBD requires the Member States to guarantee that species to which hunting laws apply are not hunted during the rearing season or during the '*various stages* of reproduction'.[66] The HD contains a similar provision in respect of priority animal species. This means that Member States must necessarily assure that the majority of young birds or species have in effect completed their rearing by demanding, as the case may be, the closure of properties hosting such species. Although the case law has not addressed this matter in terms of ownership rights, case C-38/99, *Commission v. France*, may exemplify the reach of that obligation on property ownership. The ECJ concluded that the French authorities had not complied with Article 7(4) WBD (mentioned above) by holding that in the case of mallards, in eight departments 'no more than 80 %' of young birds were able to fly by the early opening date for hunting; on the same date, in 26 other departments, a maximum of 90 % of young birds were able to fly; in the case of the coot, in eight departments, no more than 80 % of young birds were able to fly by the early opening date of hunting; in 15 other departments, no more than 90 % of young birds were able to fly by that date.[67] The strict position adopted by the ECJ was firmly based on the principle of complete protection which pervades the Directive and necessarily prevails over third parties' ownership rights.

As said above, access to breeding areas, including those which may be defined as public domain, must (not merely may) on certain occasions be banned under the WBD and HD. This situation is well exemplified by a case concerning beaches used for breeding by the marine turtle which were subject to intense human presence during that period. The ECJ ruling is important for various reasons. First, it highlighted the range of activities that may be regarded as deliberate disturbance. According to the ECJ, it was undisputed that the use

regard to the objectives of this Article. The HD refers to the 'disturbance of species' for which SCAs have been designated. Article 12(d) concerns species mentioned in Annex IV. Article 15 prohibits the use of all indiscriminate means capable of causing local disappearance of, or serious disturbance of species mentioned in Annex IV(a) and V(a).

64 Public domain lands should also be subject to similar restrictions.

65 Article 14(2) (first indent) WBD.

66 Article 7(4) (second paragraph) WBD.

67 Case C-38/99, *Commission v. France*, para. 25.

of mopeds on a beach used for breeding by the turtle was, particularly owing to the noise pollution, liable to disturb that species during the laying period, the incubation period and the hatching of the eggs, as well as during the baby turtles' migration to the sea. Even though the ECJ mainly referred to mopeds and boats, the case notes that the Commission had reported that there were a significant number of 'beach umbrellas' and 'deck-chairs' on various beaches.[68] The Greek authorities argued that nocturnal supervision of the eastern part of one of the beaches was, at the material time, particularly difficult to ensure owing to the length of the beach, the high number of access points and the low number of supervisors. These allegations did not convince the ECJ. Even though the judgment did not require the closure of the beach, at least in express terms, it could be argued that the most effective solution was to seal the beach to allow the turtles to complete their breeding. It should also be observed that the case concerned an accessible area by bathers and the general public. Whilst it may be much more unproblematic to foreclose protected areas particularly if they are slightly subject to human intervention, e.g., a nature reserve, EU law requires in effect the adoption of protection measures regardless of their status and of ownership rights exercised over them, e.g., SPAs located in urban areas.[69]

b) Habitats and species as 'common heritage' of the EU and ownership rights

According to the preamble to the CBD, the conservation of biological diversity is a 'common concern' of humankind.[70] However, this notion is not repeated anywhere in its provisions. Strictly speaking, only its *protection* would be a common concern. However, it would be rather inconsistent to proclaim that an activity related to biodiversity is a 'common concern' (no matter the meaning of this term) and at the same time detach biodiversity from that notion. Be that as it may, the States parties to the CBD have manifested that the conservation of biodiversity transcends their own boundaries.[71] However, this declaration is to be also viewed within the framework of well-established principles underpinning the Convention, i.e., that States have 'the sovereign right to exploit their *own* resources pursuant to their *own* environmental policies',[72] and that they enjoy sovereign rights over their own biological resources.[73]

The preamble to the WBD proclaims that bird species 'constitute a common heritage'.[74] This notion is not mentioned in any of its provisions. Neither the

68 Case C-103/00, *Commission v. Greece*, para. 8.

69 As Advocate Fennelly indicated in Case C-44/95, *supra* note 20, para. 88: 'Birds of such species whose habitat happens to be adjacent to an industrial development are no less deserving of protection under the Directive than those to be found in more remote areas.'

70 Third recital to the preamble.

71 Glowka, L., *A Guide to the Convention on Biological Diversity* (IUCN-The World Conservation Union, 1994) at 10.

72 Article 3, emphasis added.

73 Fourth recital to the preamble to the CBD.

74 Fourth recital to the preamble.

TFEU nor the HD contains a similar statement. However, this latter Directive declares that the adoption of measures intended to promote the conservation of priority natural habitats and priority species of Community interest is a '*common responsibility* of all Member States' a wording also mentioned in the WBD.[75] The meaning of 'common heritage' refers to resources that are not exclusively subject to a State but neither are they under the exclusive control of one State. These resources usually enjoy a biogeophysical unit being located simultaneously in the territory of two or more States also sharing geographical continuity.[76] A community of interests involving a limited number of States would therefore exercise shared rights over those resources.[77] However, the recognition that species are a common heritage of the EU as a whole also means that it is the EU, the supranational organization that is empowered to impose basic criteria on their protection, the Member States being deprived from such competence. Nevertheless, the ECJ case law has not drawn conclusions on the link between the notion of common heritage and ownership rights, including the duty to preserve such heritage for future generations as enshrined in the Bern Convention.[78] The EU would have addressed this latter issue by creating a network of areas not subjected to time constraints. However, the transfrontier categorization of species, habitats and protected sites does not alter their status in the light of ownership rights, save in the case of prohibitions concerning their killing, capture or in particular trade. In other words, the fact that species are a 'common heritage' does not mean that a new form of property has been created at EU level or has been transferred to the EU.

The transfrontier dimension was well exemplified in a case concerning national law restricting the protection to birds living in the wild state only in the Benelux countries. The ECJ held that the protective effect of the directive also covered species of naturally occurring birds in the wild state in the European territory of another Member State which were not naturally or usually to be found in the territory of the Benelux countries but which were transported there, kept there or marketed there, whether alive or dead.[79] A subsequent case against France has arguably more importance for ownership rights. The ECJ reacted against an attempt to limit the cross-border nature of the Directive as

75 Ibid.

76 Timoshenko, A. S., 'International Legal Problems of Environmental Protection in the European Region', (1989) *Connecticut Journal of International Law* 441, 446.

77 Birnie, P., Boyle, A., y Redgwell, C., *International Law & The Environment* (Oxford, University Press, 2009), 192-194; Brunnée, J., 'Common areas, common heritage and common concern', in Bodansky, D., Brunnée, J., and Hey, H., (ed.), *The Oxford Handbook of International Environmental Law* (Oxford, 2007), 550-573: Dupuy, P-M., and Viñuales, J.E., *International Environmental Law* (Cambridge, 2015), 82-86.

78 Third recital to the preamble: 'wild flora and fauna constitute a natural heritage of aesthetic, scientific, cultural, recreational, economic and intrinsic value that needs to be preserved and handed on to future generations'.

79 Case 247/85, *Commission v. Belgium*, para. 22; see also case 252/85, *Commission v. France*; case C-507/04, *Commission v. Austria*, para. 99.

a result of a French law that guaranteed the protection of birds, their habitats and their nests when a particular scientific interest or the need to preserve the 'national biological heritage' justified their conservation. After recalling the previous ruling, the ECJ held that the importance of complete and effective protection of wild birds throughout the Community caused any national legislation which delimited the protection of wild birds by reference to the concept of national heritage to be incompatible with the Directive.[80] The ruling also highlighted that wild birds have to be protected irrespective of the areas they stay in or pass through.[81] This matter is important because attention has mainly been focused on the designation of special protection areas, that is, properly demarcated terrestrial zones,[82] whilst passing corridors have largely been neglected possibly owing to the difficulties to pin them down. Needless to say, Member States are under a duty to specify flying passing areas and impose any restrictions on properties likely to be affected by such designations.

C. Concluding Remarks

The preceding paragraphs have analysed the WBD and HD from the perspective of their impact on ownership rights. The directives contain limited references to such rights, this matter apparently being left to the Member States. Even though the WBD and the HD indicate that the measures adopted to implement their objectives are to take account of 'economic requirements', they do not define this term. In principle both directives conceive such notion in a negative fashion as opposed to the environmental objectives underpinning them. It is for this reason that the ECJ has repeatedly held that economic requirements do not constitute an 'autonomous derogation' from the general system of protection set out in the directives. The preamble to the HD declares that its main aim is to promote the maintenance of biodiversity, taking account of economic, social, cultural and regional requirements and that the maintenance of such biodiversity 'may in certain cases require *the maintenance, or indeed the encouragement*, of human activities'.[83] The ECJ ruling in *Azienda Agro-Zootecnica Franchini Sarl* holds that 'the system of protection afforded by the Habitats and Birds Directives to sites forming part of the Natura 2000 network does not prohibit *all human activity* within those sites'. However, Member States' regulations must necessarily be subordinated to the objectives of the HD. Therefore, they may control, or as the case may be, curtail ownership rights to guarantee such objectives. In the same case the ECJ held that national legislation which, with a view to protecting wild bird populations inhabiting protected

80 Case 252/85, *Commission v. France*, para. 15; see also case C-240/00, *Commission v. Finland*, para. 16; and case C-507/04, *Commission v. Austria*, para. 103.

81 Case 247/85, *supra* note 79, para. 15.

82 Maritime areas must also be designated.

83 Third recital to the preamble.

areas forming part of the Natura 2000 network, imposes an absolute prohibition on the construction of new wind turbines in those areas pursues 'the same objectives as the HD'. To the extent that it provides for a stricter system of protection than that established by Article HD, it therefore constitutes a more stringent protective measure within the meaning of Article 193 TFEU.[84]

EU law does not regulate the status of species in terms of property ownership. The preamble to the WBD proclaims that bird species 'constitute a common heritage'.[85] The recognition that species are a common heritage of the EU as a whole also means that it is the EU, the supranational organization empowered to impose basic criteria for their protection, the Member States being deprived from such competence. Nevertheless, ECJ case law has not drawn conclusions on the link between the notion of common heritage and ownership rights. It may also be debatable whether the two directives demand the adoption of particular rules to classify them as special ownership rights. Nevertheless, birds and specially protected species cannot be killed or captured. Likewise, they cannot be deliberately disturbed. These prohibitions do necessarily affect property rights and require the Member States to adopt positive rules regulating the exercise of ownership rights, these not just being affected as a result of a set of prohibitions.

---

84 Case C-2/10, *supra* note 35, para. 52.

85 Fourth recital to the preamble.

Property and Environmental Protection in Investor – State Arbitration

Ole Kristian Fauchald

A. Introduction*

The consequences of international investment agreements (IIAs)[1] for environmental policies have been on the agenda of environmental bureaucrats and NGOs at least since the early 1990s.[2] A variety of legal bases may be available to an investor whose property rights are limited by measures of host states, including in particular provisions regarding expropriation, fair and equitable treatment, non-discrimination and transfer. This chapter shall focus on the combination of expropriation clauses and effective investor – state dispute settlement (ISDS) in such treaties. Expropriation clauses secure a minimum level of protection of foreign investors. Such protection may go beyond the protection afforded by national treatment clauses[3] in cases where both domestic and foreign investors are deprived of their investment without compensation. The right to initiate ISDS is provided so that investors have access to effective legal remedies without having to rely on the courts of the host state. The main alternatives to ISDS would be diplomatic protection through state – state dispute settlement or for investors to bring cases to human rights courts or treaty bodies.[4]

One dilemma for countries when drafting IIAs is to secure extensive protection of their investors while simultaneously retaining a high degree of flexibility when developing new policies. Countries that regard themselves mainly as sources of investment would generally favour extensive protection of investors, while countries that regard themselves mainly as hosts to investments would prefer to guard their policy space, but may be willing to limit the policy space in order to attract investment. Historically, IIAs have favoured the perspective of source countries. Today, however, most countries are both sources of and hosts

---

* The author grateful to Daniel Behn, Richard Macrory and Gerd Winter for insightful comments.

1 IIAs include bilateral investment treaties (BITs), multilateral investment treaties (such as the Energy Charter Treaty, 1992), and investment chapters in free trade agreements (such as chapter 11 of the North American Free Trade Agreement, 1994).

2 The topic was high on the agenda of the OECD (environmental issues were introduced in the Guidelines for Multinational Enterprises in 1991 and were also significant during negotiations of the Multilateral Agreement on Investment) and of the negotiators of the North American Free Trade Agreement (it resulted in the inclusion of environmental clauses in chapter 11 of NAFTA).

3 National treatment is treatment no less favourable than that accorded to domestic investors or investment.

4 Historically, the property rights of foreign investors have been protected through diplomatic protection. Case law in this regard has been based on treaties, customary international law, and municipal law. Examples include the Elettronica Sicula S.p.A. (ELSI) case decided by the International Court of Justice on the basis of Treaty of Friendship, Commerce and Navigation between Italy and United States (1948), cases decided by the Iran – United States Claims Tribunal on the basis of the Treaty of Amity between Iran and the United States (1955), as well as Norwegian Shipowners' Claim (Norway v. United States) (1921) 1 R.I.A.A. 307 where the tribunal applied a mix of municipal law and customary international law.

to investment and will therefore have to strike a balance between investment protection and policy space.

This chapter explores how the issue of expropriation has been dealt with in IIAs, with a main focus on a selection of model IIAs and the Energy Charter Treaty, and in recent ISDS, with a main focus on decisions during the last three years. First, the chapter will consider the scope of expropriation clauses in light of the definition of 'investment' in treaties and case law. Thereafter follows a brief discussion of whose rights are protected and the possibility of 'treaty shopping'. The main discussion of the chapter concerns the extent to which expropriation clauses extend to situations of 'regulatory taking'. Finally, the chapter considers issues regarding amount of compensation.

B. Definition of Investment

Expropriation clauses in IIAs apply to 'investment', and their scope therefore depends on the definition of investment according to 1) the IIA in question and 2) general rules developed through case law.

1) The definition of investment in IIAs is in general broadly formulated and may extend beyond what many countries would define as 'property' for the purpose of expropriation under domestic law. From an environmental perspective, it is of particular interest whether and to what extent such definitions extend to public authorities' acceptance of potentially environmentally harmful activities. Such acceptance may take different forms, including decisions (e.g. permits or concessions), contracts, other written or oral commitments, and implied acceptance through acts or passivity. To the extent that such acceptance is to be regarded as 'investment', public authorities may be prevented from withdrawing or revising the acceptance without paying compensation. This may provide foreign investors a privilege not afforded to their equivalent national competitors where environmental authorities under national law may be entitled to alter or withdraw acceptance without paying compensation.

The definitions of investment generally refer to 'every kind of asset' followed by a non-exhaustive list of assets. The starting point is consequently whether a permit, contract or implied acceptance of environmentally harmful activities is to be regarded as an asset of the investor. From the perspective of the investor, an asset could extend to all preconditions for the investment activities to continue. Items that are listed as assets in the accounts of an investor would normally qualify, but such listing is not a precondition to be treated as an investment.

Most model IIAs examined for the purpose of this article explicitly state that 'investment' extends to concessions to explore, grow (or cultivate), extract or exploit natural resources, and cover such concessions regardless of whether they are granted by law, administrative decisions or contracts.[5] While it is obvi-

[5] This is the case, with minor variations, for the model IIAs of Germany (2008), Colombia (2007), France (2006), and Italy (2003). The Indian model IIA (2003) only mentions 'concessions to search for and extract oil and other minerals'.

ous that such language extends to concessions to fish, to mine for minerals, to extract water, as well as to land-based and marine farming, it might be less clear whether it extends to permits to emit pollutants, to use environmentally harmful chemicals in production processes, or to construction permits and contracts. The reference to 'natural resources' in the definitions does not limit the definition to traditional exploitation of natural resources, since it is only provided as an example of an asset. On the one hand, it is clear from practice that construction permits could be regarded as investment.[6] Where a permit, such as a pollution permit, is decisive for whether a plant can operate, it is most likely to be assessed as an integral part of the whole investment.[7] It is probably not decisive, but might be a relevant factor in cases of doubt, whether the concession, permit or contract can be transferred to others. Implied acceptance through passivity cannot as such be regarded as an investment. To qualify as an investment, the acceptance must be in the form of an act of public authorities or actors operating on their behalf.

In cases where there is doubt about the status of an acceptance, the final determination of whether it qualifies as an investment will depend on an overall assessment of the acceptance in light of certain criteria. When seen from the perspective of the investor, it can be argued that the defining criteria should be the extent to which the activities of the investor depend on the acceptance in question, the extent to which the investor has used resources in order to obtain the acceptance, options available to the investor should the acceptance be annulled or amended, and the implications of acts of public authorities for the legitimate expectations of the investor. However, given the potential harmful ness of the investors' activities and the polluter-pays principle, it is clear that public authorities may in some cases intervene without having to pay compensation to the investor. But it is not decisive, nor arguably relevant, whether national law provides for compensation in such situations. It can be argued that the extent to which the acceptance explicitly awards a clear and unqualified right to the investor should constitute the most important criterion.

It is not clear from case law which criteria are to be regarded as relevant and how they should be weighed against each other in specific cases. The US Model BIT of 2012 provides an attempt at clarifying the criteria and their application in stating the following in a footnote to article 1:

Whether a particular type of license, authorization, permit, or similar instrument (including a concession, to the extent that it has the nature of such an instrument) has the characteristics of an investment depends on such factors as the nature and extent of the rights that the holder has under the law of the Party. Among the licenses, authorizations, permits, and similar instruments that do

6 For a discussion of some examples regarding construction permits, see OECD, International Investment Law: Understanding Concepts and Tracking Innovations (2008) pp. 63-67.

7 See Abengoa & COFIDES v Mexico (18 April 2013) paras. 572-624 (in particular para. 619) which concerned, inter alia, the relationship between a general permit to operate a plant and the need for specific environmental permits.

not have the characteristics of an investment are those that do not create any rights protected under domestic law.

This text favours a focus on the nature and extent of the rights explicitly provided by the acceptance, and seems to indicate that criteria which pay particular attention to the perspective of the investor should not be taken into account.

2) In addition to these definitions of investment, there are general rules limiting the scope of the investment concept. The legal basis for and the content of the general rules remain somewhat contested.[8] In cases where such limitations are included in the IIAs,[9] it can be argued that only the rules included in the IIA apply and that additional general rules do not apply.[10] In contrast, it can be argued that general rules following from the general reference to 'investment' in article 25 of the ICSID Convention[11] extend to all ICSID cases regardless of the wording of the specific IIA. The most famous decision in this regard is the Salini case (2001) which set out the following when discussing the implications of article 25:

> The doctrine generally considers that investment infers: contributions, a certain duration of performance of the contract and a participation in the risks of the transaction ... In reading the Convention's preamble, one may add the contribution to the economic development of the host State of the investment as an additional condition.
>
> In reality, these various elements may be interdependent. Thus, the risks of the transaction may depend on the contributions and the duration of performance of the contract. As a result, these various criteria should be assessed globally even if, for the sake of reasoning, the Tribunal considers them individually here.[12]

It has also been argued that such limitations apply generally regardless of the applicability of the ICSID Convention.[13]

One situation of interest is where investors have failed to obtain mandatory environmental permits. Such investors may lose protection under the IIAs in

---

8 See R. Dolzer and C. Schreuer, Principles of International Investment Law, 2nd ed., Oxford University Press (2012) pp. 66-76.

9 Examples are the limitation to investment done in accordance with domestic law in the model agreements of India (2003), Italy (2003) and Colombia (2007), as well as the limitations of the US model agreement (2012) to an asset that 'has the characteristics of an investment, including such characteristics as the commitment of capital or other resources, the expectation of gain or profit, or the assumption of risk.'

10 Such an argument would be particularly important where such rules as the one included in the US model agreement are included. It would be less convincing where the IIA merely requires lawfulness of the investment.

11 'The jurisdiction of the Centre shall extend to any legal dispute arising directly out of an investment ...'.

12 Salini Costruttori S.p.A. and Italstrade S.p.A. v. Morocco, ICSID Case No. ARB/00/4, para. 52.

13 See M. Sornarajah, The International Law on Foreign Investment, 3rd ed., Cambridge University Press (2010) pp. 317-318.

cases where the IIAs require the investment to be established in accordance with domestic law.[14] Arguably, they may also lose protection where the IIA in question is silent on the issue of compliance with domestic law. Where failure to comply with environmental law occurs in good faith, e.g. based on assurances from the permit issuing authority of the host state that such permits are not required, protection of the IIA would remain regardless of whether superior authorities or the courts of the host state subsequently conclude that a permit was required.[15] If such assurances are provided by public authorities other than the permit-issuing authorities, are based on erroneous implementation of clear provisions of environmental law, or are based on inadequate information provided by the investor, protection under the IIA would most likely be lost. Some tribunals have argued that loss of protection must be limited to breaches of fundamental legal principles of the host state,[16] breaches of legislation directly related to investment,[17] and cases of serious violation of domestic legislation.[18] While the legal bases for the tribunals' narrow reading of the treaty language seem weak, there are good reasons for concluding that loss of protection at least to some extent depends on the links between the investment, the legislation and the seriousness of the non-compliance.[19] The clarity of the environmental legislation may be an important factor. Where the IIA does not include any requirement regarding compliance with domestic law, loss of protection would be limited to cases of clear, significant and bad faith non-compliance.[20]

A further question is whether protection can be lost due to violation of environmental laws of the host state *after* the establishment of the investment. This could be the case where the IIA requires that the investment be carried out in accordance with domestic law. Such clauses are uncommon in IIAs. Where there is no clear basis for extending the lawfulness requirement to the post establishment phase, the protection of the IIAs would generally not be

14 This issue must be distinguished from cases where no permit was required when the investment was made and the duty to obtain a permit has been established through new legislation, see section 4 below. For a more detailed analysis of these issues, see T. Acedo, When may Foreign Investors Lose the Protection of Investment Treaties Due to Misconduct? (2014), available at http://papers.ssrn.com/sol3/papers.cfm?abstract_id=2433578, pp. 4-31. See also T. Obersteiner, 'In Accordance with Domestic Law' Clauses: How International Investment Tribunals Deal with Allegations of Unlawful Conduct of Investors, 31 Journal of International Arbitration no. 2 (2014) pp. 265-288, and Christina Knahr, Investments 'in accordance with host state law'. 4 Transnational Dispute Management no. 5 (2007).

15 Ioannis Kardassopoulos vs. Georgia, para. 182.

16 L.E.S.I. v. Algérie, para. 83; and Rumeli v. Kazakhstan, para. 319.

17 Saba Fakes v. Turkey, para. 119. See also Quiborax vs. Bolivia, paras. 263-266.

18 Tokios Tokelés v. Ukraine, para. 84-86. See also Mytilineos Holdings v. State Union of Serbia & Montenegro and Republic of Serbia, para. 137-8; Alpha Projektholding v. Ukraine, paras. 294-297; Alasdair Ross Anderson et al v. Costa Rica, para. 52; and Dolzer and Schreuer, supra note 8, p. 93.

19 See Acedo, supra note 14, pp. 15-19 and 22-23.

20 The main case of relevance in this respect is Plama v. Bulgaria paras. 135-144. See also Jan Oostergetel v. Slovak Republic; and Gustav F. W. Hamester v. Ghana.

suspended. Nevertheless, non-compliance with environmental legislation could be relevant when determining the merits of the claim of violation of the IIA and the amount of compensation.

Subsequent conduct of the host state, for example through failure to enforce environmental legislation in cases where it has had significant incentives to ensure such enforcement, may prevent the host state from invoking non-compliance with domestic legislation as a reason for suspending protection under the IIA.[21] The legal bases for such findings have been the doctrines of estoppel, good faith, and waiver. The time passed since the violation, the host state's knowledge of it, as well as the investor's legitimate expectations are important considerations when determining whether the state is prevented from invoking the unlawfulness.

In addition to lawfulness, the *Salini* case mentions contributions, duration, risk and contribution to the development of the host state as criteria for determining whether the asset is an investment.[22] The development criterion is of particular interest from an environmental perspective. However, the relevance and importance of this criterion remains contested, and the main focus seems to be on the contribution to economic development and not on the contribution to other aspects of development. It is therefore unlikely that a project that solely is harmful to the environmental aspects of sustainable development will be denied the status of investment. However, it cannot be ruled out that a project that has high environmental costs and that does not otherwise contribute to social or economic development, could be found by a tribunal not to constitute an investment due to lack of contribution to the host state's development.[23] Such considerations are most likely in cases brought under the ICSID Convention due to the reference to 'investment' in article 25. As pointed out by Acedo, recent case law seems to move away from referring to contribution to host state development as a factor when determining the scope of 'investment'.[24]

In sum, despite the limitations included in IIAs and that follow from the ICSID Convention and general rules, the expropriation clauses of IIAs extend beyond what many countries categorise as 'property' under domestic property or expropriation legislation.

---

21 Saluka v. Czech Republic, para. 217; Railroad Development Corporation v. Guatemala, para. 234; Fraport v. Philippines, para. 346; Desert Line Projects vs. Yemen, paras. 117-119; ADC Affiliate Limited v. Hungary, para. 475; Mr. Franck Charles Arif v. Moldova, para. 374-376. For a detailed analysis of case law, see Acedo, supra note 14, pp. 25-30.

22 Dolzer and Schreuer, supra note 8, state at p. 66: 'Among the five points ..., four (substantial commitment, a certain duration, assumption of risk, and a significance for the host state's development) came to be widely accepted, while regularity of profit was subsequently seldom considered relevant.'

23 For a detailed analysis of case law, see T. Acedo, supra note 14, pp. 38-61, with further references to case law. See also J.D. Mortenson, The Meaning of 'Investment': ICSID's Travaux and the Domain of International Investment Law, 51 Harvard International Law Journal, no. 1 (2010) pp. 257-318.

24 Acedo, supra note 14, pp. 59-60.

C. Whose Rights are Protected?

In order to benefit from the protection of an IIA, the investor must belong to one of the parties to the IIA, and the investment must be established in another party to the IIA. The IIA in question defines the conditions for an investor to belong to a party to the treaty. In one analysis of IIAs, the OECD identified four categories of conditions:

> i) the place of constitution in accordance with the law in force in the country; ii) the place of incorporation or where the registered office is; iii) the country of the seat, i.e. where the place of administration is; and iv) less frequently, the country of control. Most investment treaties use a combination of the tests for nationality of legal persons so that a company must satisfy two or more of them in order to be covered. The most common approach is a combination of the place of incorporation or constitution and seat, although the combination of incorporation or constitution and control and also of all three tests is also found.[25]

The model IIAs differ significantly in this respect. On the one extreme is the broad definition of the US model IIA which includes 'a branch located in the territory of a Party and carrying out business activities there.' The Italian model IIA is more restrictive as it requires that the investor shall both have its head office in and be recognized by the state. According to the definition of investment under IIAs, those owning stakes in an investment generally have the right of protection, regardless of whether they are minority shareholders. In sum, most IIAs allow investors easy access to protection through 'treaty shopping'.

D. Indirect Expropriation

Expropriation, understood as transfer of title, is prohibited under international customary law unless it is carried out in the public interest, in a non-discriminatory manner, and accompanied by compensation. The main question for cases of direct expropriation is the amount of compensation, which will be discussed in the next section. Whether and under what circumstances other kinds of intervention by public authorities, hereinafter referred to as indirect expropriation, are to be treated as if they were expropriation is contested.

The vast majority of expropriation clauses in IIAs cover indirect expropriation. Initially, case law seemed to pay little attention to differences in the wording of such clauses.[26] However, states have increasingly attempted to adjust their wording in order to avoid being sued or having to pay compensation in cases

[25] OECD, supra note 6, p. 19.

[26] Å. Romson, Environmental Policy Space and International Investment Law, Studia Juridica Stockholmiensia 88, Stockholm University 2012, pp. 249-250 and O.K. Fauchald and K.S. Thorud, Protection of investors against expropriation – Norway's obligations under investment treaties, in O.K. Fauchald,

where public policy measures are contested by affected investors. One recent example is Annex B of the US model IIA, which states that:

> The determination of whether an action or series of actions by a Party, in a specific fact situation, constitutes an indirect expropriation, requires a case-by-case, fact-based inquiry that considers, among other factors:
>
> the economic impact of the government action, although the fact that an action or series of actions by a Party has an adverse effect on the economic value of an investment, standing alone, does not establish that an indirect expropriation has occurred;
>
> the extent to which the government action interferes with distinct, reasonable investment-backed expectations; and
>
> the character of the government action.
>
> Except in rare circumstances, non-discriminatory regulatory actions by a Party that are designed and applied to protect legitimate public welfare objectives, such as public health, safety, and the environment, do not constitute indirect expropriations.

The reference to public health, safety and the environment shows the concern that environmental policy measures could be regarded as equivalent to expropriation. The text establishes the presumption that such measures are not to be regarded as indirect expropriation, and places a significant burden of proof on the claimant. Similar language has been included in other American model IIAs,[27] but not in NAFTA (see article 1110). Other countries, including important European ones, retain general references to measures having effects equivalent or tantamount to expropriation without any qualifications.[28] However, Annex X.11 of the Comprehensive Economic and Trade Agreement between Canada and the European Union (CETA, 2014) contains language similar to that of the US model IIA. This is of particular importance given that the European Union now has the authority to negotiate IIAs on behalf of its member states according to article 207 of the Treaty on the Functioning of the European Union (TFEU). These developments indicate a trend towards circumscribing the margin of appreciation of ISDS and narrowing the scope of expropriation clause in cases of indirect expropriation.

When examining case law from the past three years, we find that there is general agreement that the claimant has the initial burden of proof.[29] Moreover, the primary focus is on the effects of the contested measure for the claimant.

H. Jakhelln and A. Syse (eds.) dog Ffred er ei det Bedste ... Festskrift til Carl August Fleischer, Oslo: Universitetsforlaget (2006), pp. 121-127.

27 The Canadian and Colombian model IIAs contain similar formulations in Annex B.13(1) and article VI:2, respectively.

28 See the model IIAs of Germany, Italy and France, as well as the Energy Charter Treaty.

29 See, inter alia, Servier, Biofarma & Arts et Techniques v Poland (14 Febr 2012) paras. 582-584; Marion & Reinhard Unglaube v. Costa Rica (16 May 2012) para. 230; and Electrabel v Hungary (ECT, 30 Nov 2012) para. 6.53.

Differences in views are related to the thresholds for fulfilling the burden of proof and for a tribunal to find that the contested measure constitutes indirect expropriation. The tests applied by tribunals vary from requiring the effects of the measure for the claimant to be the same as if there had been expropriation[30] to merely requiring a 'substantial interference with rights'.[31] There seems to be agreement among tribunals that temporary measures cannot constitute indirect expropriation unless they have permanent effects for the claimant.[32] For example, when a temporary measure prohibits construction, there is no indirect expropriation as long as the rights according to a construction permit are subsequently respected. Similarly, if a permanent prohibition on construction is subsequently annulled because it is found to be unlawful, there is no basis for a claim of indirect expropriation.[33]

There seems to be agreement among the tribunals that the effects of the measure for the claimant shall be considered from the perspective of the investment as a whole.[34] In most cases, a concession to exploit natural resources or a permit to carry out environmentally harmful activities will only constitute one of several elements of an investment, for example a production plant. Where this is the case, the relevant consideration is the effects of a contested measure, *in casu* the revocation of the permit, for the future of the operation of the plant. Only in cases where a concession represents the only element of an investment can considerations of the effect of a revocation be limited to the permit as such.

Case law seems to indicate that where the claimant fails to fulfil the initial burden of proof, the tribunal needs not proceed to further considerations of the contested measure and its effects.[35] Where the initial burden of proof has been fulfilled, on the other hand, the tribunal needs to consider on a case-by-case basis whether the contested measure constitutes indirect expropriation in accordance with the standard set out in the IIA. Of relevance to the assessment is the distinction identified in the literature and to some extent in case law between the 'sole effects doctrine' and the 'police power doctrine'.[36] While the sole effects doctrine focuses on the effects of the contested measure for the investor, the police power doctrine also focuses on the need for and benefits of

30 Electrabel v Hungary (ECT, 30 Nov 2012), see in particular para. 6.53.

31 Deutsche Bank v Sri Lanka (31 Oct 2012), see in particular para. 504.

32 Achmea v Slovakia (I) (7 Dec 2012) paras. 288-93; SAUR2 v Argentina (6 June 2012) paras. 360-361; Burlington v Ecuador (14 Dec 2012) paras. 473 and 506.

33 As an illustration, see Achmea v Slovakia (I) (7 Dec 2012) para. 291: 'Had this present BIT case been decided before the decision of the Constitutional Court and the declaration that the ban on profits was unconstitutional, it is likely that this Tribunal would have held that there was a 'permanent' deprivation that could amount to an expropriation in violation of Article 5 of the Treaty.'

34 Electrabel v Hungary (ECT, 30 Nov 2012); Burlington v Ecuador (14 Dec 2012) paras. 398 and 404.

35 See SAUR1 v Argentina (11 June 2012); Achmea v Slovakia (I) (7 Dec 2012); and Electrabel v Hungary (ECT, 30 Nov 2012).

36 See e.g. OECD, International Investment Law: A Changing Landscape. A Companion Volume to International Investment Perspectives (2005) pp. 64-68 with further references.

the contested measure. However, tribunals seem to disagree as to the contexts in which the character of the measure may be relevant.[37]

The three factors mentioned in the text of the US model IIA focus mainly on the effects of the measure for the investor, and the IIA does thus arguably take the sole effects doctrine as its starting point. However, the reference to the 'character of the government action' and the presumption that 'non-discriminatory regulatory actions by a Party that are designed and applied to protect legitimate public welfare objectives' are not to be regarded as indirect expropriation implies a rather strong reliance on the police power doctrine, as well. Annex X.11 of CETA specifies what it means by the 'character' of the government measures by listing the following: 'notably their object, context and intent'. Recent treaty practice can therefore be a sign that a trend towards strengthening the police power doctrine is emerging.

When analyzing recent case law, the status of the sole effects and police power doctrines remains somewhat unclear. During the past three years, there has been some case law that points towards the sole effects doctrine. However, among the cases which concluded that there was a violation of expropriation clauses,[38] none explicitly ruled out the relevance of the character of the contested measure. One case indicated that the character could be relevant even if it was not considered in the case.[39] On the other hand, there have been several cases that take into account the character of the contested measures when determining whether they amount to indirect expropriation. Among these are cases where the character of the measure is used as an argument supporting the conclusion that there is indirect expropriation,[40] and against indirect expropria-

37 By way of example: On the one hand, Burlington v Ecuador (14 Dec 2012) sets up the following test to be applied (para. 473, see also para. 506): whether the contested measure '(i) substantially deprived Burlington of the value of its investment, (ii) on a permanent basis, and (iii) found no justification in the police powers doctrine.' Here the character of the contested measure would only be relevant as a 'justification'. On the other hand, El Paso Energy v. Argentina (31 Oct 2011) sets out the following test (para. 241): 'If general regulations are unreasonable, i.e. arbitrary, discriminatory, disproportionate or otherwise unfair, they can, however, be considered as amounting to indirect expropriation if they result in a neutralisation of the foreign investor's property rights.' Here the character of the measure would (also) be part of the basic criteria determining indirect expropriation.

38 Marion & Reinhard Unglaube v. Costa Rica (16 May 2012), see in particular paras. 217-218 and 223; SAUR2 v Argentina (6 June 2012), see in particular para. 366; and Abengoa & COFIDES v Mexico (18 April 2013), see in particular para. 610.

39 See Marion & Reinhard Unglaube v. Costa Rica (16 May 2012), see in particular para. 218.

40 El Paso Energy v. Argentina (31 Oct 2011), see in particular para. 241; Servier, Biofarma & Arts et Techniques v Poland (14 Febr 2012), see in particular para. 575; Deutsche Bank v Sri Lanka (31 Oct 2012), see in particular paras. 522-523.

tion.[41] It is rare for tribunals to declare the character of the contested measure to be irrelevant.[42]

One situation of interest is where increasing scarcity or competition for natural resources or deteriorating environmental qualities necessitate new requirements concerning existing investment. On the one hand, it can be argued that existing investments that have operated without concessions or permits have established a right to operate, and that to (partly) remove such rights by denying investors permits or award limited permits would constitute indirect expropriation of (parts of) the rights to operate. On the other hand, it can be argued that, unless public authorities have made commitments not to introduce specific requirements, investors have not established any rights to continue to operate the investments under existing conditions. The initial burden is on the investors to prove that there are *prima facie* cases of indirect expropriation in accordance with the standards set out in the IIA in question. Where such proof exists, the difference between the sole effects and police power doctrines becomes apparent. If focus is to be solely on the effects of new requirements for existing investors, tribunals will not take appropriately into account the need to ensure maximum sustainable yield from the natural resource, the need to avoid harmful environmental deterioration, and the need to allow new investors to compete with existing investors on equal terms. On the one hand, it can be argued that public authorities rather than investors should cover costs from measures taken to promote general public interests such as maximum sustainable yield of natural resources and prevention of environmental harm. On the other hand, it can be argued in accordance with the polluter or user pays principle[43] that the investors should cover such costs related to their investment. Awarding compensation to existing investors in such cases will constitute favourable treatment of them when compared to potential new investors, and may lead to economic and

[41] Antoine Goetz & others v Burundi (21 June 2012), see in particular para. 258; Burlington v Ecuador (14 Dec 2012), see in particular paras. 401, 404 and 430-433.

[42] Burlington v Ecuador (14 Dec 2012) comes close when declaring that 'international tribunals have generally applied the sole effects test and focused on substantial deprivation' (para. 396 with further references).

[43] One formulation of the polluter pays principle can be found in principle 16 of the Rio Declaration on Environment and Development (1992): 'National authorities should endeavour to promote the internalization of environmental costs and the use of economic instruments, taking into account the approach that the polluter should, in principle, bear the cost of pollution, with due regard to the public interest and without distorting international trade and investment.' The United Nations Glossary of Environment Statistics, Studies in Methods, Series F, No. 67 (1997) contains the following definitions: 'The polluter-pays principle is the principle according to which the polluter should bear the cost of measures to reduce pollution according to the extent of either the damage done to society or the exceeding of an acceptable level (standard) of pollution.' 'The user-pays principle is the variation of the polluter-pays principle that calls upon the user of a natural resource to bear the cost of running down natural capital.' See also D. Collins, Reliance Remedies at the International Center for the Settlement of Investment Disputes, 29 Northwestern Journal of International Law & Business (2009) pp. 211-12.

environmental inefficiencies since existing investors may continue operations that should have been replaced by more efficient operations.

In sum, there are strong arguments in favour of the police power doctrine and such arguments seem to receive significant support in treaty practice and recent case law. However, case law still seems to differ as to how to consider the character of the measure and as to the relative importance of the character of the measure when compared against the effects of the measure for the investor. Hence, it remains unclear how tribunals will resolve a broad range of issues, including the introduction of new requirements concerning concessions and permits.

Given the significant differences in standards and approaches of IIAs and tribunals in relation to indirect expropriation, it is of interest to explore the extent to which states and tribunals refer to customary international law. The only references to customary law in the treaties examined for the purpose of this article can be found in the annexes to the US model IIA and the BIT between the US and Uruguay. These provisions state that: 'The Parties confirm their shared understanding that: [the article on expropriation and compensation] is intended to reflect customary international law concerning the obligation of States with respect to expropriation.' Such statements can be interpreted either as ensuring a restrictive interpretation of the expropriation clauses, or as a means of promoting the definition of indirect expropriation as part of customary international law. When considering the significant differences in case law as well as the few references to customary international law in recent case law,[44] it seems most appropriate to consider such clauses as a means of promoting relevant countries' view on the rights and duties relating to expropriation under customary international law.[45]

E. Amount of Compensation

When considering the question of compensation, a distinction must be drawn between the compensation to be paid for an expropriation to be lawful and the compensation to be paid because there is a violation of the IIA.

44 The only references to customary law found in case law regarding indirect expropriation the past three years include the following: Marion & Reinhard Unglaube v. Costa Rica (16 May 2012) para. 219; Burlington v Ecuador (14 Dec 2012) para. 393; and Electrabel v Hungary (ECT, 30 Nov 2012) para. 6.60.

45 See also M.C. Porterfield, State Practice and the (Purported) Obligation under Customary International Law to Provide Compensation for Regulatory Expropriations, 37 North Carolina Journal of Int'l Law and Commercial Regulation (2011-2012) pp. 159-197, who concludes (p. 196) that the standard set out in IIAs reflects customary international law 'growing out of the general and consistent practice of states is not supported by an examination of the actual practice of states with regard to the protection of property from regulatory expropriations. There is no general and consistent practice on this issue even among capital exporting states that presumably share a strong interest in robust standards of investor protection.'

Cases concerning direct expropriation are more likely to focus on whether the compensation paid was in accordance with the requirement of the expropriation clause. In contrast, cases concerning indirect expropriation focus on whether the contested measures generate duties to pay compensation and not on whether the amounts of compensation paid were according to the standards required by the IIAs' expropriation clauses. In these cases the tribunals determine the amounts of compensation based on the violations of the IIAs. However, in practice, tribunals do not in general distinguish between compensation based on expropriation clauses and compensation based on treaty violation.[46]

While many expropriation clauses require the compensation to be 'prompt, adequate and effective', thus reflecting the 'Hull formula',[47] other clauses are more open-ended.[48] Moreover, while many clauses specify the amount of compensation to be calculated on the basis of 'fair market value',[49] other clauses can be read to indicate somewhat differing standards.[50] Finally, compensation shall in general be calculated on the basis of the value immediately before the expropriation or before the expropriation became publicly known. Hence, while IIAs differ somewhat in how compensation shall be calculated, the general trend seems to favour 'prompt, adequate and effective' compensation[51] based on 'fair market value'.[52]

The issue of prime interest here is the extent to which environmental effects of the contested measure are taken into account when tribunals determine the amount of compensation. One starting point is the principles of polluter pays and the user pays.[53] Arguably, it would be contrary to these principles if an investor receives compensation for losing the opportunity to carry out environmentally harmful activities.

Since tribunals do not distinguish between cases concerning expropriation clauses and treaty violations, our discussion of the role of environmental effects will be based on all existing cases involving significant environmental consequences regardless of whether the violation in question concerned expropriation clauses. Of the eight environmental cases in which the host state was required to pay compensation, five did and three did not take into account environmen-

46 See Marion & Reinhard Unglaube v. Costa Rica (16 May 2012) paras. 306-307, with further references to case law.

47 See Canada art. 13.1; US art. 6.1.c; Italy art. V.2 ('immediate, full and effective compensation'); Colombia art. VI.1; CETA art. X.11.1; and ECT art. 13.1. For a brief introduction to the Hull formula and associated discussions, see OECD, supra note 37, p. 44 footnote 1.

48 See France art. 5.2 ('prompt and adequate compensation'); Germany art. 4.2 ('compensation'); and India art. 5.1 ('fair and equitable compensation').

49 Italy, US, Canada, CETA, ECT.

50 Colombia: 'market value', India: 'genuine value'; France: 'real value'; Germany: 'value'.

51 OECD, supra note 36, p. 44 footnote 1.

52 One controversial topic that remains is the extent to which future expectations shall be compensated, see Collins, supra note 43, pp. 195-216.

53 See supra note 43.

tal effects as a reason for limiting the amount of compensation.[54] None of the cases made reference to the principles of polluter pays or user pays. However, it can be argued that five cases included elements of the principles. These cases concerned housing development on environmentally sensitive land,[55] establishment and operation of hazardous waste landfills,[56] and establishment of a mine.[57]

Two of these cases concerned denial of permits by local authorities in cases where national authorities had provided permits and made assurances that the activities would be lawful. In the first, which involved the construction of a landfill, the tribunal stated: 'The fact that the site may require remediation has been borne in mind by the Tribunal and allowance has been made for this in the calculation of the sum payable by the Government of Mexico.'[58] In the second, the tribunal found that the risks taken by the investor, including the risk associated with the lack of development permits, meant 'that the Claimants should bear part of the damages suffered and the Tribunal estimates that share to be 50 %'.[59] A third case with significant similarities concerned expropriation of beaches to be included in a national park. When considering the amount of compensation, the tribunal concluded that the fair market value 'should refer not to high density usage – appropriate to a large city or factory area – but rather to a usage appropriate to the environmentally-sensitive surroundings'.[60]

The fourth case concerned the refusal of environmental authorities to renew an authorization to operate a landfill containing hazardous industrial waste and a subsequent request to submit a program for the closure of the landfill. These measures were responses to local protests against the landfill. In this case, the findings of the tribunal paid more attention to refuse deduction of profit due to 'a decision attributable to the Respondent that the Arbitral Tribunal has found to be in violation of the Agreement' than to allow deduction for profits that would result from environmentally harmful activities.[61]

Finally, a recent case concerned loss of rights to exploit mineral resources, in part due to slow processing of the environmental permit. In this case, the tribunal was faced with several environmental issues when determining the compen-

54 The three that did not take into account environmental effects were: Saar Papier Vertriebs GmbH v. Poland (UNCITRAL); S.D. Myers, Inc. v. Canada (UNCITRAL, Second Partial Award 21 Oct. 2002, see paras. 181, 221 and 270); and Abengoa S.A. y COFIDES S.A. v. Mexico (ICSID Case No. ARB(AF)/09/2, 18 April 2013.

55 MTD Equity Sdn. Bhd. and MTD Chile S.A. v. Chile (ICSID Case No. ARB/01/7 award 25 May 2004) and Marion Unglaube v. Costa Rica (ICSID Case No. ARB/08/1 award 16 May 2012).

56 Metalclad Corporation v. Mexico (ICSID Case No. ARB(AF)/97/1 award 30 Aug 2000) and Técnicas Medioambientales Tecmed, S.A. v. Mexico (ICSID Case No. ARB (AF)/00/2 award 29 May 2003).

57 Gold Reserve Inc. v. Venezuela (ICSID Case No. ARB(AF)/09/1 award 22 Sep 2014).

58 Metalclad v. Mexico para. 127.

59 MTD v. Chile paras. 242-243.

60 Unglaube v. Costa Rica para. 309.

61 Tecmed v. Mexico paras. 193 and 195.

sation. It considered that costs to address environmental problems of stockpiles should be taken into account, but concluded that there was not sufficient proof that environmental hazards would occur as a consequence of oxidization, thus ignoring the possibility of allowing for a precautionary approach.[62] Moreover, the tribunal found it 'reasonable to factor in some time allowance for relevant approvals', but it was 'not, however, convinced that a two year delay [was] necessary', and concluded that a one year delay was reasonable.[63] The tribunal rejected suggestions that fuel and electricity costs would double over the forecast period given 'Venezuela's long-standing policy of subsidizing low electricity and fuel prices'.[64]

In sum, tribunals do not seem sensitive to environmental issues when determining the amount of compensation. There are few, if any, traces of the principles of polluter pays and user pays. In some cases, this may be due to a lack of focus on such arguments by host countries. However, even in cases where such arguments are brought forward, the tribunals seem to place a significant burden of proof on the host countries. In the cases involving failure to obtain the required permits, the tribunals conclude that the host state should nevertheless cover substantial elements of the damages caused. And host state arguments that compensation should take into account strict(er) environmental requirements are met with skepticism. The tribunals thus attribute more weight to property interests of investors than to the environmental interests of the host state.

F. Concluding Remarks

Despite significant attention during negotiation of treaties, in jurisprudence and in the doctrine, the issues of indirect expropriation and compensation remain controversial in international investment law. Recent developments may point in the direction of limiting the discretion of tribunals and expanding the freedom of governments to regulate the activities of investors without incurring responsibility to compensate. However, we have also seen that significant uncertainty remains and that treaty practice and jurisprudence are rather far from establishing common approaches.

There is a tendency of paying particular attention to countries' regulatory freedom in relation to measures taken to protect the environment in the IIAs of certain American and European countries. So far, there does not seem to be significant effects of this tendency in jurisprudence, despite the fact that the issue has been on the agenda for more than twenty years. A significant number

62 Gold Reserve v. Venezuela paras. 762 and 766.

63 Ibid. paras. 771-772.

64 Ibid. para. 847.

of cases brought by European investors against Spain,[65] the Czech Republic[66] and Italy[67] under the Energy Charter Treaty concerning measures to support the production of renewable energy (solar power), as well as two cases brought against Canada under NAFTA concerning feed-in tariffs for renewable energy[68] may constitute significant opportunities for ISDS to clarify relevant provisions, including expropriation clauses. Little information is available concerning the claims and status of proceedings in these cases.

Against this background, we may ask whether IIAs are appropriate for establishing basic rules concerning expropriation and whether ISDS is appropriate for resolving expropriation disputes between investors and countries. As has been discussed elsewhere in this volume, such disputes can also be brought before the European Court of Human Rights (ECtHR). The main differences are the wording of the relevant provisions, that domestic remedies must be exhausted before bringing a case to the ECtHR while such requirements are virtually non-existent in IIAs, ISDS is ad hoc while the ECtHR is a permanent institution consisting of judges from all member states of the Council of Europe, and ISDS provides for a relatively prompt, easily accessible but expensive remedy while the ECtHR provides a relatively inexpensive but hard to access and slow remedy. Hence, these remedies can hardly be regarded as substitutable from the perspective of international investors.

As has been demonstrated by this volume, countries within the same region and subject to significant regulatory harmonization have diverging rules regarding expropriation. If we take into account the significant differences between European countries and countries of other regions of the world when it comes to rules regarding expropriation and associated judicial remedies, we can clearly see why investors and their NGOs promote international rules backed by ISDS. The main problem is that the level of protection offered by current IIAs and the associated ISDS procedures goes beyond the level offered by most countries, including many OECD countries. This means that foreign investors in many

65 There are eleven cases against Spain: *PV Investors v Spain* (UNCITRAL), 1 November 2011; *Charanne v Spain* (Stockholm Chamber of Commerce), 2013; *Isolux v Spain* (Stockholm Chamber of Commerce), 2013; *CSP v Spain* (Stockholm Chamber of Commerce), 2013; *Antin v Spain* (ICSID Case No. ARB/13/31), 11 November 2013; *RREEF v. Spain* (ICSID Case No. ARB/13/30), 22 November 2013; *Eiser v Spain* (ICSID Case No. ARB/13/36),, 23 December 2013; *Masdar v Spain* (ICSID Case No. ARB/14/01), 11 February 2014; *NextEra v Spain* (ICSID Case No. ARB/14/11), 23 May 2014; *InfraRed v Spain* (ICSID Case No. ARB/14/12), 3 June 2014; *Renergy v Spain* (ICSID Case ARB/14/18), 1 August 2014.

66 There are seven cases against the Czech Republic: *Antaris v Czech Republic* (Permanent Court of Arbitration, UNCITRAL), 8 May 2013; *Natland v Czech Republic* (UNCITRAL), 8 May 2013; *Voltaic v Czech Republic* (UNCITRAL), 8 May 2013; *ICW v Czech Republic* (UNCITRAL), 8 May 2013; *Photovoltaik v Czech Republic* (UNCITRAL), 8 May 2013; *WA v Czech Republic* (UNCITRAL), 8 May 2013; *JSW Solar v Czech Republic* (UNCITRAL), 1 June 2013.

67 *Blusun v Italy* (ICSID Case No. ARB/14/3), 21 February 2014.

68 *Mesa Energy v Canada* (UNCITRAL), 4 October 2011; *Windstream v Canada* (UNCITRAL), 5 November 2013.

cases enjoy more extensive protection than do domestic investors. Such favourable treatment becomes apparent in a few ISDS cases, but may also constitute a broader phenomenon in the form of negotiations between investors and public authorities based on IIAs. Such negotiations are hard to trace due to lack of transparency.

It can be concluded that the current IIAs, under which the ISDS has extensive powers to define rules concerning expropriation and investors can use IIAs as bargaining tools in relation to host states, are ripe for reform. The efforts so far to elaborate expropriation clauses of IIAs and to safeguard regulatory freedom in selected fields of public interests are a first step. On the one hand, the slow pace of reforms to date taken together with efforts by investors and their NGOs to resist limitations on their rights, are signs that solutions to current problems are unlikely to emerge in the near future. On the other hand, the facts that the European Commission has been awarded competence to negotiate IIAs under article 207 of the TFEU, that members of the European Union are parties to a high number of existing IIAs,[69] that ISDS is on the agenda of the current trade and investment negotiations between the EU and the USA,[70] and that UNCTAD is promoting reform of IIAs based on the objective of sustainable development[71] indicate that there is currently a window of opportunity for major reforms. Experience with jurisprudence so far shows that reforms should not be left to *ad hoc* tribunals based on existing IIA rules and ISDS procedures.

---

69 See UNCTAD, Investor-State Dispute Settlement: An Information Note on the United States and the European Union, IIA Issue Note No. 2 June 2014, p. 3: 'In total, the 28 EU Member States are currently parties to 1,356 extra-EU BITs, of which 1,160 are in force. There are also 199 intra-EU BITs, of which 198 are in force. Thus, EU Member States currently have 1,228 active extra-EU BIT relationships (i.e. about 44 relationships on average per Member State) and 211 active intra-EU BIT relationships, which come to 1,426 if extra-EU and intra-EU BIT relationships are combined. Aside from BITs, the EU and its Member States are parties to the ECT, a multilateral agreement with 53 signatories, which protects investments in the energy sector and includes an ISDS mechanism.' Worldwide, there existed more than 3,200 IIAs at the end of 2013, see UNCTAD, World Investment Report 2014, pp. xxiii-xxiv.

70 The Transatlantic Trade and Investment Partnership.

71 See UNCTAD, Reform of the IIA Regime: Four Paths of Action and a Way Forward, IIA Issue Note No. 3 June 2014.

PART III

EU and EEA Member States

The following national reports are generally structured according to a questionnaire which can be found on pages 362-363.

Property and Environmental Protection in Belgium

Luc Lavrysen

A./B. Objects of Private Property, Private Property in Natural Resources

Both movable and immovable goods, material and non-material things, personal rights and rights *in rem* may be the object of property rights. This may include shares in corporations, clientele, goodwill, operating licences, licences to deliver telecom services, etc... .[1] Also most natural resources may be the object of property rights. An exception has to be made for the *res communes* (art. 714 Civil Code) (the sea, the atmosphere, the air space...) which cannot be the object of property rights, only of public law provisions regulating their use.[2] A further exception has to do with minerals. According to public mining law, which dates back to the 19th century, the property rights of the owner of land are restricted to the upper layers of the subsoil (without specification of a clear underground distance). So, e.g. according to the Decree of the Flemish Region of 8 May 2009 concerning the deep subsoil,[3] the Flemish Region is the owner of the hydrocarbons which are naturally present in the deep subsoil. The ownership of the hydrocarbons which are extracted from the deep subsoil on the basis of an extraction licence will pass over to the holder of the licence, provided that compensation is paid to the Flemish Government (Art 3). The owner of the land or the buildings thereon has to tolerate that a holder of a licence explores or extracts hydrocarbons, prospects for potential storage complexes for carbon dioxide or effectively stores carbon dioxide when those activities take place at least 100 metres below the surface. The holder of the licence must compensate for damage to the surface and the buildings thereon, as well as for the loss of productivity of the land (Art 4). Similar provisions can be found in the Mining Decree of the Walloon Region of 7 July 1988[4] which has a broader scope, as it is applicable to a broad range of minerals and fossils (Art 2).

C. Private Property Used in Defense of Environmental Protection

Private owners of land, including nature conservation organisations that manage nature reserves, or of other immovable goods, such as buildings of all kinds, that are damaged by environmental pollution or other forms of environmental harm will find in this situation a sufficient interest to bring a case before the courts provided that this damage or harm is the result of

---

[1] M Pâques and C Vercheval, 'Le droit de propriété' in M Verdussen and N Bonbled (eds), *Les droits constitutionnels en Belgique*, Vol. 2 (Bruylant 2011) 791-793; M Pâques, 'Propriété et zonage écologique, compensation et indemnisation' in CEDRE (ed), *Le zonage écologique* (Bruylant 2002) 248.

[2] A. Lebrun, 'Le droit civil d'usage sur les 'res', éléments vitaux de l'environnment' in L Lavrysen (ed), *Milieurecht. Recente Ontwikkelingen. Deel II – Droit de l'environnement. Développements récents. Volume II* (E Story-Scientia 1989) 389-431.

[3] *Moniteur belge* 6 July 2009.

[4] *Moniteur belge* 27 January 1989.

some form of unlawful behaviour by a third party. This can be done in the form of civil liability actions against the polluters and in some circumstances against the public authorities that are believed not taking action against it in a wrongful manner, but it can also take the form of public law actions directed against e.g. permits delivered by public authorities that are believed to be illegal.

Sectoral environmental law may more specifically provide judicial action against environmental harm. Let's take the imaginary example of a factory, situated near a town that has been operating for decades. People are slowly realizing that statistically the inhabitants in the city and in the vicinity do not live until the average age and that cancer is more prevalent among them and is also the frequent cause of death. They have no direct proof that the factory could be responsible, although it is fairly clear that the soil around the factory is poisoned and that the heavy metals found in vegetables grown in that soil could be linked to the factory. However, credible evidence is lacking.

Soil remediation is regulated by specific legislation in the three regions of Belgium. As far as the Flemish Region is concerned, the applicable legislation[5] makes a distinction between historical (occurring before 29 October 1995), new (occurring after 28 October 1995) and mixed soil pollution. New soil pollution must be remediated if the soil pollution exceeds the soil remediation standards, while historical pollution must be remediated if the government decides that it poses a 'serious hazard'. In the case of mixed pollution, it has to be determined whether the largest part is historical or new. Let's assume in this case that it is historical and that the government decides on the basis of a risk analysis that there is a serious hazard, so that the whole pollution has to be treated as historical under the Decree. The remediation obligation lies in the first place with the *operator*, if on the land where the pollution *originated*[6] an establishment is located for which an environmental licence or notification is required. In this case the operator of the factory has the obligation to remediate the soil pollution (not only of its own property) at its own expense, provided of course that it can be proven that the soil is contaminated by its emissions. For other forms of damage, civil fault based liability will be involved, and the question will arise if a fault can be proven, as well as the causal connection between that fault and the damage.[7]

---

5 Decree of 27 October 2006 on soil remediation and soil protection, replacing the initial decree of 22 February 1995 on Soil Remediation. See on the initial legislation: L Lavrysen, 'Legislation on soil remediation in Belgium (Flemish Region)' in G Cordini and A Postiglione (eds), *Prevention and Remedying of Environmental Damage*, (Bruylant 2005) 71- 87. See on the new legislation: E De Pue, L Lavrysen and P Stryckers, *Milieuzakboekje 2013* (Wolters Kluwer Belgium 2013) 593-647.

6 According to the definitions of the Decree that it is the land where the emissions took place that directly or indirectly caused the soil pollution.

7 See for a case in which the operator of an asbestos plant was held liable for health damages caused in the period 1960-2000 and compensation of € 250,000 was awarded to the children of a couple that died from asbestos related cancer: District Court of Brussels, 28 November 2011, *Consorts J v nv E, Tijdschrift voor Milieurecht* (2012) 167-184.

If the licence is withdrawn by the authorities and this is clearly motivated by e.g. the violation of environmental standards or the general duty of (environmental) care there would not be a case for liability of the authorities, provided that this measure is not found disproportionate, in other words if it is obvious that another measure could not solve the problem in a less burdensome way.

D. Property in Public Aids for Beneficial Use of Natural Resources

The subsidization of a beneficial use of natural resources, such as a guaranteed feed-in tariff for renewables, is under Belgian law not considered as 'property' as such. But at the same time this does not mean that the legislator is completely free to withdraw subsidies for budgetary or other reasons, as other constitutional principles should be observed as well. There is some case law on the system of green energy certificates, a financial incentive to promote the production of electricity on the basis of renewable sources, which are defined in the legislation concerned as 'transferable intangible assets'. After some years of application the system as set up in the Flemish Region became too costly. By a Decree of 13 July 2012, the Energy Decree of the Flemish Region was amended, in order to reduce the number of certificates allocated to the producers of renewable energy (according to a very complex system supposed to reflect the cost-efficiency of the technology applied) and also limited in time, whereas originally those certificates were granted for the whole life span of the installation. This limitation in time was also applied to existing installations built at the time when the certificates were granted without limitation in time. The Constitutional Court affirmed that the legislator has the right to review its system at any time. However, it was of the opinion that one of the new measures applied to existing installations violated nevertheless Art. 10 and 11 of the Constitution, because the time during which certificates were granted under the new rules depended on decisions taken by the operator at a time when the rules were different, and he could not predict that the rules would change. There was indeed no proper justification of this sudden change of the legal framework. The Court found, with reference to the case law of the ECtHR, for the remainder no violation of Art 1, Protocol No 1, ECHR. According to the ECtHR:

> 'the concept of 'possessions' referred to in the first part of Article 1 of Protocol No. 1 has an autonomous meaning which is not limited to the ownership of physical goods and is independent from the formal classification in domestic law: certain other rights and interests constituting assets can also be regarded as 'property rights', and thus as 'possessions' for the purposes of this provision. In each case the issue that needs to be examined is whether the circumstances of the case, considered as a whole, conferred on the applicant title to a substantive interest protected by Article 1 of Protocol No. 1 (see *Iatridis* v. Greece [GC], no. 31107/96, § 54, ECHR 1999-II; *Öneryıldız*, cited above, § 124; and *Hamer*, cited above, § 75). [....]

> The concept of 'possessions' is not limited to 'existing possessions' but may also cover assets, including claims, in respect of which the applicant can argue that he has at least a reasonable and legitimate expectation of obtaining effective enjoyment of a property right (see *Hamer*, cited above, § 75). A legitimate expectation of being able to continue having peaceful enjoyment of a possession must have a 'sufficient basis in national law' (see *Kopecký* v. Slovakia [GC], no. 44912/98, § 52, ECHR 2004-IX).'[8]

The Constitutional Court was of the opinion that the previous legislation could not be understood as creating a legitimate expectation concerning the conservation, without change, of the conditions under which the certificates are granted.[9]

E. Expropriation

Article 16 of the Belgian Constitution that has remained unchanged since 1831, reads as follows: 'No one can be deprived of his property except in the case of expropriation for a public purpose, in the cases and manner established by the law and in return for fair compensation paid beforehand'. According to Article 17: 'Assets may not be confiscated as a means of punishment'. The National Congress that prepared the 1831 Constitution explicitly provided five guarantees for protection against an arbitrary deprivation of property by the public authorities: 1. Deprivation of property is only possible *in the public interest*, with a view to enlarging or improving the public domain of the public authorities; an explicit legal authorization is required for expropriation of private persons; judges must examine whether a compulsory purchase decision meets the requirements of public interest; 2. Deprivation of property is only possible *in the cases laid down by law*; the legislature has authorized the Executive Branch on the federal level and on the level of the Regions and Communities to decide on expropriations under certain conditions; they may empower subordinate authorities, such as municipalities and provinces, to proceed with an expropriation; 3. Deprivation of property should take place *in the manner prescribed by law*; unless there is an amicable settlement, there is always a prior intervention by a judge; most expropriations proceed along the lines of the 'urgency procedure' to allow the public authorities to take possession of property expeditiously; 4. There must be *fair compensation* to indemnify the owner in full, allowing him at least to acquire an immovable asset of the same value; 5. The *compensation* must be paid *in advance*; only after payment of the compensation by the public authorities may the latter order the courts to take possession of the property.[10]

---

8 Depalle v France, 29 March 2010, paras 62-63.

9 Constitutional Court, n° 8/2014, 23 January 2014, *nv Aspiravi and vzw Federatie Belgische Biogasinstallatie and Others v Flemish Government.*

10 A Alen (ed) *Treatise on Belgian Constitutional Law* (Kluwer 1992)207-208; Pâques and Vercheval (n 1) 800-806.

Traditionally, the field of application of Art 16 of the Constitution has been restricted to expropriations for a public purpose. To be applicable, there must be a complete dispossession of the private owner, together with a transfer of ownership to a public authority.[11] More recently the Constitutional Court has however – in a case concerning legislation that gives the right to tenants of social housing (housing provided by virtue of government intervention and rented out on favourable terms to less-well-off sections of the population) to purchase the dwelling they rent, subject to compliance with a number of conditions – widened the scope of Art 16 of the Constitution by observing that Article 16 provides *a general safeguard against loss of enjoyment of property, regardless of the legal status of the party deprived of the property*. In this case there was an – in certain cases compulsory – transfer of ownership from public bodies to private persons. With regard to the question of fair compensation within the meaning of Article 16 of the Constitution, the Court considered that compensation equal to the market value was justified on the grounds that social housing associations, by virtue of their specific features, were in a different situation with regard to their property from a private owner, with the result that certain forms of harm or loss of amenity, such as inconvenience, harm stemming from the existence of a sentimental attachment and removal expenses, could be considered irrelevant in their case. The Court further took account of the fact that the Decree also provided for a special compensation system, with housing associations taking part in a government investment programme. With regard to the question of prior compensation, the Court considered that the seller enjoyed safeguards similar to those attached to compensation in the event of expropriation, given the particular nature of the forced sale and the fact that the transfer of ownership took place only once the tenant was prepared to pay, to that end, a price equal to the market value of the dwelling, as defined in the Decree.[12] The applicants also contended that the proportionality requirement laid down in Article 16 of the Constitution and Article 1 Protocol 1 ECHR had been violated. The Court held that any interference in the right of ownership must strike a fair balance between public-interest requirements and the need to protect the right to respect for property. The means used had to be proportionate to the end. In the case of housing policy, which was a central plank of the social and economic policies of modern societies, the Court, when checking that the right to decent housing (Article 23(3)(3) of the Constitution) had been observed, was bound to respect the assessment of the public interest made by those who drafted regional laws, unless that assessment was manifestly unreasonable. After establishing the circumstances in which the measure had been taken and the conditions attached to the social housing tenant's right to buy, and taking account of the

[11] Pâques and Vercheval (n 1) 794; Pâques (n 1) 248-249; E Orban de Xivry, 'Droit de propriété et établissement du réseau Natura 2000 (Région wallonne)' in M Pâques (ed), *Le droit de propriété et Natura 2000 – Natura 2000 and Property Rights* (Bruylant 2005) 65.

[12] Constitutional Court, n° 33/2007, 7 Mach 2007, *vzw Vereniging van Vlaamse Huisvestingsmaatschappijen and Others* v *Flemish Government*.

guarantee of fair compensation afforded to the social housing association, the Court concluded that the contested provision did not disproportionately undermine the right of ownership of the applicants and dismissed the application to have it set aside.

The question if there is a *transfer of ownership* or not seems crucial to distinguish expropriation from *limitation of ownership.*[13] The obligation to rent out its land for maximum 1 year against compensation to allow the military to renew a NATO pipeline[14] or the obligation to accept the construction/replacement of a pipeline by a third party over its land[15] is not to be considered as an expropriation. In principle, according to traditional Belgian case law, *limitations of the use of property in the general interest,* when they are not to be considered as a *de facto* expropriation, must be accepted without compensation, except when the legislator decides otherwise.[16] However, the legislator must also respect the equality principle.[17] If it decides to compensate wholly or partially certain restrictions, it cannot refuse to do so in situations which are in all aspects similar, without a reasonable and pertinent justification.[18] The Court found a violation of Art 16 of the Constitution in conjunction with Art 1 of Protocol No 1 to the ECHR in so far as the Brussels Town Planning Code did not provide for compensation in the case of an interdiction to build as a result of a decision to protect an area as landscape for which previously an allotment permit had been delivered, while the same code provides for compensation[19] if the interdiction to build is the result of the adoption or the review of a land use plan. The Court also found no justification for the fact that the owner of land in the dunes along the North Sea coast is compensated[20] when he loses the right to build on the land, while someone who is not the owner, but had a valid building permit and made some costs to prepare the terrain for building, will not be compensated when he loses the right to use this permit.[21]

Furthermore, since the legislative amendment of 9 March 2003, the Constitutional Court is competent to review the constitutionality of federal and regional laws directly with reference to all provisions of Title II of the Constitu-

---

13 Pâques and Vercheval (n 1) 794 -796; Orban de Xivry (n 11) 65.

14 Constitutional Court, n° 97/2001, 12 July 2001, *ML Dubois* v *Belgian State;* M Pâques (n 1) 253-254.

15 Constitutional Court, n° 62/2006, 26 April 2006, *NV Aquafin* v *cvba Pligas.*

16 Hof van Cassatie 16 March 1990, *Arr Cass* (1989-1990) 922; Constitutional Court, n° 50/93, 24 June 1993, *B Vander Voordt and Others* v *Belgian State, Flemish Region and Flemish Community* (restrictions on the basis of the legislation on landscape protection); Pâques (n 1) 249.

17 M Pâques (n 1) 258-259.

18 Constitutional Court, n° 12/2014, 23 January 2014, *nv Immobiliën Vennootschap Verkavelingen and Others* v *Brussels Capital Region and Commune of Sint-Agatha Berchem.*

19 The compensation is limited to 80% of the difference in value of the land before and after the interdiction to build.

20 The same restriction applies.

21 Constitutional Court, n° 55/2012, 19 April 2012, *Vlaamse Gewest* v *nv MAFAR.*

tion, containing the Belgian Fundamental Rights Catalogue.[22] The Court took the view that it is also competent to take into account those provisions of international law which secure analogous rights or freedoms.[23] Article 1 of Protocol No.1 to the ECHR is believed to have a scope which is similar to that of Art 16 of the Constitution, so that the guarantees it contains form an inseparable whole with those contained in the Constitution, and that the Constitutional Court has to take into consideration all those guarantees. Article 1 of Protocol No. 1 reads as follows:

> 'Every natural or legal person is entitled to the peaceful enjoyment of his possessions. No one shall be deprived of his possessions except in the public interest and subject to the conditions provided for by law and by the general principles of international law.
>
> The preceding provisions shall not, however, in any way impair the right of a State to enforce such laws as it deems necessary to control the use of property in accordance with the general interest or to secure the payment of taxes or other contributions or penalties.'

According to the case law of the ECtHR, Article 1 of Protocol No.1 in substance guarantees the right of ownership.[24] In its judgment of 23 September 1982 in the case *of Sporrong and Lönnroth*, the Court analysed Article 1 as comprising 'three distinct rules': the first rule, set out in the first sentence of the first paragraph, is of a general nature and enunciates *the principle of the peaceful enjoyment of property*; the second rule, contained in the second sentence of the first paragraph, covers *deprivation of possessions and subjects it to certain conditions*; the third rule, stated in the second paragraph, is concerned, amongst other things, with *the right of a State to control the use of property*. However, the Court made it clear in its *James and Others* judgment of 21 February 1986 that the three rules are not 'distinct' in the sense of being unconnected: the second and third rules are concerned with particular instances of interference with the right to peaceful enjoyment of property and should therefore be construed in the light of the general principle enunciated in the first rule. Not only must a measure depriving a person of his property pursue, on the facts as well as in principle, a legitimate aim 'in the public interest', but there must also be a *reasonable relationship of proportionality* between the means employed and the aim sought to be realised. This latter requirement was expressed in other terms in the above-mentioned *Sporrong and Lönnroth* judgment by the notion of the 'fair balance' that must be struck between the demands of the general interest of the commu-

[22] Before its competence was restricted to some Articles of that Title, but with a (very) broad scope, such as the equality and non-dicrimination clauses.

[23] Constitutional Court, n° 136/2004, 22 July 2004, *OM* v *R. Vergauwen and Others*; L Lavrysen and J Theunis, "The Belgian Constitutional Court: a satellite of the ECHR?" in A Alen, V Joosten, R Leysen and W Verrijdt (eds), *Liberae cogitationes : Liber Amicorum Marc Bossuyt (*Intersentia 2013) 332.

[24] Marckx v Belgium (1979) *Series A* no. 31, para 63.

nity and the requirements of the protection of the individual's fundamental rights. The requisite balance will not be found if the person concerned has had to bear 'an individual and excessive burden'. Although the Court was speaking in that judgment in the context of the general rule of peaceful enjoyment of property enunciated in the first sentence of the first paragraph, it pointed out that 'the search for this balance is ... reflected in the structure of Article 1 (P1-1)' as a whole. Clearly, compensation terms are material to the assessment whether *a fair balance has been struck between the various interests at stake and, notably, whether or not a disproportionate burden has been imposed on the person who has been deprived of his possessions.*[25] The Constitutional Court has fully endorsed this case-law.[26]

F. Indirect Expropriation by Environmental Regulation?

The Belgian Constitutional Court generally follows very closely the case law of the EctHR.[27] In its Grand Chamber Judgment in the case of *JA Pye (Oxford) Ltd and JA Pye (Oxford) Land Ltd*[28] the ECtHR summarized its approach in this respect as follows:

> '54. The taking of property under the second sentence of the first paragraph of Article 1 without payment of an amount reasonably related to its value will normally constitute a disproportionate interference that cannot be justified under Article 1. The provision does not, however, guarantee a right to full compensation in all circumstances, since legitimate objectives of 'public interest' may call for less than reimbursement of the full market value (see *Papachelas* v. Greece [GC], no. 31423/96, § 48, ECHR 1999-II, again with further references).
>
> 55. In respect of interferences which fall under the second paragraph of Article 1 of Protocol No. 1, with its specific reference to 'the right of a State to enforce such laws as it deems necessary to control the use of property in accordance with the general interest ...', there must also exist *a reasonable relationship of proportionality between the means employed and the aim sought to be realised*. In this respect, *States enjoy a wide margin of appreciation* with regard both to choosing the means of enforcement and to ascertaining whether the consequences of enforcement are justified in the general interest for the purpose of achieving the object of the law in question (see *AGOSI* v. the United Kingdom, 24 October 1986, § 52, Series A no. 108).
>
> [...]
>
> 71. As to the existence, over and above the general interest in the limitation period, of a specific general interest in the extinguishment of title and the attribution of new title at the end of the limitation period, the Court notes that in discuss-

25 Lithgow and Others v United Kingdom (8 July 1986) para 120; Pâques (n 1) 259-262.

26 Orban de Xivry (n 11) 66; Pâques (n 1) 267.

27 Lavrysen and Theunis (n 23) 349-353.

28 JA Pye (Oxford) Ltd and JA Pye (Oxford) Land Ltd v United Kingdom(30 August 2007).

ing the public interest present in *Jahn and Others* v. Germany, in the context of a deprivation of property, it stated that, 'finding it natural that the margin of appreciation available to the legislature in implementing social and economic policies should be a wide one, [the Court] will respect the legislature's judgment as to what is "in the public interest" unless that judgment is manifestly without reasonable foundation' ([GC], nos. 46720/99, 72203/01 and 72552/01, § 91, ECHR 2005-VI, with reference back to *James and Others*, cited above, and *The former King of Greece and Others* v. Greece [GC], no. 25701/94, ECHR 2000-XII, and to *Zvolský and Zvolská* v. the Czech Republic, no. 46129/99, § 67, ECHR 2002-IX). This is particularly true in cases such as the present one where what is at stake is a long-standing and complex area of law which regulates private-law matters between individuals.

[...]

75. The second paragraph of Article 1 is to be construed in the light of the general principle enunciated in the opening sentence. There must, in respect of a 'control of use', also exist a *reasonable relationship of proportionality between the means employed and the aim sought to be realised*. In other words, the Court must determine whether *a fair balance* has been struck between the demands of the general interest and the interest of the individuals concerned. In determining whether a fair balance exists, the Court recognises *that the State enjoys a wide margin of appreciation, with regard both to choosing the means of enforcement and to ascertaining whether the consequences of enforcement are justified in the general interest for the purpose of achieving the object of the law in question* (see *AGOSI*, cited above, § 52, and, for a more recent authority concerning a deprivation of possessions, *Jahn and Others*, cited above, § 93). In spheres such as housing, the Court will respect the legislature's judgment as to what is in the general interest unless that judgment *is manifestly without reasonable foundation* (see *Immobiliare Saffi* v. Italy [GC], no. 22774/93, § 49, ECHR 1999-V). In other contexts, the Court has underlined that it is not in theory required to settle disputes of a private nature. It can nevertheless not remain passive, in exercising the European supervision incumbent on it, where a domestic court's interpretation of a legal act appeared '*unreasonable, arbitrary or ... inconsistent ... with the principles underlying the Convention*' (see *Pla and Puncernau* v. Andorra, no. 69498/01, § 59, *ECHR* 2004-VIII). When discussing the proportionality of a refusal of a private television company to broadcast a television commercial, the Court considered that a margin of appreciation was particularly essential in commercial matters (see *VgT Verein gegen Tierfabriken* v. Switzerland, no. 24699/94, § 69, *ECHR* 2001-VI). In a case concerning a dispute over the interpretation of patent law, and at the same time as noting that even in cases involving litigation between individuals and companies the State has obligations under Article 1 of Protocol No. 1 to take measures necessary to protect the right of property, the Court reiterated that its duty is to ensure the observance of the engagements undertaken by the Contracting Parties to the Convention, and not to deal with errors of fact or law allegedly committed by a national court unless Convention rights and freedoms may have been infringed (see *Anheuser-Busch Inc.*, cited above, § 83).'

The Belgian Constitutional Court will allow the federal and regional legislators the same wide margin of appreciation, especially in socio-economic matters,[29] without making distinctions according to the type of legislation at stake or the policy area concerned. In that respect the Court was e.g. of the opinion that a right of redemption against a capped price of the authority in cases of ceasing of a business activity without limitation of time, when plots of land were sold to businesses in industrial area's developed by that authority, was justified in the light of the aim of public interest pursued by that authority.[30] In another case the Court held that the reduction of authorized car parking places in case of renewal of an environmental permit in the Brussels Capital Region was justified by reasons of mobility and air quality policy.[31] The cases in which the Court found a disproportionate restriction are rare.[32] The *fair balance* test includes a proportionality test: the more stringent the restriction is, the more there will be a need to compensate.[33]

G. Dissolution of Property for Environmental Protection

The only relevant example of dissolution of vested rights for reasons of environmental protection without compensation is the case of the high tax on nuclear energy production. Article 65 of the Federal Act of 22 December 2008 required nuclear power producers to pay a single 'distribution contribution' of 250 million Euros for 2008. The aim of this contribution was to 'finance the country's energy policy and government measures to cover expenditure on promoting investments in electrical power generation, to meet expenses and investments relating to nuclear power, to reinforce security of supply, to combat energy price rises and, lastly, to enhance competition in the power market in the interests of consumers and industry.' The company Electrabel SA, asserting that it had to pay 89 % of the total contribution and that this tax repre-

[29] Constitutional Court, n° 173/2008, 3 December 2008, *nv Linopan* v *cvba West-Vlaamse Intercommunale* and *nv Imver* v *Intercommunale Ontwikkelingsmaatschappij voor de Kempen*; L Lavrysen and J Theunis (n 23) 350; Pâques and Vercheval (n 1) 810-811.

[30] Constitutional Court, n° 173/2008, 3 December 2008, *nv Linopan* v *cvba West-Vlaamse Intercommunale* and *nv Imver* v *Intercommunale Ontwikkelingsmaatschappij voor de Kempen.*

[31] Constitutional Court, n°170/2014, 27 November 2014, *vzw Federatie van de Belgische parkings* and *Beroepsvereniging van de Vastgoedsector.*

[32] E.g. Constitutional Court, n° 107/2005, 22 June 2005, *P Renkin* v *Walloon Government* (an inheritance tax of more than 80%; see on this judgment: Lavrysen and Theunis (n 23) 350-351); Constitutional Court, n° 145/2013, *nv All Projects & Development* v *Flemish Government* (the obligation to provide a certain quantity of social housing in each private housing development project and to transfer these houses to the public sector without proper compensation, after the ECJ had held that the compensation provided for was state aid that was not notified for approval to the Commission: Cases C-197/11 and C-203/11, *Libert and Others* and *All Projects & Developments NV and Others).*

[33] Pâques and Vercheval (n 1) 811; Pâques (n 1) 272-285.

sented about one quarter of its total net profit, sought the annulment of this legislation. Other companies required to contribute also lodged appeals seeking the Act's annulment. After dismissing a number of objections on grounds of inadmissibility, the Court first examined whether there was discrimination (Articles 10 and 11 of the Constitution) between, on the one hand, nuclear power operators and other companies having a share in power generation through fission of nuclear fuel, who were required to pay this contribution, and, on the other hand, non-nuclear power producers and 'other Belgian electricity market operators' such as importers, transporters, distributors and suppliers of electricity and other intermediaries in the Belgian power market, who were not required to pay the contribution. The Court cited at length the preparatory documents justifying this measure. It considered that when, in such matters, the legislature decided to impose a contribution on certain categories of entities, this approach was part and parcel of its overall economic, tax and energy policy and the Court could censure differences in treatment resulting from such decisions only if there was clearly no reasonable justification for them. The Court concluded that the Parliament could consider that nuclear power operators and other companies, having a share in power generation through fission of nuclear fuel, were in a situation different from that of the entities with which the appellants compared themselves. The Court then ruled on a limb of the ground of appeal complaining that 'small nuclear power producers' which were required to pay the distribution contribution and the 'dominant nuclear power operator' were treated in the same way. It replied that the situations of the nuclear power operator and of the other two companies having a share in power generation through fission of nuclear fuel, who were affected by the two grounds of appeal in question, were not fundamentally different from the standpoint of the challenged legislation, since these three taxpayers had in common the fact that they controlled part of the nuclear power generation industry. The parties also complained of discrimination between the entities concerned by this legislation and all other taxpayers liable for corporate income tax. In this connection, the Court recalled the scope of the constitutional principle of equality and non-discrimination. In the light of the aim laid down in the impugned legislation, the Court considered that 'ordinary' taxpayers liable for corporate income tax were not in a comparable situation from the standpoint of a measure of this kind. The Court also rejected the arguments concerning the principle of lawfulness in tax matters, the non-retrospective effect of legislation and the right of ownership and dismissed the appeal. Concerning the right of ownership, the Court observed that Article 1 Protocol 1 ECHR was similar in scope to Article 16 of the Constitution and that the safeguards laid down therein were indistinguishable from those secured by the constitutional provision. The Court pointed out that a tax in principle constituted an interference with the right to peaceful enjoyment of one's property. The Court referred to the aim of the contribution and held that, in the light of the profits engendered by nuclear power generation on account of the accelerated depreciation of nuclear power plants, parliament could consider that this contribution was not 'exorbitant' and that the fair balance between the demands of the general interest and the requirements of the right to peaceful enjoyment of one's property was not upset.[34]

It should be noted that meanwhile the Nuclear Power Phase out Act of 31 January 2003 has been amended by an Act of 18 December 2013, postponing the phased closure of Nuclear Power Plants to the period 2015-2025. This Amendment was coupled with an increase (more than doubling) the nuclear power production tax. That increase was again challenged before the Constitutional Court by *nv EDF Luminus* and *nv Electrabel*. The Court rejected the appeal on similar grounds.[35] It should be noticed that the phasing out as such was not challenged before the Constitutional Court.

H. State Liability for Environmental Damage to Private Property

Civil liability in Belgium is in the first place fault based (Art. 1382 *et seq* of the Civil Code),[36] however, there are various specific regimes, also in the environmental field, in which some form of strict liability is applied (e.g. toxic waste, exploitation of groundwater, nuclear energy, soil contamination...).[37] Also the state and its subdivisions are subject to the various civil liability regimes, in principle[38] under the same conditions as private parties.

How the system functions can be illustrated by the following imaginary case. A waste disposal site is located not far away from a place with approximately 150 houses. Inhabitants assert that they smell bad odour and they would like to sell their property, but of course there are no potential buyers. Their property has decreased in value. The waste disposal site has the necessary permits.

---

34 Constitutional Court, n° 32/2010, 30 March 2010, *nv Electrabel and Others* v *Council of Ministers*.

35 Constitutional Court, n° 106/2014, 17 July 2014, *nv Electrabel and Others* v *Council of Ministers*.

36 M Deketelaere, 'Deel VII. Aansprakelijkheidsrecht' in K Deketelaere (ed), *Handboek Milieu- en Energierecht*, (die Keure 2006) 1330-1336; E De Pue, L Lavrysen and P Stryckers, *Milieuzakboekje 2014* (Wolters Kluwer Belgium 2014) 1225-1241.

37 M Deketelaere and T Vanden Borre in K Deketelaere (ed), *Handboek Milieu- en Energierecht* (die Keure 2006) 1336-1344; De Pue, Lavrysen and Stryckers (n 34) 1243-1248.

38 See, however, the particularities of the civil liability of the judiciary (Constitutional Court, n° 99/2014, 30 June 2014, *Commune de Schaarbeek v Belgian State*) and of the legislator (Hof van Cassatie, 1 juni 2006, *Belgische Staat v Universele Kerk van het Koninkrijk Gods and Others*; Cour de cassation, 28 september 2006, *Etat belge v FJML*; Hof van Cassatie, 10 September 2010, *Belgische Staat v CG*; A. Van Oevelen, 'De aansprakelijkheid van de staat, de gewesten en de gemeenschappen voor onrechtmatige wetgeving', *Tijdschrift voor wetgeving* (2006) 400-416); A Alen, 'De overheidsaansprakelijkheid voor fouten van de wetgever. Over de Cassatiearresten van 1 juni 2006 en 28 september 2006' in W Pintens, A Alen, E Dirix and P Senaeve (eds), *Vigilantibus ius scriptum. Feestbundel voor Hugo Vandenberghe* (die Keure 2007) 1-14.

In this case, the operator of the waste disposal site most probably violates applicable standards. According to Art. 5.2.1.6. VLAREM II (Order of the Flemish Government of 1 June 1995 concerning General and Sectorial provisions relating to Environmental Safety), a provision applicable to the operator of any waste management facility:

> Using appropriate means particular to the responsible operation of the establishment, the operator *prevents and controls* dust, gas, aerosols, smoke *or unpleasant odours*. The operator takes all possible measures to minimise polluting emissions. *Any nuisance caused may not exceed acceptable limits nor should it go beyond the normal nuisance caused by neighbours.*

Violating a legal provision is considered to be a fault within the meaning of Art. 1382 of the Civil Code concerning fault based liability. So if the victims can prove their damage and the causal link between the damage and the fault of the operator, the operator has to restore the situation. Given that causing such an odour is illegal, a civil judge can impose its cessation, under the threat of a penalty per day of non-observance of the court order and of financial compensation for past damage (given the fact that reaching a final judgment will take time). Since the environmental permit cannot authorize such odour, there is no need to challenge the permit itself. Naturally the situation can also be addressed by administrative measures and sanctions, ranging from the withdrawal of the permit for violating applicable operating conditions to criminal sanctions.

I. Proprietor's Liability for Environmental Damage

The question may arise whether one can be responsible for environmental damage solely on account of ownership of the property (i.e. for instance, the owner of the land where the waste is illegally deposited by a third (unknown) party). Recently the Constitutional Court had to decide on such a case. The Court held that Articles 12 and 37 of the Decree of the Flemish Region of 2 July 1981 concerning the prevention and management of waste would violate Articles 10 and 11 of the Constitution (the equality principle) in the case that those articles would be construed in such a way that the public waste company may recover the costs incurred for *ex officio* removal of the waste from the owner of the land that has been contaminated by the waste, if said owner did not know and should not have known that the property was polluted by the waste the day he became owner. In the interpretation, however, that the owner can only be made liable for those costs if he knew or should have known that the land was polluted by that waste the day he acquired the land[39], there is no violation of the

[39] Constitutional Court, n° 15/2014, 29 January 2014, *cvba Haras* v *Openbare Vlaamse Afvalstoffenmaatschappij*.

equality principle. The solution found by the Constitutional Court comes close to the solution that is used in the Flemish Soil Remediation legislation. It is up to the operator, when there is an installation subject to environmental permit on the land, or to the landowner, when there is no operator or another user on the land, to take remedial action in case of historical or new soil pollution. In case of historical pollution there is an exemption for the so-called 'innocent owner', that is the person who can show that he has not caused the pollution himself and that at the time when he became the proprietor or user of the piece of land, he was not or could not be assumed to have been aware of the pollution.[40]

The situation is, however, different for waste that is disposed of by third parties while someone else is the owner of the land, with or without its consent. According to Art. 12 of the Decree of the Flemish Region of 23 December 2011 concerning sustainable management of material cycles and waste[41], it is forbidden to dump waste or to manage waste in a manner contrary to the Decree and its Implementing Orders. Such a conduct is punishable by criminal sanctions[42] and by a court order to restore the site.[43] In the Belgian case law it is assumed that the polluter is not only criminally liable by actually dumping the waste, but also if the necessary measures are not taken to end the violation,[44] even if the waste was dumped by another person.[45]

J. Permit Excuse in Environmental Liability

In the different regional legislations on environmental permits there is an explicit provision that the permit has no influence on the rights of third parties.[46] This means that civil liability can occur, even when an operator is acting completely in conformity with the conditions of its environmental permit[47], e.g. when the general duty of care obligation is stricter in a given case than the conditions of the environmental permit. However, in the past the idea prevailed that the judiciary could in such a case not order measures to repair the damage that would hamper the activities of the operator concerned. They could

40 Lavrysen (n 5) 76-77.

41 A similar provision could be found in the former Decree of 2 July 1981.

42 Penal sanctions from € 600 to € 3,000,000 and/or imprisonment for 1 month to 5 years (Art 16.6.3 Decree of 5 April 1995) or an alternative administrative fine of max. € 1,500,000 (Art 16.4.27).

43 Art 16.6.6 Decree of 5 April 1995.

44 Hof van Cassatie, 22 February 2005, *Arr Cass* (2005) nr. 109; Hof van Cassatie 11 January 2011, *Arr Cass* (2011) nr. 26; Council of State, n° 168.992, 15 March 2007, *cvba Haras* v *OVAM*.

45 Court of Appeal, Ghent, 26 April 2013, *Tijdschrift voor Milieurecht* (2013) 534.

46 E.g. Art 8 Decree of the Flemish Region of 28 June 1985 concerning the environmental permit; Art 49 of the Decree of the Walloon Region of 11 March 1999 concerning the environmental permit.

47 A Van Oevelen, 'Civielrechtelijke aansprakelijkheid voor milieuschade', in Centrum voor Beroepsvervolmaking in de Rechten – UIA, *Rechtspraktijk en milieubescherming. Antwerps Juristencongres 1991* (Kluwer rechtswetenschappen 1991) 139.

only order the operator to compensate the damage financially. Since a judgment of the Supreme Court of 26 June 1980, in which the Court held that ordering the reparation in kind was not incompatible with the separation of powers, this approach was gradually abandoned to a certain extent.[48]

K. Direct or Indirect Expropriation by EU Measures

In a case in which indirect or direct expropriation may be caused by EU legislative acts or their implementation, the validity of an EU legislative act could be directly (e.g. Regulation) or indirectly (domestic legislation transposing directives) challenged. The Constitutional Court would in that event most probably[49] refer the case to the ECJ, asking the ECJ to check the validity of the EU legislative act against Art. 17 of the Charter of Fundamental Rights of the EU.

Unlike most of the Constitutional Courts of the Member States that seem to be more than reluctant to start a dialogue with the ECJ,[50] the Belgian Constitutional Court has shown considerable openness to EU law and the case law of the ECJ. In the period 2009-2010 15.6 % of the cases of the Belgian Constitutional Court were EU related cases.[51] Until mid-2014 the Constitutional Court has referred 23 cases for a preliminary ruling to the ECJ and adjudicated 19 of them after having received the answer of the ECJ. This is a very high number compared with other Constitutional Courts, most of which never referred a

48 Van Oevelen (n 45) 151-154; H Bocken, 'Aansprakelijkheid voor schade veroorzaakt door milieuverontreiniging naar Belgisch recht' in H Bocken and D Ryckbost (eds), *Verzekering van Milieuschade/ L'assurance des dommages causés par la pollution/Insurance of Environmental Damage* (E Story-Scientia 1991) 63.

49 However, in the emission trading case (Constitutional Court, n° 92/2006, 7 June 2006, *nv Cockerill Sambre and sa Arcelor)* the Court did not question the ECJ on the validity of the ETS Directive (G Winter, 'Anmerkung zum Urteil des Belgischen Schiedshofes vom 7. Juni 2006, Urteil Nr. 92/2006, Geschäftverzeichnisnummer 3715, *ZUR* 9/2006, 419-420). The Court was in that case of the opinion that the domestic legislator could itself avoid a supposed discrimination by applying the domestic scheme also to industries that were exempted from the ETS Directive. So in constitutional terms it was irrelevant if the ETS Directive was invalid or not in this respect. The Constitutional Court came however to the conclusion that the domestic exemptions were justified, a conclusion that was reached some years later also by the ECJ in answer to a validity question raised by the French Supreme Administrative Court (Case C-127/07 *Arcelor Atlantique and Lorraine and Others* [2008] ECR I-9895; in the same sense: Case T-16/04, *Arcelor v. Parliament and Council* [2010 ECR II-211). See on this issue: L Lavrysen, 'Chapter 10. Belgium' in J H Jans, R Macrory & A M Moreno Molina, *National Courts and EU Environmental Law* (Europa Law Publishing 2013), 236 and 239-243.

50 P Popelier, 'Judicial conversations in multilevel constitutionalism. The Belgian case', in M Claes, M de Visser, P Popelier and Others (eds), *Constitutional Conversations in Europe. Actors, Topics and Procedures*, Ius Commune Europeaum:107 (Intersentia 2012) 82-83.

51 Ibid, 81-82.

case.[52] The Court applies the answers received from the ECJ, without reservation, while utilizing the room for manoeuvre left to the fullest extent possible. Also in cases where on the basis of the *CILFIT* criteria the Court feels no need to refer interpretation or validity questions to the ECJ, the case-law of the ECJ is quoted and applied frequently. In the period 2009 – 2010 the Constitutional Court referred in 20.75 % of the EU law related cases to the case law of the ECJ.[53]

52 Only the Constitutional Courts of Austria (4 cases), and the Courts of Italy (1 case), Lithuania (1 case), Spain (1 case) and, very recently, Germany (1 case) have referred cases to the ECJ. Some Courts even display an aggressive resistance to the ECJ: J Komárek, 'The Place of Constitutional Courts in the EU', *European Constitutional Law Review* (2013) 420-450.

53 Popelier (n 47) 85-86.

Property and Environmental Protection in Czechia

Ilona Jancarova, Jakub Hanak & Vojtech Vomacka

The legislation in the Czech Republic underwent substantial changes after the Communists seized power and started to suppress democratic principles in the country. During the Communist era, the government struggled to gain complete control over the society including the use of land and other environmental resources. Therefore, it was generally accepted that environmental resources and other environmental components were in possession of the state and the state gave permission to use them (through its authorities) and charged fees for their exploitation (e.g., fees for emitting polluting substances into the air). The 1960 Communist Constitution explicitly declared principal water resources to be the state property.

After the 1989 revolution, the Communist legislative system was substantially changed to fit the needs of a democratic society, and later on, to comply with the EU requirements. As early as the beginning of the 1990's the system of modern environmental law was established and changes in the field of civil law were not so abrupt, though. The 1964 Communist Civil Code (amended many times since then) was effective until 1 January 2014 when the new Civil Code (Act No. 89/2012 Coll., hereinafter NCC) entered into force. In the period of 1989-2013 only material things, not rights, were considered to be things in the legal sense and buildings were not considered part of land; the *superficies solo cedit* principle (abandoned in the Communist era) was not adopted again because of distorted property rights and due to the need to complete the process of their restitution and privatization.

In the NCC, the conception of things in the legal sense (as objects of property rights) and many other issues were changed substantially (return to the *superficies solo cedit* principle, among others) with the aim to establish a new Czech civil legislation on the traditional civil law principles and to harmonize it with other European countries. Therefore, there has been virtually no experience with the practical application and interpretation of the NCC provisions so far. Nevertheless, it seems that many provisions of the NCC are, without doubt, not interrelated properly with other parts of the Czech legal regime (including environmental laws), which will probably create significant obstacles in the practical application and is worth being researched properly.

A. Objects of Private Property

Potential objects of property are defined in § 1011, NCC.[1] According to it, both movable and immovable material things and non-material things including rights are defined as things in the legal sense and all these things may be objects of ownership. The main character of a thing in its legal sense is its usefulness and the possibility of control exercised over it. The NCC expressly excludes some objects from the definition of the term 'thing'. These are human bodies and their parts, living animals, and rights which are not

1 NCC § 1011: Everything that belongs to someone, all of its tangible and intangible things, is his property.

objects of property rights, e.g. personal rights and creations of personal character (e.g. an author's works, inventions, etc.).[2] Immaterial things are rights whose character enable them to belong to somebody. It means that not all rights are things in the legal sense. For the right to become an object of property rights, it has to have the character of property. Therefore, private and public law rights should be distinguished. Private subjective rights and private subjective duties are characterized as mutual private rights and mutual private duties of private persons. They arise between persons in their mutual contacts in the private sphere, not between a private person and a public authority.[3] Subjective public rights, on the other hand, are established by an act of a public authority (a permit to operate). Public law rights do not substitute private law rights (e.g. a construction permit itself does not provide the right to build a house on another person's lot).[4] Therefore, it can be concluded that public law rights – according to the authors' opinion – are not supposed to be a thing in the legal sense and they are not an object of property.

The NCC provisions relating to material things are applicable (beside others) to those environmental components eligible to gain control over, and accordingly, to manageable natural forces which are objects of commerce. Most natural resources may be objects of property rights, including those serving the public purposes. Public domain/commons[5] are things which are subject to common use and objects of the general public use are typically immovable things (mostly real-estates, e.g., roads, parks, etc.). These real things can be owned by different kinds of persons (the state, municipalities, private legal persons and also natural persons). Moreover, an object of the public use does not have to be an object of property rights at all (e.g., according to the Water Act No. 254/2001 Coll., as amended, anybody has the right to use surface waters for his own needs without any technical device, this being called 'common use of waters'[6] (about the legal character of waters see more below). Therefore, the criterion for the defining of an object of the public domain is not the property right (Constitutional Court, I.ÚS 451/11). The right to use private property as a public domain is usually established by public laws (e.g., the Forest Act No. 289/1995 Coll., as amended, and many others).[7] According to the Constitutional Court (Pl. ÚS 15/96), a healthy environment is an example of the public domain. Lately, the same court (Pl. ÚS 21/04) declared explicitly cultural heritage to be part of the public domain as well.

---

2 Explanatory report to the Act No. 89/2012 Coll., Civil Code. Documents of the Chamber No. 362. 6th term of office of the Chamber. Available at http://www.psp.cz [last visited in April 20, 2014].

3 J. Švestka, J. Dvořák, J. Fiala et al.: *Občanský zákoník. Komentář.* Praha: Wolters Kluwer, 2014, p. 2.

4 Ibid., p. 13.

5 Public domain/commons are defined as a thing designated to the general use of the public.

6 Surface and ground waters are not objects of property rights according to the 2001 Water Act.

7 Act No. 289/1995 Coll. on Forests, as amended, gives the right to anybody to enter forests and pick small branches, mushrooms and berries there.

On the basis of environmental laws exceptions from the NCC rules have to be made in relation to specific natural resources. Surface and ground water resources and caves are not subject to property rights (according to special environmental laws) and their exploitation is based either on the right to common use (surface waters for a person's own needs drawn without technical devices) or on public law permits/licences. For example, in order to draw surface water with a pump a permit is required by the Water Act.

Living animals are not considered to be things, nevertheless, provisions relating to things are applicable to living animals to a certain extent. On the other hand, wild living animals such as game may be kept in closed preserves and in this case, (even if not being things in the legal sense) they belong to the person who bought or raised them (the Decision of the Supreme Court 22 Cdo 980/2005). Otherwise, wild living animals do not belong to anybody until they have been caught/taken on the basis of a licence to hunt. The Constitutional Court dealt with this question in its findings (e.g., Pl. ÚS 34/03 of 13.12.2006). The court took the view that wild game moves freely without regard to boundaries and therefore it cannot be a part of the land (lot). According to the Court, game is considered to be '*res nullius*'[8] and the state is entitled to regulate the execution of the right to hunt. The execution of this right is a legitimate restriction of the owner of the land.

According to the Mining Act No. 44/1988 Coll., the state is an exclusive owner of the exclusive deposits of minerals (listed as exclusive deposits by the Mining Act) and only the state authorities may award licences/concessions to exploit them.

The use of natural resources or other environmental components is regulated by environmental laws. Nevertheless, this protection has its limitations arising from the constitutional freedom to carry out enterprising activities Many environmental laws provide for the public authorities' discretion in their decision-making. The discretion, however, does not mean arbitrariness. For example, no land owner can be deprived of his right to construct a building on his land if his project is consistent with the legal requirements (for example, it complies with the adopted land-use plan and environmental law conditions). If some development activities are projected and carried out according to an approved plan, the protection of the agricultural or forest land expressed in the public interest in not losing forests or agricultural land is overcome by the owner's will that is consistent with the public interest in the development of specific area, expressed in the land use plans (environmental requirements should be considered during the planning process).

In the cases where the public interest in environmental protection and other public issues (to construct a highway) are in conflict in a certain territory, the state authorities will decide which public interest will prevail and establish conditions under which a project can or cannot be carried out. Such a decision

8 This opinion was formulated before the NCC came into effect and animals were considered a thing.

can be appealed against and, consequently, reviewed by an independent administrative court.

B. Private Property in Natural Resources

The right to use some natural resources is a part of ownership. The natural resource, as mentioned above, has to have the character of a thing in the legal sense as an object of property, e.g. it has to be manageable and useful for man (for example, a forest), and at the same time another condition must be met, i.e. that special laws (mostly environmental ones) do not exclude the natural resource as an object of ownership or otherwise establish different legal rules in relation to it. If the natural resource is an object of property rights (for example, a piece of land), the owner himself is restricted in its use by constitutional and public laws. These restrictions can encompass permits/consents that the owner (or another person entitled to use his/her property) must get in order to exploit the natural resource in a specific way.

The use of other natural resources which belong to the state or which are not objects of ownership rights (for example, waters) is either allowed directly by the law (the so-called 'common use of a natural resource' or a 'public domain' – for example the right to pick up berries and mushrooms in the forest by natural persons) or it is based on a permit or a licence.

Permits/licences to exploit natural resources in a specific way awarded to applicants (owners of the natural resource and/or other persons without property rights to it) are generally conceived as subjective public rights. Specifics relating to conditions of these rights are established by environmental laws.

According to some authors,[9] permits to use surface or ground water, once awarded according to the Water Act, represent a permanent obstacle other future uses of the given water source. The only way is to confer the right voluntarily on another person by means of a request to change the permit to enable the other person to use the water. The Water Act does not obstruct possible compensation paid by the new user to the previous one for the withdrawal from that subjective public right.

The Mining Act enables private persons to apply for the decision on 'delimitation of the mining area' which establishes the right to exploit exclusive deposits of minerals.[10] These persons can transfer their right to other ones on the basis of a mutual contract and a previous consent granted by the competent mining authority. This opinion was supported by the decision of the Supreme Court which was adopted 15.1.2013 (23 Cdo 721/2011). The Court held that transferring the right to exploit the resource does not mean transferring the property right to the deposit. The Court stressed further that the decision on delimita-

9 M. Sobotka: Řešení potencionálních konfliktů při nakládání s vodami. In I. Průchová, I. et al.: *Voda v právních vztazích*. Brno: Masaryk University, 2014, p. 20.

10 Exclusive deposits of minerals belong exclusively to the state.

tion of the mining area is a legal act made by the district mining authority and the mining authority is entitled to establish the mining area and to change or abolish this decision. This supports the idea that delimitation of the mining area and the consequent right to use the state deposits of exclusive minerals was not considered to be a thing in the legal sense (subjective public right) by the previous Civil Code (1964) because legal things cannot be established or changed or cannot expire by administrative decisions. The Court opinion can be considered consistent with the current legal doctrine introduced by the NCC, according to which immaterial thing are meant to be rights whose character renders it possible. This rule would be applicable to other permits to use natural resources. At the same time it is held that public rights are not immaterial things (objects of property rights) because they are not transferable by private legal acts. Public rights may be transferred by the so-called 'administrative agreement' adopted by the addressees of public administration with the previous consent of a competent administrative authority[11], as specified in the Administrative Code (§ 162).[12] The findings of the Constitutional Court of the CR (III.ÚS 66/97, IV. ÚS 499/98) and the decisions of the Supreme Administrative Court (6 A 93/2001, 8 Afs 56/2007) confirmed that subjective public rights are established as primary and not secondary rights.[13] Transfers of the public right (to use water, to exploit deposit of minerals) are mostly characterized as public law agreements (administrative agreements).[14/15] This opinion, however, is opposed by some authors.[16]

One may agree that the above mentioned may also concern other activities relating to the use of natural resources, even if other laws do not state explicitly any possibility of transferring a public right. The transfer in such a case is based directly on the Administrative Code but conditions set by other laws must also be complied with.[17]

In general, it can be concluded that permits to use natural resources are not objects of property rights because of their public law character. They are not considered to be a thing in the legal sense because they cannot be transferred by private legal acts. In practice, however, there are often some financial benefits accompanying the transfer of the right between private parties, which are basically not excluded by the law.

The right to emit polluting substances into the environment is not an object of property rights for the same reasons. Environmental laws generally do not regulate the possibility of transferring the right to pollute. However, in regions where air quality limits are being exceeded, the permit to emit those polluting substances may be granted only if the planned increment to the existing

[11] The administrative authority is not obligated to grant the consent.

[12] Act No. 500/2004 Coll., Rules of Administrative Procedure as amended.

[13] P. Lavický et al: *Občanský zákoník I. Obecná část (§ 1-654). Komentář.* Praha: C. H. Beck, 2014, p. 1758.

[14] J. Vedral: *Správní řád: komentář.*2. vydání, Praha: Bova Polygon, 2012, p. 1274.

[15] L. Jemelka, K. Pondléíčková, D. Bohadlo: *Správní řád. Komentář.* Praha: C. H. Beck, 2013, p. 687.

[16] Z. Horáček: *Vodní zákon: komentář.* Praha: Sondy, 2013, p. 44.

[17] J. Vedral: *Správní řád: komentář.* Praha: Sondy, 2012, p. 1275.

pollution from the new source of pollution would be compensated by emission reductions in the existing sources of air pollution that are owned by another person or entity. These compensatory measures are imposed by an air protection authority on the basis of a request by their operators (see the sources listed in Appendix 2 to the Air Act) to change the permit in order to operate the existing source. Compensatory measures not included in the sources listed in the Appendix are carried out on the basis of an administrative agreement made among a regional air protection authority, an applicant for the consent to establish a new source of air pollution and the operator of the existing source. It is obvious that the voluntary emission reduction would provide financial compensation to the owner/operator of an existing source of air pollution on the basis of their mutual private law agreement.

Another exemption from the above mentioned rule is tradeable allowances to emit carbon dioxide (CO_2). These allowances are the property of the state according to § 17 of the Act No. 383/2012 Coll., on Conditions of Trade in Greenhouse Gases Emission Allowances. This Act is not consistent with the NCC terminology because the allowance is defined here as the so-called 'other property value' which equals to the right of the operator to emit an equivalent of 1 ton of CO_2 into the air. Since the NCC came into the effect, this 'other property value' can be considered a thing in the legal sense which is freely transferable within EU ETS.

Regarding the time validity of authorizations it can be said that some permits are time limited and must be renewed after their expiration. If the permit is not time limited, then it cannot be changed or abolished if the authorized person complies with the conditions set in the permit. However, this is a general rule and environmental laws contain specific exemptions to it which are based on very strict conditions.

It is necessary to point out that the Constitutional Court of the Czech Republic repeatedly ruled on the principle of legitimate expectation[18] stating that, in accordance with ECHR, the legitimate expectation is conceived as a property right which has been specified by particular legal acts (decisions) or based directly on the law. The Constitutional Court held the view that the 'property' definition in Art. 1 of Protocol 1 to the Convention has its own scope and cannot be limited to material property without regard to the formal qualification in the national law. The object of protection in Article 1 is thus not only existing property but also a legitimate expectation to gain the property. It can be concluded that the Czech Constitutional Court ruling, when interpreting the term 'property' in Art. 1 of the Protocol, is consistent with the ECHR and the protection would have been probably provided to the property in accord with this international treaty even if the object of protection had not been defined as property in the Czech law. The abolishment of the permit is not considered disproportion-

18 See judgements Pl. ÚS 2/02 of 9 March 2004, Pl. ÚS 50/04 of 8 March 2006, Pl. ÚS 9/07 of 1 July 2010, Pl. ÚS 17/11 of 15 May 2012. Available at http://nalus.usoud.cz/Search/Search.aspx [last visited August 20, 2014].

ate, however, if it is consistent with the conditions of the permit as in the ECHR *Fredin v. Sweden.*[19]

C. Private Property Used in Defense of Environmental Protection

Private property can be used for environmental protection indirectly. The owners of real- estate are participants of administrative procedures concerning the use of different environmental components. This position enables participants to get access to all information gathered during the decision-making procedure, to comment upon it, to submit evidence, to appeal against the decision and to file a complaint with an administrative court if it is necessary for the protection of their subjective rights. Moreover, if some activity requires the property rights to the land, then the owner of the land can use his property rights to prevent this activity (for example, he refuses to sell the land suitable for mining activities on the land surface).

The owner or the user (the tenant) of the real-estate can also sue for private nuisance in relation to other property owners' activities that are causing 'unreasonable' interference with their individual rights to use their own land (for example, excessive emissions of substances and/or noise/odour coming out of an adjacent land to their real-estate). They can also sue polluters in tort law for any damage caused to their property and health (for example, damage to the forest caused by emissions of polluting substances, damage to their right to use ground waters, etc.).

The NCC established the rule (Art. 1013.2) that if the nuisance (pollution, odour, noise, etc.) comes out of a legally authorized activity, the neighbour is entitled just to monetary compensation of the damage. This rule is aimed at protection of entrepreneurs and excludes a private nuisance suit. However, it does not concern all kinds of interference with the owner's rights. For example, direct discharge of pollution onto another person's land is prohibited in general and the neighbour (operator of polluting activity) can be sued for causing a private nuisance. A private nuisance action is also allowed in the case of pollution coming from operational activities exceeding the authorized limits.[20]

As far as the case in question is concerned, it can be dealt with either at the public law level or at the private law level. The solution will depend on the legal existence of the operator of the factory. If the operator still exists:

- People can claim damages for the damage to their health and property in a civil law suit. In this case they need some evidence to establish a *causal*

[19] *Fredin v. Sweden.* (Application no. 12033/86). Judgement of 18 February 1991. Available at http://hudoc.echr.coe.int/sites/eng/pages/search.aspx?i=001-57651#{"itemid":["001-57651"]} [last visited August 1, 2014].

[20] J. Spáčil a kol.: *Občanský zákoník III. Věcná práva (§ 976-1474). Komentář.* 1. vydání, Praha, C.H.Beck, 2013, p. 145-162.

nexus between the operation of the factory and the damage.
- People can file a private nuisance complaint if emissions of noxious substances exceed an authorized level.
- People can draw the criminal or administrative authorities' attention to the problem of excessive pollution. These authorities have a duty to investigate such a complaint. Illegal behaviour of the polluter could be probably punished as a crime (it applies to both natural persons and legal persons), or at least as an administrative offence. Along with it, taking corrective measures to clean the site could be ordered by an administrative authority. This procedure could be used only if the polluter does not comply with the public law requirements.
- People (owners of the contaminated land) can claim that they have suffered an 'ecological (e.g. environmental) damage'. If the factory is on the list (see Appendix 1 , Act No. 167/2008 Coll., on Ecological Damage Liability[21]), the contamination of the land can have the character of 'ecological damage'. If the contamination was caused by an activity which was carried out after 18.8.2008 (the day the Act came into effect), the operator has a duty to take preventive and remedial measures according to the Act.

The permit may not be revoked unless conditions set for revocation by the law would be met (for example, a previous imposition of a fine and/or corrective measure being ineffective). No compensation or property guarantee can be claimed in this regard (prohibition of the operation represents a sort of punishment).

If the operator does not exist anymore, remedial measures will be taken by the state. Different situations are anticipated by the law regarding the duty of the state to carry out the remedy. The old environmental damage caused by enterprises during the Communist regime was dealt with in specific programs concerning mostly the privatization processes.[22]

D. Natural Resources as Public Property or Interest

Natural resources are defined as living and not-living parts of nature which are used or can be used by man to satisfy his needs. It means that, for example, land, trees, animals, rocks, water, etc., are considered natural resources according to the Act No. 17/1992 Coll. on the Environment. Interpretations of this definition differ, though.[23]

---

21 The Act No. 167/2008 Coll. was adopted to introduce Directive 2004/35/EC of the European Parliament and of the Council of 21 April 2004 on environmental liability with regard to the prevention and remedying of environmental damage (ELD).

22 See more in I. Jančářová: *Právní prostředky a cesty k řešení starých ekologických zátěží.Brno*: Masarykova univerzita, 2008.

23 See more I. Jančářová, L. Bahýl'ová, M. Pekárek, I Průchová, V. Vomáčka: Odpovědnost v právu *životního prostředí – současný stav a perspektivy*. Brno: Masarykova univerzita, 2013, p. 17.

According to the Art. 11.2 of the Charter of Basic Human Rights,[24] the law may establish a property which is necessary to accommodate the needs of the whole society, to ensure the economic development and the protection of public interests and to designate persons who may become exclusive owners of such property (for example, the state, municipalities or specific legal persons). This delimitation concerns the deposits of exclusive minerals (enumerated by the Mining Act[25]). These deposits are often found on the land which is privately owned; in such a case, an agreement must be reached with the land owners to get the right to exploit the deposit on their land. The ownership of some land in specially protected natural areas is also reserved for the state because protection of nature is considered a public interest.

Some natural resources (as mentioned above) are not subject to property rights according to the Czech law. In order to exploit these resources, some kind of authorization (permit, consent, etc.) is generally required by the law. Similar requirements concern the exploitation of other natural resources which are privately owned and apply to the owner of a resource as well. To exploit the natural resource, a permit/licence must be granted or other legal requirements must be met (for example, in order to log timber in the forest, the owners of the forest must not exceed the quantity of timber set by the forest management plans and they have to meet many other requirements set by the Forest Act;[26] in order to construct a building on a private land; the development consent and construction permit are generally required according to the Act No. 183/2006 Coll., Construction Code, as amended, etc.). During the permitting procedure, many preconditions must be fulfilled (usually in the cases of a significant impact on the environment), such as a consent granted by various environmental authorities (air protection authority, agricultural land protection authority, nature protection authority, EIA authority, water protection authority, state forest administration, etc.) which can be substituted with an integrated permit (IPPC).[27] If all legal conditions and requirements are complied with, the authorization must be granted; however, it may be cancelled if the resource is not used for a long time or if these legal requirements are not met.

E. Property in Public Aids for Beneficial Use of Natural Resources

According to the general provisions of Act No. 218/2000 Coll., on the Budgetary Rules, decisions on a grant or repayable financial assistance are not subject to general regulations on administrative proceedings and a

24 Constitutional Act No. 2/1993 Coll., as amended.

25 Act No. 44/1988 Coll., Mining Act, as amended.

26 Act No. 289/1995 Coll.

27 This permit substitutes environmental authorities' consents required under different environmental laws for deciding on a construction/building permit.

judicial review is not permissible. Hence, almost unlimited state discretion applies here. The state financial assistance in environmental matters is, however, mostly regulated by specific rules (for example, Act No. 388/1991 Coll., on the State Environmental Fund) and the applicants can claim state support and defend their rights based usually on a public contract in court. These rights are conceived as subjective public rights (see the decision of the Supreme Administrative Court 7 As 173/2012) and the same applies to the subsidisation of a beneficial use of natural resources guaranteed directly by the law. The recent controversy following an unprecedented expansion of solar power plants and the newly introduced taxes upon the operators resulted in a series of legal and academic disputes.

Constitutional complaints were filed against taxes introduced by Act No. 402/2010Coll., amending the Act on the Promotion of the Use of Energy from Renewable Sources. They were based on a conflict between Czech constitutional law and EU law because the tax concerns just those photovoltaic power plants which started their operation within the period of 1.1.2009-31.12.2010. The Constitutional Court (Pl.ÚS 17/11 of 15.5.2012) took the view that the legislation is in harmony with the principle of legitimate expectation and the principle of equity, since the renewable sources of energy kept to be subsidised. According to the court, different approaches to different groups of persons/individuals are acceptable if based on reasonable grounds, unless in a particular case, one of the contested provisions will have liquidating effects ('suffocating effects') on the producer, or will interfere in the very essence of the producer's property. (In the given period of time, the costs of individual components of photovoltaic power plants decreased dramatically by more than 40%. Therefore this group of operators took the biggest advantage of the subsidy which the state deemed necessary to reduce by an additional tax (the decision of the Supreme Administrative Court 1 Afs 80/2012-40[28]). This case law indicates that the *pacta sunt servanda* principle does not apply absolutely and the principle of legal certainty cannot be considered a requirement for absolutely excluding any change in the legislative framework; it is also subject to other social-economic changes and demands for the stability of the state budget.

F. Expropriation

The legal regulation of expropriation is derived from the basic rule which is contained in the Charter of the Basic Human Rights (Const. Act No. 2/1993 Coll., as amended, CBHR).

Art. 11(3) of the CBHR establishes:

---

[28] The decision of the Supreme Administrative Court 1 Afs 80/2012-40 of 20 December 2012. Available at http://www.nssoud.cz/mainoCol.aspx?cls=JudikaturaSimpleSearch&pageSource=0 [last visited August 5, 2014].

> The property is an obligation. It must not be used to harm rights of others or in breach of interests protected by the law. Realization of the property rights must not harm human health, nature and environment above the level set by the law.

Art. 11(4):

> Expropriation or limitation of the property is allowed only in the public interest, based on the law and in return for a fair compensation.

This basic constitutional right is implemented in other legislation, too. Deprivation of property is possible only in cases laid down by the law and in the manner prescribed by the law. Special laws, including environmental laws, establish purposes for which the expropriation is allowed. Among those purposes, environmental friendly investments can be found (redevelopment/rehabilitation of the territory, establishment of the system of ecological stability, archaeological heritage protection, measures aimed at reduction and prevention of floods and other natural disasters, etc.). Expropriation or limitation of the property for the sake of energy production of renewable sources of energy is not the reason for expropriation; on the other hand, expropriation is possible for the purposes of technical and transportation infrastructure. These are the reasons, or purposes of expropriation, set by the law. The public interest in each individual case must be proved in a special administrative procedure. The legislature has authorized a special expropriation authority at the district level to decide on expropriation in each individual case.

According to the Act No. 184/2006 Coll. (Expropriation Act) expropriation means not only complete dispossession of the private owner, but also limitation of the property rights in the form of easements. The owner of the property is compensated in both cases. Based on the decision of the expropriation authority, the ownership of an expropriated real-estate or an easement right is transferred to the proposer of expropriation (e.g., the state and/or a private individual).

G. Indirect Expropriation by Environmental Regulation?

In the Czech legal system restrictions to use property with or without compensation can be found. According to T. Kocourek, the difference is based on Art. 11.3 and Art. 11.4 of the CBHR (see above). A consequence of the restrictions is, in the sense of Art. 11.4, an exclusion of execution of a certain part of property right and/or establishment of inequality among different groups of owners of similar real estates. Such intense restrictions of property rights are admissible only if they are substantiated by a strong public interest. On the other hand, restrictions of execution of property rights in the sense of Art. 11.3 are not followed by any deprivation or limitation of execution of parts of property right by inequality among owners of similar real-estates, because they concern all real-estate of the same character.[29] No compensation is paid to the owners of the forests who are restricted by the right to 'common use of the forest' according to which everybody has the right to enter forests, pick up berries, mushrooms and small branches. Moreover, owners and users (legal persons only) of the land in the open landscape are restricted by anybody's right to open access.

Land use planning restricts owners of land in the future use of their property (any change in the use of the land must be in compliance with the existing land use plan) without any compensation. However, in a situation when the site formerly designated for a development activity (building site) is according to the new/changed land use plan designated to another use disabling the development there (for example, a city park), then the owner of the land is entitled to financial compensation, because the value of his property was decreased (Art. 102 of Construction Code (Act No. 183/2006 Coll., as amended)).

The Supreme Administrative Court took the view (the decision of NSS of 19.5.2011, 1 Ao 2/2011-16) that owners of the land are not restricted in their rights by the land use plan which is not supposed to change the current use of land. On the other hand, interests of an owner of agricultural land which is supposed to be (according to the plan) used for the development purposes against his will are always affected (therefore he may ask an administrative court for annulment of the land use plan).

In another decision (NSS of 5.2.2009, 2 Ao 4/2008 – 88), the Supreme Administrative Court applied the principle of proportionality. The court ruled that the planned change in use of the land does not mean direct intervention to property rights; the indirect effect cannot be excluded in relation to limited use of property. Even though owners must accept a certain level of restriction, it is necessary to consider situations when those restrictions exceed the principle of equity between public policy and imperatives aimed at protection of basic human rights of individuals. In such a situation, the owner must be compensated according to Art. 11.4 of CBHR. On the basis of the test of proportionality the court is entitled to repeal part of the plan in which the excessive restrictions are anticipated without adequate compensation.

Protocol No.1 to the ECHR guarantees the right to property to every natural or legal person and provides for adequate protection of this right. The Constitutional Court of the Czech Republic (findings of the Constitutional Court of 26.4.2012 IV.ÚS 2005/09) pointed out that the property right is not absolutely unlimited, which is consistent with ECHR. Legal restrictions of this right for the sake of protection of other persons' rights and for the sake of protection of public interests (protection of environment and human health) is legitimate. The property right, on the other hand, must not be restricted more than it is necessary. Therefore, a restriction concerning logging of forest trees in a National Nature Reserve without financial compensation (amounting to the

29 T. Kocourek: Omezení vlastnického práva k pozemkům ve prospěch ochrany životního prostředí, Praha, Leges 2012, p. 23-29.

value of potentially unlogged timber) is not an excessive intervention in rights of individuals according to the Constitutional Court view.

Owners of the land situated in specially protected areas (including NATURA 2000) face many restrictions concerning their land. Among others, they are restricted from logging the timber and in carrying out intensive agriculture/ forestry activities. The recent judicial decisions indicate however, that the owner of the agricultural/forest land is entitled only to compensation for increased expenses relating to the protected forest areas management. Restrictions relating to the loss of profit in this regard do not represent any breach of constitutional rights, since the CBHR in Art. 35.3 establishes the duty not to endanger or damage the environment, natural resources and cultural heritage above the limits set by the law.[30]

The Czech Supreme Court, on the other hand, took the opposite view in its later decision (Case No. 25 Cdo 3837/2011) and ruled that the owners are entitled to compensation for limitation of their property right.

H. Dissolution of Property for Environmental Protection

According to Czech law, limitation or prohibition of operational activity is one of the basic public-law sanctions contained practically in all environmental law. In the administrative law theory, they are called 'sanctions with renewable character'[31] and they are usually imposed in case of breach of duties (excessive emissions of polluting substances) when other penalties (fine, corrective measures) were not effective. No compensation in such a case is a natural consequence.

According to some environmental laws, permits (to do some activity) are issued only for a limited period of time (for example, a permit to take surface or ground waters and to discharge waste waters). Moreover, according to § 12 of the Water Act (Act No. 254/201 Coll., as amended), the water protection authority is empowered to change or abolish the permit to use ground and surface waters based on conditions set by the Water Act. Cases in which this authority is entitled to change or abolish the permit (an authority has the right to do that) should be distinguished from cases when the water protection authority has a duty to act.

A similar provision is contained in the Air Act (Act No. 201/2012 Coll.). Pursuant to § 13 of this Act, an air protection authority is entitled to decide on a change of a previously issued permit to operate under the conditions set by the law (for example, a change leading to improvement of air quality in the given region without demanding excessive financial expenses on the part of the polluter). In those cases, no compensation is anticipated by the law. Similar

30 E. Wagnerová, V. Šimíček, T. Langášek, I. Pospíšil: *Listina základních práv a svobod. Komentář*. Praha: Wolters Kluwer, 2012, p. 312.

31 P. Průcha: *Správní právo: obecná část*. Brno: Masarykova univerzita, 2012, p. 125.

regulation is contained in the Integrated Prevention and Pollution Control Act (IPPC Act No. 76/2002 Coll., as amended).

Unanticipated archaeological, cultural or natural finds that were discovered during development activities are regulated in § 176 of the Construction Code (Act No. 183/2006 Coll.) According to it, the developer has a duty to stop construction work, to protect the site against any damage and to report such finds to a construction authority. On the basis of it, the authorities may decide on a change of the construction permit. Significant finds can be declared a part of the cultural heritage. In such a case, the construction permit may be changed or repealed. The developer is entitled to compensation.

I. State Liability for Environmental Damage to Private Property

If the operation of the disposal site was authorized, the inhabitants can sue the waste disposal site for private nuisance demanding financial compensation. *Restitutio in integrum* is not possible because the operation was permitted. A state authority is empowered to impose corrective measures if the disposal site does not comply with legal requirements.

Compensation reflecting the decrease of the property value has not been generally awarded by Czech courts so far (even though it was not prohibited by the previous Civil Code), but according to the NCC such compensation is possible.[32]

J. Proprietor's Liability for Environmental Damage

The owner is not responsible for illegal behaviour of a third (unknown) person; that is the general rule. Under specific circumstances (for example, the privatization process), the owner of property may be required to take remedial measures to clean up contamination which was caused by the previous property holder/s.

K. Permit Excuse in Environmental Liability

Conditions of liability for damage are established by civil law (NCC). Since the permits concern operational activities (which are governed by public law), non-compliance with permits gives rise to administrative law liability. Liability for damage is regulated by civil law and in general, it is a fault-based liability. Nevertheless, liability for damage caused by operational activities/

32 J. Spáčil a kol.: *Občanský zákoník III. Věcná práva (§ 976-1474). Komentář.* 1. vydání, Praha, C.H.Beck, 2013, p. 160.

hazardous activities is governed by specific provisions (§§ 2924 and 2925 NCC) and it is liability without regard to fault. According to those rules, the mere compliance with public law requirements is usually not a direct reason for being relieved from liability.

L. Direct or Indirect Expropriation by EU Measures

There is neither a specific legal approach to this issue nor corresponding case law. Any forthcoming cases would be probably dealt with in accordance with the basic legal principles and protection of the constitutional rights depending also on the nature of a particular EU legal act.

Property and Environmental Protection in Croatia

Lana Ofak

A. Objects of Private Property

The main legal sources that regulate the right of ownership in Croatia are:

- the Constitution of the Republic of Croatia,[1]
- European Convention for the Protection of Human Rights and Fundamental Freedoms (ratification date: 5 November 1997),
- Act on Ownership and Other Real Rights (AOORR),[2]
- Act on Expropriation and Determining Compensation (Expropriation Act).[3]

The right of ownership applies to an object, which may as an individually specified thing (Art. 5/1 of the AOORR) refer to: (1) a movable thing, (2) an immovable (real property) thing, and (3) a certain kind of right or anything else that is considered by law to have an equal status as a thing (Art. 2 AOORR). For instance, non-physical securities can be the object of ownership although they do not exist as a tangible item, but as an electronic record of a securities account in the computer system of the central depository agency (see: Art. 124-130 of the Act on Securities Market[4]). Accordingly, the right to build is by law on equal terms with real property (Art. 280/2 AOORR).

Basically all things have the capacity of being the object of the right of ownership and other real rights, except those which cannot belong to an individual due to their natural characteristics or if legal provisions preclude them from belonging to an individual (Art. 3/1 AOORR). Natural objects whose characteristics prevent them from being in control of only one natural person or legal entity, but are used by all (common things), such as the air, water in rivers, lakes and the sea, as well as the seashore, cannot be the object of the right of ownership or other real rights (Art. 3/2 AOORR). From a legal point of view, buildings and other structures built on a common thing based on a concession are not part of the common things, and they form a distinct real property for the duration of the respective concession (Art. 3/4 AOORR).

B. Private Property in Natural Resources

The Constitutional Court of the Republic of Croatia holds that ownership 'must be very broadly interpreted' because it encompasses 'in principle all property rights',[5] including the economic interests connected to the

---

1 Official Gazette (Narodne novine (NN)), no. 56/90, 135/97, 113/00, 28/01, 76/10 and 5/14.

2 NN no. 91/96, 68/98, 137/99, 22/00, 73/00, 114/01, 79/06, 141/06, 146/08, 38/09, 153/09, 90/10 and 143/12.

3 NN no. 74/14.

4 NN no. 84/02, 140/05, 138/06 and 88/08.

5 See for example the decisions of the Constitutional Court nos.: U-III-661/1999 of 13 March 2000; U-III-72/1995 of 11 April 2000; U-III-551/1999 of 25 May 2000; U-III-476/2000 of 14 June 2000, etc.

property and the legitimate expectations of parties that their property rights, grounded on legal acts, will be respected and their realization protected.[6] The Constitutional Court often bases its decisions on the view of the European Court of Human Rights that legitimate expectations of the parties must – under certain conditions – be considered as 'property' under the protection of Article 1 of Protocol no. 1 of the European Convention.[7] Therefore, rights of using natural resources such as a concession to exploit a resource or an authorisation/allowance to emit noxious substances may be interpreted as property.

C. Private Property Used in Defense of Environmental Protection

The cases of private property usage in defense of environmental protection typically involve land-owners who challenge authorizations for infrastructure or industrial developments.

In the case of the factory that has been operating for decades, there is a possibility for the State to revoke the permit under the conditions that are set in the

---

6 Decision of the Constitutional Court, U-IIIB/1373/2009, para. 7, available in English: http://www.codices.coe.int/NXT/gateway.dll/CODICES/full/eur/cro/eng/cro-2009-2-010?fn=document-frame.htm$f=templates$3.0.

7 For instance, see judgment in the case *Pine Valley Developments LTD and others v. Ireland* and judgment of the Grand Chamber in the case *Kopecký v. Slovakia*. In its decision U-IIIB/1373/2009, the Constitutional Court summarized these cases:
The European Court first mentioned the concept of 'legitimate expectation' in the context of Article 1 of Protocol no. 1 to the Convention in the judgment in the case of Pine Valley Developments LTD and others v. Ireland of 29 November 1991 (application no. 12742/87). In this case the applicants were entrepreneurs whose principal business was the purchase and development of land; in 1978 they bought land on the site in reliance on an outline for planning permission for industrial warehouse and office development, which the Irish Supreme Court later found *ultra vires* and therefore *ab initio* a nullity because it contravened relevant laws. In that case, the Court found that a 'legitimate expectation' arose when outline planning permission had been granted, in reliance on which the applicant companies had purchased land with a view to its development. The planning permission, which could not be revoked by the planning authority, was 'a component part of the applicant companies' property' (§ 51 of the Pine Valley judgment and § 45 of the judgment of the Grand Chamber in the case Kopecký v. Slovakia of 28 September 2004, application no. 44912/98, 2004-IX). In the Kopecký v. Slovakia judgment the Grand Chamber of the European Court condensed the views explained in the Pine Valley judgment and in the newer Stretch v. the United Kingdom judgment of 24 June 2003 (application no. 44277/98, § 35). It explicitly stated that in the above cases, the persons concerned were entitled to rely on the fact that the legal act on the basis of which they had incurred financial obligations would not be retrospectively invalidated to their detriment. In this class of case, the 'legitimate expectation' is thus based on a reasonably justified reliance on a legal act which has a sound legal basis and which bears on property rights (§ 47 of the Kopecký judgment).

General Administrative Procedure Act (Art. 130).[8] A lawful decision by which a party has acquired a certain right may be revoked if it is necessary to avert any serious and immediate danger to the life and health of people and public safety, if the said cannot be successfully averted by other means that would impinge upon the acquired rights to a lesser extent. A party suffering damages as a result of the revocation of a decision for the purpose of averting a serious and immediate danger to the life and health of people and public safety is entitled to receive compensation of actual damages.

D. Natural Resources as Public Property or Interest

Art. 52 of the Constitution stipulates:

> The sea, seashore, islands, waters, air space, mineral resources, and other natural goods, as well as land, forests, flora and fauna, other components of the natural environment, real estate and goods of particular cultural, historical, economic or ecological significance which are specified by law to be of interest to the Republic of Croatia shall enjoy its special protection.
>
> The way in which goods of interest to the Republic of Croatia may be used and exploited by holders of rights thereto and by their owners, as well as compensation for the restrictions imposed on them, shall be regulated by law.

Art. 52/2 of the Constitution is elaborated in Art. 32/2 of the AOORR, which reads as follows:

> The owner of a thing, which was proclaimed to be of interest to the Republic in a particular piece of legislation, pursuant to the Constitution and with respect to which a special way of its use and utilization – by its owner and by persons authorized to other rights on it – is laid down, is bound to exercise his right of ownership accordingly; however, he is entitled to compensation for the limitations imposed on his right of ownership.

Since the restrictions pursuant to Art. 52 are not determined with respect to all owners of particular things, but only for some of the owners, these restrictions require 'greater sacrifice' from the latter. Thus, the Constitution stipulates that they are entitled to compensation. As an example, special provisions of the Nature Protection Act[9] demanding compensation for limitations of the property in protected areas shall be demonstrated here:

---

[8] NN no. 47/09.

[9] NN no. 80/13.

(1) Land hosting speleological sites (Art. 108)

The holder of the right to or the owner of the land hosting a speleological site must permit access and visit to such a site for authorized purposes. The owner or holder of the right on land hosting the speleological site shall have the right to compensation for restrictions to which he/she is subjected, in an amount proportional to the reduced earnings. The compensation level shall be determined by agreement and in case of dispute concerning the level of compensation the matter shall be referred to the courts. The compensation shall be disbursed from State Budget Funds.

(2) Visitation of protected areas (Art. 146 and 147)

Protected natural areas may be visited and toured in a manner that will not endanger their assets or the implementation of protection. The holder of the right to or the owner of a protected area shall be bound to permit access to a particular natural asset, if a specific regulation does not stipulate otherwise. If the owner or right-holder is subject to limitations due to visitation, the Minister for environmental and nature protection may determine compensation. Such decision of the Minister shall stipulate compensation to the owner or right-holder for any restrictions to which he is subjected.

(3) Owner's right to compensation (Art. 148)

If the use and exploitation of a protected area for particular designated purposes is restricted or prohibited, then the holder of the right to or the owner of such protected area shall have the right to compensation for any restrictions to which he/she is subject. The amount of remuneration shall be established by agreement. The amount of compensation depends on the purpose of use, its duration, type and extent of restrictions or prohibitions. In the case of dispute concerning the amount of compensation, the matter shall be referred to the courts. The compensation shall be disbursed from the State Budget or budget of the county, the City of Zagreb, city or municipality (depending on the type of protected area). Art. 148 (the owner's right to compensation) is based on Art. 52/2 of the Constitution that explicitly calls the legislator to regulate compensation for the restrictions imposed on the owners and other holders of rights.

(4) Indemnity (Art. 169)

A legal or natural person whose prevailing opportunities for earning income are significantly impaired shall be entitled to compensation resulting from restrictions to which he/she is subjected by the Nature Protection Act or due to the acts on protection passed on the basis of this Act if such impairment cannot be compensated by authorized activity within the framework of the statutory protection regime in the protected area. The compensation may be disbursed if the Ministry for environmental and nature protection or competent administrative authority has previously ascertained that the legal or natural person implemented prescribed nature protection requirements. The amount of compensation depends on the degree of deterioration of existing conditions for the acquisition of income and the duration, type and extent of restrictions or prohibitions. The level of compensation shall be established by agreement, and in the case of a dispute concerning the level of compensation, the matter shall be referred to the courts. The compensation shall be disbursed from the State Budget or budget of the county, the City of Zagreb, city or municipality (depending on the type of protected area). Unlike Art. 148, Art. 169 is not based on the provision of the Constitution. This is a case of the State's liability for damage caused without any unlawful or improper act, when the legislator decided to grant compensation, even though the State acted in accordance with the law, but a person suffered loss of earnings. Art. 169 is a new provision that did not exist in the previous Nature Protection Act.[10] The reasons for introducing this kind of State's liability were not explained in the Final Draft of the new Nature Protection Act.

E. Property in Public Aids for Beneficial Use of Natural Resources

One of the principles of the General Administrative Procedure Act is the principle of protection of vested rights of parties (Art. 13). When a certain right has been obtained by a final decision of an administrative body, such decision may be annulled, revoked or changed only in the cases provided by law i.e. for reasons of lodging extraordinary legal remedies prescribed by a General Administrative Procedure Act or some other special Act. The legislator is free to withdraw subsidies for any reasons in cases this applies *pro futuro*.

F. Expropriation

The Croatian Constitution contains provisions regarding the possibility of taking or restriction of ownership: 'In the interest of the Republic of Croatia, ownership may be restricted or taken by law, subject to compensation equal to the market value of the property.' (Art. 50/1).

The Expropriation Act is the main piece of legislation that regulates the expropriation procedure. Expropriation shall be authorized if the taking or the limitation of a person's ownership right is needed in order to build facilities or perform works in the interest of the Republic of Croatia and if it was evaluated that the new use of the real estate will achieve greater value than the prior usage. The condition prescribed by the Constitution (as well as by Expropriation Act) is that the previous owner must receive compensation for the expropriated real estate in the amount of the market value. Property may be expropriated for performing works or construction of economic infrastructure (transport,

[10] NN no. 70/05, 139/08 and 57/11.

telecommunications, water management or energy), health, educational and cultural facilities, industrial, energy, transport and telecommunication facilities, facilities for the Croatian judiciary, the military and police as well as research and exploitation of minerals and other resources. There are no special provisions in this matter relating to the environment or of environmental friendly investments.

In general, the Croatian Government is the competent authority for deciding that performing works or construction is in the interest of the Republic of Croatia, subject to the recommendations of two committees of the Croatian Parliament (committee competent for promotion of efficient use and spatial planning and committee whose responsibility covers the area of harmonization and improvement of economic life).

There are two types of expropriation prescribed by the Expropriation Act (Art. 5 to 7):

- Taking of the ownership = complete expropriation which means that the right of ownership passes from the property owner to the new owner i.e. expropriation beneficiary;
- Restriction of the ownership = incomplete expropriation that can be established in two forms: a) easement (servitude) or b) temporary lease.

As a rule, the compensation for expropriated real estate (in case of complete expropriation) is determined through another real estate of corresponding value. If the beneficiary of the expropriation cannot secure the real estate or if the previous owner does not accept the real estate offered, the compensation is to be determined in cash or another allowed form (e.g. shares, bonds, commodities).

G. Indirect Expropriation by Environmental Regulation?

The Croatian Constitution distinguishes allowable restrictions without compensation and allowable restrictions with compensation. The criteria of their distinction are not sector-specific.

1) Allowable restrictions without compensation

The bases for allowable restrictions without compensation are:

- Art. 48/2 of Constitution: Ownership shall imply obligations. Holders of the right of ownership and its users shall contribute to the general welfare.
- Art. 50/2 of the Constitution: Entrepreneurial freedom and property rights may be exceptionally restricted by law for the purposes of protecting the interests and security of the Republic of Croatia, nature and the human environment and human health.

However, there are boundaries to which these restrictions may be imposed. The principle of proportionality must be observed:

> Any restriction of freedoms or rights shall be proportionate to the nature of the need for the restriction in each individual case. (Art. 16/2 of the Constitution).

The Constitutional Court expressed this view in its decision U-I/763/2009 of 30 March 2011:

> Ownership rights may not be restricted beyond what is necessary to achieve the legitimate aim of a legislative measure. As long as a legislative measure ensures the individual's personal freedom in ownership rights it conforms with the guarantee in Article 48 para. 1 of the Constitution.[11] The restriction of ownership rights that results from the social bounds of ownership (Article 48 para. 2 of the Constitution) must in principle be accepted without any compensation, except in cases when the Constitution itself provides for compensation for them. If a statutory measure oversteps these boundaries, it is not in conformity with the Constitution.[12]

In addition, the

> [...] rule, contained in Article 50 para. 2 of the Constitution, empowers the legislator to 'exceptionally' restrict ownership rights (and entrepreneurial freedom, which are inherent to ownership) by law, without the obligation to pay any kind of compensation, when the restriction is necessary for the protection of some particular values or assets protected by the Constitution (protecting the interests and security of the Republic of Croatia, nature, the human environment and

---

11 The right of ownership shall be guaranteed (Art. 48/1 of the Constitution).

12 Para. 17 of the decision U-I/763/2009, Publication data: Official Gazette no. 39/11, available in English: http://www.codices.coe.int/NXT/gateway.dll/CODICES/full/eur/cro/eng/cro-2011-1-002?f=templates$fn=document-frame.htm$3.0. The case concerned the question of conformity with the Constitution of certain provisions of the Agricultural Land Act. There were three main arguments. Firstly, this Act regulated the legal possibility of leasing privately-owned agricultural land, for a particular time period, to other natural or legal persons after the administrative authority of the municipality, city or the City of Zagreb has found that this land is not being cultivated in accordance with agro-technical measures and was not cultivated in the preceding vegetative period, or that it is overgrown with vegetation of several years. The Constitutional Court examined whether the particular legislative solutions satisfied the requirements of the principle of proportionality and the principle of the rule of law, in the light of the constitutional guarantee of the right of ownership. The Court concluded that there was a disproportionate interference in the rights of the owner of agricultural land. Secondly, the Agricultural Land Act also regulated a one-time charge for the conversion of agricultural land in such a way that it created inequality among the owners of agricultural land on the basis of their property. The regulation imposed disproportionate burden on the owners depending on the location of their agricultural land on the day when the Act entered into force. Thirdly, the Agricultural Land Act regulated selling and leasing privately-owned agricultural land. In reviewing the legislative solutions from the aspect of the restriction of ownership rights and entrepreneurial freedom permitted under constitutional law, the Constitutional Court found that they were not in conformity with the Constitution.

human health). Article 50 para. 2 of the Constitution thus refers to the protective function of ownership (and entrepreneurship), in which the public interest of the community as a whole, or some of its parts is inherent. The Constitution does not guarantee compensation for this kind of restriction.

The Constitutional Court reiterates that the principle of proportionality (Article 16 of the Constitution) holds for all the rules of ownership. Every regulation on ownership must ensure a fair balance and harmonious relationship between the right of private persons to ownership and general interests, i.e. public interests. Interference in the right of ownership must be proportional to the nature of the need for the restriction in each individual case.[13]

2) Allowable restrictions with compensation

The bases for allowable restrictions with compensation are the following articles of the Constitution:

- Art. 50/1: In the interest of the Republic of Croatia, ownership may be restricted or taken by law, subject to compensation equal to the market value of the property.
- Art. 52: The sea, seashore, islands, waters, air space, mineral resources, and other natural goods, as well as land, forests, flora and fauna, other components of the natural environment, real estate and goods of particular cultural, historical, economic or ecological significance which are specified by law to be of interest to the Republic of Croatia shall enjoy its special protection. The way in which goods of interest to the Republic of Croatia may be used and exploited by holders of rights thereto and by their owners, as well as compensation for the restrictions imposed on them, shall be regulated by law.

The Constitutional Court explained the difference between this compensation based on Art. 52/2 of the Constitution and the compensation regulated in Art. 50/1:

> Namely, in Article 52 para. 2 the Constitution stipulates that the owners of assets of interest of the Republic of Croatia receive 'compensation' regulated by law for the restrictions imposed on them, while the restriction of ownership in the interest of the Republic of Croatia in Article 50 para. 1 of the Constitution unconditionally requires that the owners shall receive 'compensation equal to its market value'.
>
> Because there is a connection in substantive law between these two constitutional articles, the Constitutional Court does not exclude the constitutional possibility that the 'compensation' in Article 52 para. 2 of the Constitution could also be 'compensation equal to its market value', which depends on the particular legislative solutions and how intensely they interfere in the ownership rights of the owner of assets of interest of the Republic of Croatia. From this aspect, the Consti-

[13] Ibid. (para. 17/1).

tution would as a rule demand compensation amounting to the market value of the asset when a particular legislative measure restricted the owner of the asset of interest of the Republic of Croatia to such a measure that it resulted in depriving the owner of his ownership rights.[14] [...]

The Constitutional Court also notes that a legislative measure restricting the right of ownership in the interest of the Republic of Croatia with the aim of realising the general welfare (Article 52 para. 2 and Articles 50 para. 1 taken with Article 48 para. 2 of the Constitution) need not a priori be acceptable in constitutional law just because the owner is to receive 'compensation' (Article 52 para. 2 of the Constitution), or 'compensation equal to its market value' (Article 50 para. 1 of the Constitution), for the restrictions imposed on him. The guarantee of the right of ownership in Article 48 para. 1 of the Constitution first requires that everything possible should be done to retain the private usability of the property without disproportionately burdening the owner. The objective of these measures is to secure that the property remains in the owner's hands, which is the basic expression of the guarantee of the right of ownership in a social state based on the rule of law.[15] [...]

In conclusion, it is the legislator's task to effectuate the guarantee of the right of ownership (Article 48 para. 1 of the Constitution) and, bearing in mind a socially just regulation of ownership, i.e. the protected interests of private owners and the general or public interests, to establish a just condition in which owners will enjoy a balanced relationship. The guarantee of ownership rights does not protect malpractice in property use, but neither does the social function of ownership justify a disproportionate and excessive restriction of private ownership.[16]

H. Dissolution of Property for Environmental Protection

There has been one case before the Constitutional Court regarding the dissolution of vested rights – U-I-1156/1999 of 26 January 2000.[17] In the Act on the Use of Tobacco Products[18] (which came into force on 8 December 1999) there was a provision according to which the sale of tobacco products from vending machines was prohibited from 1 January 2000. That was an obvious restriction of entrepreneurial freedom and ownership rights, although undertaken towards a legitimate aim (protection of health), with a specific aim to control whether tobacco products are sold to minors. However, entrepreneurs had a deadline of only 20 days to shut down their operations. The Act actually imposed a ban on a specific economic activity, and that was done without notice

14 Ibid. (para. 19).

15 Ibid. (para. 19/1).

16 Ibid.

17 Summary available in English: http://www.codices.coe.int/NXT/gateway.dll/CODICES/precis/eng/eur/cro/cro-2000-1-003?fn=document-frame.htm$f=templates$3.0.

18 NN no. 128/99.

and without leaving a reasonable time in which the entrepreneurs could liquidate or reorganize without danger for the rights of the owner, employee rights, etc. The decision of the Constitutional Court was that a law which prohibits a previously legal economic activity or introduces restrictions on it, without leaving a reasonable period of time during which the affected subjects might adjust to the newly established conditions of business, is unconstitutional. There is no proportionality between the legitimate aim and the measures undertaken to ensure that aim if constitutional rights are restricted to a greater extent than necessary.

The new Act on the Use of Tobacco Products[19] that introduced the same prohibition was again challenged (case: U-I/951/2000 of 11 October 2000). This time, however, the Constitutional Court stated that in the process of harmonization with the previous Court's decision of 26 January 2000, the legislature amended the statutory provisions in such a way that the prohibition was postponed until 2001, which amounted to one year and one month since the formally expressed will of the legislature to ban the sale of tobacco products from vending machines. The Court determined that the amended provision struck a fair balance between the protection of entrepreneurial freedom and property rights of affected businesses, on the one hand, and the requirements for achieving the public interest for the protection of human health, on the other hand. In the Court's opinion, the disputed provision prescribed a sufficiently long period for the adaptation of the entrepreneurs to the new conditions.

I. State Liability for Environmental Damage to Private Property

No one may exploit or use a piece of real property in a way that as the result smoke, unpleasant odours, soot, sewage waters, earthquakes, noise etc. reach the property of another, either by accident or by forces of nature, if they are excessive in view of the purpose appropriate for the real property in question considering the place and time, or if they cause more substantial damages or if they are impermissible based on the provisions of a particular piece of legislation (excessive indirect emissions) (Art. 110/1 of the AOORR). The owners of properties exposed to excessive indirect emissions are authorized to request the owner of the real property from which such emissions originate to eliminate the causes of the emissions and to compensate the resulting damages, as well as not to continue what was the cause of the excessive emissions until he takes all measures required to eliminate the possibility of excessive emissions (Art. 110/2). However, where excessive emissions are the product of activities for which there is a permission by the competent authority, the owners of the exposed property do not have the right to request the owner to stop the activity as long as the permission is in force; however, they are authorized to claim com-

[19] NN no. 55/00.

pensation of damages caused by the emissions, as well as demand the emitter to take appropriate measures to prevent or minimize future damages (Art. 110/3).

Croatia has major problems with landfills that do not comply with the legislation ('non-compliant landfills'). There is a provision in the Act on Sustainable Waste Management[20] that grants the right to compensation due to the proximity of non-compliant landfills.

Compensation due to the proximity of non-compliant landfills (Art. 41)

- The owner of an existing residential, or a residential-commercial building permanently occupied by residents, which is situated at a distance of up to 500 m measuring from the vertex of the cadastral plot on which a non-complaint landfill is located to the vertex of the cadastral plot on which the residential and the residential-commercial building is located, shall be entitled to financial compensation due to the proximity of a non-compliant landfill, under the condition that he had acquired ownership of the real estate before the construction of the landfill facility began.
- The operator of the non-compliant landfill shall be liable to pay the compensation referred to in paragraph 1 of this Article.
- Upon request of the real property owner referred to in paragraph 1 of this Article the competent body of the local self-government unit in whose territory the non-compliant landfill is located shall issue a decision determining the right to compensation and the amount of the financial compensation to be awarded on account of the proximity of the non-compliant landfill.
- An appeal may be lodged to the Ministry against the decision referred to in paragraph 3 of this Article.
- The criteria and the method for defining the amount of the compensation, the manner in which the compensations referred to in paragraph 1 of this Article shall be paid, shall be laid down by an ordinance[21] issued by the Minister.[22]

J. Proprietor's Liability for Environmental Damage

Pursuant to the Civil Obligations Act,[23] the owner shall be liable for damage resulting from a dangerous thing, and the person engaged in the respective activity shall be liable for damage resulting from a dangerous activity (Art. 1064). There is a presumption of causality: Damage caused in relation with a dangerous thing or dangerous activity shall be considered as resulting from

20 NN no. 94/13.

21 Ordinance on the criteria, procedure and manner of determining compensation to real estate owners and local self-government units (NN no. 59/06 and 109/12).

22 Translation: http://www.mzoip.hr/doc/Propisi/Act_sustainable_waste_management.pdf.

23 NN no. 35/05, 41/08 and 125/11.

that thing or activity, unless it has been proved that the damage was not caused by it (Art. 1063). There exists a possibility of release from liability (Art. 1067):

- The owner shall be released from liability if he proves that the damage results from an unforeseeable cause unrelated to the thing and which could not be prevented, avoided or eliminated.
- The owner shall be released from liability if he/she proves that the damage has occurred exclusively due to an action of the injured party or a third party, which the owner could not anticipate and the consequences of which could not be avoided or eliminated.
- The owner shall be partly released from liability if the injured party has partly contributed to the occurrence of damage.
- If a third party partly contributed to the occurrence of damage, that party shall be liable to the injured party jointly with the owner of the thing, and shall make compensation proportionately to the degree of its fault.
- The person of whom the owner has made use in the usage of the property shall not be considered a third party.

K. Permit Excuse in Environmental Liability

The permit does not exclude the holder from the liability towards third persons. However, if damage is the result of performing an activity of public interest for which an approval has been obtained from the competent authority, only a compensation for damage exceeding the usual limits may be required (excessive damage). Nevertheless, in that case adaption of socially justified measures may be required in order to prevent the occurrence of damage or to reduce damage (Art. 1047 of the Civil Obligations Act).

L. Direct or Indirect Expropriation by EU Measures

Croatia became an EU Member State on 1st of July 2013. There have been no cases yet regarding the question of expropriation that may be caused by EU legal acts or their implementation.

Property and Environmental Protection in Denmark

Peter Pagh

A. Constitutional Aspects

The Danish Constitution contains one provision (section 73) regarding the protection of private property but since the Constitution has not been changed since 1953 the Constitution does not contain any provision direct or indirectly addressing the protection of the environment. Section 73(1) of the Constitution states (private translation):

> The right of private property is inviolable. No one can be obliged to surrender his private property except when this is needed because of public interest. This can only happen if mandated by a legislative act and the owner is fully compensated.

The wording of section 73 is rather old fashioned and goes back to the original first Danish Constitution in 1849. The notion '*inviolable*' in the first sentence is interpreted as just a programmatic statement stressing that interference in private property rights can only be accepted if needed which already follows from the second sentence.

The wording '*private property*' is in theory and in case law interpreted widely as including: real estate, private physical things, intellectual property rights, economic demands, concessions and as a right to continue legal use of land in so far as this use does not harm private or public interest.

The last reservation is important because a wider interpretation of property combined with the wording would indicate that any intervention in private use of land is expropriation and will require full compensation for economic loss to the owner, since such an intervention in private property rights is only lawful if justified by public interest and only if the owner is fully compensated. This is, however, not the legal meaning of section 73 of the Constitution.

1. Expropriation and not expropriation

It follows clearly from case law that intervention in the use of private land and other private property can be lawful without compensation and therefore should not be seen as expropriation. The distinction between *expropriation* and what is named '*public intervention without compensation*' is according to case law related to four criteria invented in legal theory.

The *first criterion* is whether the intervention with the use of private property is *general or individual*. For example section 3 of the Nature Protection Act prohibiting any changes in nature with specific characteristics (e.g. swamps and lakes) is considered a *general* interference indicating no expropriation (with reservations for citizens strongly affected). Section 33 of the Nature Protection Act on conservation of land granting the environmental authorities the right to decide restrictions on the use of individual designated land for the improvement of nature protection is considered an *individual* measure and therefore expropriation, giving the owner the right to full financial compensation for the economic loss caused by the decision.

The *second criterion* is if the intervention means a transfer of the property right to another physical or legal private person or public body. Such transfer indicates strongly that the intervention is an expropriation requiring full compensation. In fact there is no example in Danish case law in which a compulsory transfer of property right has not been considered expropriation withdrawing the owner's right to full compensation.

The *third criterion* is the *character of the public interest justifying the intervention*. If the intervention is to prevent damage which could give victims the right to compensation, this strongly indicates that the intervention is not considered expropriation and does not require compensation. The application of this criterion can be illustrated by the Supreme Court ruling in case on granite mining (MAD 1996.888). The granite is considered part of the private property belonging to the owner of the land. By a new legislative Act in 1977 the right to further exploitation after 1986 was cancelled if no new permit was granted. The mining company applied for a new permit but this was rejected by the authority arguing that further extraction could cause pollution of the ground water. The mining company claimed this was expropriation because the pollution of groundwater was not caused by the mining but by extraction of ground water for drinking water supply. Based on the evidence presented, the Supreme Court found that the mining activity did not cause a serious threat in the form of pollution of the groundwater and hence the rejection of a new permit could be seen as a ban of mining. The ban was found to be an expropriation according to the meaning of section 73 of the constitution and compensation was granted.

The *fourth criterion* is the *intensity of the impact on the owner* of the intervention. The application of this criterion can be illustrated by a case raised by the farmers' union regarding section 69 of the Watercourse Act which banned farming within a zone of two meters from watercourses and lakes. The case was raised on behalf of two farmers claiming compensation for a yearly economic loss of 40 € (250 € respectively). In this case, the intervention was general and did not transfer the property right. Furthermore the intervention was reasoned as a necessary preventive measure to avoid pollution of streams and disputably lakes. However, the Supreme Court did not decide on the third criterion but stated that since the intensity of the intervention on the two farmers was so minor, there was no doubt that this was not expropriation leaving it open whether other farmers might be affected so intensively that it could be considered expropriation under section 73 of the Danish Constitution (MAD 1998.902).

The application of the four criteria was reviewed by an advising committee in 1976 regarding the Environmental Protection Act adopted in 1973. In accordance with the polluter-pays principle the Environmental Protection Act includes a provision granting the environmental authority the discretion to direct restrictions on pollution and if necessary the closure of polluting industrial installations. The committee concluded that such public order to an individual industrial installation was with reservation in case of extraordinary circumstances, not expropriation.

2. The Legislative Approach to Protection of Private Property and the Environment

It follows from section 73 of the constitution that expropriation requires a mandate by a legislative act adopted by the Parliament and that full compensation for economic loss to the owner is required. Before a new legislation is adopted the Parliament therefore has a constitutional duty to consider whether the legislation empowers expropriation; this must be reflected in the legislation adopted, but the Parliament decides how. In practice different legal designs are used to address expropriation.

Regarding environmental legislation the protection of private property is reflected in five different legislative designs or patterns.

The main and traditional system is that the environmental legislation adopted by parliament includes a provision granting the environmental authority the power to expropriate when certain conditions are met and the amount of compensation is decided by an independent committee (*'taksation committee'*). In the traditional system, the legislator decides which interventions are considered expropriation and asks the *taksation committee* to decide on compensation providing a simple and not expensive procedural system to ensure compensation for the affected landowners. This system is applied in the Planning Act section 47 (local plans), the Soil Contamination Act section 22 (public cleaning of private land), the Environmental Protection Act section 58 (sewage, restrictions on farmers use of pesticides and fertilizers), the Drinking Water Supply Act section 37 and 38 and the Nature Protection Act section 45.

The problem to decide whether an intervention is expropriation or not is, however, not always easy to answer. This uncertainty is addressed in four different legislative designs. One is the Planning Act section 48 and 49 which gives the owner of property the right to require the Municipal Council to take over the owner's land if the local plan or the municipal plan significantly prevents the owner from the normal economic benefits of his land. If the conditions are met, the Municipal Council must buy the land and pay the owner the price equivalent to the value of his land before the plan was adopted. As in the main system, the compensation is decided by the *taksation committee.*

The second legislative solution concerns restrictions of land use because of the protection of Natura 2000 sites. In this case the Parliament acknowledges that such restrictions will in some – but not in all – cases be expropriation. The Parliament is not specific on this distinction but indicates that it is expropriation if Natura 2000 protection requires the farmer to close a pig farm while it is no expropriation if Natura 2000 protection only affects a minor part of his land. In order to avoid uncertainty, the Parliament decided in the Nature Protection Act section 19g that full compensation to the owner must be given in all cases – provided the restriction of land use did not follow from other legislation – and compensation is decided by the *taksation committee.*

The third legislative design is seen in the Nature Protection Act section 29a implementing the protection of Annex IV species under the Habitat Directive art. 12-16. In this case the Parliament recognizes that restriction of land use to protect endangered species and their habitats in some cases will be expropriation. But in contrast to the Natura 2000 protection, the legislation does not provide any procedural system to review if the restriction of land use is expropriation. Instead the owner is asked to initiate civil proceeding before a civil court and ask the court to decide whether the restriction of land use is expropriation. This gives the owner the right to compensation and therefore substantially increases the procedural cost for the claim.

The fourth legal response to the uncertainty on whether intervention is expropriation can be found in the Contaminated Soil Act section 44. This provision concerns public orders to the polluter to clean up land owned by a third party. Since the polluter is not the owner of the polluted land, section 44 gives the environmental authority the right to demand the owner of the polluted land to accept that the polluter cleans up the pollution. The Parliament found that such clean-up on foreign land will be expropriation if the owner of the polluted sites rejects such a intervention on his land. If this is the case, the public order to clean up is legally invalid.

In sum, the environmental legislation design for addressing expropriation varies and the same pattern is resembled in the implementation of EU environmental legislation.

B. The Scope of Private Property Protection

As mentioned above, the protection of private property under section 73 of the Constitution is interpreted widely as not only including real estate, things and intellectual property rights but also including the right to stay in business and profit loss if this is prevented or substantially reduced by public intervention. The market share itself is however not recognized as a property right.

The right of using natural resources on private land is considered a property right to the extent the use is lawful. However, oil and gas and other minerals which are placed in the deep underground are under the Underground Act defined as the property of the State. But when the right to exploitation has been given as a permit, this permit is considered a property right protected under section 73 of the Constitution. The same legal concept applies with minor modification to the extraction of water from ground water and watercourses. To avoid compensation, only permits for 10 years exploitation are granted under the recent Drinking Water Act and Water Course. To solve the problem of compensation for old permits without any time limits when further extraction of water is denied, the legislator in 1977 decided by legislative Acts that the old permits expired in 2005. The same scheme was adopted regarding mining on private land but as the above mentioned case in MAD 1996.888 demonstrates, such expiry of old permits does not always mean that the right to further exploitation is not protected as a property right.

Even the right of the owner not to be exposed to substantial nuisance from noise or other pollution is considered a property right which gives the owner rights to compensation when the threshold for nuisance is exceeded by new infrastructure projects such as highways, railways and sewage plants. Compensation to land owners has also even been granted for the reduction of property value because of the establishment of high tension cables near the property. Although the Supreme Court did not find it proven that radiation from high tension cables could cause health damage, compensation was granted because the public debate on such potential health damage has caused uncertainty which significantly reduced the value of the land.[1] It is disputed in legal theory whether the creation of nuisance itself should be considered an expropriation or whether the compensation just should be seen as a result of neighbour law principles. In my opinion, the compensation follows from neighbour law principles. But since the compensation is granted by the *taksation committee* as an integrated part of the expropriation process in establishing new infrastructure projects, some other Danish scholars argue that the nuisance should to this extent be considered an expropriation.

Although it is disputed how compensation for new infrastructure project should be categorized it is clear that the right not to be exposed to substantial pollution on private land is protected – also if this exposure comes from old installations and even closed installations. The last can be illustrated by a case on neighbour law principles regarding a closed landfill which had been operated by the municipal council.

The neighbour was compensated for nuisance when the site was established by the municipality. 15 years later, the site was closed in accordance with the environmental protection act. After the disclosure of the site, the Western High Court granted the neighbour 65.000 € compensation for the reduction of the property value due to the potential danger from underground emissions of methane. The ruling is based on strict liability since the court stated that it recognizes that the danger was first acknowledged after the site was closed.[2]

Under neighbour law principles it is the operator – not the authority – who can be held liable. This does also apply if the nuisance is in accordance with a permit issued by the authority, but the permit is an indication that the nuisance is not exceeding the acceptable threshold. The authority can, however, be held liable for the nuisance under neighbour law principles, if the permit is unlawful. The last could be the case, if the permit is granted in conflict with planning legislation or if the permitted pollution goes beyond what can be accepted in that particular area. In these cases the public authority can be held liable under

1 Supreme Court ruling of 22 January 1996 Höjby (UfR 1996.540), Supreme Court ruling of 7 November 1997 Tjele (UfR 1997.105) and Supreme Court ruling of 13 August 1998 Vissenbjerg (UfR 1998.1515).

2 Wester High Court ruling of 25 January 1999 Randers Waste Deposit (MAD 1999.88).

neighbour law principles. If the operation of the factory does not require a permit under the Environmental Protection Act, the operation of the factory can be subject to an administrative order to reduce pollution from the factory under the Environmental Protection Act section 42, and the environmental authority has the obligation to issue an administrative order if the guiding thresholds regarding noise, smell or air pollution are exceeded. If the authority fails to act, the authority can be held liable for the passivity or for accepting too much pollution as lately demonstrated in a case on noise from a sawmill which however ended negatively because the legal action was raised too late before the court.[3]

If an industrial facility is closed by the authority because the pollution exceeds the acceptable level under the Environmental Protection Act and preventive measures are technically or economically not feasible, this is not considered expropriation and the owner of the facility has no right to compensation – provided the authority follows the administrative law procedures. In deciding how to respond to serious pollution the environmental authority has a wide discretion but if the authority goes beyond this discretion, the authority can be held liable towards neighbours as illustrated in the sawmill case mentioned above.

C. Natural Resources as Legal Concept

There is not one overall legal status of natural resources under Danish Law. Raw materials like sand and clay are part of the property of the private land and the mining right belongs to the owner, provided mining is permitted. The same concept applies regarding hunting on private land and fishing in private lakes or streams.

The Danish legislation on nature protection and use of natural resources is not based on the concept of public trust or public property or land stewardship but is based on the regulatory power of the state leaving it to the parliament to decide what part of nature shall be protected and how. In so far as such regulation is general, the restrictions on the use of private land will not interfere with existing legal use of the land and will therefore normally not give the landowner rights to compensation. Reservations to this are made for landowners which suffer substantial loss because of the interference, as shown in the Supreme Court ruling in the mining case (UfR 1997.157 H).

Regarding pollution, the concept is different, since restrictions on pollution will also affect existing activity without compensation – and again with reservation for extraordinary burdensome intervention.

The Danish legislation does not contain legally binding duties for the national or local environmental authorities to protect the natural resources or wildlife in any specific way subject to legal review, except when such duties follow from EU legislation on nature protection.

---

3 Supreme Court ruling of 22 November 2011 Hvalsö Sawmill (UfR 2012.574).

D. The Legal Status of Subsidies For Environmental Friendly Use

Subsidies for environmental friendly farming and for renewable energy are well known in Danish Law. Regarding environmental friendly farming the subsidy is given based on a contract between the Nature Agency under the Minister of Environment and the farmer on the way of managing the farming land and such contracts cover a specific period of year. During these years the farmer's right to receive a subsidy is protected as a property right provided that the farmer complies with the condition for the management laid down in the contract.

Regarding windmills or sun energy the system is different and the protection relates to the legislation in place when the windmill project or sun energy installation was permitted. The legal concept is that to make the conditions of such investment foreseeable, the subsidy system in force when the project was permitted, cannot be reduced when a new subsidy system for renewable energy has been adopted with lower subsidies. This means that the new subsidy system with lower subsidies only applies for new installations, while the old system still applies for some years for old installations to ensure the expected benefit of the investment is not lost. Thus, to a certain extent the subsidies to renewable energy installations are considered protected property rights.

E. Landowner Liability, State Liability and Operator Liability

Danish law does not include any sort of landowner liability regarding polluted land or waste. The concept of landowner liability regarding polluted land was presented by the Environmental Protection Agency but was rejected by the Supreme Court in the so called *Rockwool* case. In this case, the company Rockwool had purchased a site and during the construction of new buildings pollution from closed oil tanks was discovered. The municipality ordered Rockwool to clean up the pollution and after appeal this administrative order was upheld by the Environmental Protection Agency (EPA). Rockwool complied with the administrative order and cleaned the site up but then raised legal action against the municipality and the EPA claiming the two authorities were liable for the clean-up cost arguing that there was no legal basis to order the company to clean up pollution caused by the previous owner of the land. The Supreme Court agreed that the administrative order was legally invalid and contrary to the polluter-pays principle, since Rockwool was not the polluter. The EPA and the municipality were therefore jointly liable for the full clean-up cost without reduction for the increasing value of the property after cleaning up pollution since *Rockwool* has been under the obligation to comply with the administrative order.[4]

---

[4] Supreme Court ruling of 18 June 1991 Rockwool (UfR 1991.674).

The rejection of landowner liability in the *Rockwool* case was later upheld by the Parliament when strict liability for environmental damage caused by IPPC installations was adopted in the Environmental Liability Act from 1994 and when the Contaminated Soil Act was adopted in 1999 establishing a strict administrative liability system regarding soil pollution caused by commercial activities after 2001.

While the landowner is not liable for waste deposited illegally by a prior owner or by third parties, the operator of an industrial installation can be held liable for cleaning up waste originating at the industrial facility under a prior operator. But this succession is restricted to the operator, not the landowner and does not apply to soil pollution except when the installation is covered by article 22 under the Industrial Emission Directive (2010/75).

Compliance with conditions in the IPPC permit for an industrial installation will not exclude the company operating the facility from liability. Under the Environmental Liability Act from 1994 and under the Contaminated Soil Act from 1999 the operator can be liable for environmental damage and respectively the cleaning-up of soil pollution even when all conditions in the permit are met.

The allocation of responsibilities differs under the Nature Protection Act which holds the owner and user of the land responsible for illegal acts committed by a previous owner or user. The scope of a new owner's succession in unlawful acts committed by previous owner under the Nature Protection Act is restricted to cases where the previous owner had made constructions or new management of land offending the Nature Protection Act.

Property and Environmental Protection in France

Matthieu Galey

A. Objects of Private Property

The province of potential objects of property, which French law calls *'les biens'*, includes real things as well as incorporeal rights or properties.

For a long time, the issue has been blurred due to the influence of the German theory of subjective rights on French legal literature. Anyhow, the theoretical attempt to reduce the province of property to real things and to analyse incorporeal rights as subjective rights, has proven to be unable to provide a satisfactory description of the rules set out by the French Civil Code as well as of their contemporary evolutions. Although some authors still criticize this opinion,[1] the vast majority of French legal scholars as a consequence admits the ability of incorporeal rights to be owned.[2]

Potential objects of property include assets such as:

- Real things;
- Incorporeal rights, such as: any real right other than the right of property as defined by the article 544[3] of the French Civil Code, claims based on contract or tort liability, civil actions, shares and interests in partnership or a company, ...;
- Incorporeal properties, such as: ministerial offices (notaries and auctioneers, among others), commercial as well as agricultural establishments (which comprises good will, right to the lease, the physical installation, merchandises,...), intellectual property rights (copyright, patent).

According to this prevailing view, the right of property is the only right *in rem* to be also a subjective right. As such, it cannot be owned.

As to real things, it should be noted that article 714 of the French Civil Code acknowledges the existence of a class of real things, deemed to be *res communis*, that is: unable of property and subject to an open access regime, their use being organised by public regulations. Anyhow, the scope of this article is fairly narrow, if not shrinking. Its scope is now limited to the air and to running waters. For examples, since 1986 Hertzian waves have become the object of public property on the ground of statute law.[4]

One should also bear in mind that today, the French Civil Code as such is unable to provide with a valid ground, the formal recognition of the many new incorporeal rights that arise along the development of new streams of wealth.

[1] W. Dross, *Droit des biens*, 2è éd., Paris: Montchrestien 2014, p. 353.

[2] J. Carbonnier, *Droit civil, vol. II: Les biens, les obligations*, Paris: PUF Quadrige, 2004, 2574 p., n° 712 et 713, pp. 1603 à 1607; F. Terré, P. Simmler, *Droit civil: les biens*, 9è éd., Paris: Dalloz, 2014, 863 p., n° 53 à 63, pp. 66 à 80; Y. STICKLER, *Les biens*, Paris: PUF, 2006, n° 53 à 68, pp. 94 à 113; F. Zénati-Castaing, T. Revet, *Les biens*, 3è éd., Paris: PUF, 2008, n° 8, pp. 27 à 30, p. 33.

[3] According to the article 544 of the Civil Code: *'La propriété est le droit de jouir et de disposer des choses de la manière la plus absolue, pourvu qu'on n'en fasse pas un usage prohibé par les lois ou par les règlements'.*

[4] Code général de la propriété des personnes publiques, art. L.2111-17; N. Foulquier, *Droit administratif des biens*, Paris: Lexis-nexis, 2013, n° 193, p. 85.

This formal recognition is usually provided either directly, through particular statutes, or indirectly, through tort case law.[5]

First, this uneasiness of French law with new incorporeal rights and properties stems from an old rural bias of the French Civil Code, at the expense of industry, according to which the fruiting rural land is the fundamental source of all wealth. Accordingly, acquiring rights on newly created wealth is under the Civil Code only possible through production. Hence it is not applicable in cases where the wealth is the pure product of human industry.[6] The other reason for this uneasiness is the administrative law principle according to which all administrative permits are delivered *intuitu personae* and cannot be transferred without prior public authority approval, let alone being bought or sold. For example, a special statutory provision was necessary to recognise the fact that the emission quota of greenhouse effect gas is a freely negotiable object of property.

Although the right of property is protected by the Constitution on the ground of article 17[7] of the French Bill of Rights (*déclaration des droits de l'homme et du citoyen*),[8] there is no equivalent in French law like the case law of the American Supreme Court. Indeed, the state power to regulate the exercise of the right of property in pursuit of the public interest is embedded in the very legal definition of this right. According to article 544 of the French Civil Code, property is the right to enjoy and to dispose of property in the uttermost manner, provided this exercise is not contrary to law and public regulation. This definition relies on a sharp distinction between *dominium*, that is: *ownership*, the absolute economic control of the source of wealth, which is the object of property, and *imperium*, that is: sovereignty, the ultimate power to command people. The legislator's intent in setting out this distinction within the legal definition of the right of property, was to prevent any revival of feudality. This definition of the Civil Code has been confirmed by the French Constitutional Council case law[9] and has proved to be very inspirational of its case law. Article 544's definition entails a distinction between the vesting of property title (*jouissance*) and its use (*exercice*), according to which, the use of the right of property might be severely restricted by public regulation, as soon as this restriction has a purpose of general interest and does not go as far as denaturing the meaning and scope of the property title.[10] In any case, the title itself is not deemed to be

5 T. Revet, 'Les nouveaux biens en droit français", in *La propriété*, Travaux de l'association Henri Capitant, vol. LIII, Paris: Société de législation comparée, 2003, p. 273 et s.

6 T. Revet, *ibid.*, n° 9, p. 177.

7 According to article 17, '*La propriété est un droit inviolable et sacré, nul ne peut en être privé, si ce n'est lorsque la nécessité publique, légalement constatée, l'exige évidemment, et à la condition d'une juste et préalable indemnité.*'.

8 CC, n° 81-132 DC, 16 janvier 1982, R. p. 18.

9 CC, n° 2001-169 QPC, 30 sept. 2011, *AJDI* 2011.885, note N. Le Rudulier.

10 CC, n° 89-303 DC, 25 juill. 1989, R. p. 53.

taken.[11] Accordingly, one cannot resort to the taking argument in order to freeze the enforcement of a public regulation. Nonetheless compensation might be claimed.

B. Private Property in Natural Resources

The right of property includes the right to use all natural resources included in the assets owned. As far as land ownership is concerned, the owner owns in principle everything above and below the ground, although the *cuius est solum* maxim undergoes severe legal restrictions. Accordingly, the landowner is presumed to own all trees, plants or flowers growing on its land,[12] but the underground minerals, qualifying as *'mines'* according to the article L.111-1 of the *code minier*, are the only domain in French law where the State claims a right of eminent control over an asset of private property.[13] Wild animal and fish are *res nullius*, which means they are in principle the property of the local municipality, if not the State,[14] unless they get acquired through occupation. Any wild animal or fish passing onto the landowner's land becomes part of his property by way of accession.[15] Accordingly, the rights to hunt and to fish are impliedly recognized by French law as incidents of the right of property.[16] Based on the right of occupation wild animals and fish may be acquired through their killing and seizing by hunters and fishermen; even on the land of someone else. Indeed, hunting or fishing on someone else's land, while far from being a right as such, is tolerated by French law: it is deemed to be accepted by the landowner, unless he or she expressly forbids it. This implied licence to hunt on one's property is linked to what French lawyers know as the *chasse banale'*.[17]

---

11 F. Biglione, La notion de privation de propriété. Etude relative à la propriété immobilière, Aix-en-Provence, 1999, 482 p.

12 Code civil, art. 552.

13 F. Terré, P. Simmler, *op. cit.*, n° 338, p. 285.

14 Code civil, art. 713. *'Les biens qui n'ont pas de maître appartiennent à la commune sur le territoire de laquelle ils sont situés. Par délibération du conseil municipal, la commune peut renoncer à exercer ses droits, sur tout ou partie de son territoire, au profit de l'établissement public de coopération intercommunale à fiscalité propre dont elle est membre. Les biens sans maître sont alors réputés appartenir à l'établissement public de coopération intercommunale à fiscalité propre. / Toutefois, la propriété est transférée de plein droit à l'Etat si la commune renonce à exercer ses droits en l'absence de délibération telle que définie au premier alinéa ou si l'établissement public de coopération intercommunale à fiscalité propre renonce à exercer ses droits.'*

15 Code civil, art. 564.

16 Code de l'environnement, art. L.422-1: *'Nul n'a le droit de chasser sur la propriété d'autrui sans le consentement du propriétaire ou de ses ayants-droits'*; F. Terré, P. Simmler, op. cit., n° 415, p. 334.

17 J. de Malafosse, 'La liberté et l'appropriation des *res nullius* ou les défis de la liberté', in M. VOVELLE (dir.), *La révolution et l'ordre juridique privé, Rationalité ou scandale?*, Colloque d'Orléans 1986, Paris: CNRS/PUF, 1988, 836 p., t. II, p. 725 s.

The landowners also own riparian rights of use over the running waters of rivers passing by their properties as long as those rivers do not belong to the fluvial public domain of the state.

Besides being components of the right of property, the right to use and enjoy natural resources may also be framed as a right *in rem* (*droit réel*) granted on the private property of someone else. A typical example is the right of surfaces (*droit de superficie*), whose object might be the plants (trees or grass roots) or the fruits growing on someone else's land.

Whether framed as a component of the right of property, as a right *in rem* on someone else's land or merely as freedom (in the case of *res communis* and *res nullius*), the exercise of the right to use natural resources will always be subject to administrative regulation (*police administrative*). Administrative authorisations granted on that basis, whether planning permission or environmental permits, can never become a negotiable asset for their holder, unless the French legislator decides otherwise. As a consequence, neither planning permission nor environmental permits are deemed to run with the land. In French law indeed, the object of landownership is exclusively made of the corporeal immovable (and of all its accessories).[18] Accordingly, the transfers of such permits along with the conveyance of land always need the prior approval of public authorities.

There are nevertheless some exceptions. Both mining permission (*permis d'exploitation*)[19] and mining concession[20] give rise to an immovable and negotiable right *in rem*, distinct from the property of the surface land, even when they are granted to its very owner. This right of exploitation is able of being sold, subject to the prior approval of the state on the ground of its right of eminent domain over mines. The same is true, but to a far lesser extent, of the administrative authorisations and public concession delivered to a private operator as to the use of running waters in order to run hydroelectric facilities. The administrative permits to run a hydroelectric plant may not be negotiated nor sold,[21] but the rights deriving from such an administrative permit or such a concession may be mortgaged.[22]

18 A.M. Patault, 'Regard historique sur l'évolution du droit des biens. Histoire de l'immeuble corporel", in *L'évolution contemporaine du droit des biens, 3è journées Paul Savatier*, Paris : PUF, 1991, 192 p., p, 6.

19 Code minier, art. L.131-1: *'le permis d'exploitation crée un droit immobilier, indivisible, non susceptible d'hypothèque"* (à vérifier: la dernière version en vigueur).

20 Code minier, art. L.132-8: *'L'institution d'une concession, même au profit du propriétaire de la surface, crée un droit réel immobilier, distinct de la propriété de la surface. Ce droit n'est pas susceptible d'hypothèque'.*

21 Code de l'énergie, art. L.312-1 & L.311-5, al.2 (consultés le 27 avril 2015).

22 Code de l'énergie, art. L.511.10.

C. Private Property Used in Defense of Environmental Protection

Private property may be used for the sake of environmental protection. Landownership gives standing at court to challenge planning permission for infrastructure or industrial development on neighbouring land. Besides, trust-like devices, like the *conservatoires régionaux des espaces naturels* rely on the private ownership of land in order to protect spaces of outstanding natural beauty or special scientific interest.[23]

It remains anyhow that in French law the private property regime suffers major shortcomings as a tool of environmental protection, due to some loopholes in the protection that private property of land can gain from trespassory rules as well as from the French law of nuisance.

First, the private ownership of land may not give satisfactory control over the access to a natural resource. Indeed, the mere unlawful incursion onto land in possession of someone else does not qualify as trespass and remains outside the scope of possessory actions, if it is not meant to be a challenge of the exclusive rights on land stemming from possession or ownership. Furthermore, the statutory right to oppose hunting on one's own land, recognized to the owner of a land situated on the territory of an agreed hunting society (*association de chasse agréée*), is grounded not so much on one's right of property than on one's freedom of consciousness. As a consequence, the owner is not free to hunt on his/her own premises, if he/she has formally notified to the hunting society his opposition to hunting practices.[24]

Secondly, the landowner's right to sue one's neighbour in case of nuisance resulting in abnormal interferences with one's peaceful enjoyment of land (*troubles anormaux de voisinage*) is subject to the right of anteriority of one's neighbour. The so-called 'pre-occupation principle' means that a private landowner cannot resort to a private law action in nuisance against polluting activities on neighbouring land in order to get an injunctive relief or even compensation for environmental damage, if these activities, whether agricultural, industrial, commercial or traditional, took place in the area before the landowner settled

[23] The conservatoires régionaux des espaces naturels are non governmental organisations ruled by the Statute of the 1st july 1901 on Societies (*loi du 1er juillet 1901 sur le contrat d'association*) and article L. 414-11 of the environmental code. From a legal point of view, they differ both from public interest foundations and from public organisation like the *Conservatoire des espaces littoraux et des rivages lacustres*. In particular, in case of winding up of a *conservatoire régional* due to its bankruptcy, there is no guaranteed preservation of the environmental protection of its properties. Their legal status is thus far less environmentally friendly than for example the one of British charities. Nevertheless, these *conservatoires régionaux* have also become a fundamental partner of the state and departmental Councils for the management of environmentally sensitives areas (*espaces naturels sensibles*) acquired by them through the use of their public right of preemption in these areas.

[24] Code de l'environnement, art. L.422-10.

there and are complying with public regulations and statutes.[25] This principle was passed in statute law through some planning act in 1976, on the demand of farming organisations grumbling against abusive (or deemed to be so) litigations introduced by residential owners. The French Constitutional Council recently held that the pre-occupation rule did comply with the requirements of the environmental charter.[26]

Nevertheless, in the wake of passing the environmental charter and the constitutional value it gives to the prevention principle,[27] the landowner's legal position regarding environmental liabilities was lately reinforced. Indeed, the mere risk of harm is now recognized by civil case law as a valid ground for suing neighbours in an action for negligence or private nuisance.[28]

How would the factory case be treated in your country?

Under French law, this factory qualifies as a plant regulated for the sake of environmental protection (*installation classée pour la protection de l'environnement*). Accordingly, the *préfet*, who is the local representative of the central government, may require at any time any studies or controls regarding the state of soils and water.[29] If this industrial plant falls within the scope of the Directive n° 2010/75/EU, he *must* reconsider and update the permits conditions when the pollution caused by the installations is of such significance that the existing emissions value of the permit need to be revised or new values need to be included in the permit.[30]

Besides, and on a more general basis, the *préfet* may prescribe the assessment and the implementation of any remedies required in case of *'any other danger or inconvenience threatening to damage any public interest pursued by the regulation'*[31] among which are public health and the environment.[32] The *préfet* has thus the power to require at any time the operator of a regulated plant to proceed with any necessary remediation of soils contaminated by the operator through the operation of the plant.[33] According to most of the legal authors, the

---

25 Code de la construction et de l'habitation, art. L.112-16.

26 CC n° 2011-116 QPC du 8 avril 2011, *Michel Z et autres*, R. p. 183.

27 B. Parance, 'Le sort du propriétaire dans la responsabilité environnementale', in C. Cans (dir.), *La responsabilité environnementale: prévention, imputation, réparation*, Paris: Dalloz, 2009, 421 p., p. 319 à 322.

28 For example: Civ. 2è, 10 juin 2004, req. n° 03-10.434; Civ. 1è, 28 nov. 2007, req. n° 06-19.405; Civ. 2è, 15 mai 2008, *Billy v. Valmory*, req. n° 07-13.453.

29 CE, 26 mars 1997, *Société Elf Antargaz*, req. n° 135974; CAA Lyon, 12 mars 2002, *ministre de l'aménagement du Territoire et de l'Environnement c/ Diebolt*, req. n° 00LY00636; CAA Nancy, 23 avril 1998, *SA Prochimest*, req. n° 94NC01534.

30 Code de l'environnement, art. R.515-70, § III, transposing § 5 of the article 21, directive n° 2010/75/EU, 24th November 2010, *on industrial emissions.*

31 Code de l'environnement, art. L.512-20.

32 Code de l'environnement, art. L.511-1.

33 CE, 26 novembre 2010, *Société ArcelorMittal*, req. n° 32354.

wide drafting of the article L.521-20 of the environmental code is designed to empower the *préfet* to take some *'arrêtés d'urgence'*, in order to implement the precautionary principle, in cases of scientific uncertainty.[34]

The *property guarantees* reasoning does not fit here to give an account of the rationales behind the guarantees, which are given to the permit holder in case of a closure of his/her factory.

What is primarily protected at the constitutional level, as well as embedded in the legal procedure ruling the operation of the administrative regulation, is the *economic freedom of commerce and industry* principle, according to which economic freedom must remain the principle and the administrative restriction or constraint the exception. Accordingly, there is, formally, no statutory power to revoke the environmental permit conceived as an ordinary tool of administrative monitoring of the operation of the industrial plant. Although it appears to be an archaism,[35] powers to suspend or close the factory are to be found in the chapter of the environmental code relating to administrative sanctions. The guarantees granted to the economic freedom of the permit holder are of a strictly procedural nature. Thus, in case of a danger or an inconvenience, threatening to damage the public interests protected by statute *and unknown at the time of the deliverance of the authorisation*, and if the first step described above is not sufficient, the power lies, not with the *préfet*, but with the minister in charge of the environment to suspend, or with the prime minister to close, the operation of the plant.[36]

The other principle to be implemented is *equality before public burdens*. Thus, in case of the prime minister taking a *décret en Conseil d'état* ordering the closure of the factory, its operator could not claim any property guarantee, as such, against the State. But, if he can demonstrate that he has suffered a special and abnormal harm, he would have a right for compensation, enforceable against the State on a strict liability basis, on the ground of the breach of the principle of equality before public burdens.[37]

Finally, it should be remembered that any environmental permits delivered on the ground of the administrative control of plants regulated for the sake of environmental protection (*installations classées pour la protection de*

[34] D. Deharbe, *Les installations classées pour la protection de l'environnement*, Paris: Litec, 2007, n° 372, p. 303; J.P. Boivin, F. Defradas, *Sites et sols pollués: Outils juridiques, méthodologiques et financiers*, 2è éd., Paris: Le Moniteur, 2013, 332 p., p. 66.

[35] M. Pennaforte, *La réglementation des installations classées pour la protection de l'environnement: Pratique du droit de l'environnement industriel*, 2è éd., Paris: Le Moniteur, 2011, 517 p.

[36] Code de l'environnement, art. L.514-7. One should be bear in mind that, within the framework of the *police des installations classées*, there is no power of revocation of environmental permits as a tool of administrative monitoring of the operation of a regulated plant. From a formal point of view, the suspension or closing of a regulated plant intervenes as an administrative sanction, in case of breach of the regulation.

[37] CE, 2 novembre 2005, *Société coopérative agricole Ax'ion*, req. n° 266564.

l'environnement) are subject to the rights of third parties.[38] Accordingly, third parties may have standing to challenge any refusal of the State to use its power, and the administrative judge may act as an appeal authority, with full jurisdiction not only to quash or confirm, but also to modify any decision of the administrative authority.

D. Natural Resources as Public Property or Interest

Public management of natural resources is either direct or indirect. Direct public management of natural resources relies on public property, which is deemed to provide the environment with a greater protection than the private property regime, insofar as the benefit of the public domain regime (*domanialité* publique) is subject to the public nature of the owner of the land. Indeed, there is no equivalent in French law of legal mechanisms such as the *Öffentliche Sache* in German law. For the public law to protect the allocation of land to a public use, it has to be publicly owned.

The public domain regime is made of a package of immunities, privileges and duties, that altogether aim at protecting the allocation of the asset publicly owned to its use or purpose of public interest. It is widely believed to frame a sounder environmental management of natural resources. Thus, the assets of the public domain cannot be sold (rules of inalienability) nor acquired by prescription; its public owner is under a legal duty to maintain the asset fit for its purpose and may be given, by a legal clause, the power to regulate its private uses accordingly (*police de la conservation*). Any private occupation of the public domain is subject to an authorization which remains precarious and revocable in principle, unless statutes decide otherwise. If so prescribed by statutes or regulations, the unauthorized commission, whether by a trespasser or a lawful occupier, of any action or inaction which permanently alter the physical character of the land within the public domain, qualifies as a statutory violation (*contravention de grande voirie*),[39] that is: an *offence* of a derogatory nature, which

[38] Code de l'environnement, art. L.514-19.

[39] The expression *'contraventions de grande voirie'* is an archaic legal formula. It literally translates as *'great highway offences'* but its scope goes far beyond the public highways and includes every part of the public domain. Although they are concerned with the deeds of the users of the public domain and although their legal effects are repressive, the *'contravention de grand voierie'* play, in the context of French public domain, a function similar to the one played by the common law 'doctrine of waste' in the context of private *estate* and trust of land. According the *Osborn's Concise Law Dictionary* (8th ed., London: Sweet & Maxwell, 1993, 392 p., p. 347) waste is defined as 'generally any alteration of a tenanted property which is attributable to the tenant's action or neglect' According to Professor K. Gray, "waste' is defined [in the context of land law] as any action or inaction on the part of the estate owner which permanently altered the physical character of the land. The unauthorised commission of waste operates implicitly as a compulsory transfer of wealth from the remainder to the limited owner, and for this reason, the law relating to waste was designed 'primarily to police the temporal boundary between the two.' (*Elements of*

the *préfet* has the power, and indeed the duty, to sue directly before the *tribunal administratif*, on behalf of the public owner and without resorting to a public prosecutor. In some cases public owners, such as the director general of *Voies navigable de France* or the Conservancy of coastal shoreline and lakeside shore (*Conservatoire du littoral et des rivages lacustres*), are even empowered by statute to prosecute by themselves offences of statutory wastes. The administrative judge is bound not only to fine the offender but also to order him to restore the premises to their initial state.

Anyhow, not all public property belongs to the public domain. For example, lands acquired in order to protect suburban natural or agricultural spaces remains in the private domain of public authorities[40] whereas all the land belonging to the conservancy of coastal shoreline and lakeside shore are deemed by statute to be part of its public domain.[41] When statutes remain silent, the matter is settled by case law, which requires, besides the public ownership, an allocation of the premise to public use or to a public service, subject, in this last case, to the existence of some special fittings laying-out. Accordingly, there is no systematic connection between the environmental protection status of assets owned by a public authority and they being part of the public domain. For example, public forests remain part of the private domain of local authorities.

Furthermore, environmental protection is not an explicit purpose of the public domain regime.[42] Accordingly, there is no protection for lands of environmental interest against the discretionary power of public authorities to change their use or to favour their economic development by granting long term leases or occupation permits providing their holder with a right *in rem* upon them.[43] Most authors hold the opinion that the full enhancement of the environmental potential of the public domain regime is yet to come.[44]

Indirect public management of natural resources relies either on administrative restrictions on the use of private property of land, which are grounded on some environmental zoning (such as in national parks, nature reserves, etc.) or, in the case of underground minerals, a mechanism of eminent domain (see first question).

Land Law, 5th ed., Oxford: Oxford University Press, 2009, 1434 p, n° 1.3.13, p.62) The same is true in the French context concerning the relations between the offender and all the other members of the public which are users of the public domain. Hence the translation is 'statutory wastes'.

40 Code de l'urbanisme, art. L.143-3, al. 5.

41 Code de l'environnement, art. L.322-9.

42 S. Caudal-Sizaret, *'La domanialité public comme instrument de protection de l'environnement'*, *AJDA* 2009.2329, pp. 2332-2334; See also: M. Deffairi, *La patrimonialisation en droit de l'environnement*, Thèse, 2013, Université Paris I (Panthéon-Sorbonne), 861 p.

43 V. Inserguet-Brisset, *Droit de l'environnement*, Rennes: PUR, 2005, 292 p., pp. 164-165.

44 S. Caudal-Sizaret, *op. cit.*; V. Inserguet-Brisset, *La domanialité publique et la protection de l'environnement*, Paris: LGDJ, 1994, 315 p., p. 131 et s.

E. Property in Public Aids for Beneficial Use of Natural Resources

The subsidisation of a beneficial use of natural resources is not conceived as property in French law, even if the grant of a subsidy qualifies as an individual administrative decision giving rise to vested rights, whether or not it is subject to conditions.[45] Thus, when it is illegal, a decision granting a subsidy might be withdrawn without compensation only within four months after its signature, whether or not it is subject to conditions. But the decision granting a subsidy subject to conditions may be withdrawn at any time, in case of a non-compliance with these conditions by the beneficiary.[46] Such a withdrawal, which involves the reimbursement of all the sums received, might even happen ten years after the first grant.[47] The conditions, to which the grant of a subsidy is subject, might be either explicit or implicit. Implicit conditions might be constructively discovered by the judge[48] if they are clearly identifiable.[49]

Besides, it has been held by the *Conseil d'Etat* that the mere right of renewable energy producers, using solar photovoltaic technology, to conclude a guaranteed purchase agreement based on a feed-in tariff did not qualify as '*a legitimate hope, grounded on a sufficient legal basis, to get a sum of money*' and could not therefore be considered as property according to the first article of the first protocol of the European Convention for Human Rights.[50]

Indeed, no one is entitled to the current preservation of a general regulation, which the legislator or the government has the discretion to modify at any time within the limits of the principle of legal certainty security. According to this principle, any passing of a new regulation must be accompanied by transitional provision in order to prevent excessive hardship for public or private interests.[51]

For example, a decree temporarily suspending the implementation of a feed-in tariff, in the field of solar energy, has been held to respect the rule of legal certainty, insofar as were already signed purchase agreement as well as current application to get one (according to their degree of completion) were excluded from its scope.[52]

---

45 CE, 6 nov. 2002, *Mme Soulier*, Rec. p. 369, *AJDA* 2002, p. 1434, Chron. Donnat et Casas, *AJFP* 2003, p. 20, note A. Fuchs.

46 CE, 26 nov. 1993, *Société industrielle française du tout-terrain*, Rec. p. 593. See also: CE, 7 août 2008, *Crédit coopératif*, req. n° 285979.

47 CE, 8 février 1985, *Syndicat intercommunal de la Marana*, AJDA 1985, p. 293.

48 CE, 8 juillet 1988, *SABDEC*, Rec. p. 280.

49 CE, 21 mars 2001, *SICOMI Bail-investissement*, req. n° 198232.

50 CE, 16 nov. 2011, n° 344972 et a., *Société Ciel et Terre et a.: Juris data* n° 2011-025346, *RJEP*, n° 695, mars 2012, comm. 14.

51 CE, 24 mars 2006, n° 288460, *KPMG: JurisData* n° 2006-069857, Rec. p. 154; *CE, 13 déc. 2006, n° 287845, Lacroix* : *JurisData* n° 2006-071180 ; Rec., p. 540.

52 CE, 16 nov. 2011, n° 344972 et a., *Société Ciel et Terre et a.* , *op. cit.*

The rule of legitimate expectation is not recognised as such in French law and applies only when the implementation of the law of the European Union is at stake.[53]

F. Expropriation

1. Notion of expropriation

According to French law, the expropriation for public purposes is the procedure by which the state compels a private or public owner to assign his real rights to the beneficiary of the expropriation, whether as an absolute right of property or a mere right *in rem*, such as an *usufruct*, a servitude or a long term lease, on movables or immovables, against a prior and just compensation.[54]

In order to be deemed to take place, the expropriation requires the formal and compulsory transfer of the property title to the patrimony of the beneficiary designated by statute, which can be either public or private.[55] In this respect, it must be distinguished from requisition, which involves only a temporary dispossession. Also, a mere administrative restriction on private property, however severe it may be, cannot be held to be an expropriation, in the absence of a formal transfer of title.[56] Accordingly, a compulsory purchase procedure is not necessary to establish such a restriction.

2. Precondition of expropriation

The expropriation is known by administrative case law as a complex operation (that is: made of several different administrative decisions), whose taking place must be authorised by an enabling statute.

The procedure itself is designed to ascertain that three other preconditions are satisfied: the existence of an overriding public interest attached to the project requiring the resort to the compulsory purchase of land, the fairness of the designation process of the properties concerned and the full compensation of the loss due to the compulsory transfer of the land.

It is built in two phases: the administrative phase and the judiciary one. The administrative phase deals with the first two preconditions. It involves the taking place of a first public inquiry, designed to establish the existence of an overriding public interest (*utilité publique*), through a statement of overriding

---

53 CE, 9 mai 2001, n° 210944, *Entreprise personnelle de transports Freymuth* : *JurisData* n° 2001-062376 ; Rec., tables p. 865. – CE, Ass.,11 juillet 2001, n° 219494, *FNSEA* et a.: *JurisData* n° 2001-062815 ; Rec., p. 340.

54 N. Foulquier, *Droit administratif des biens*, Paris: LexisNexis, 2013, 748 p., n° 929, p. 363: *'L'expropriation pour cause d'utilité publique est la procédure par laquelle l'Etat impose à une personne privée ou publique de céder un droit immobilier ou mobilier, dans un but d'utilité publique, moyennant le paiement d'une juste et préalable indemnité'*.

55 P. Subra De Bieusse, *Les servitudes administratives*, Paris: Berger-Levrault, 1976, 372 p., p. 73.

56 CE, 13 avril 1983, *Association pour le Tourisme de Plein Air à Belle-Île-en-Mer*, Tables, p. 902.

public interest (*déclaration d'utilité publique*). Judicial review of the legality of this statement has been including a control of proportionality since 1971. According to the administrative judge, an overriding public interest can be validly stated to be attached to an operation, only if its impact on private property, its financial cost and, possibly, social inconveniences or any impact of other public interests, are not excessive regarding the public interest that is pursued through it.[57] The impact of an operation on the environment was taken into account by the administrative judge into the balance sheet in 1972.[58] Besides, the purpose of environmental protection was declared by statute of July 1976 to be of general interest, and it is now recognised as being able to qualify as an overriding public interest.[59]

The second step involved by the administrative phase is another public inquiry consisting in a land survey (*enquête parcellaire*), designed to list all the lands included in the perimeter of the operation, to identify all their owners, as well all the rights *in rem* pertaining to them, and to check their amenability to compulsory purchase. Land parts of the public domain are not amenable to expropriation, due to the rule of inalienability. As a conclusion, the *préfet* takes an *arrêté de cessibilité*, which compiles the list of all the lands to be purchased and all the owners and rights holders concerned. Once notified to the owner concerned, this second administrative decision equates to a 'notice to treat', in the British procedure of compulsory purchase.

The judiciary phase deals with the last of the preconditions, that is: a just and prior compensation. Thus the civil judge determines the sum to be paid and pronounces the transfer of title for each land. It is dealt with on an individual basis, according to the principle that the owner is entitled to the full compensation of its harm.

G. Indirect Expropriation by Environmental Regulation?

There is no clear general principle or criteria relating to the question of compensation for regulatory restrictions to the use of private property of land in French law.

The cornerstone of the law governing the right to compensation in this field is the distinction between regulatory restrictions on the exercise of the right of property, which put some prerogative of the owner in abeyance, without extinguishing the property title (*servitudes d'utilité publique*), and expropriation, which involves the compulsory purchase of the land and results accordingly in the formal transfer of the property title. Article 545 of the Civil Code considers the right to compensation only in the case of compulsory purchase of land, but remains silent as to the regulatory restrictions. Likewise, article 17 of the decla-

57 CE, Ass., 28 mai 1971, *Ville Nouvelle-Est*, R. p. 409, concl. Braibant, *AJDA* 1971, p. 405.

58 CE, 12 avril 1972, *Pelte*, R. p. 269.

59 For example: CE, 25 juill. 1975, *Conservatoire de l'espace littoral et des rivages lacustres*, AJDA 1995, p. 660.

ration of the rights of men and citizens is held by the Constitutional Council to provide for a right to a just and prior compensation in the sole case of dispossession. According to its case law, article 17 does not hinder the legislator to provide for regulatory restrictions on the use of private property without compensation, as long as these restrictions do not equate to dispossession, that is: as long as it has a purpose of general interest and does not go as far as depriving the right of property of its substance or putting undue restrictions to any other constitutionally entrenched rights and liberties of its occupiers.[60] In such a case, the public authority has the duty to resort to a compulsory purchase of the land concerned.[61] On the contrary, a statute that does not intend nor result in depriving the landowner of its right of property remains outside the scope of article 17 of the declaration of the rights of men and citizens, even if it provides for regulatory restrictions on its exercise.[62] As a consequence, constitutional law provides the legislator with no guidance as to the question of compensation for regulatory restrictions on the exercise of the right of property.

In the absence of a general principle, the legislator deals with the compensation issue on a case by case basis. As a consequence, the law is made of a patchwork of different provisions that no general criteria can put into order, so that we could speak of a legislative lottery.

A first group of statutory provisions set out a rule of no compensation.

For example, article L.160-5 of the *code de l'urbanisme* sets out a no compensation principle for all planning restrictions established on the basis of the code, with two direct exceptions: the removal of vested rights and the modification of the previous state of the land. A third exception has been set out by the *Conseil d'État*, in order to comply with the requirements of the European Convention for Human Rights,[63] in case of a special and exorbitant planning restriction that is out of proportion with its purpose of general interest.[64] In light of this last case law, the *Conseil d'État* held that the claim questioning the constitutionality of article L.160-5 of the *code de l'urbanisme* and its conformity to article 17 of the *declaration of the rights of man and citizen* was neither serious nor new and refused accordingly to transmit it to the constitutional council.[65] Another exception stems from article L.160-6 of the *code de l'urbanisme*, which provides for compensation regarding public rights of providing pedestrian with an access to the shoreline.

A second group of statutory provisions provides landowners with a right to compensation, which includes very different hypothesis, such as, among others,

60 CC, n° DC 85-198 du 13 décembre 1985, R. p. 78.

61 G. Liet-Veaux, *Servitudes administratives: théorie générale*, J. Cl. Adm., fasc. n° 390, 28 january 2011, n° 45.

62 CC, n° DC 85-189 du 17 juillet 1985, R. p. 49.

63 ECHR, 23 sept. 1982, *Sporrong & Lönroth v. Sweden*, Series A, n° 52.

64 CE, Sect., 3 juillet 1998, req. n° 158592, *Bitouzet*, R. p. 288.

65 CE, 16 juillet 2010, n° 334665, *SCI La Saulaie*, *JurisData* n° 2010-011682, *AJDA* 2010.1453.

national parks,[66] nature reserves,[67] natural sites and monuments,[68] protection zones around regulated industrial plants,[69] or sites dedicated to the underground storage of nuclear waste.[70]

A third group of statute remains silent as to the compensation issue. In this case, the administrative judge may recognise a right to compensation, on a strict liability basis, if it appears that a special and abnormal harm results from the implementation of the regulatory restrictions,[71] unless the legislator's intent was to exclude completely such compensation, as it was held in the case of natural risks prevention plans.[72] The case law tends to presume such intent, as regards the activities directly regulated by the statute, unless material considerations derived from legislator's deliberation indicates otherwise.[73] But this tacit rule of non-compensation remains subject to the exception, derived from the European case law, of a special and exorbitant regulatory restriction, out of proportion with its purpose of general interests.[74]

H. Dissolution of Property for Environmental Protection

As it has been already said above, that no one is entitled to the preservation of a general regulation currently in force. The protection of vested rights arising from lawful permits consists in, firstly, a prohibition of retrospective administrative regulations and, secondly, guarantees of a due process of law, in case of modification of a valid permit or suspension or closure of a lawfully run industrial plant, whether on a general or an individual basis (see above, as regard the second hypothesis).

As a consequence, the lawful dissolution of vested rights for reason of public interest such as environmental protection would not give rise, as of right, to a right to compensation. The principle is one of non compensation. However, as it has already been said above, a right to compensation might be claimed on a

66 Code de l'environnement, art. L. 331-17.

67 Code de l'environnement, art. L. 332-5.

68 Code de l'environnement, art. L. 341-6, al. 2.

69 Code de l'environnement, art. L. 515-11.

70 Code de l'environnement, art. L.542-8, al. 2.

71 CE Ass., 14 janv. 1938, *Société anonyme des produits laitiers 'La Fleurette'*, R. p. 25, GAJA 19è éd., n° 49, p. 313; CE, Sect., 18 décembre 1981, *Ministre de la culture et de la communication c. Cie d'aménagement et de promotion immobilière*, R. p. 478, in respect of a right of entry of the ministry of culture to visit archaeological remains situated on a private property; CE, Sect., 14 mars 1986, Commune de Gap-Romette, R. p. 73, *AJDA* 1986.317, in respect of protection zones around cimeteries.

72 CAA Nancy, 10 avril 2003, n° 97NC02711, *Société Le Nid*, *AJDA* 2003.1619, note Cassin.

73 CE, Sect., 30 juillet 2003, *Association pour le développement de l'aquaculture en région centre et autres*, R. p. 367, *RFDA* 2004.144, concl. F. Lamy, note P. Bon.

74 CE, Sect., 29 décembre 2004, *Société d'aménagement des coteaux de Saint – Blaine*, *AJDA* 2005.423, Chron. C. Landais & F. Lenica.

strict liability basis, if the legislator's intent is construed as not excluding any right to compensation and the holder of the dissolved vested rights can prove that he or she is undergoing a severe, special and abnormal economic hardship, as a direct consequence of the dissolution.

In this respect, it should be borne in mind that the conditions governing this strict liability regime are narrowly construed by the administrative judge. For example, the economic hardship undergone by the operator of a closed industrial plant will deemed to be neither special nor abnormal, if the State can prove, first, that the operator was aware of the gravity of the hazard posed by his or her plant and, secondly, that the operator can raise a fair or even partial compensation for this hardship from the market price of the land supporting the closed plant (especially if it is located in an urban area).[75]

I. State Liability for Environmental Damage to Private Property (incl. Case of Communal Waste Disposal Site)

Side effects of lawful measures on activities other than those directly regulated by these measures, may raise a right to compensation on a strict liability basis, on the ground of a breach of the rule of equality before public burdens, insofar as the legislator's intent is not judicially construed as excluding such liability. Such was finally the case regarding damage caused to agricultural lands or to fisheries by wild birds and wild species protected by virtue of the statute of 10th July 1976 on nature protection. It was held by the *Conseil d'État* that nothing in the object or the terms of this statute, nor in the legislative debates conducing to it, could be construed as purporting to exclude state liability in respect of abnormal harm caused by its implementation to activities other than those statutorily deemed to endanger the fulfilment of the statutory aim of wild animals protection.[76]

How would the case of the communal waste disposal site be treated in your country?

According to the administrative case law, a communal waste disposal site qualifies as a public facility (*ouvrage public*), insofar as it is made of a building devoted to a purpose of general interest,[77] for instance: the public service of waste disposal. Although the inhabitants of the neighbourhood may well be the beneficiaries of this public service, they would be considered by the administrative judge as third parties and not as users of the public facility.[78] As a consequence, the litigation would fall within the jurisdiction of the administrative judge. The bad odour emanating from the waste disposal site would be held

[75] CE, 27 juillet 2009, *Ministre de l'écologie et du développement durable c. Société coopérative Ax'ion*, req. n° 300040.

[76] CE, 20 juillet 2003, *Association pour le développement de l'aquaculture en région Centre et autres*, op. cit.

[77] CE, 29 janvier 1969, *Ville de Saint-Tropez* CE, 3 juillet 1970, *Commune de Dourgne*, R. p. 462.

[78] CE, 17 mai 1974, *Commune de Bonnieux*, R. p. 295.

to be public work damage (*dommage de travaux publics*), if the inhabitants can demonstrate that the interference they suffer is abnormal as regards the general character of the neighbourhood.[79] The local authority would then be held liable to pay compensation.[80] As to the economic harm consisting in the blight of their land, the inhabitants would have to demonstrate their selling project as a fact as well as their inability to proceed to it, the French administrative case law refusing to take into account the mere loss of a chance.[81]

As it was said above, environmental permits delivered on the ground of the administrative control of plants regulated for the sake of environmental protection (*installations classées pour la protection de l'environnement*) is subject to the rights of third parties.[82] The inhabitant of the neighbourhood would not have to search for the withdrawal of the permit first or, at least for its modification, unless they did settle in the area after the communal waste disposal.

Although article L.112-16 of the *code de la construction* is formally held to be irrelevant as regards damages caused by the operation of public facilities, the administrative case law is very much inspired by the pre-occupation principle,[83] which is implemented in an even tighter way by the administrative judge. Indeed, the change in the operation as well in the conditions to which the environmental permits is subject may be no exception to this principle, although they occurred after the settlement of the victims in the neighbourhood.[84]

Anyhow, third parties living in neighbouring areas may also ask the *préfet* for some changes in the prescriptions regulating the operation of the plant. Accordingly, they may have standing to challenge any refusal of the state to use its power, and the administrative judge may act as an appeal authority, with full jurisdiction not only to quash or confirm, but also to modify any decision of the administrative authority.

J. Proprietor's Liability for Environmental Damage

The owner of the land where some waste is illegally deposited by a third unknown person might be held responsible for the pollution caused by it. The respective positions of the civil and administrative judges are broadly similar in this respect. The administrative judge holds that the landowner is to be regarded as the holder of the wastes discarded on his/her land, in respect of

79 *Contra:* CAA Nantes, 17 mai 2010, *Mirault c. Syndicat mixte intercommunal de traitement des ordures ménagères*, n° 09NT00910.

80 CAA Bordeaux, 20 mars 2014, *Commune d'Auch*, n° 12BX01944.

81 *Ibid.*, considérant n° 4.

82 Code de l'environnement, art. L.514-19.

83 CE, 12 juillet 1969, *Lejeune, R.T.* p. 981. – CE, 27 mai 1988, SETMIT, R.T. p. 1013.

84 CAA Nancy, 4 août 2005, *X*, n° 04NC00274, *Environnement*, n° 11, novembre 2005, comm. 70.

article L. 541-2[85] of the environmental code, especially if he or she is proven to have been negligent.[86] He or she will also deemed to be negligent, if he or she could not ignore both the existence of the waste on the land sold and the lack of any known holder, on the conveyance date.[87] According to the civil judge, the landowner will be held responsible in that case, unless he demonstrates that he or she did not take any part to their discards on his/her property, nor did he or she authorise or facilitate their discards by way of leniency or negligence.[88] In any case, the landowner's responsibility remains subsidiary.

K. Permit Excuse in Environmental Liability

In French law, any administrative permission, whether planning permission or environmental permits, is granted subject to the rights of third parties. The landowner is therefore entitled to sue one's neighbour in case of nuisance resulting in abnormal interferences with one's peaceful enjoyment of land (*troubles anormaux de voisinage*), even if one's neighbour's activities are duly authorised by a state permit. The holding of a valid permit from the state is no defence for the polluter as such. Anyhow, as it has been said above, the landowner's right to sue is subject to the right of anteriority of one's neighbour. Once again: the so-called 'pre-occupation principle' means that a private landowner cannot resort to a private law action in nuisance against polluting activities on neighbouring lands in order to get an injunctive relief or even compensation for environmental damage, if these activities, whether agricultural, industrial, commercial or traditional, took place in the area before the landowner settled there. This pre-occupation rule is subject to the compliance of the authorised activities causing nuisance with all public regulations and statutes, in general, and with the conditions of their environmental permit, in particular, under the very same conditions and without any change, since the complainant settled in the vicinity.[89]

---

85 According to article L.541-2 of the envrionmental code, *'Tout producteur ou détenteur de déchets est tenu d'en assurer ou d'en faire assurer la gestion, conformément aux disposition du présent chapitre. / Tout producteur ou détenteur de déchets est responsable de la gestion de ces déchets jusqu'à leur élimination ou valorisation finale, même lorsque le déchet est transféré à des fins de traitement à un tiers. / Tout producteur ou détenteur de déchets s'assure que la personne à qui il les remet est autorisée à les prendre en charge.'*

86 CE, 26 juillet 2011, n° 328651, *Commune de Palais-sur-Vienne*, T. R. p. 1035; CE, 1 mars 2013, *Société Natiocrédimus*, n° 354188; CE, 25 septembre 2013, *Société Wattelez*, n° 358923.

87 CE, 24 octobre 2014, *Société Unibail-Rodamco*, n° 361231.

88 Cass. 3è civ., 11 juillet 2012, n° 11-10.478, *D* 2012.2208, note M. Bouthonet.

89 Code de la construction et de l'habitation, art. L.112-16.

L. Direct or Indirect Expropriation by EU Measures

Such a question has not been raised for now in the French case law. Contrary to what happened in German law, the French regulatory transposition of the directive 2003/87/EC establishing a scheme for greenhouse gas emission allowance trading was typically challenged, not on the ground of a breach of the constitutional property guarantee, but on the basis of a violation of the constitutional principle of equality before the law, regarding the incremental approach adopted as the implementation of the European scheme. After a preliminary ruling of the European Court of Justice confirming the validity of the directive as regards the European principle of equal treatment, the Conseil d'état held that there was no breach with the constitutional principle of equality before the law.[90]

90 A. Levade, 'Affaire Arcelor: Epilogue d'un dialogue emprunt de loyauté', *Constitutions* 2010, p. 50.

PART III CH 6

Property and Environmental Protection in Germany

Gerd Winter

A. Objects of Private Property

The notion of property is different in civil and constitutional law.[1] Property in civil law can only be related to things (*'Sachen'*). In constitutional law – which is more relevant in our context – property covers many more assets:

- civil law property (in things)
- claims based on contract or tort liability,
- intellectual property rights (patent, copyright)
- public law rights if they were obtained through the work and/or capital of the right-holder, such as
  - rights to retirement payment (but not rights to social aid payments)
  - permits/licences/authorisations (within the limits of what they warrant)
- an established business (*'eingerichteter und ausgeübter Gewerbebetrieb'*), i.e. the ensemble of real assets (land, buildings, machinery) and know how

Not considered as property are market opportunities and cost reduction factors, such as the demand for a product, the profitable location of a business,[2] easy access of a farmer or fisherman to his working ground, etc.[3]

It is important to note that according to the doctrinal conception of the Federal Constitutional Court (BVerfG) what can become the content of the property guarantee is not given by 'pre-state' natural law but framed by democratic legislation. However, the legislator is not absolutely free in that regard but must respect some essential requirements embedded in the constitution such as that individuals must be able to possess some property assets needed for a decent personal life. Social life must be characterised by allowing for private property. In relation to property in the economic sphere the legislator has more discretion to grant property rights. The larger the enterprise the more so. The constitution has since its inception of 1949 been interpreted to be neutral concerning capitalist or socialist economic concepts, i.e. to leave it to the legislator to decide. (Of course this question is presently of low importance). The limits posed to the legislatorial discretion are labelled the guarantee of the institution of property (*Institutsgarantie*).

The state and local communities may also possess private property (e.g. in land, as shareholders etc.) (sometimes being called fiscal property) but this property is not protected by the constitutional property guarantee because basic

1 There is even a notion of public law property (*'öffentlich-rechtliches Eigentum'*). For instance, in the Land of Hamburg dikes are public property. The concept expresses the political will to make something a common good and convey the necessary powers to manage it. Those powers can however also be established if the property is (fiscal) civil property in public hands.

2 See BGHZ 55,261 – Soldatengaststätte: the construction of a throughway between a restaurant and military barracks hindered soldiers to visit the restaurant.

3 See BGHZ 45, 150 – Elbeleitdamm: a dam cut a fisherman off easy access to his fishing grounds.

rights are construed as rights 'against', not 'of' the state. Local communities are – dubitably – considered to be part of the state in that regard.

B. Private Property in Natural Resources

Private property in natural resources is possible if the natural resources are implied in the assets listed above, such as:

- private property in land includes property in the plants growing on it; however, the genetic programme contained in a plant is as such not included, neither is it the species character of a specimen growing on it
- contractual or tort law rights e.g. to deliver a plant or to compensate for the damage to a plant
- a concession (*Bewilligung*) to use public waters such as for extraction of water, introduction of drained water, utilization of rivers for power generation etc.
- an established business entitled by law or licence to using natural resources (a fisherman, a nature camp, an installation discharging waste water into a river)

It should be noted that the distinction between a concession and an authorisation to use natural resources is difficult to draw. A major example is water law. The concession (*Bewilligung*) to utilise public waters is the traditional form of allocating a proprietary right. It used to be granted upon formal public participation procedures and was conditioned by the applicant's showing that without a secure right the investment was not feasible (§ 14 Water Act – *Wasserhaushaltsgesetz* – WHG). In contrast, the authorisation (*Erlaubnis*) only provided an entitlement (*Befugnis*), not a right. The blurring has happened in the following ways: On the one side the *Bewilligung* was excluded for any utilization that entails the introduction of substances into waterbodies, on the other the *Erlaubnis* was in a way strengthened because it was for larger projects also subject to a public participation procedure, and court case law developed it to a kind of property if the *Erlaubnis* was used to establish a business such as a factory discharging waste water into a waterbody.

C. Private Property Used in Defense of Environmental Protection (incl. Case of Polluting Factory)

The typical cases of use of private property in defense of natural resources involve land-owners (farmers, landlords living in or letting their houses, etc.) who challenge authorisations for infrastructure or industrial developments. More traditional are cases of nuisance in neighbourhood relationships that are treated under private, not public law. In recent times conventional and organic farmers have defended their land against the influx of pollen from genetically modified plants growing on neighbouring fields.

The use of private property to defend natural resources is in the German legal system restricted in certain ways. Concerning civil law claims (contractual or tort based) a victim can theoretically ask for injunction of or compensation for damage to the environment as such if the damage coincides with individual damage. But in practice victims will focus on the prevention or compensation only of their individual damage. For instance, if the grazing ground of a farmer was polluted the farmer will ask for restoration of the grass but not necessarily of the endangered plant species that may have grown on the ground. .

Concerning public law rights, property holders can challenge administrative acts permitting damaging activities (or administrative omissions concerning such activities) only to the extent they are individually concerned. They are not considered to be individually concerned if environmental damage as such is at stake. For instance, in our case the farmer can challenge the responsible administrative body to take measures so that the usability of her land is restored, not however that rare species shall be reintroduced.

However, in cases where private property is not just adversely affected but shall be taken for public purposes (such as for the construction of a road) the land-owner can challenge the related administrative authorisation also in relation to environmental damage as such. This can be explained by the fact that the taking of property is a very serious intrusion that necessitates legality in all respects of the public action.

Environmental NGOs can, apart from their rights to file an association action as representatives of public interests, also act as property holders. The device they use is to buy a piece of land in the neighbourhood of a contested development just for the purpose of searching legal protection as a land-owner (the plot is called '*Sperrgrundstück*'- 'halting estate'). It has been controversial if such strategic behavior provides legal standing. The Federal Administrative Court (BVerwG) denies standing if the property was acquired mala fide, which it considers to be the case if the former owner retains the usufruct right, or if the price is far lower than the value of the land, or if the NGO does not plan to use the property e.g. for agricultural or nature protection purposes.[4]

If the adverse effects on natural resources in private property is caused by public bodies (such as air, particle and noise pollution from public roads, odors from public waste deposits or sewage treatment plants, etc.) property holders can claim compensation for 'expropriating encroachment' ('*enteignender Eingriff*'). The preconditions (and even the very existence) of this right to compensation for '*enteignender Eingriff*' are highly controversial. The preconditions center around criteria of gravity and of inequality of impact.[5] The controversy has become

4 BVerwGE 112, 135 (137); 131, 274 (286). The BVerfG is concurring and even a bit more open for strategic purchases, see BVerfGE 134, 242 (287=No 153).

5 Chr. Külpmann, Enteignende Eingriffe? Das Entschädigungsinstitut des enteignenden Eingriffs und die neuere verfassungsrechtliche Dogmatik der Eigentumsgarantie, Berlin: Duncker & Humblot 2000, 143-148.

somewhat random because more and more sectoral laws include provisions which specify the conditions of compensation. For instance, Art. 42 BImSchG rules concerning noise from public roads:

> (1) Where the emission limits laid down in Article 43 (1) first sentence No. 1 are exceeded [...], the owner of a building affected thereby shall be entitled to claim adequate financial compensation from the entity responsible for the construction, except where such impairment is deemed to be reasonable in view of the specific purpose for which the building is used.
>
> (2) The compensation shall be paid for sound-proofing measures at the building covering the actual expenditure incurred where such expenditure is within the limits determined by an ordinance [...]. [...].

Note, that the right to compensation for *'enteignender Eingriff'* only concerns cases where the damage has already been caused. If the encroachment can still be prevented the proprietor must seek primary legal protection.

Concerning the case:

If the factory is a regulated industry under Directive 2010/75/EC, Art. 21 of this Directive should be applied. It requires that permit conditions shall be adapted to existing BREFs or other best available techniques, even independently of whether environmental adverse effects are proven.

The transformation of this clause into German law is contained in Art. 17 BImSchG which reads:

> ***Article 17***
>
> *Subsequent Orders*
>
> (1) In order to perform the obligations resulting from this Act or from any ordinance issued hereunder, orders may be issued following the granting of the licence [...]. If after the issuance of such a licence [...]the protection of the general public or the neighbourhood against any harmful effects on the environment or any other hazards, significant disadvantages and significant nuisances turns out to be inadequate, the competent authority should issue subsequent orders.
>
> (2) The competent authority may not issue any subsequent order if such order would lack proportionality, above all if the effort needed to comply with an initial order is not commensurate with the desired effect; in this respect, special attention shall be paid to the nature, volume and hazardousness of the emissions originating from the installation and the emissions released by it as well as to the useful life and the characteristic technical features of the installation. Where a subsequent order is not permitted for lack of proportionality, the competent authority should revoke the licence wholly or in part in accordance with the provisions of Article 21 (1) Nos. 3 to 5 ; Article 21 (3) to (6) shall be applicable.

Art. 17 (1) 1st sentence refers, among others, to the precautionary principle which allows[6] for preventive measures even in situations of uncertainty. The competent authority is empowered to intervene in such cases, e.g. by requiring BAT. It is obliged[7] to intervene if harmful effects on the general public or the neighbourhood can be proven (Art. 17 (1) 2nd sentence). In any case, however, proportionality must be kept (see Art. 17 (2) 1st sentence). If proportionality is denied the administrative body shall revoke the permit and must pay compensation (Art. 17 (2)

D. Natural Resources as Public Property or Interest

The protection of natural resources is considered as a public interest justifying the taking of appropriate measures serving it. There is no concept of public trust in Germany.[8] In principle, natural resources can be an object of the private property of individuals. However, public entities (a local commune, a *Land*, the federal state, a university, etc.) can also acquire private property in natural resources. In relation to specific resources, a public entity will normally be the proprietor. This is for instance the case for the federal water courses and federal highways (owned by the *Bund*[9]). Other resources such as most of the minerals are excluded from individual ownership and form a kind of property without being called property. They are public goods and as such allocated to the management of public entities, in particular the *Länder* in the case of minerals.[10] This kind of property of or allocation to public entities aims at ensuring that the benefits from exploiting the resource are socialised such as by payment of royalties. It also serves to determine who bears the burden of maintaining the resource, for instance, by dredging navigable rivers and constructing highways.

There is a legal category transporting the idea that an object shall be open for public use: the *öffentliche Sache* (public thing). A thing is made *öffentliche Sache* by a special administrative decision called *Widmung* (consecration). The thing can be in individual property but will normally be in private property of a public entity. Things qualifying for *öffentliche Sache* are publicly usable assets such as streets, squares, parks, railways, ports, dikes, sewage purification plants, etc.).

6 Cf the 'may' in Art. 1 1st sentence. The administrative thus has discretion to act or not.

7 Cf the 'should' ('*soll*') in Art. 1 2nd sentence. The 'should' signifies an obligation which is more than discretion but less strict than a 'shall'. In German legal doctrine this is termed 'obligation in the normal case'.

8 See, however, H. Kube, Eigentum an Naturgütern. Zuordnung und Unverfügbarkeit, Berlin: Duncker & Humblot 1999, for an interesting attempt to transfer the US concept of public trust to German nature protection law.

9 § 1 para 3 Federal Water Courses Law (*Bundeswasserstraßengesetz*); § 2 para 2 Federal Roads Law (*Bundesfernstraßengesetz*).

10 §§ 3 & 6 Federal Minerals Act (*Bundesberggesetz*).

The status as *öffentliche Sache* involves a special public regime that determines the rights of the public to its free common use (*Gemeingebrauch*), the allocation of and payment for special uses (*Sondernutzung*), but also the obligation of government to provide them.[11]

While private property of public entities as well as '*öffentliche Sache*' have traditionally been legal concepts supporting public use they can of course also be employed to restrict uses in cases of scarcity, such as if the public use of a nature park is restricted. However, the environmental media which have traditionally been the concern of environmental protection, such as the atmosphere, the space, water bodies and the underground are in nobody's private property. Neither has a separate category of public property been created.[12] These natural resources are free goods the use of which is however regulated in the public interest of protection.

E. Property in Public Aids for Beneficial Use of Natural Resources

The granting of a subsidy is not conceived as property because property presupposes that the beneficiary has invested labour or capital into the position that shall qualify for property. Nevertheless, if a subsidy was granted such position is protected by the principle of legitimate expectation (*Vertrauensschutz*). The principle has been codified in relation to individual administrative acts such as an allowance. For instance, if an operator was granted a certain subsidy for investing in pollution reduction technology such allowance cannot be withdrawn but for certain given reasons, including breach of laws, non-attainment of investment targets, diversion of funds for other purposes etc. In relation to general subsidy schemes (such as the guaranteed feed in tariff for electricity from renewable sources) the principle of *Vertrauensschutz* is less precisely framed. Factors to be considered include whether the subsidy scheme has become politically controversial, how much capital and labour an operator spent trusting that the subsidy scheme would endure, if the investment is close to amortisation, if the public budget can afford continuation, how important the protected environmental good is, etc.

F. Expropriation

1. *Notion of expropriation*

Expropriation is constructed in a formal sense: a property right must have been removed from the property holder, such as the private property

11 For details see H.-J. Papier, Recht der öffentlichen Sachen, in: Hans-Uwe Erichsen, Dirk Ehlers (eds.) Allgemeines Verwaltungsrecht, 13th ed. Berlin: De Gruyter.Papier 2005.

12 An exception is the public property in dikes that was established by the Land Hamburg.

in a piece of land or a legal title. The restriction of land property by a registered servitude also counts as expropriation. The taking of a right is undoubtedly expropriation if it involves the transfer of the right to another (private or public) person or body (as, for instance, the transfer of land to the government or a private person for the sake of the construction of a road). This case is called expropriation for acquisition of an object (*Güterbeschaffung*). Expropriation for the dissolution or invalidation of a property right constitutes a second case of which it is not yet conclusive if this counts as expropriation or as *Inhaltsbestimmung*. The more recent jurisprudence of the BVerfG takes the latter position so that expropriation in the genuine sense is always construed to aim at *Güterbeschaffung*.[13]

2. Preconditions of expropriation

The preconditions of expropriation are: (1) It must be based on an empowering law (2) It must be needed for an overriding public interest (3) Full compensation must be paid (4) The law must declare that it enables expropriation (the so-called *Zitiergebot* ('cite requirement') which shall alert the legislator to the fact that expropriation is at stake.

The expropriation will normally be ordered by individual administrative decision. It is however also constitutionally possible that it is ordered by the law itself, such as in the case when a Land took all private property in dikes and transferred it to the state.[14]

The overriding public interest can be determined by the executive but the legislator needs to somewhat specify the allowable reasons. A general law that would allow the executive to expropriate for any public interest would convey too broad powers. For instance, the BVerfG found § 79 of the German Minerals Act (*Berggesetz*) constitutional in which expropriation was allowed if, among other reasons, there is a demand for the minerals that shall be exploited.[15] In addition, the public interest supporting the expropriation must be weighed with possible conflicting interests, such as nature and landscape protection in the case of open pit mining of brown coal.[16]

The public interest must be the more significant the more the expropriated object belongs to the personal sphere of a person rather than her economic sphere.[17]

If the expropriation leads to the transfer of property to private persons it must be ensured and supervised that the beneficiary satisfies a public interest.[18]

[13] BVerfGE 104, 1 (10). By contrast, BVerfGE 83, 201 (212) advocated the former opinion. BVerfGE 134, 242 (289=No. 162) leaves the question open.

[14] BVerfGE 24, 367 (398-403) (Hamburger Deichgesetz).

[15] BVerfGE 134, 242 (303-305=Nos. 201-204) (Garzweiler).

[16] BVerfG 134, 242 (307-310=Nos. 210-218) (Garzweiler).

[17] BVerfGE 134, 242 (294=No177) (Garzweiler).

[18] BVerfG 134, 242 (295=Nos. 179-180) (Garzweiler).

In the environmental policy context expropriation is normally used for development purposes (construction of infrastructure projects, public purpose buildings in planning law, etc.). As a means of environmental protection expropriation is a rare phenomenon. It can happen, for instance, if a farmer's land must be used for specific intensive nature protection measures which exclude any private exploitation. In such cases the landowner has even the right to ask for the expropriation and compensation of the land.

G. Indirect Expropriation by Environmental Regulation?

1. Preconditions of any use restriction

Use restrictions must be based on a parliamentary law (so-called legislative reservation, *Gesetzesvorbehalt*), legitimated by a public interest, and meet the proportionality test. As a general rule the use regulation can be more restrictive the more important the objective (here: protectable environmental goods, serious endangerment of them) and the less important the property and its use are.

2. Use restrictions entailing compensation

The German legal system does distinguish between allowable use restrictions with and without compensation. Other than in many legal systems use restrictions involving compensation are, however, not named indirect or regulatory expropriation but rather *'entschädigungspflichtige Inhaltsbestimmung des Eigentums'* (determination of property content mandating compensation). I believe the difference in terms implies a difference in concept in three respects:

- By categorising use restrictions as legislatorial determinations of property content the legislator is conceded more freedom of political action than if it must always reckon with being blamed to transgress the border to expropriation.
- The concept of content determination allows employment of the proportionality principle as a sophisticated instrument of fine tuning the border between non-compensation and compensation. In contrast the concept of indirect expropriation suggests the border is to be drawn solely in terms of severity or inequality of impact.
- Applying the proportionality principle a balance can more easily be drawn between the importance of the public interest (here: environmental protection) and the severity of impact. In addition, compensation can be considered as just one among other possible ways the legislator may take to reduce the gravity of use restrictions. For instance, rather than granting financial compensation it may allow for exceptional uses.

3. Criteria of distinction between compensable and non-compensable use restrictions

When assessing whether a use restriction must be accepted without compensation, German property doctrine distinguishes between different functions of protectable property: if the property serves a personal purpose (an apartment, personal belongings, pension rights etc.) it has more weight than if the property is used for commercial interests or is tied into a public interest.

Further criteria include the severity of impact and the inequality of treatment. Some specific criteria have been developed in different sectors:

(a) Nature protection

In relation to land use restrictions for nature protection purposes courts apply a concept of implied boundedness of a site (*Situationsgebundenheit*): where a plot of land is situated in valuable nature the owner must acquiesce to restrictions that conserve this situation.

Case *Thüringer Oberverwaltungsgericht*, Urteil vom 15. August 2007 – 1 KO 1127/05 –, ThürVGRspr 2008, 97-104. The case concerns the prohibition of gravel removal from a site in a landscape protection area. The court rejected the appeal of the landowner against this restriction.

> 'Every piece of land is distincted by its location and characteristics and the imbedding in its environment, in other words by its situation. This *situation boundedness* can legitimate legislatory restrictions of property rights, because the discretion of the legislator according to Article 14 sec. 1 sentence 2 GG is the broader the stronger the social relationship of the object of property is which again is dependent on its characteristics and function. If the conditions of nature and landscape of a site are worth preserving in the public interest and need to be protected this results in a restriction of property rights which are *immanent*, i.e. *adhered to the site* and are only retraced by nature and landscape protective regulation'. (my emphasis)

The case would be different if the site was destined for public purposes such as recreation facilities, playing grounds etc., i.e. for purposes which do not reinforce the immanent protectable properties of the site.[19]

However, to the extent the use restrictions are very severe nature protection law provides that some compensation shall be paid, but only insofar as the excessive burden shall be alleviated.

My own opinion is that agricultural land should be considered to be bound not only situationally but more generally by its very function as land of primary agricultural production. Such production is dependent on and embedded in natural life cycles. It cannot be managed as a pure techno-industrial undertaking without seriously disturbing natural cycles and thus – in the long run

[19] See BVerwGE 94, 1 (5) concerning restrictions of using valuable moorish land for (among others) camping purposes. See also A. Mengel, A. Naturschutz, Landnutzung und Grundeigentum, Baden-Baden: Nomos 2004.

– damaging itself. Therefore primary production must share its processes and yields with the non-cultivated nature. In practical terms this implies, for instance, that part of the products must be tolerated to be consumed by insects which again feed birds etc.

(b) Dangerous technology

The authorisation of dangerous installations (as regulated by Directive 2010/75 and *Bundesimmissionsschutzgesetz* – BImSchG) does not grant a property right in the once authorised technology because it is conceived as a privilege to cause risks to human health and the environment. It implies that the operator must adapt the installation to new best available technology and prevent newly detected dangers. However, the proportionality principle may require that the operator is granted appropriate time to write off his/her investment (Art. 17 BImSchG). In contrast, the permit to construct a normal building for dwelling purposes is not subject to subsequent alteration. However, if important interests such as energy saving so require new buildings can be required by legislative act to meet certain isolation standards.

(c) Land-use planning

Landownership does not entail the right to construct a building. Rather, this is dependent on whether land-use plans allow this. Where no plan has been enacted constructions are in principle not allowed outside settlements (except for agricultural buildings e. a.); within settlements they are allowed if fitting to the dominant intensity and shape of existing constructions. However, compensation is due if the right under an existing land-use plan to construct is removed or seriously restricted by a new plan.

H. Dissolution of Property for Environmental Protection

Yes, there is such a category. The stepping out of nuclear energy can be regarded as a case in point (although the question is still to be decided by the BVerfG). If the legislator re-structures an entire legal area for the future, it is first of all authorised to decide that certain categories of property shall not be accepted. This means for nuclear energy, that the legislator is able to ban property in new nuclear power plants (NPPs)—in other words, to refuse to license new NPPs. In addition, and most importantly in our context, the legislator is allowed to remove existing rights without paying compensation. This was approved in a landmark decision of the BVerfG concerning old rights of land-owners to gravel mining. The court ruled that such rights can be dissolved without compensation, if overriding reasons of the public interest (in casu: groundwater protection) exist and the right holders are given a sufficient grace period, which allows them to switch to other economic activities (*Auflösung von*

Rechtspositionen).[20] In doctrinal terms the court categorises this dissolution of rights (*Auflösung von Rechtspositionen*) as a variant of '*Inhaltsbestimmung*' but I believe it is in fact a variant of expropriation – one without compensation.

It may be noted that also the ECtHR exceptionally accepts non-compensation of removal of property rights in cases of a basic reorientation of the law. See Case of Jahn and Others v. Germany (Appl. nos. 46720/99, 72203/01 and 72552/01):

> '94. [...]In this connection, the Court has already found that the taking of property without payment of an amount reasonably related to its value will normally constitute a disproportionate interference and a total lack of compensation can be considered justifiable under Article 1 of Protocol No. 1 only in exceptional circumstances' [cites]
>
> '113. In that connection, the Court reiterates that the State has a wide margin of appreciation when passing laws in the context of a change of political and economic regime (see, inter alia, Kopecký v. Slovakia [GC], no. 44912/98, § 35, ECHR 2004-IX, and Zvolský and Zvolská, cited above, §§ 67-68 and 72). It has also reiterated this point regarding the enactment of laws in the unique context of German reunification (see, most recently, Von Maltzan and Others v. Germany (dec.) [GC], nos. 71916/01, 71917/01 and 10260/02, §§ 77 and 111-12, ECHR 2005-V).'

I. State Liability for Environmental Damage to Private Property (incl. Case of Municipal Waste Disposal Site)

Assuming first that the operator of the waste deposit is a private person the law of nuisance applies. The relevant provisions are sec. 1004 and 906 Civil Code (*Bürgerliches Gesetzbuch* – BGB) which read:

> *sec. 1004 Claim for removal and injunction*
>
> (1) If the ownership is interfered with by means other than removal or retention of possession, the owner may require the disturber to remove the interference. If further interferences are to be feared, the owner may seek a prohibitory injunction.
>
> (2) The claim is excluded if the owner is obliged to tolerate the interference.
>
> *sec. 906 Introduction of imponderable substances*
>
> (1) The owner of a plot of land may not prohibit the introduction of gases, steam, smells, smoke, soot, warmth, noise, vibrations and similar influences emanating from another plot of land to the extent that the influence does not interfere with the use of his plot of land, or interferes with it only to an insignificant extent. An insignificant interference is normally present if the limits or targets laid down in statutes or by statutory orders are not exceeded by the influences

[20] BVerfGE 58, 300 (351).

established and assessed under these provisions. The same applies to values in general administrative provisions that have been issued under section 48 of the Federal Environmental Impact Protection Act [*Bundes-Immissionsschutzgesetz*] and represent the state of the art.

(2) The same applies to the extent that a significant interference is caused by a use of the other plot of land that is customary in the location and cannot be prevented by measures that are financially reasonable for users of this kind. Where the owner is obliged to tolerate an influence under these provisions, he may require from the user of the other plot of land reasonable compensation in money if the influence impairs a use of the owner's plot of land that is customary in the location or its revenue beyond the degree that the owner can be expected to tolerate.

(3) [...]

The provision is rather complex. Like in an algorithm it proceeds along certain criteria that lead to different claims of injunction and compensation. The neighbours have a right of injunction if the odour causes 'significant interference' ('*wesentliche Beeinträchtigung*'). The judge will have to determine what is significant, but if public law thresholds exist and were obeyed it is rebuttably presumed that the interference was not significant. In addition, if the interference is significant, it must be more serious than what is customary in the location ('*ortsüblich*'). If, for instance, the location is characterised by many industrial activities the level of odour may be customary. If the customary level is exceeded only the taking of preventive measures can be claimed, not however the stopping of operations. If the preventive measures are financially too costly the neighbours can claim reasonable compensation, provided the customary use of the land and the revenue from it is seriously impaired.

Besides trying private law nuisance claims the neighbours can also try public law means. This can be done by filing a mandamus action against the competent supervisory authority asking the court to condemn the same to serve an improvement order on the operator. The authority has such powers under Art. 39 *Kreislaufwirtschafts-/Abfallgesetz* (formerly such powers derived from general police law), and it can be mandated by the court to take action if the plaintiffs can prove that the preconditions are given, i.e. if their health and well-being is seriously affected.

The legal situation changes in structure but less so in effect if the disposal site is run by a public entity, such as the local authority. Public law remedies apply rather than the private law nuisance claim.[21] Action for injunction or improvement is possible if the authority acts unlawfully, such as if the site was not duly authorized or was run in breach of permit conditions and applicable threshold values. Compensation can be claimed for past damage if the operation was unlawful. If the operation was lawful, in particular, if no applicable threshold was exceeded, compensation may nevertheless be claimed if the pollution

21 BVerwGE 79, 254 (257).

rendered the profitable use of the land impossible, this constituting a de facto expropriation (*'enteignender Eingriff'*). Criteria applied here would be the seriousness and the unequal treatment of the neighbours in comparison with the general public.[22]

J. Proprietor's Liability for Environmental Damage

Under traditional police law the causer and the property holder are responsible for a nuisance. The administrative body has discretion from whom to require remediation but is considered to be bound to address the causer rather than the proprietor. The latter can seek redress from the former.

These principles have been held up but specified by legislation concerning soil protection (*Bodenschutzgesetz*), and in particular in relation to contaminated sites.

K. Permit Excuse in Environmental Liability

If an IPPC permit was issued and has become valid a concerned neighbour can no longer ask for an injunction under civil law. The neighbour can however ask for technical improvements according to BAT provided this is economically feasible.[23] He/she can also, under administrative law, ask the competent administrative body to modify the permit and order the operator to improve the installation if it causes emissions having adverse effects on his/her health.

L. Direct or Indirect Expropriation by EU Measures

In a case concerning the emissions trading regime the BVerwG was asked to check whether the capping of climate gas emissions from coal power plants breached the constitutional property guarantee. The court ruled that the capping was fully determined by EU law (Directive 2003/87/EC)and were therefore to be tested against the EU property guarantee rather than the national one. The BVerwG considered how the ECJ would answer this question and concluded that it was likely to approve the constitutionality of the Directive. For this reason the court did not submit a related question to the ECJ.[24]

---

22 F. Ossenbühl, M. Cornils, Staatshaftungsrecht, München: Beck 6th ed. 2013, 339-348.

23 Art. 14 BImSchG.

24 BVerwGE 124, 47 (57).

Property and Environmental Protection in Hungary

Gyula Bándi

Introduction: the Concept of Environmental and Property Rights

The right to environment as a human right has been a part of the Hungarian Constitution since 1989, but the first direct reference to the right to environment was introduced in 1976 into the Environmental Act (Act. II of 1976). While the earlier provisions did not receive any merits, the constitutional rights proved to be successful. The Constitution included two appropriate articles:

- Art. 18 on the right to 'healthy' environment as such, and
- Art. 70/D the protection of public health, within which environmental protection has been taken as a perfect tool or guarantee of such a right.

The Constitutional Court in its several decisions examined the details of the right to environment, affirming this right as a fundamental right and emphasizing that the state should specify the actual content of the right and formulate its necessary institutional and regulatory guarantees, taking prevention into the centre. The non-retrogression principle, which will not be discussed here in detail, established the lower limit.

A characteristic example of the case-law of the Court, concerning environmental vis-á-vis other constitutional rights is the decision (106/2007. (XII. 20.) AB *határozat*) on the constitutionality of the Act on National Physical Planning, using the necessity/proportionality test. The Court concluded that any limitation of the right to healthy environment may exceptionally be restricted by the necessity to protect an equally important constitutional right – such as national defence or public health, etc. Thus, any such limitation must be well founded, considering all possible aspects and assuring that there are no other means available for the protection for an equally important other fundamental right. Although environmental protection may in theory be limited under extraordinary conditions, the case law of the Court did not mention any example, which may support the supremacy of other rights – inter alia, property rights – over the environmental right.

The same necessity/proportionality conditions are also applicable for the possible limitations of the right to property. The Constitutional Court in several decisions agreed with the limitation of property rights due to overriding public interests (such as in the decision 64/1993. (XII. 22.) AB *határozat*). This judgment and other decisions emphasize that different public and private law limitations may exist in connection with the right to property and public authorities also have the right to become involved if needed.

Several judgments of the Court discuss the 'unequal equilibrium' of environmental and property rights. As a result, environmental interests may serve as grounds for limitations of property rights, but – as it is generally understood by interpreters – environmental rights practically may not be limited in order to protect property rights (e.g. decision 50/2007. (VII. 10.) AB *határozat*). In this case and in some similar cases, the Court discusses the proportionality and necessity test in connection with any limitation of fundamental rights. The Court always refers to the possible limitations of property rights, but does not really mention the limitation of environmental rights, while environmental interests are always taken as major grounds for restricting property rights.[1] Environmental obligations are relatively broad constitutional requirements and may be taken as sources of necessary restrictions over property rights (e.g. decision 33/2006. (VII. 13.) AB *határozat*).

The former Constitution has been replaced by the Fundamental Law in 2011. Many of the provisions of this Law (in fact a constitution) refer to both environmental rights and property rights. We may mention the preamble ('Credo') as a good example with references to the interests of future generations, national heritage and human dignity. Also Art. P) refers to the same elements and furthermore contains the general duty of the state and everybody to safeguard these interests. From the chapter on human rights of the Fundamental Law the following elements shall be stressed:

- Art. XIII. on the right to property, together with the general social responsibility of property;[2]
- Art. XX. is largely similar to the former Art. 70/D, thus environmental protection is taken as a tool for protecting public health,[3] while
- Art. XXI resembles the former Art. 18, so it is a stand-alone environmental right.[4]

A. Objects of Private Property

Since 2010 almost all major existing laws have substantially been amended or replaced by new laws. This is also true for the Civil Code. The new Civil Code – Act V. of 2013 – entered into force in March 2014. Book Five of the Code covers property issues, with most provisions similar to the previous Civil Code. The basis of property issues today is Art. 5:13, referring both to the full and exclusive rights of the owner and, at the same time, the possible limita-

1 The decision is in this respect characterized by the point III.3.2.: 'The content of property as a fundamental right shall always be understood together with the effective (constitutional) public and private law limitations.' On the other hand, similar conditions or references of limiting environmental rights have not been mentioned by the Court.

2 (1) Every person shall have the right to property and inheritance. Property shall entail social responsibility.

3 (1) Every person shall have the right to physical and mental health. (2) Hungary shall promote the exercise of the right set out in Paragraph (1) by ensuring that its agriculture remains free from any genetically modified organism, by providing access to healthy food and drinking water, by managing industrial safety and healthcare, by supporting sports and regular physical exercise, and by ensuring environmental protection.

4 (1) Hungary shall recognise and enforce the right of every person to a healthy environment.

tions of property rights. These limitations include the respect of the rights of others as a minimum, but also other potential legal restrictions.

The Code stipulates in Art. 5:14. § as general rules:

- any physical object which can be possessed may also belong to a property,
- the term material object covers money, securities
- it also extends to natural resources that are utilized as physical objects
- animals are regarded as objects of property, although within the limits of other legal provisions that take the specific nature of animals into consideration.

The Code also regulates the property rights of immovable objects (Art. 5:17.) covering the airspace over the soil and the ground/soil below the ground-level, but it does not extend to the natural resources and mineral resources that belong to the scope of state ownership.

The part of the Code on property also contains the protection of the right of possession against disturbances according to 5:5. § and 5:21. §, while 5:23. § regulates the so-called neighbourhood rights, forbidding needless disturbances of neighbours.

B. Private Property in Natural Resources

The rights of using natural resources, including concessions, are taken as property rights according to the Civil Code. Inter alia, the emission allowances under the ETS scheme of greenhouse gases are taken as material assets.

C. Private Property as Opponent and Defense of Environmental Protection

The Environmental Act of 1995 introduced the environmental review process (Arts. 73-76 of the Act LIII of 1995) which basically is comparable with the EU IPPC permit in case of ongoing activities. Later this review process became the procedure of the IPPC permitting in the same situations. According to the original and still existing legal conditions, as complemented by the IPPC requirements, the environmental authority has the right to oblige the operator to undertake an environmental review, if certain relatively broad conditions are met – for example, if there are signs of significant pollution like in the case assumed in the question. The environmental review may cover the whole operation or may only be partial, based upon the attributes of the given situation and according to the decision of the authority. The review shall also focus on the possible corrective measures to be taken in order to improve the environmental conditions. The outcome may be the granting of an environmental operational permit if there are no significant environmental consequences, but may also be the refusal of the permit, and consequently the termination of the operation. This procedure checks the broad scope of concerns, while certain sector-specific concerns are subject to further procedures, for example in the field of water protection. The possibility for an overall review of the authorization of ongoing operations has at first been introduced 20 years ago into the Hungarian legal system, and the transposition of the IPPC directive in 2001 could refer to this instrument, instead of introducing a similar other measure.

If the operation does not meet the standards or other environmental requirements or if there is a likelihood of significant damage – we should not forget that the precautionary principle is also part of the Hungarian Environmental Act and is widely used – the consequence is that, having no operational permit, the given operation may not be continued. So the failure of the review might have a serious consequence on the operation.

Public administration law in general can, even apart from the environmental review process, induce the conclusion that, in case of changes of the legal situation – for example due to a new environmental law standard – or of changes of the factual situation, the already existing permits may be amended or revoked in order to meet the new conditions. This decision is not taken as a consequence of an unlawful operation realized in the past, but as a consequence of the current, newly materialized unlawful situation – that the new standards can not be met. In case of general compensatory regime, the Hungarian scheme does not refer to a general right to receive a compensation as a consequence of changes in the legal setting of the given activity or operation, but the right to receive a compensation shall always be clearly stipulated in law. If there is no reference to receive a compensation, this actually means that compensation is not provided for. For example, the Act on Nature Conservation (Act LIII of 1996) in Art. 72(1) prescribes that the actual damage of the land user may only be compensated, if the limitations or prohibitions directly are imposed on the user of a nature protection area due to nature conservation interests or if due to the reasons the changes of the production structure of the given area are significant.

This also means that all the current permits in the field of environmental protection – be it a general authorization, a water use license, a permit for discharging into the aquatic environment, or an authorization for emission into the air, etc. – are subject to a revision by the authority which may end up in the suspension, revocation or modification of the permit or its conditions and compensation may only be provided for if directly prescribed by the law.

The Environmental Act also contains a separate chapter on public participation – Chapter VIII. According to Art. 99 environmental associations have the right to file a lawsuit against any user of the environment in case of an environmentally hazardous situation, environmental pollution or damage. The lawsuit may either be filed in order to prohibit the unlawful conduct, or to issue an obligation to take the necessary steps to mitigate the damage. This is the outcome of a civil law procedure, also answering the problem of the case assumed in the questionnaire.

Besides this opportunity of a public lawsuit, the prosecutor has the right – and in many cases is using this right effectively – to file a lawsuit against the operator on the basis of Art. 109 (3) of the Environmental Act and claim that the court prohibits the unlawful operation and/or oblige the operator to compensate the damages caused.

The operator may only require some kind of compensation if there is an infringement or fault on behalf of the authority (see question no. 9 below for details) – for example, the permit has been granted against the current legal conditions and this leads to a revocation or limitation and the damage suffered goes beyond the acceptable level of business-as-usual expectations. Therefore the compensation is exceptional, i.e. due only under specific circumstances, while the general rule is that compensation is not provided for. This certainly means that generally property rights in defence of environmental protection may not be referred to. The provisions of the Fundamental Law in Art. XIII on the social responsibility of the property[5] underlines this concept, while Art. P[6] of the Fundamental Law reinforces these obligations as part of the overall responsibility towards environmental interests.

D. Natural Resources as Public Property or Interest

Public property is the general concept of managing natural resources. The basis of state property and also of national assets is again the Fundamental Law. It says in Art. 38:

> '(1) The properties of the State and local governments shall be national assets. The management and protection of national assets shall aim to serve the public interest, to satisfy common needs and to safeguard natural resources in consideration of the needs of future generations. The requirements for the preservation, protection and responsible management of national assets shall be defined by a cardinal Act.
>
> ...
>
> (3) National assets shall only be transferred for the purposes and with the exceptions determined by law and in consideration of the requirement of proportionate values.'

5 (1) Every person shall have the right to property and inheritance. Property shall entail social responsibility.

6 Art. P: All natural resources, especially agricultural land, forests and drinking water supplies, biodiversity – in particular native plant and animal species – and cultural assets shall form part of the nation's common heritage, and the State and every person shall be obliged to protect, sustain and preserve them for future generations.

The specific regulations of national assets are to be found in a separate act.[7] The list of national assets is provided for in Art. 1 (2) of this act, covering among others assets which are part of the exclusive state ownership and of the exclusive property of local governments, the non-exclusive property of the state and of the local governments.

Art. 4 (1) lists the items of the exclusive ownership of the state, covering in connection with natural resources the mineral resources in their natural state, groundwater, most of the surface water, rivers, lakes and their watercourses (listed in the annex), abandoned watercourse and new islands within rivers and lakes, several flood protection and water use installations (listed in the annex), national roads, national basic railroads (listed in the annex), caves, etc. Some of them (which are also listed in a separate annex) are regarded as privileged property.

There is a separate act on the management of state ownership,[8] regulating the management and use of state property, referring back again to the items which belong to such ownership, underlining that it covers natural resources which may be used as objects of property. Also the general rules of using this property are listed.

Game and fish are part of the state property while they are in their natural environment. The protected species and protected mineral resources also belong to state property. Otherwise protected areas do not necessarily form a part of state ownership.

E. Property in Public Aids for Beneficial Use of Natural Resources

Subsidies and any other forms of state support are normally not regarded as property. Rather, they are considered as a kind of donation by the state, which is provided if certain conditions are met, but which may also be withdrawn or modified when the underlying conditions are changing. Underlying conditions here may mean changes in the legal environment, budgetary limitations of the state, etc. Of course, under certain circumstances, compensation may be sought, for example, the feed-in tariff for renewables is an obligatory payment, a counter value of definite services or goods, meaning a special contractual relationship imposed by the state. Budgetary or other reasons may end up in the amendment of such financial incentives.

7 Act CXCVI of 2011 on national assets.

8 Act CVI of 2007.

F. Expropriation

The Fundamental Law in its Art. XIII. Par. 2 refers to the major conditions and limitations of expropriation,[9] while the details are provided for in Act CXXIII of 2007. Real estate may only be expropriated exceptionally on the basis of a public interest and it must be followed by a full and immediate compensation/indemnification. There is an exhaustive list of possible grounds of public interests in Art. 2 of the act, within which subpar. k) covers nature protection, l) water management, m) sustainable forestry, p) environmental protection. Art. 3 enumerates the general legal conditions, such as the need to begin the whole procedure of acquiring the property first with a normal purchase offer and only in case of failure may the process of expropriation be started. Another condition is to limit the scope of expropriation to the necessary minimum. Also the necessity that only the given area is suitable for the specific public purpose shall be demonstrated.

The detailed list of cases – being a kind of repetition of the general framework – within the specific environmental grounds are provided for in Art. 4, such as:

> 'j) heritage protection (archaeological site, national monument or national memorial site),
>
> k) nature conservation (if the current activity on the site may not be harmonized with the nature conservation interest, leading to a likely destruction of the area, or the conservation status must be restored, or in case of habitat reconstruction operations),
>
> l) water management and water utility reasons (such as safety operations – in case of drought, flood or inland inundation – public utility water supply or sewage treatment operations, etc.)
>
> m) sustainable forestry, shielding forest or public interest forest development,
>
> ...
>
> p) environmental protection (such as the remediation of durable environmental degradation, waste management site development or recultivation, or green area development in urban areas)'.

Expropriation belongs to the competence of county government offices, which also decide on the question of compensation. The procedure is regulated in every detail. Both the decision on expropriation itself and the decision on compensation are subject to a judicial review.

There are also some further environmental conditions of expropriation in specific cases – for example, if the given plot belongs to a nature protection area, a prior approval of the nature protection authorities is needed.

[9] (2) Property may only be expropriated in exceptional cases and in the public interest, in legally defined cases and ways, and subject to full, unconditional and immediate indemnity.

G. Indirect Expropriation by Environmental Regulation?

There are several regulations related to the use of property and the problems of compensation. Sometimes these restrictions do not entail compensation, sometimes they do. As it has already been mentioned, a general compensation right does not exist. It is always special legislation that provides the conditions of compensation. The Fundamental Law in its Art. XIII, par. 1 emphasises the social responsibility of property and in Par. 2 only refers to expropriation as such a restriction which definitely ends up in full and unconditional compensation. Otherwise all other compensatory regimes are specific.

The most important environmental examples are:

- The Act CXXXIV. of 2013 on some public services in Art. 3 allows the use temporarily of the equipment necessary for waste management services in emergency situations. This entails compensation.
- The Act CCIX of 2011 on water utility service covers the rights of servitude on land, necessary for the water supply, mostly in connection with the use of pipelines. This may not serve as the basis for compensation.
- The Act CXXVIII of 2011 on natural and industrial disasters (catastrophes) also contains some obligations, for example, companies may be subjected to a direct state supervision (see, for example the red-mud disaster in 2011). This may entail compensation if there is a direct damage.
- The Act XXXVII of 2009 on forestry and forest management usually does not require compensation in case of limitations due to nature conservation or water management reasons.
- The Act LXIV of 2010 on cultural heritage does not allow compensation for limitations or obligations which do not extend beyond the actual needs of conservation.
- There are several obligations and restrictions, regulated in Act LXXVIII of 1997 on the protection of built environment (Act on Physical Planning and Building), mostly connected with the needs of implementing the local physical planning obligations. As a general rule, compensation is due – for example if there is a limitation related to construction, due to the changes of local planning, etc. No compensation is needed if the limitations are necessary in order to prevent damage from nature conservation hazards, etc.
- The Act LV of 1996 regulates hunting and the protection of game. On the one hand there are compensation measures connected with game – damages caused by animals – and on the other hand limitations due to the needs of game management.
- The Nature Conservation Act (Act LIII. of 1996) regulates compensation and also subsidies. Compensation may cover the actual damages in case of limiting economic activities due to nature conservation interest. But there are some cases where no compensation is given – for example in nature conservation areas for limitations in order to avoid damage to nature or if a subsidy is used instead of a compensation, etc. There are specific regula-

tions on the compensation of damages caused by protected species, with several conditions.
- The Act XCIII of 1995 on the appropriate level of nature protection generally allows compensation only if the limitations make the use of the given land unfeasible or if they establish significant restrictions.
- There are also several compensation aspects in the Act LVII of 1995 on water management. For example, if the available water quantity is reduced due to natural or other unavoidable reasons, water use may be restricted without compensation. In case of obligatory public interest water management operations and installations compensation is possible.
- The Environmental Act – Act LIII of 1995 – regulates in general terms the preventive and restorative obligations in connection with environmental interest, which usually entails compensation.
- The Act XLVIII of 1993 on mining also covers several conditions of compensation due to mining operations or limiting such operations, for example as a consequence of pipelines, etc.

H. Dissolution of Property for Environmental Protection

Until now we have not had a similar case like in the 'Plantanol' judgment,[10] but the outcome would in Hungary most likely be the same.

I. State Liability for Environmental Damage to Private Property

The question actually comprises two sub-questions, which do not necessarily overlap. One segment of the first part of the question – state liability – has already been dealt with under question G, discussing the possible compensation measures in connection with regulatory restrictions. There, compensation is the potential consequence of lawful actions of the state vis-à-vis the regulated community. If the question is whether third parties may get any compensation as a consequence of lawful regulatory activities of the state, then the answer is negative.

As to the second segment of the first sub-question, the new Civil Code mostly follows the previous conditions related to damage caused by public authorities within their sphere of competence. It is regulated in Art. 6:548 of the Code. The primary legal basis is Art. 6:518 of the Code, which reads: 'The act prohibits causing any damage in violation of law.' The idea behind it is that in some cases, causing damage is not taken as an unlawful act – see the indemnifi-

10 C-201/08 Plantanol GmbH & Co. KG v Hauptzollamt Darmstadt. Reference for a preliminary ruling: Hessisches Finanzgericht – Germany. 2009 I-08343.

cation or compensation in case of nature conservation limitations, etc. Compensation is only possible if the following conditions are met:

- if the damage has been caused by using the powers of a public authority either actively via an action (e.g. permitting) of an authority or inactively via omission to act and
- the damage could not be avoided
  -by using the normal procedure of legal remedy (usually appeal) within the administrative procedure and/or
  -by referring the case to court review.

As to the second sub-question, third parties may receive compensation for lawful operations if they cause damage. Some details are also given under question K. There are also several cases of compensation or of non-pecuniary damage due to environmental pollution. We mention under question K a court judgment (Debreceni Ítélőtábla Pf.II.20.242/2011/5. szám), where it was clear that the noise and the particulate pollution deriving from an authorized activity caused the deterioration of living conditions and also had a harmful effect on the original agricultural activities (vineyards), which could lead to the depreciation of the value of real estates in the neighbourhood. The court accepted the claim and obliged the operator to pay compensation for the devaluation and non-physical damage in the form of changed living standards.

Likewise non-physical damage was the outcome of several other judgments, also due to the deterioration of living conditions (e.g. Fővárosi Ítélőtábla, 6.Pf.21.995/2009/3). The operator of a local road is liable for the environmental damage caused by the traffic of heavy vehicles (Fővárosi Ítélőtábla, 5.Pf.21.390/2010/3.), unless he/she names the one who is directly liable for the given damage. Among the different reasons for compensation, there is also the lack of mitigating measures that could have been adopted.

In our last example the defendant received a permit for industrial activities, contrary to the conditions of physical planning. The operation was expanded, causing significant noise pollution, ending in the depreciation of the value of the houses in the neighbourhood (Komárom-Esztergom Megyei Bíróság, 9.P.20.338/2007/9. szám). The court underlined that even an authorized activity may cause unnecessary disturbance of the neighbours and may establish the claim for compensation. Here we should not forget that the Hungarian private law regulations use the no-fault liability standard for activities dangerous to the environment. The defendant could have had the chance to build such a noisy plant at a greater distance from the housing area; thus they could not refer to any escape clauses.

J. Proprietor's Liability for Environmental Damage

The Environmental Act (Act LIII. of 1995) in Chapter IX contains the major provisions related to the different conditions of liability. There are also some important rules within this chapter – in Art. 102 – helping the damaged persons in the implementation of liability rules. These are:

- the presumption of joint and several liability of the polluter and of the landowner. The landowner may escape from liability if he/she designates the effective user (polluter) and proves without doubt that the latter is solely responsible;
- the same presumption applies in theory for mobile polluting sources, but this has never been used in practice;
- there is a joint and several liability rule which applies for the joint companies, where the company and its founders share the liability in connection with environmental obligations or debts;
- plus there is an extra option in Art. 52 of the Environmental Act, a special provision which applies to real estate: durable environmental damage must be entered into the land register on the basis of the decision of the authorities or of the court.

The above general provisions cover liability in the wider context. There are also some provisions where the liability is limited to the costs of different measures, such as making assessments, monitoring, proper treatment, etc. In case of waste, deposited on land, either legally or illegally, the landowner is obliged to take care for the proper treatment, if the one who is responsible remains unknown.[11] The landowner may escape liability if she/he names the responsible person and also proves that the waste had illegally been deposited or left derelict on the land. The same applies for water pollution – particularly groundwater pollution.[12] The landowner may be obliged to take the necessary steps for assessing the factual situation and make plans of action, but he/she may prove (actually the proof is not necessary, the probability is enough) that there is no responsibility on his/her side.

K. Permit Excuse in Environmental Liability

The simple answer is: this may not happen. Third party liability is regulated by civil law and there are many judgments of Hungarian courts – see question I above – which underline without doubt that under the civil law regime the permit or authorization may not influence liability or the protection of third party rights – for example property rights, personal integrity rights, human dignity or the right to get compensation in case of damage. These judg-

[11] Act CLXXXV. of 2012 (the Waste Act) Art. 61.

[12] Gov. Decree 219/200. (VII.21.) on the protection of groundwater.

ments always emphasize that the two protected legal interests – regulated by public law and the other regulated by civil law – are not necessarily matching, one may not overrule the other. The regulated interests are different, consequently also the conditions of their implementation. An activity may be authorized under public law if it meets the different legal requirements and satisfies the conditions of the public authority, but even if the different interests are carefully balanced and evaluated, this may still impair the rights of neighbours.

A recent example is the judgment of the Debreceni Ítélőtábla (Pf. II.20.242/2011/5.) – a regional high level court below the Curia – in connection with the depreciation of a real estate due to industrial activities in the neighbourhood, causing air pollution and noise. According to the court, the damage is proven, as 'an operation having a permit of the public authority should by no means cause unnecessary disturbance in the neighbouring properties.'

L. Direct or Indirect Expropriation by EU Measures

There is not distinction made in terms of EU law implementation and domestic law, consequently there is no specific solution for this situation.

Property and Environmental Protection in Italy

Massimiliano Montini

A. Objects of Private Property

In the Italian legal system, article 42 of the Constitution contains the basic provisions on the protection and regulation of property ownership and use. Article 42(1) reads as follows:

> 'Property is public or private. Economic assets may belong to the State, to public bodies or to private persons. Private property is recognised and guaranteed by the law, which prescribes the ways it is acquired, enjoyed and its limitations, so as to ensure its social function and make it accessible to all.'

The basic provisions contained in the Italian Constitution are supplemented by the specific norms of the Italian Civil Code, which list the objects belonging to the public property of the State (article 822 to of the Italian Civil Code) and distinguish them from the objects that can be subject to private property. For the latter ones, no specific list is provided by the Civil Code.

In particular, article 822 of the Civil Code identifies and lists the objects which belong to the State (or to other local territorial public authorities), which are said to include the following: seashore, beaches, natural harbours, ports, rivers, creeks, lakes and all public waters. As far as the latter are concerned, the present provision of the Civil Code was supplemented by Law 36/1994 which determines that all superficial and underground waters are to be considered public goods and belong to the State. Beside the objects listed in article 822 of the Civil Code, there are other goods which may be under both public and private property law and are subject to some sort of public interest regulation. All goods belonging to natural and cultural heritage as well as landscape protected areas may fall in this category.

Some of the objects which are subject to public property may be managed and exploited by private persons by means of a 'concession' (*concessione*) given by the State, for a certain period of time, which confers on him/her the right to exclude third parties from its use and exploitation.

In recent times, a widespread debate has developed in Italy on the opportunity to revise the traditional distinction between public and private property contained in the Italian Civil Code. To this effect, the Government set up in 2007 the so-called *Commission on Public Goods*, also called *Commissione Rodotà*, by the name of its chairman. The Commission prompted and guided a very broad discussion on the revision of public and private property concepts in the Italian legal system and proposed the institution of a third category of goods, which ought to be identified as 'common goods'. The common goods should include all the goods which are aimed at satisfying common general interests and are functional to the exercise of fundamental rights, for the benefit of present and future generations. Common goods may be subject to public or private property, but their common and collective use must be guaranteed. The new category of common goods should include most natural resources, such as rivers, lakes and their sources; all waters; the air; parks, forests and other woods, high mountains, glaciers, environmentally protected coasts and seashores, wild fauna and protected flora; and, more generally, all archaeological, cultural and environmental heritage as well as landscape protected areas.

The reason for the institution of the new category of 'common goods' lies in the fact that the State or the other local territorial public authorities, which presently exercise property rights on those goods, are often not able to provide them with adequate protection, insofar as they are sometimes in a conflict of interest position. For instance, the State might have an interest to protect parks and other cultural, environmental or landscape protected areas on the one side, which may possibly compete and conflict with the parallel interest to gain profits from their commercial exploitation. For this reason, the proposal of the *Commission on Public Goods* aims at reinforcing the protection of those goods, while enhancing their collective use, in the interests of present and future generations. Therefore, in the proposal of the *Commission*, the possibility to give a 'concession' to private parties for the exclusive exploitation of those goods should be restricted, as compared to the current Civil Code regulation of public goods.

The ultimate aim of the proposal of the *Commission on Public Goods* is to lead to an amendment to the relevant provisions on property of the Italian Civil Code. So far, despite broad support gained by the proposal, this has not happened yet. However, the work of the *Commission*, since its publication, has given rise to an intense scholarly debate, which may eventually exercise a certain influence on the interpretation of the existing legislation on property by Italian courts.

Going back to the Italian legislation on property currently in force, it should be mentioned that, under the present regulation of public and private property, it is possible for a private party to have ownership over natural resources. However, in this case, the relevant property rights must be exercised within the limits set by the law and the administrative regulations which may be enacted by public authorities, for the protection of the environmental and cultural heritage and as well as for the protection of archaeological, artistic and landscape values.

B. Private Property in Natural Resources

The right to use of natural resources, consisting in authorisations or concessions, cannot be considered as equivalent to property rights, although they constitute in some way an 'asset' that can be transferred together with the land.

Concessions, in particular, create an exclusive right of use with respect to a certain land or resource, which gives the concession holder (*'concessionario'*) the right to exclude all others from use. However, despite this right of exclusive use, there is no general right of trust or legitimate expectation in the future continuation of the authorisation/concession, which always has a fixed duration and whose renewal depends on the discretionary decision of the competent public administration.

It is noteworthy to mention, however, that a sort of trust in the future continuation of a concession existed, until recently, in the domain of the concessions for the use of public beaches, which were framed as giving exclusive rights of exploitation for the provision of touristic services in a certain beach or in a given part of the beach. In such a case, the concession was periodically reviewed, but the owner of the concession enjoyed a 'right of preference' (*diritto di insistenza*) over other possible interested parties, which *de facto* rendered the concession almost permanent. This feature of such types of concessions, however, was contested by the European Commission by means of the infringement procedure No. 2008/4908 and this prompted Italy to modify the relevant regulatory regime of concessions, thus abolishing such a right of preference for the concession holder in relation to the exclusive right of use of public beaches.

C. Private Property Used in Defense of Environmental Protection (incl. Case on Industrial Pollution)

To my knowledge, there are no cases under Italian law when private property has been successfully used in defence of environmental protection. However, private property defenses may be used to protect the health of property owners, following the line of reasoning of the ECHR in the well known *Guerra* and *Lopez Ostra* cases.

The fictional case regarding the factory presents some similarities with a real case that happened in Italy in the last few years and that is still not completely settled. This is the case regarding the steel factory Ilva, located in the town of Taranto, in southern Italy. In such a case, there was a criminal prosecution started against the managers of the factory for the alleged damage to human health caused by the continuing operation of the factory in violation of applicable health and safety standards. The criminal prosecution is still on-going at the time of this writing. In the meantime, however, the Ministry for the Environment (MOE), prompted by the existence of the criminal prosecution and the limitations that the competent criminal court, through interim measures, had imposed on the plant production, acted for the revision of the IPPC permit which had been previously issued by the same Ministry to the factory, imposing higher standards for the maintenance of the economic activity. The MOE acted on the basis of the allegation that some provisions contained in the permit had not been correctly complied with by the industrial installation. There is no evidence that the company claimed any sort of compensation for damage with respect to the revision of the permit by the MOE. Quite the contrary, it can be assumed that the intervention of the MOE was actually aimed at finding a reasonable balance between the economic and commercial interest of the company to continue its production and the conflicting public interest related to environmental and health protection.

D. Natural Resources as Public Property or Interest

In Italy, the public management of natural resources is normally legally framed as public property (*'demanio'*). The goods belonging to the public property cannot be normally transferred, but a concession may be given to private persons for the use (e.g. for mines and quarries, public waters, public beaches, etc.). In such cases, the concession holder may sometimes enjoy an exclusive right of use.

E. Property in Public Aids for Beneficial Use of Natural Resources

The subsidisation of a beneficial use of natural resources (such as a guaranteed feed-in tariff for production of renewable energy) is not conceived as a property right *strictu senso*. It is rather a contractual right. As a consequence, in some cases, such a right may also not be strictly related to the property of the concerned goods. For instance, the Italian national support scheme for energy efficiency can be relied upon not only by the owner, but by the tenant as well, depending on the person who incurred the relevant costs. In general terms, under Italian law, the legislator may withdraw for budgetary reasons (and, in fact, in recent years it has firstly reframed and then substantially removed) the previously existing subsidies for production of renewable – mainly photovoltaic – energy. In such cases, compensation may be normally due, for violation of the contract with the beneficiary, in case subsidies are removed with respect to plants which are already in operation (i.e. are actually producing energy) at the time when the incentives are modified or removed. On the contrary, Italian administrative courts (see (Tar Lazio, Rome, sec. III Ter, No. 3143/2013 and Tar Lazio, Roma, sec. III ter, No. 9732/2013) have held that no compensation is due for those plants which had already received an authorisation for construction, with a view to get the incentives provided by the law, in case the said incentives were modified or removed before their such plants started to operate.

F. Expropriation

Expropriation is the greatest limitation to private property existing in the Italian legal order. It is regulated by Decree 327/2001 (*Single Text on Expropriation*), in accordance with the general provisions of article 42 of the Italian Constitution and article 834 of the Italian Civil Code. In particular, article 42(2) of the Constitution reads as follows:

> 'In the cases provided for by the law and with the provision of compensation, private property may be expropriated for reasons of general interest.'

Expropriation is normally preceded by a 'declaration of public necessity' (*dichiarazione di public utilità*), issued in relation to the specific property at stake. This is the basis for the expropriation act itself.

In recent years, however, a special track procedure of expropriation was introduced in the Italian legal system, by means of article 12(1) of Decree 387/2003, adopted as the implementing measure of EC Directive 2001/77 on the promotion of renewable energies, with the aim of harnessing the construction of renewable energy plants and related infrastructures. The special track procedure aims at speeding up the expropriation procedure by removing the requirement of a prior declaration of public necessity. In fact, the construction of renewable energy plants is considered *ipso facto* an activity to be carried out under a 'public necessity' circumstance.

G. Indirect Expropriation by Environmental Regulation?

Generally speaking, it is commonly understood that the legislature (or the public administration) has a certain margin of appreciation, which may result in regulatory restrictions for which no compensation is normally due. For instance, when Law 36/1994 was adopted, which declared that all superficial and underground waters ought to be considered as falling within the 'public property', the legislature did not foresee any kind of compensation for the private owners of such resources. In such a case, to the best of my knowledge, this regulatory restriction was not contested before national courts.

As far as regulatory restrictions on the use of property are concerned, the relevant case-law of Italian courts has consistently tried to establish a clear distinction between expropriation and restrictions related to expropriation on the one side (for which compensation is normally due) as opposed to restrictions to property not related to expropriation on the other side (for which compensation is normally not due) (see *Corte Costituzionale*, No. 179/1999).

As to the specific restrictions to property not related to expropriation, Courts have held that land planning restrictions regarding the modalities of the right to build on a land normally do not require any compensation. However, compensation may be required for absolute restrictions of the right to build (*ius aedificandi*), particularly in cases when they are re-iterated over a long period of time without any clear justification or in case legitimate expectations have been created on the right to build. Just in the latter case, a duty to compensate may arise (see *Corte Costituzionale*, No. 6/1966, No. 55/1968, No. 133/1971, No. 417/1995, No. 419/1996, No. 179/1999).

Similarly, compensation is normally not due for restrictions based on environmental and landscape grounds (see *Corte Costituzionale*, No. 179/1999), even in case of regulatory changes, which modify a previously existing situation and restrict owners' property rights. This is now also explicitly foreseen by article 145 of the so-called Italian Cultural Heritage and Landscape Code (Decree 42/2004, as amended by Decree 63/2008).

H. Dissolution of Property for Environmental Protection

In Italy there is no evidence of circumstances in which legislative or administrative acts adopted by public authorities for reasons of environmental protection, caused the sudden or gradual dissolution of vested rights of private parties, along the line experienced in Germany with the stepping out of nuclear power. However, there have been cases related to the phasing out of subsidies to green electricity, produced by renewable (photovoltaic) energy, with regard to which Italian administrative courts have stated that compensation is due only if a subsidy is withdrawn with respect to a plant already in operation, as mentioned in § E above.

In any case, it can be assumed that should such a dissolution of vested rights of private parties for reasons of environmental protection occur, the general rules on expropriation and regulatory restrictions (explained above under § F and G) would apply.

I. State Liability for Environmental Damage to Private Property (incl. Case of Municipal Waste Disposal Site)

In Italy, compensation is normally not provided for environmental deteriorations of private property which occur as side effects of lawfully authorised activities. On the contrary, compensation may be due for negative side effects of unlawful measures (e.g. invalid authorisation), in case the relevant administrative act have been previously declared void by an administrative court. In such cases, for instance when the property owner claims that the value of his/her property has decreased in connection with the construction or operation of an industrial installation located nearby or with the construction or operation of an energy plant or in connection with other infrastructures for the distribution of energy, the possibility to file a claim for compensation may be dependant on the prior annulment of the permit which allows the performance of a certain economic activity or which authorises the construction of certain plant or infrastructure.

Moreover, compensation may be due in case the conditions of the authorisation are not respected or in case the relevant industrial activity gives rise to a crime against the environment or public health (i.e. a violation of a criminal law provision). In such circumstances, the prior annulment of the permit would not be necessary in case the property owner claims to have suffered damages in connection with the violation of criminal law provisions related to environmental or health protection.

As far as environmental damages are concerned, private parties cannot claim compensation, insofar as the relevant competence lays exclusively with the State, according to article 311 ff. of the Italian Environmental Code (Decree 152/2006, as amended several times).

For instance, in a case a communal waste disposal site, it seems that the property owners whose property value has decreased in relation to the operation of the waste disposal site in the vicinity of their properties may be allowed to claim compensation for the suffered damages only in connection with the above mentioned circumstances. In particular, they could claim compensation only if they could demonstrate that the waste disposal installation was operating without a valid permit, or in violation of specific provisions thereto, or in violation of a criminal law provision protecting the environment or public health. In reality, however, it may be said that, arguing on the basis of similar cases decided by Italian courts, it seems very unlikely that they could successfully obtain compensation for the damages suffered with regard to the mere decrease of value of their property.

J. Proprietor's Liability for Environmental Damage

In general terms, according to the relevant provisions of the Italian Environmental Code (Decree 152/2006, as amended several times), the owner of a land cannot be held responsible for the environmental damage caused by the illegal deposit of waste within his/her land, for the mere fact of being the landowner. However, the landowner may nonetheless be subject to some duties and obligations in such cases. In fact, in several cases Italian courts have dealt with the interpretation of the provisions (art. 244, 245 and 253) of the Italian Environmental Code concerning the duties and obligations of a landowner in case of illegal deposit of waste on his/her land. Recently, the Italian Supreme Administrative Court, that is the Council of State (*Consiglio di Stato*), by means of Order No. 21/2013, has stated that the land owner has no duty to prevent or minimise environmental damage in such a circumstance, but an encumbrance (*onere reale*) may be imposed on the value of his/her property, which is equivalent to the costs of the clean-up operations performed by the State on the contaminated land. The Council of State, however, with the same Order 21/2013, has submitted a reference for a preliminary ruling to the CJEU regarding the interpretation of such duties, in particular with reference to their conformity with the EU environmental law principles listed in art. 191(2) TFEU (in particular the polluter pays principle) as well as with the provisions contained in art. 1 and 8(3) of EC Directive 2004/35 (ELD Directive).

The Court of Justice decided on the preliminary ruling (Case No. C-534-13) on 4 March 2015. In particular, the Court held, with regard to the application of the polluter pays principle, that 'it should be noted, however, that the "polluter pays" principle is capable of applying in the main proceedings to the extent that it is implemented by Directive 2004/35' (§ 42). Moreover, with specific regard to the interpretation of the relevant provisions of the ELD Directive it confirmed the interpretation of the Italian Council of State, by stating that 'the answer to the question referred is that Directive 2004/35 must be interpreted as not precluding national legislation such as that at issue in the main proceedings, which, in cases where it is impossible to identify the polluter of a plot of land or to have that person adopt remedial measures, does not permit the competent authority to require the owner of the land (who is not responsible for the pollution) to adopt preventive and remedial measures, that person being required merely to reimburse the costs relating to the measures undertaken by the competent authority within the limit of the market value of the site, determined after those measures have been carried out.' (§ 63).

K. Permit Excuse in Environmental Liability

In presence of a valid permit to operate an installation, the holder of the permit would be normally excluded from liability towards third persons. In such cases, as mentioned above, claims for damages could be successful only if claimants were able to demonstrate that the installation was operating without a valid permit or was acting in violation of specific provisions thereto. In such a case, claims for damages could be filed only after the annulment of the permit by an administrative court. Obviously, the situation would be different and the permit defence would normally not operate if a criminal law violation against public health or environmental protection has been committed by the installation management.

L. Direct or Indirect Expropriation by EU Measures

To my knowledge, there is no evidence in the Italian legal order of case-law in which direct or indirect expropriation has been caused by the implementation of EU legal acts. However, it can be presumed that, should such a case be brought before an Italian court, the usual rules (seen above) on the regulation of expropriations and regulatory restrictions will apply.

Property and Environmental Protection in Latvia

Zaneta Mikosa

A. Objects of Private Property

According to the 'Civil Law' (CL) of Latvia, the object of 'property' can be everything that is not removed by law from general circulation (Art. 929 CL). Thus, the definition is indeed very broad. To answer whether something particular could not be regarded as 'property' we need to look whether there is any limitation established by law (so, which 'things/rights' may not be put in general circulation). 'Rights to property' as well as 'rights to favourable environment' are both protected by the Constitution of Latvia under chapter VIII on 'Human rights'. 'Rights to property' is protected by Art. 105 of the Constitution[1] and 'rights to favourable environment' is protected by Art. 115.[2]

There are a number of cases that have been settled by the Constitutional Court of Latvia in connection with property rights versus environmental rights, especially as regards restrictions stemming from territorial planning and from nature protection. From one of those cases we can conclude that 'property' protected by the Constitution also includes 'compensation' provided by the environmental legislation.[3] The Court held that Art. 105 of the Constitution covers the right to receive compensation due to damages caused by protected species.

'Private law rights', like the use of property 'in a way that gives the highest economic benefit',[4] have been 'tested' time to time before the Constitutional Court, with the majority of judgments, especially of recent years, ruling in favour of property rights. One example is case no. 2009-09-03 about a dispute concerning Art. 105 of the Constitution and the legality of modifications of territorial planning of Riga. By the plan[5] the allowed usage of a particular property (territory of 44 000 m2) was changed from an area where construction of buildings is allowed to an area where it is banned, due to the risk of flooding. In case limitations to property rights are established, the Constitutional Court will check: 1) whether this is done by law; 2) whether the aim of the limitation is legitimate; 3) whether the limitation is proportional to achieve that legitimate aim.[6] In this case it was recognised that the limitations were adopted by law and the aim was legitimate. However, the particular change had no proper justification.[7] Thus, the Court concluded that by amending the allowed use of property the municipality has breached Art. 105 of the Constitution.

1 Art. 105: 'Everyone has the right to own property. Property shall not be used contrary to the interests of the public. Property rights may be restricted only in accordance with law. Expropriation of property for public purposes shall be allowed only in exceptional cases on the basis of a specific law and in return for fair compensation.'

2 Art. 115: 'The State shall protect the right of everyone to live in a benevolent environment by providing information about environmental conditions and by promoting the preservation and improvement of the environment.'

3 Constitutional Court case Nr. 2013-13-01, further explanation see section E.

4 Constitutional Court case Nr. 2009-09-03, judgment of 19.11.2009, para 11.2.

5 It was adopted by binding rule Nr. 34 of Riga's municipality of 20.12.2005.

6 Ibid. para 12.

7 Ibid, para 18.

There are some more cases with similar bearing. On the one hand they acknowledge the right of municipalities to exercise broad discretion in planning of their territory, including the power to decide about conditions to use property rights. On the other hand the Constitutional Court does check that discretion in the light of such principles as proportionality, legal certainty, etc.[8]

One more case is worth mentioning as regards property versus environment. It is connected with odour nuisance from pig farms. The municipality of Laza adopted a territorial plan for the years 2007 to 2019 which introduced some restrictions concerning livestock farms including conditions on existing farms and a ban on expansion of existing and development of new ones. Those restrictions were disputed before the Constitutional Court referring to the 'right to property' (Art. 105).[9] The Constitutional Court conceded that the restrictions were based on law, that their purpose was legitimate as well as that appropriate means were chosen to achieve the aim (i.e. the protection of living conditions for inhabitants). However, the municipality had not assessed whether there are mechanisms to achieve that aim with minor restrictions to the rights of property of the applicant (para 15 of the judgment). Thus, the Court held that Art. 105 was violated.

An opposite approach could be found in the case about wind farm sites, where the municipality of Rucava had devoted some areas within their administrative territory for potential wind farms. It was disputed by local inhabitants before the Constitutional Court referring to both articles: the 'rights to property' (Art. 105) as regards neighbours of a potential wind park area and the 'rights to favourable environment' (Art. 115). The Constitutional Court admitted that the territorial planning concerning potential places for wind parks is in conformity with both articles of the Constitution.[10] This case is also interesting due to the fact that the Constitutional Court stated that 'in general a development of production of energy from wind is targeted to the fulfilment of positive obligations to improve living conditions stemming from Art. 115 [of the Constitution]'.[11]

Finally, one positive example as regards environment versus property is the case about the violation of Art. 115 of the Constitution by a territorial plan of Saka concerning a forest area and nature reserve. The case was initiated by the NGO 'Friends of the Earth Latvia', which claimed the plans of the municipality threaten to destroy significant environmental values and living conditions for local inhabitants. The Constitutional Court admitted that the territorial plan of

---

8 There has not been any discussion or assessment whether the 'right to build' is a 'natural property right' protected by the Constitution in any of those many cases where exactly those rights (or rather restrictions to build) are under dispute. It seems that it is due to the broad concept defining 'rights to property' mentioned above.

9 Constitutional Court case Nr.2008-05-03 (judgment of 12.11.2008).

10 Constitutional Court case Nr.2010-48-03 (judgment of 24.02.2011).

11 This is a statement which raised broad debate.

Saka, by allowing the construction of houses and forest logging in a coastal area protected by law, violated legislation on Protected Zones, the Environmental Protection Law and thus Art. 115 of the Constitution.[12]

'Public law rights', like a permit to build some particular object (or other type of permits), have not been recognised as a part of 'property rights.' However, rights to compensation stemming from the legislation[13] could be recognised as rights which may be protected as 'property rights' by Art. 105 of the Constitution.[14]

B. Private Property in Natural Resources

According to the Civil Law and the Law on Subterranean Depths (SD Law) of Latvia the underground natural resources are, unlike in other EU member states, property of the owner of the overlying land. However, how those resources may be used is regulated by the state.

For example, an owner needs to get a permit if he wants to make a borehole for groundwater deeper than 20 m. Additionally, there is a regulation on permitting and limiting extraction of widespread mineral resources.[15] Furthermore, there are additional conditions set, for example, by the SD Law which defines the 'territories (plots) of subsurface resources of national importance' (at the moment 27 territories). A special order applies on how one could extract underground resources within those territories.

In any case, as regards rights to use (exploit) public natural resources (like fish, rivers/water, etc.) they are rather constructed as 'public law rights' issuing permits according to conditions established by law (e.g. fishing permits or hunting permits). Those rights would not be treated or regarded as 'property rights' protected by Art. 105 of the Constitution. However, the Administrative Procedural Law includes some elements of protection (more precisely, administrative acts: legal, illegal, positive, negative) which set tight conditions for the cancellation of permits.

---

[12] Constitutional Court case Nr.2010-56-03 (judgment of 12.05.2011), paras 13, 19.

[13] E.g. the law on Conservation of Species and Biotopes (Art. 10) provides rights to receive compensation due to damages caused by protected species.

[14] Quoted in footnote 3.

[15] Government enactment Nr. 696 of 06.09.2014. Procedure for the Issue of Licences for the Use of Subterranean Depths and Authorisations for the Extraction of Widespread Mineral Resources. 'Widespread mineral resources' as defined by the SD Law are "mineral resources spread throughout the territory of Latvia and present in sufficient amount" (Art. 1), for example, clay or sand.

C. Private Property Used in Defense of Environmental Protection (incl. Case on Pollution from Industrial Installation)

Private property has rather been used in defense of environmental protection (e.g. example of the Constitutional Court case on wind power farms, see Question A). Nonetheless there exists a number of cases where the opposite is true, environmental protection legislation being used (along other arguments) in defence of property rights (e.g. as regards air quality or odour).

In the exemplary case of industrial pollution the neighbours may submit a claim to the Environmental State Service and request its action to that regard.[16] Inspection authority would be obliged (in such case of indirect but serious indication of damage) to examine the situation and request information from the factory. It may conduct inspections including the factory's compliance with the permit.

As a second step, the neighbours may initiate a case at the Administrative Court claiming violation of particular legislation or the conditions of the permit. According to 'the principle of objective investigation'[17] the court may conduct its own investigation or decide the situation to be assessed.

It seems that the 'strict liability' regime will apply in this particular situation.[18] Concerning the 'property guarantee' for the industrial installation: In case the competent authority decides to revoke the permit, the 'property guarantee' will not impede it if the decision is based on conditions included in the Law on Environmental Protection. Moreover, there exists a provision in the Law on Pollution stating that under certain circumstances (which are defined by the law) the permit shall be reviewed and conditions may be added/changed.[19]

D. Natural Resources as Public Property or Interest

Unfortunately there is no unitary 'formula' or legal construction about all natural resources, although the general principle could be 'public

[16] According to the Law on Environmental Protection Art. 30 titled 'Society rights in case of environmental damage or threat of environmental damage.'

[17] Art. 107(4) of the Administrative Procedural Law.

[18] If that particular activity is covered (as majority of dangerous activities) by Art. 25 (4) of the Law on Environmental Protection (which transposes the Directive on Environmental Liability 2004/35/EC).

[19] According to Art. 32 on 'Review, Renewal and Extension of Permits': '(3) The matter regarding the issue of a permit or permit conditions shall be reviewed in the following cases: (...) 1) when information regarding the negative effects of pollution on human health or the environment have been received, the limit values of environmental quality requirements have been exceeded or amendments to the regulatory enactments determining the environmental quality requirements have been made'. According to the same article 'the conditions of the permit (in certain circumstances defined by law) may be reviewed, renewed or added to during the whole period of validity of the permit.'

property'. Different approaches regarding the 'management' of resources are taken. For instance, the state forest is managed by the state company (JSC State Forests of Latvia) that operates based on a contract system. Concerning the coast there are still disputes between the state and municipalities (and society) of the best way to manage it. A draft law on land management (including inland public waters) is now pending at the Parliament. The use of other resources like fishes and game animals are based on a 'permitting' system with specific requirements (including limits) to be followed in order to receive a permit.

As mentioned above under Question B in Latvia (unlike in other EU member states) 'underground natural resources' are, according to the Civil Law and the Law on Subterranean Depths (SD Law), owned by the owner of the overlying land.

E. Property in Public Aids for Beneficial Use of Natural Resources

'Subsidies' are less regarded as 'property' but more as a 'right' which may be changed/withdrawn by the state. However in this process all relevant principles stemming from the 'rule of law' (like the principle of proportionality, the principle of legal certainty and expectations, etc.) must be taken into account.

As a result of political changes the system of 'feed-in tariffs' became less popular as it was claimed to be too expensive. Nonetheless the Government could not abolish it since cancellation was considered a disproportional measure. In 2014 a new tax[20] on energy produced from renewables was introduced. Additionally, in 2013 the Ministry of Economy requested all project developers holding licences for 'feed-in-tariff' but still being at a 'project stage' to submit a building permit and the approval of funding till the end of 2013; otherwise they would lose their licences.

Concerning the second part of the question whether the legislator is free to withdraw subsidies: an answer would be rather negative especially taking into account some Constitutional Court cases where different types of payments were partly or fully withdrawn by the state due to budgetary reasons in 2008-2012. The Constitutional Court acknowledged that in principle the state may limit payments (e.g. amount) but it always has to take into account the principles of proportionality, legal expectations etc. So far these cases rather concerned state payments (like pensions) than subsidies of natural resource use.

One example for the suspension of rights to compensation is a case of compensation from damages caused by protected (non-game and migratory) species, which was recently adjudicated by the Constitutional Court.[21] The case

[20] 5 %, 10 % or 15 % depending on type of renewable used.

[21] Constitutional Court case Nr. 2013-13-01 judgment of 19 March 2014. http://www.satv.tiesa.gov.lv/?lang=1&mid=19&lid=1049.

had in the first place been submitted to the Administrative Court and concerns the damages to a fish farm caused by migratory species. The case was initiated by the Supreme Administrative Court in connection with a case before this court. In the case before the Administrative Court a dispute was about refused compensation to cover damages occurring to a fish farm caused by migratory species (heron etc.)

According to the law there is a right to receive compensation for such type of damages. However, due to budgetary constrains during the economic crises the state amended the law, stating that there would be no compensation for such types of damages in 2009, 2010 and 2011. The Administrative Supreme Court raised questions on potentially 'disproportional restrictions of the property right' and the violation of legitimate expectations. The Constitutional Court admitted that the cancellation of the rights to compensation breaches the principle of legitimate expectation. But the Court also stated that the aim of that measure, to protect society's interests during the economic crises, was legitimate. However, that particular measure (to cancel compensation) was not proportional as the state could adopt a less restrictive measure like to postpone compensation or reduce compensation proportionally (para 15.2). The Constitutional Court noted that besides an interest in budget consolidation the state and the society are also interested in ensuring nature protection. Thus, in the long-term the benefit for the public would be higher if the legislator would choose a measure which is less restrictive for the owner – who had still obligations not to disturb migratory birds (para 16.2). Hence the Constitutional Court ruled that the norm (on cancelled compensation) provides disproportional restriction to the rights and thus violates Art. 1 and Art. 105 of the Constitution. The Court granted retrospective effect for the annulment of the norm since the particular fish farm. Additionally, they invited the legislator to reconsider regulation on suspended compensation.

Another example indicates the answer to this section's question to be negative: About twenty years ago the state concluded an agreement with a gas company allowing it to 'utilise useful characteristics of subterranean depths' for 25 years. Attempts to restrict the 'free use', even if only though a natural resource tax, have remained without results.

F. Expropriation

The 'right to property' is defined in Art. 105 of the Constitution as following: 'Everyone has the right to own property. Property shall not be used contrary to the interests of the public. Property rights may be restricted only in accordance with law. Expropriation of property for public purposes shall be allowed only in exceptional cases on the basis of a specific law and in return for fair compensation.'

In relation to land property the 'Law on Expropriation of Real Estate for Public Purposes' (EREPP Law) determines: 'Real estate expropriation for public purposes may be allowed only in exceptional cases and only with fair compensation and in accordance with a special law.' (Art 5, Law from 01.01.2011).

So far there have been some cases of expropriation for the construction of infrastructure objects like roads, bridges, the National Library, etc. in Latvia. However, there has not been any expropriation due to environmental protection at least concerning cases where the formal procedure of expropriation has been followed (i.e. law is adopted).

Usually, it is difficult to agree on a 'fair compensation', as the example of Latvia loosing a case at the European Court of Human Rights concerning 'fair compensation' for the expropriation of land in the territory of Riga port, illustrates.[22] It needs to be noted that this case was about a situation in 1994 and that the regulation which created the basis for that particular case is not in force any more. However, the issue of compensation is quite often a reason why those cases last quite long or create court cases.

G. Indirect Expropriation by Environmental Regulation?

No formal criteria can be found in legislation as regards cases when the legislator decides about regulatory restrictions to use property with or without compensation (except for direct expropriation as mentioned above). There is no coherence between those two kinds of situations in the legal system of Latvia. However, 'general interests' are often used as the main reason to argue in favour of no compensation, like one can see from the 'Law on Protected Zones'. According to this law four types of protected zones are distinguished (with different types of restrictions therein):

1) environmental and natural resource protection zones – those are established to protect, for example, the coastal area, surface waters, sites of water extraction, forests around cities; no compensation is provided as regards the 'allowed regulatory restrictions' that are established by law; it may include for example a building prohibition within 300 m of the coastal line.

2) area of operation (zone) – mainly around different infrastructure objects like roads, railways, electric cables, water pipes, heating systems etc.; no compensation is provided although there is an obligation to avoid any damages to owners; if there are damages due to 'operational works' those need to be compensated by the owner of the infrastructure object.

3) sanitary protection zones – mainly around objects where higher sanitary requirements need to be observed like around landfills and cemeteries – no compensation.

---

[22] ECtHR judgment of 25.10.2012. Vistins and Perepjolkins v. Latvia 71243/01, admitted violation of Art. 1 of Protocol Nr.1.

4) security zones – around objects of high-risk like factories of chemical industry and wind power stations (if 20 kW or more). Those zones are aimed to ensure security of the public and environment as well as other objects in the vicinity. According to Art. 35(9) of the 'Law on Protected Zones' the owner of that object (around which the protected zone is established) is entitled to use the territory (defined zone) without paying compensation except for damages which occurred to owners of real estate due to usage of that zone.

It is to be noted that in some of those cases restrictions are so 'heavy' that the owner is deprived of the rights to use his/her property. Such a situation was addressed by the Supreme Administrative Court judgment[23] on restrictions due to a protected zone for water extraction according to the 'Law on Protected Zones'. The Supreme Court concluded that compensation for restrictions introduced by the law (which does not provide for a compensation) may not be granted by the Court. However, the Supreme Court adopted an 'additional decision' addressed to the Government which highlighted the imperfection of the legislation on compensations in the situations where owners are de facto deprived of the of use of their property. The Government then drafted amendments to this law, which introduce an exception from the general rule of 'no compensation' if there is a 'high security' protected zone established for water extraction site. In case no agreement with the landowner can be achieved, the municipality would be entitled to initiate expropriation of the particular part of land. This draft for amendments of the law seems to be highly disputable as it has been pending in the Parliament since November 2013.

In connection with 'protected zones' there is a 'partial compensation mechanism': if there is any protected zone established by the law on protected zones the state reduces the cadastral value of property (using some fixed calculation mechanisms). As a consequence the tax on the real estate is reduced, since the tax is calculated taking into account the cadastral value of the particular real estate.

Concerning legislation for nature protection there are both, restrictions with and without compensation. In fact, a compensation mechanism was recently established after the adoption of the new 'Law on Compensation for Restrictions on Economic Activities in Protected Areas' (in force since 2006). It introduces compensation for restrictions on forestry and agricultural activities in some types of nature protected areas (like reserves). The law provides for two types of compensation and details what kind of restrictions have to be compensated by the state.

Additionally, according to a draft legislation on land management (aimed to be adopted by October, 2014) more detailed provisions shall be introduced on the planning of infrastructural objects of public interests and the rights of owners to compensation for damages resulting from restrictions of economic activities.

---

[23] Supreme Administrative Court judgment of 08.05.2012. Nr. SKA-16/2012.

H. Dissolution of Property for Environmental Protection

Question H will rather be denied as could be concluded from the above mentioned example of usage of 'useful characteristics of subterranean depths' (under Question E). A recent court case may be pertinent: it concerned a permit to build a small hydropower station at a river. The permit was issued in 2002 and afterwards prolonged 9 times to avoid its expiration. It was issued before the introduction of a law in 2003 which prohibits building any hydropower station at that public river (among some others) for environmental reasons.[24] The owner of the permit has not used his rights before he started to build in 2010. In the same year the permit (in fact the prolongation of it) was disputed by NGOs before the Administrative Court. The two instances of the Administrative Court admitted that the prolongation of the permit was illegal since particular legal circumstances had changed (prohibiting the building of such objects). According to the court a competent authority would have been obliged to assess whether the construction was still legal including an environmental impact assessment for such kind of objects which has not been performed. During this process the hydropower station was built, so now there is a request to the municipality to decide on the demolition of the building. The issue is pending as the case is also pending before the Supreme Court.[25]

I. State Liability for Environmental Damage to Private Property

Firstly, there exist conditions as regards the withdrawal of a 'lawful administrative act' and revocation of an 'unlawful' administrative act. A 'lawful administrative act' may be withdrawn if e.g. 'the actual or legal circumstances of the matter have changed such that had they existed in such a way at the time the administrative act was issued, the institution may have not issued such administrative act, and the continuation of the administrative act being in effect affects significant interests of the public.'[26] In this case there is the possibility to apply for a compensation according to APL Art. 85(3): 'the relevant public law legal person shall, in accordance with Chapter 8 of this Law, compensate the addressee for losses and personal harm caused to him or her as a result of revocation of the administrative act.' Concerning an 'unlawful administrative act' the situation could be similar for the right to compensation. According to APL Art. 86(2)3 the unlawful (but favourable) administrative act may be revoked if e.g.: 'the continuation of the administrative act being in effect affects essential interests of the public. If the addressee on the basis of such administrative act

[24] There is no compensation provided in that law prohibiting constructions of hydropower stations at the public rivers listed in that legislation.

[25] Case Nr.A420580211, judgment of the second instance of the Administrative Court on 31 March 2014.

[26] Administrative Procedure Law (APL), Art. 85(2)4.

has received money or other benefits, the administrative act shall cease to be in effect as of the day it is revoked. The relevant public law legal person shall, in accordance with Chapter 8 of this Law, compensate the addressee for losses or personal harm caused him or her as a result of revocation of the administrative act.'

Chapter 8 ('Compensation') of the Administrative Procedural Law (APL) provides the 'right to compensations' stating quite broadly that 'everyone is entitled to claim due compensation for financial loss or personal harm, including moral harm, which has been caused him or her by an administrative act or an actual action of an institution.' However, court cases on compensation from the public authority due to a breach of environmental requirements are very rare.

How would the case of the communal waste disposal be treated in Latvia?

Firstly, it has to be noted that such kind of cases (with bad odour from landfill) would not be classified as 'state activity' allowing compensation intended in the APL provisions mentioned above (except in the case of illegal/legal authorisation which may be revoked due to one of the conditions provided in the APL), although waste disposal sites are operated usually by a company owned (or controlled) by a municipality. Regarding activities with waste they will be treated as 'private actors' (operators) which have to comply with all relevant legislation. If they breach the 'odour limits', which is stated in their permit (in accordance with a Government enactment), the activity may be stopped or forced to be changed. Inhabitants would not be entitled to compensation like annual revenue but would rather have to request withdrawal or changes of the permit. In theory they may request damages according to the Civil Law (if they could prove 'fault' criteria). Therefore first of all they have to appeal the permit (or request the environmental authority to act as mentioned under Question C).

J. Proprietor's Liability for Environmental Damage

Two laws could be mentioned here as examples to give a rather positive answer. Firstly, according to the Law on Waste Management Art. 15(4) there is an obligation of the land owner to remove illegally deposited waste from his property and hand it over to a waste management company.

At the moment there is an interesting case under consideration before the Administrative Court[27] in connection with waste illegally deposited in the territory of the municipality of Riga. The Environmental State Authority issued a decision (administrative act) – initiated/requested by an NGO at the first stage – to the municipality of Riga (as owner of the particular land) to remove illegally deposited construction waste from the land close to the lake Kisezers. The municipality partly fulfilled that task by removing waste from the land. But

[27] Case Nr. A42689508, judgment of the second instance, Administrative Court on 1 July 2014. It seems that there will be an appeal before the Supreme Court.

the dispute remains about that part of the waste which now finds itself in the state-owned lake due to faulty work of the municipality (as the NGO claims). The judgment of the second instance (1 July 2014) states the municipality's duty to finalise the clean up works and remove all illegal construction waste (so to comply with the authority decision requesting such action). Hence the answer to this Question 10 would be rather yes when illegal waste is concerned.

The second example is about 'contaminated sites/territories' that are registered or have to be registered according to the 'Law on Pollution' (01.07.2001. as amended until 21.02.2014.). According to Art. 33-35 of this law there is a general obligation of municipalities together with Regional Environmental state authority to identify and register all contaminated or potentially contaminated sites/territories in a specific public register. According to Art. 38 (about persons who would be obliged to cover costs of remediation) the land owner may under certain circumstances be requested to cover the costs of remediation, i.e. in case he bought the land after it was registered in the public register as contaminated. In all other cases an owner has to agree to cover those costs of remediation (Art. 38(2)).

K. Permit Excuse in Environmental Liability

The state permit does not entirely preclude liability towards third persons. However, liability is limited to fault-based and the existence of 'illegal action'. Thus, if an operator strictly followed the requirements of the state permit and nonetheless damage occurred to a third person, there will rather not be a chance to recover those damages from the permit holder since all four conditions, which are needed to hold somebody liable on 'fault based approach', will not be met: illegal action (or omission), fault, damages and causal link (see Civil law Part IV). According to Civil Law there may in general not be a violation of other person's rights if somebody just uses his rights (Art. 1636). But apart from this general law there are also some specific conditions regarding activities with a 'high risk source' The owner (or holder) of such object would be liable for damages if they occurred to a third person due to usage of that high risk source (Art. 2347) except if the owner (holder) proves that those damages occurred due to 'force majeure' or due to the fault of the victim. There is no definition of 'high-risk sources' although some examples are mentioned such as 'transport, building, dangers substances etc. in Art. 2347 of the Civil Law. Hence notwithstanding the existence of a state permit there could be an obligation by the holder of a permit to compensate damages if he operates a 'high-risk source' or faultily.

As regards 'environmental damage' due to a 'permit defence', the operator would be exempted from an obligation to cover the costs for remedying measures (Art. 31 of the Environmental Protection Law). Nonetheless, he is still under 'liability' i.e. obligation to take preventive measures or immediately needed measures to stop further damage.

L. Direct or Indirect Expropriation by EU Measures

Although there is no pertinent case yet, I would presume that there is no difference from situations stemming from national level.

Property and Environmental Protection in the Netherlands

Jan H. Jans & Annalies Outhuijse

A. Constitutional Framework

The Dutch Constitution (*Grondwet; Gw*) contains no explicit right to property. The 'official' argument is that such right is so fundamental that it is not necessary to explicitly mention it in the Constitution. We will not debate the lack of logic of this argumentation any further, but the premise of it is that the Dutch Constitution only provides for non-fundamental provision. However, the Constitution does contain provisions on expropriation (Article 14(1)) and on restrictions to the use of property (Article 14(3)).

Article 14 of the Dutch Constitution provides, translated into English, as follows:

> 1. Expropriation may take place only in the public interest and on prior assurance of full compensation, in accordance with regulations laid down by or pursuant to Act of Parliament.
>
> 2. Prior assurance of full compensation shall not be required if in an emergency immediate expropriation is called for.
>
> 3. In the cases laid down by or pursuant to Act of Parliament there shall be a right to full or partial compensation if in the public interest the competent authority destroys property or renders it unusable or restricts the exercise of the owner's rights to it.

Procedure expropriation (14(1) Gw)

Expropriation, in the meaning of Article 14(1), is governed by the Act on Expropriation (*Onteigeningswet*). The procedure consists of 3 stages. The first stage is that the public authority should try to reach an agreement with the proprietor.[1] If a voluntary agreement is not possible, the next step is that by Royal Decree – in most cases based on a proposal of the city council and after advice of the Council of State – a decision on expropriation is taken.[2] Such a decision needs to be affirmed by the court and the court will be responsible to set the amount of compensation. The ruling of the court is subject to cassation (i.e. review on points of law only) by the Supreme Court. This 'heavy' procedure must be seen as *ultimum remedium* and should only be used if no other, more amicable, solutions are possible.

Restrictions on the use of property (14(3) Gw)

Restrictions on the use of property are governed by Article 14(3) *Gw*. The formulation of the provision (in the cases laid down by or pursuant to Act of Parliament) makes it clear that this provision does not in *itself* grant a right to full or partial compensation and cannot be used by an individual to claim such a compensation.[3] Such a right can only be based by or pursuant to an Act of

[1] Article 17 *Onteigeningswet*.

[2] Article 18 *Onteigeningswet*.

[3] See for example CBb 15 June 1990, AB 1992, 229, with case note R.M. van Male, ECLI:NL:CBB:1990:AN2397.

Parliament. But the provision does not require the legislator or the administration to provide for rules of compensation. An example can be found in Article 6(1) of the Dutch Spatial Planning Act. If an individual suffers a loss of income or if there is a decrease of the value of (immovable) property caused by certain planning decisions the municipal public authority will provide for an allowance (*'tegemoetkoming'*), in so far as the damage cannot be reasonably attributed to the individual and is not ensured otherwise.[4] There is prolific literature and case law on this provision (and similar provisions in other acts). We will leave this aside. However, there seems to be a certain consensus that 'standard societal risks' will not be compensated, only excess risks (see below the remarks on the concept on *'égalité devant les charges publiques'*). Also the foreseeability of damage can lead to a limitation of the compensation.[5]

The scope of 'property'

'Expropriation' is only possible with respect to 'property', i.e. physical objects. The procedure cannot be used to expropriate 'rights', such as lease rights. This implies that the substantive scope of this provision is more limited than Article 1, Protocol 1 ECHR. As we know, the property-guarantee of that provision is not limited to physical objects, but stretches to rights/interests with an economic value.[6] In the Netherlands a permit/license is not regarded as 'property', nor is it defined in terms of 'subjective rights'.[7] In other words, revoking a permit or *ex officio* changing permit conditions is not seen as 'expropriation' or as 'regulating property'. This is consistent case law.

One recent example of 'expropriation' in its formal meaning concerns the Scheldt river estuary (in the Dutch/Belgium border area) where it was found necessary (in view of the obligation to compensate ex Article 6(4) Habitats Directive) to flood the Hedwige-polder. That means that the proprietors of the land in the polder (mostly farmers) have to be compensated in full according the rules of the *Onteigeningswet*, since this flooding will leave them with no reasonable use of the land as it had to be expropriated.

B. Article 1, Protocol 1 ECHR

Above it was demonstrated that the Dutch Constitutional provisions on expropriation have only limited practical significance due to the fact that the Constitution does not in *itself* grant a right to full or partial compensation and cannot be used by an individual to claim such a compensation.

4 Article 6(1) and (2) Spatial Planning Act.

5 Article 6(3) Spatial Planning Act. Cf. e.g. Dutch Council of State 27 December 2006, ECLI:NL:RVS:2006:AZ5163.

6 See Bernhard Wegener's paper on the ECHR.

7 For example Dutch Council of State 21 March 1996, M en R 1997, 83, with case note Ch. Backes, ECLI:NL:RVS:1996:AP8216.

And such a right can only be based on an Act of Parliament. Also in view of the Dutch constitutional rule that Acts of Parliament cannot be reviewed on their constitutionality by the Dutch courts, the significance of Article 14 of the Dutch Constitution for day-to-day environment-based policy-making is limited. Having said that, matters are different with respect to the property-guarantee of Art. 1, Protocol 1 ECHR. In view of Articles 93 and 94 of the Dutch Constitution 'self-executing' provisions of international treaties can be relied upon in Dutch courts and those provisions have precedence over conflicting national law. In short, according to Dutch constitutional law one cannot claim compensation based upon Art. 14 *Grondwet*, but can claim the same damage by relying on Art. 1P1. Also, as shown by Bernhard Wegener's contribution in this book, it must be noted that the Art. 1P1 definition on 'property' seems to be much wider than that of its Dutch equivalent. Furthermore, also shown by Wegener, Art. 1P1 is, to a certain extent, also applicable in 'horizontal' situations. While the Dutch constitutional guarantee is limited to the vertical relation state v. private individual.

It is therefore no surprise that, once again from a practical perspective, the role of Art. 1P1 is more important than Art. 14 *Grondwet*. Art. 1P1 has been relied upon in a couple of cases where individuals sought judicial review of national environmental measures affecting their interests.

Examples in Dutch case law concerning Art. 1P1

One of the most notorious cases in this respect is the so-called *Pig Quota* case.[8] In order to reduce phosphate and nitrogen contamination in the environment, the Act on the Restructuring of the Pig Rearing Industry (*Wet herstructurering varkenshouderij*; Whv) introduced a system of pig quotas for individual pig rearing undertakings, by which *de facto* a maximum number of pigs were set for individual pig rearers. This act was challenged before the Dutch courts as being an 'illegal act of the legislator' and pig rearers relied upon Art. 1P1 in particular. The District Court Den Haag argued that this act, which resulted in a 25% reduction of the number of pigs, without offering adequate compensation, was incompatible with Art. 1P1. According to the District Court this was a case of expropriation and therefore not allowed without compensation.[9] This judgment was upheld in appeal.[10] However, the Dutch Supreme Court thought otherwise. It argued that it was a case of 'regulation of property' and not of 'expropriation'.[11]

8 Dutch Supreme Court 16 November 2001, AB 2002, 25, with case note P.J.J. van Buuren, ECLI:NL:HR:2001:AD5493.

9 District Court Den Haag 23 December 1998, M en R 1999, 28, ECLI:NL:RBSGR:1998:AA1085.

10 Court of Appeal Den Haag 10 June 1999, M en R 1999, 72, with case note J.E. Hoitink, ECLI:NL:GHSGR:1999:AH6846.

11 Dutch Supreme Court 16 November 2001, AB 2002, 25, with case note P.J.J. van Buuren, ECLI:NL:HR:2001:AD5493.

Another example concerned a Governmental Decree (*Algemene Maatregel van Bestuur*) to create, in certain areas, crop-free and manure-free zones.[12] As a result farmers are no longer allowed to use their full property for their business purposes. 'Biological farming', however, was still allowed. The Decree intended to limit the discharge into surfacewater of phosphates and nitrogen. Some farmers challenged this decree and relied upon Art. 1P1. The District Court Den Haag argued that the objective of the legislation (protection against water pollution) is a legitimate objective and that the measures taken were not disproportionate to their aim. The size of the crop-free and manure-free zones was limited, and there was a special rule for 'small' properties and biological farming was excluded. In particular noteworthy was that the court did use the 'polluter pays principle' to argue that the costs for taking measures against water pollution had to be borne by the person who caused it (in this case the farmers). The district court ruled that there was no need for compensation.

A *Sahlsted*[13]-like case was dealt with by the Dutch Council of State. The decision to designate land as an SPA under the Birds Directive and the Dutch Nature Conservation Act, landowners argued that the decision violated Art. 1P1 as they were not longer allowed to hunt on their own property.[14] According to the Council of State the decision could not be regarded as 'expropriation', but as 'regulation' of property. It was also argued that the regulation of property served a general interest and that there were insufficient reasons to support the idea that the restrictions were disproportionate. Therefore no compensation was required, although the Council of State did not completely rule out that afterwards, in concrete and individual cases, the decision could have disproportionate effects and in those cases compensation is required. However, there was no need to establish a priori a general compensation scheme.

A somewhat peculiar case where Art. 1P1 was relied upon concerned someone who lived in a nature conservation area.[15] According to the rules applicable in the municipal zoning plan certain restrictions applied on the use of that property. After repeatedly having violated these user-restrictions the public authority issued a 'penalty payment order'. This order was challenged with the argument that the user-restrictions in the municipal zoning plan were incompatible with Art. 1P1. The Council of State was not impressed and ruled that 'even if' the user-restrictions were to be regarded as a restriction to enjoy property, these restrictions are deemed to be necessary to regulate property in the light of the general interests at stake and that no evidence was presented to argue that the applicable rule were disproportionate.

---

12 District Court Den Haag 20 March 2002, M en R 2003, 79, with case note H.F.M.W. van Rijswick, ECLI:NL:RBSGR:2002:AE7269.

13 Case C-362/06 P *Sahlstedt*, [2009] ECR I-2903, ECLI:EU:C:2009:243.

14 Dutch Council of State 19 March 2013, M en R 2003, 70, ECLI:NL:RVS:2003:AF5992.

15 Dutch Council of State 14 November 2001, ECLI:NL:RVS:2001:AD6818.

C. The *Égalité*-Principle

The principle as such

Although the basic rule in Dutch law is that, in absence of explicit statutory provisions, the administration is only liable to pay/compensate for damages in case of illegal acts/omissions, it is now acknowledged by the courts that in specific circumstances there can be a duty to compensate for lawful acts.[16] The legal basis for this obligation goes back to the French principle '*égalité devant les charges publiques*', in short: the *égalité*-principle. This principle of unwritten origin is now being codified in Article 4:126 of the Dutch General Administrative Law Act (*Algemene wet Bestuursrecht*; Awb).[17]

The basic idea behind this principle is that there should be equality for public charges. If the administration takes a measure in the 'general interest' and as a consequence an individual suffers in a 'specific' and 'abnormal' manner, this might trigger liability. 'Specific' in this context means that only a limited group of individuals has carried the burden in the general interest. 'Abnormal' means that the burden exceeds what can be considered a 'normal societal risk'. The *égalité*-principle in essence means that although the measures taken by a public authority in the general interest, for instance for reasons of environmental protection, are as such valid and legal, there is a duty to compensate for the excess loss. By definition this does not mean full compensation.

Once again, the importance of Art. 1P1 must be noted. Acts of parliament cannot be challenged by relying on the *égalité*-principle, but can be reviewed against Art. 1P1.[18] On the other hand, the *égalité*-principle seems, in a certain way, broader than Art. 1P1. As shown by Wegener, certain 'hazards of economic life' do not qualify for compensation under Art. 1P1, but could qualify for compensation under the *égalité*-principle. One might think of the following example. As a result of the *Waddenzee*-judgment[19] the Dutch government decided to phase out cockle-fishing completely. It is debatable whether or not such a decision would qualify for compensation under Art. 1P1. Arguably not. Compensation under the *égalité*-principle might prove to be more promising. However, it can also be argued that compensation for the phasing out of certain economic activities (cockle-fishing, but in the Netherlands also mink-farming) is not required by law at all. That compensation has been given by the government in situations like these could be called: compensation by 'leniency'.

---

16 Dutch Council of State 6 May 1997, AB 1997, 229, with case note P.J.J. van Buuren, ECLI:NL:RVS:1997:AA6762.

17 Not yet in force, but probably 1 January 2016.

18 Dutch Supreme Court 14 April 2000, AB 2001, 135, with case note T.A. van Kampen, ECLI:NL:HR:2000:AA5527.

19 Case C-127/02 *Landelijke Vereniging tot Behoud van de Waddenzee and Nederlandse Vereniging tot Bescherming van Vogels v Staatssecretaris van Landbouw, Natuurbeheer en Visserij* [2004] ECR I-07405, ECLI:EU:C:2004:482.

The égalité-principle in planning and environmental law

Earlier we already mentioned that Article 6(1) of the Dutch Spatial Planning Act is a specific 'legislative' application of the *égalité*-principle. With respect to environmental law a similar provision can be found in the Articles 15.20 and 15.21 of the Environmental Management Act (*Wet milieubeheer*). These provisions provide in essence that in the case a public authority takes a decision with respect to a permit-holder and as a result of this decision this permit-holder suffers damages that reasonably should not be attributed to him, the public authority is required to compensate on a bona fide basis. Article 15.20 deals with compensation if damages occur due to a single administrative act; Article 15.21 (even more exceptional) provides for compensation if the damage is caused by general legal provisions.

In environmental law compensation ex Articles 15.20 and 15.21 of the Environmental Management Act is governed by the so called '*Circulaire schadevergoedingen*'.[20] These policy rules give rather detailed instructions to the public authority in question on all aspects of the compensation to be paid. The requirements for compensation are the same in both articles. The scope of the articles can not be limited by policy rules.[21] According to Art. 4:84 of the Dutch General Administrative Law Act these policy rules are binding for the administration, except for special circumstances.

The general idea of the *Circulaire schadevergoedingen* is that whenever for reasons of environmental protection action is required the public authority in question is under an obligation to see whether or not the consequences of this for individuals are disproportionate. The *Circulaire schadevergoeding* is however rather restricted towards compensation. Broadly speaking, a request for compensation must meet four conditions, whilst the burden of proof is on the applicant. At first, there should be a *direct causal link* between the measures taken by the administration and the damage occurred.[22] If the measures to be taken for environmental reasons are as such legitimate, the permit-holder must be compensated financially for the disproportionate burden he has to carry. The second condition is that the applicant must show that it is *unreasonable* that the applicant bears the full or partial burden of the cost of remedial or preventive action to be taken. However, this will only be the case in exceptional circumstances because, in general, undertakings have, in view of the polluter pays principle, to bear the costs of those measures necessary for environmental protection reasons. To show disproportionality the applicant must show that without compensation there will be a significant negative impact on his ability to compete on the market.[23] According to the *Circulaire schadevergoedingen* there is

[20] *Stcrt.* 1997, 246 jo. *Stcrt.* 1998, 168.

[21] Dutch Council of State 22 December 2000, AB 2001, 70, with case note F.C.M.A. Michiels, ECLI:NL:RVS:2000:AN6591.

[22] For example Dutch Council of State 14 January 2000, AB 2000, 142, with case note F.C.M.A. Michiels, ECLI:NL:RVS:2000:AA4973.

[23] *Parliamentary Papers II* 1986/87, 19 752, nr. 3, p. 15.

a disproportionate burden if the costs of the measures to be taken are at least 20 % higher than the costs of standard measures. The benchmark is the costs other competitors have to make. Damage below 20% is not be compensated, since this is considered as a 'standard business risk'. Compensation is excluded if any other possibility to be compensated exists. The compensation is meant as a *ultimum remedium*.[24] Finally, compensation under the *Circulaire schadevergoedingen* is not in full, but based on *equity*. The maximum compensation is 80 % of the total costs.[25] The criteria of the *Circulaire schadevergoedingen* are being applied – and upheld by the courts – rather restrictively. Derogation is only allowed if a strict application of the rules lead to an obviously unreasonable outcome.

The *Circulaire schadevergoeding* makes also clear under which conditions no compensation will be given. No compensation will be given for:

- new activities,
- if a permit-application is refused, and
- after the expiration of temporary permits.[26]

In general no compensation will be given if the permit-holder applies for the broadening/changing of existing activities, unless these changes are necessary to comply with exceptional environmental standards. Revision or revoking of 'old' permits or permit-conditions can give grounds for compensation. Third parties are able to submit a request to the permitting authority for such changes. Foreseeability of the damage is a key element. When making investment decisions reasonable and prudent, actors have to be aware that changes in law and policy might occur.[27] The 'older', the less compensation. Accepting foreseeable damages will not be compensated ('active risk acceptance'). Finally, it is relevant to what extent a permit-holder had the opportunity to anticipate and to adapt to the changes in the legal regime, for instance by granting a period for the transition to take place.[28] There is hardly any possibility to claim, based on the principle of legitimate expectations, that the existing *status quo* must be maintained.

With respect to compensation for decisions of a general nature, Art. 15.21 *Wet milieubeheer* makes clear that only in exceptional circumstances compensation is required. The reason for this is that *general* measures hardly ever affect competition between individual persons and undertakings.[29]

---

24 Dutch Council of State 3 September 2003, AB 2004, 51, with case note A.B. Blomberg, ECLI:NL:RVS:2003:AI1745.

25 Dutch Council of State 23 October 1993, AB 1994, 653, ECLI:NL:RVS:1993:AN3939.

26 Cf. also, prior to the *Circulaire schadevergoedingen*: Dutch Council of State 18 March 1996, M en R 1997, 26, with case note Ch. Backes.

27 E.g. Dutch Council of State 23 October 1993, AB 1994, 653, ECLI:NL:RVS:1993:AN3939.

28 Dutch Council of State 21 March 1996, M en R 1997, 83, with case note Ch. Backes, ECLI:NL:RVS:1996:AP8216.

29 Dutch Council of State 18 January 1991, AB 1991, 241, with case note F.H. van der Burg, ECLI:NL:HR:1991:AC4031.

D. The Two Cases According to Dutch Law

A factory, situated near a town, has been operating for decades. People are slowly realizing that statistically the inhabitants in the city and in the vicinity do not live average age and the cancer is more frequently present among them, also the frequent cause of the deaths. They have no direct proofs that the factory could be responsible, although it is rather clear that the soil around the factory is poisoned and that the heavy metals found in the vegetable could be linked to the factory. However, credible proofs are missing.

Assuming that the factory operates within the permit conditions the primary obligation for the state is to consider whether there is a need for a revision of the permit. This according to Article 13(5) and (7) of the IED Directive 2010/75/EU.[30] Revising permit conditions can be triggered on the request of the inhabitants or *ex officio* by the administration. If the factory causes serious negative effects for the environment and a change of permit conditions do no provide a reasonable solution, the administration is required to close the factory. This, however, is rarely the case.[31]

A waste disposal site is located not far away from a place with app. 150 individual houses. Inhabitants assert that they smell bad odour and they would like to sell their property, but, of course, there are no potential buyers. Their property is worth less. The waste disposal site is equipped with the necessary permits.

If the waste dump is being built as a result of a change in the local building plan(s), compensation is possible ex Article 6(1) of the Dutch Spatial Planning Act (see above). We can refer to older case law where the owner of a milkfarm had to be compensated in view of the location nearby of a waste site.[32] If one buys a house next to an existing waste dump site, there is no compensation ('active risk acceptance'). If the permit conditions are violated 'standard' enforcement remedies vis-à-vis the administration are available.

E. Summary

The Dutch Constitutional guarantee of Article 14 *Grondwet* concerning 'property' is rather weak. The procedure leading to expropriation is complex, but more importantly Art. 14 *Grondwet* does not in *itself* grant a right to full or partial compensation and cannot be used by an individual to claim such a compensation. The normative value of the Constitution for compensation is therefore very limited indeed. For day-to-day environmental policy-making the role of Article 1 Protocol 1 ECHR is more important. Art. 1P1 does provide a

---

30 OJ 2010 L 334. And its implementation in Dutch law: Article 2.31(1) *Wabo.*

31 Article 2.33(1)(d) Wabo. *Parliamentary Papers II* 2006/07, 30 844, nr. 3, p. 18.

32 Dutch Council of State 17 December 1999, ECLI:NL:RVS:1999:AA4628.

direct legal basis for compensation and also its scope – it encompasses 'rights' – is wider than the Dutch constitutional provision.

With respect to restrictions of the use of property, the *égalité*-principle is of some importance. The basic idea behind this principle is that there should be equality for public charges. If the administration takes a measure in the 'general interest' and as a consequence an individual suffers in a 'specific' and 'abnormal' manner, this might trigger liability. Recently, this principle has been codified in the Dutch General Administrative Law Act. In planning law and environmental protection law, specific legal provisions based on the *égalité*-principle apply.

Property and Environmental Protection in Norway

Ole Kristian Fauchald*

A. Objects of Private Property

Article 105 of the Norwegian Constitution contains the basic provision on protection of property in cases of expropriation. It states that: 'If the welfare of the State requires that any person shall surrender his movable or immovable property for the public use, he shall receive full compensation from the Treasury.' Article 105 is closely linked to article 97 which simply states: 'No law must be given retroactive effect.' A main issue under this provision is the extent to which new legislation can remove or limit existing property rights.

As a starting point, the wording of article 105 is limited to ownership to physical objects and land. However, the wording has been interpreted broadly to include user rights in such objects, as well as immaterial rights. Hence, private law rights will generally be regarded as property for the purpose of section 105. Concessions to exploit natural resources can also constitute property for the purpose of the provision, as was indicated by the minority in a Supreme Court decision (not contested by the majority) concerning permanent fishing concessions that were made time limited. The minority paid particular attention to the intention of the legislator as expressed in the preparatory works.[1] The interpretation of article 105 is likely to be influenced by the interpretation of the term 'possessions' in article 1 of the Additional Protocol to the European Convention for the Protection of Human Rights and Fundamental Freedoms (ECHR) by the European Court of Human Rights (ECtHR).[2] In one case where a concession to explore for petroleum was lost due to the establishment of a nature reserve, the Supreme Court commented on the broad interpretation of 'possessions' and concluded that it was questionable whether a concession that provided an exclusive right to search for but not rights to carry out necessary test drilling or to exploit resources was to be regarded as a possession.[3] Whether article 105 extends to concessions to exploit natural resources must consequently be based on a case-by-case assessment of the concession's legal character, relevant acts of public authorities, and the expectations of the private parties.

Some permits to carry out environmentally harmful activities, such as pollution permits and permits to use motor vehicles outside of roads, will generally not fall within the scope of article 105. An exception is permits issued under the Greenhouse Gas Emission Trading Act (Act no. 99 of 2004). Other permits, such as construction permits, will generally fall within the scope of article 105.

There is a presumption that article 97 of the Constitution on retroactivity extends at least to all rights covered by article 105. Whether the scope of article 97 of the Constitution extends beyond that of article 105 cannot be answered in general. Case law has applied article 97 on a case-by-case basis where a core

---

1 Rt 2013, p. 1345, at paras. 173-4.

2 The ECHR has been incorporated into Norwegian law by the Human Rights Act of 1999 no. 30.

3 Rt 2008, p. 1747, at paras. 41-4.

issue has been the expectations of private parties, as was made clear by the majority of the Supreme Court in the case concerning fishing rights.[4]

B. Private Property in Natural Resources

We may distinguish three main situations. First, rights to use natural resources may be based on customary use. Courts frequently frame such rights, for example rights to hunt or fish, in terms of exclusive rights rather than as property. Secondly, where rights of using natural resources are linked to ownership of land, such rights can be framed as property, for example the right to use timber or gravel, or in terms of rights, for example the right to produce hydropower from a river that runs across privately owned land. How such rights are framed seem to be related to whether a concession is needed before the resource can be used by the owner of the land. But there is significant lack of consistency in this regard in Norwegian legislation. Finally, rights of using natural resources based on authorisations from public authorities, such as the right to exploit petroleum resources or to emit pollutants, are generally not framed as property.

C. Private Property Used in Defense of Environmental Protection

The main legal basis for using private property as a defence of environmental protection is section 2 of the Neighbouring Properties Act (1961) which prohibits activities that may unreasonably or unnecessarily cause damage or be a nuisance to neighbouring property. One example is a case brought by property owners concerning noise from an airport. The Supreme Court concluded that the nuisance was contrary to the standards of section 2 and awarded compensation to property owners.[5] However, it is not common for property owners or their associations to use this legal basis in defence of environmental protection. It is essentially used in disputes between neighbours concerning removal of trees and buildings.

Brief case study

'A factory, situated near a town, has been operating for decades. People are slowly realizing that statistically the inhabitants in the city and in the vicinity do not live average age and the cancer is more frequently present among them, also the frequent cause of the deaths. They have no direct proofs that the factory

4 Rt 2013, p. 1345, at paras. 73-78, where the Court concludes that the rights established can enjoy protection under article 97. Similar issues were discussed by the Supreme Court in relation to payment for rights to exploit petroleum resources, see Rt 1985, p. 1355, at pp. 1377-9.

5 Rt 2006, p. 486.

could be responsible, although it is rather clear that the soil around the factory is poisoned and that the heavy metals found in the vegetable could be linked to the factory. However, credible proofs are missing.'

The obligations of Norwegian authorities according to section 48 of the Pollution Control Act (1981 no. 6) are to monitor the general pollution situation and the pollution from the factory, and they shall ensure compliance with the general prohibition against pollution according to section 7 of the Act. Inhabitants could bring a case to courts claiming that the pollution authorities must fulfil their duties under the Act. While the courts could order pollution authorities to take measures to fulfil their duties, the courts would generally refrain from providing detailed instructions to authorities.

If the pollution authorities want to revoke the pollution permit of the factory, they can do so according to section 18 of the Pollution Control Act provided that the damage or nuisance caused by the pollution proves to be significantly greater than or different from that anticipated when the permit was issued. If more than ten years have passed since the permit was issued, the authorities have broader discretionary power. They stand free to withdraw or alter the permit as long as they have taken into account the costs that alteration or reversal will involve for the polluter and any other advantages and disadvantages the alteration or reversal will involve.

In addition to the Pollution Control Act, chapter 3 of the Public Health Act (2011 no. 29) authorises the municipality to take measures to prevent and remedy environmentally related health problems and risks, such as pollution or exposure to harmful chemicals. The municipality may order that a situation be rectified provided that 'the inconvenience caused by rectification is in a reasonable proportion to the health considerations' (section 14). Due to the broad discretion of municipalities, courts are unlikely to conclude in favor of inhabitants' claims that the municipal authorities must issue such an order.

D. Natural Resources as Public Property or Interest

There are particular regimes for public property rights to certain natural resources under Norwegian legislation:

- Hydropower resources belong to and shall be managed to the benefit of the public according to section 1 of the Industrial Licensing Act (1917);
- Petroleum resources on the continental shelf belong to Norway according to section 1-1 of the Petroleum Act (1996 no. 72);
- Section 2 of the Marine Resources Act (2008 no. 37) states: 'Wild living marine resources belong to Norwegian society as a whole'. The same applies to marine genetic resources.
- Metals with a specific gravity of 5 grams/cm3 or greater as well as titanium, arsenic, pyrrhotite and pyrite belong to the state according to section 7 of the Minerals Act (2009 no. 101); and

- Section 57 of the Nature Diversity Act (2009 no. 100) states: 'Genetic material obtained from the natural environment is a common resource belonging to Norwegian society as a whole'.

The legal framing of the management of these resources thus varies from property rights of the state to property rights of the society. There are few specific duties and rights regarding the management of such resources beyond general statements of purpose:

- Under the Petroleum Act (section 1-2): Management shall be carried out in a long-term perspective for the benefit of the Norwegian society as a whole. In this regard the resource management shall provide revenues to the country and shall contribute to ensuring welfare, employment and an improved environment, as well as to the strengthening of Norwegian trade and industry and industrial development, and at the same time take due regard to regional and local policy considerations and other activities.
- Under the Marine Resources Act (section 1): To ensure sustainable and economically profitable management of wild living marine resources and genetic material derived from them, and to promote employment and settlement in coastal communities.
- Under the Minerals Act (sections 1 and 2): To promote and ensure socially responsible administration and use of mineral resources in accordance with the principle of sustainable development, and to ensure that the following interests are safeguarded: a) value creation and industrial and commercial development; b) the foundation of Sami culture, commercial activity and social life; c) the surroundings and nearby areas while operations are being carried out; d) the environmental consequences of extraction; and e) long-term planning relating to subsequent use or reclamation of the area.
- Under the Nature Diversity Act (section 57): To utilize the genetic resources to the greatest possible benefit of the environment and human beings in both a national and an international context, also attaching importance to appropriate measures for sharing the benefits arising out of the utilisation of genetic material and in such a way as to safeguard the interests of indigenous peoples and local communities.

In addition, public authorities have the main responsibility for management of protected areas, which cover approximately 17 per cent of the Norwegian mainland. Such responsibility has been extensively delegated to local management boards composed of local and regional politicians. Their main obligation is to ensure that the objectives of the protected areas are fulfilled, as formulated in chapter V of the Nature Diversity Act and in the decisions establishing the protected areas.

E. Property in Public Aids for Beneficial Use of Natural Resources

The starting point is that subsidies are decided as part of the general budget every year. The Parliament's budgetary freedom follows directly from article 75 of the Constitution. The Parliament is consequently free to withdraw subsidies for budgetary or other reasons. However, this does not necessarily rule out the possibility that subsidies for beneficial use of natural resources can be designed so that they can be characterised as property. This is most commonly done by imposing specific taxes within a sector, the proceeds of which are earmarked to support measures to improve environmental performance within the sector. One example can be found in chapter 4 of the Forestry Act (2005 no. 31) which provides for payments to a Forest Trust Fund which is to finance forest owners' measures aimed at sustainable forest management. The Act indicates that the forest owners have property rights to what has been paid to the Fund from forestry on the property in question. Another example is certificates issued to producers of renewable energy according to the Act on Electricity Certificates (2011 no. 39). Those to whom such certificates are issued gain property rights to the certificates, and distributors of electricity are obliged to purchase a number of certificates depending on the amount of electricity that they distribute.

F. Expropriation

The general rule according to article 105 of the Constitution is that only expropriation understood as transfer of ownership title triggers a right of compensation. Expropriation must be authorised by law. Norway has a general Act on Expropriation of Land (1959) which authorises expropriation for 55 purposes provided that the benefits of expropriation are clearly greater than the disadvantages (section 2). There is no general reference to expropriation for environmental purposes in the Act, but expropriation is allowed for nature restoration and for management measures in protected areas. In addition, there are some specific provisions authorising expropriation in other legislation, such as the possibility for municipalities to expropriate when adopting plans that involve nature protection (see sections 12-5 no. 5 and 16-2 of the Planning and Building Act (2008 no. 71)).

Hydropower plants have a special legal position in Norway, as the plants are transferred to the state without cost after termination of the concession, normally 60 years after the concession was provided. This arrangement was challenged before the EFTA Court and found to violate articles 31 and 40 of the EEA Agreement on the basis that it discriminated between private and public owners of hydropower plants.[6] Norway responded by eliminating certain

6 Case E-2/06E/.

discriminatory aspects of the legislation, but maintained the general policy of favouring public ownership.[7]

G. Indirect Expropriation by Environmental Regulation?

The general rule is that public authorities may restrict the freedom to enjoy property rights without having to pay compensation. There are two exceptions to this starting point. The first is a general customary rule that significant restrictions on property rights may generate a right of compensation. According to case law, the threshold for a right to compensation in such cases is very high, and the courts have almost never accepted claims for compensation on this basis. Relevant considerations are the extent to which the owner may still benefit from the property rights, whether the restrictions are aimed at one particular owner or a limited group of owners, and whether the restrictions are reasonable (e.g. whether they were to be expected and the extent to which enjoyment of the property rights would lead to environmental damage).[8]

The second exception is specific entitlements to compensation set out in legislation. The most important such provisions from an environmental perspective are sections 50 and 51 of the Nature Diversity Act (2009 no. 100), the former of which states that:

> A landowner or a holder of rights in property that is wholly or partly protected as a national park, protected landscape, nature reserve, habitat management area or marine protected area is entitled to compensation from the state for financial losses incurred when protection makes current use of the property more difficult.

According to the Act, all these categories of protected areas may be established on private property. Compensation is restricted to current use. Expectations regarding future use will only be compensated when right holders have obtained permits to carry out the relevant activities and the permits were acquired prior to the announcement of the protected areas. The threshold for access to compensation is rather low, as there is only a requirement that current use be made 'difficult'. Minor difficulties would not qualify, and the owner must be willing to adjust the use in ways that would minimize the need to compensate. Other provisions of interest can be found in chapter 15 of the Planning and Building Act (2008 no. 71), according to which owners can claim compensation in cases where land is designated for certain purposes in municipal master plans or zoning plans. The condition for compensation is that the property can no longer

7 Revisions were made through Act 2008 no. 78 which inter alia amended the Industrial Licensing Act (1917).

8 See Rt 2005, p. 469 which concerned claims for compensation as a consequence of the establishment of protected areas. The legislation at the time referred to general principles as the legal basis for the duty to compensate. The Supreme Court came to the conclusion that there was no right to compensation.

be 'utilized profitably'. As above, the owner must adjust the use to minimize the need to compensate.

Where permits and concessions are required, the question that arises is whether they can be revoked or amended to benefit environmental concerns without compensation. The general rule which is laid down in section 35 of the Public Administration Act (1967) is that such permits or concessions cannot be revoked or amended to the disadvantage of the private party save in a very limited range of situations. Hence, the general possibility of revising permits and concessions to benefit the environment remains limited. However, some environmental acts extend this possibility significantly. Section 18 of the Pollution Control Act (1981 no. 6) opens up for revising pollution permits to benefit the environment on certain conditions, and public authorities have full freedom to revoke or amend the permit 10 years after it was awarded. A similar provision can be found in the section 67 of the Nature Diversity Act (2009 no. 100). Other examples of resource legislation that allow for extensive revisions of concessions and permits are section 9 of the Aquaculture Act (2005 no. 79), section 25 of the Water Resources Act (2000 no. 82) and section 10-4 of the Energy Act (1990 no. 50).

In other cases, essentially concerning exploitation of natural resources, the right to revoke or amend concessions or permits is made part of the system of sanctions against improper or unlawful acts of the concessionaire or permit holder (e.g. section 65 of the Mineral Act (2009 no. 101), section 10-13 of the Petroleum Act (1996 no. 72) and section 11 of the Act relating to the Right to Participate in Fisheries (1999 no. 15)). The restrictive rule of the Public Administration Act (1967) applies to some important sectors, including the forestry sector (Forestry Act, 2005 no. 31), hunting (Wildlife Act, 1981 no. 38) and construction permits (Planning and Building Act, 2008 no. 71).

In sum, the possibility of revoking or amending concessions and permits vary widely in the Norwegian legal system. It seems that environmental legislation provides for most flexibility. Otherwise, no clear pattern emerges. The issue seems to be resolved on an ad hoc basis where negotiation between relevant ministries probably is an essential factor. Where the revocation or amendment of a concession or permit is in accordance with the legislation, no compensation would be required. Otherwise, revocation or amendment would simply not be allowed unless consent can be obtained from the concessionaire or permit holder.

H. Dissolution of Property for Environmental Protection

Whether rights can be withdrawn or revised without having to pay compensation depends on the legal nature of the rights. Rights based on concessions or permits may in most cases be modified or withdrawn through new legislation or through individual decisions where such decisions are authorized in the existing legislation.[9]

I. State Liability for Environmental Damage to Private Property

The issue of who may be liable to pay compensation for environmental damage is addressed in section 55 of the Pollution Control Act (1981 no. 6), which states that:

> The owner of real property, an object, an installation or an enterprise that causes pollution damage is liable to pay compensation pursuant to this chapter regardless of any fault on his part if the owner also operates, uses or occupies the property, etc.

Moreover, the provision extends liability to any person 'that by supplying goods and services, carrying out control or supervisory measures or similar means has indirectly contributed to pollution damage' in cases of intention or negligence. These rules do not distinguish between private parties and public authorities, and could consequently be a legal basis for state liability.

It can also be asked whether public authorities may incur liability as a consequence of having authorised environmentally harmful activities. As long as the authorisation is lawful, the starting point is that public authorities would not incur liability. However, as indicated in a Supreme Court judgement regarding a permit to import smolt (young salmon) that caused damages to a number of salmon farms due to an infectious disease, liability may in some cases extend to cases where the decision was lawful.[10] Liability of public authorities in such cases is based on their responsibility for errors committed by employees in accordance with section 2-1 of the Act relating to Compensation in Certain Circumstances (1969).

Brief case study

'A communal waste disposal site is located not far away from a place with appr. 150 individual houses. Inhabitants assert that they smell bad odour and they would like to sell their property, but, of course, there are no potential buyers. Their property is almost worthless. The waste disposal site is equipped with the necessary permits.'

The inhabitants would be entitled to compensation according to chapter 8 of the Pollution Control Act (1981 no. 6). The main rule is a one-time compensation, but there is a possibility of providing for payment in instalments. There is

9 See section G.

10 Rt 1992, p. 453, at pp. 475-6.

no requirement to seek annulment of the permits before claiming compensation.

J. Proprietor's Liability for Environmental Damage

The Pollution Control Act (1981 no. 6) does in general assign responsibility to 'the person responsible for the pollution' (see in particular section 7 and chapter 8). The issue of responsibility is partly a question concerning who is responsible for cleaning up the property. According to section 51, public authorities may order 'any person that possesses, does, or initiates anything that results in or that there is reason to believe may result in pollution' to carry out investigations and similar activities. The extension of such responsibility to a mother company was discussed in a case before the Supreme Court concerning an order by environmental authorities to investigate a contaminated site. The Court stated that the word 'possess' extends to the owner regardless of whether the owner has carried out activities that led to the pollution. The decisive factor was whether the owner had control over the polluting activities.[11] The Supreme Court answered the question of whether responsibility could extend to the mother company in the affirmative, despite the fact that the two companies were distinct legal subjects and that the daughter company was a shareholding company.[12] The rule on liability in section 55 has a more limited scope than section 51, as it requires that the 'owner also operates, uses or occupies the property' in order to incur liability. The Supreme Court discussed the link between the two provisions and acknowledged that section 55 could not extend liability to the mother company in the case at hand, but that this did not restrict the authorities' ability to order the mother company to investigate the contaminated site under section 51.

K. Permit Excuse in Environmental Liability

The general approach would be that those carrying out the activities would remain liable towards third persons regardless of the existence of a permit. According to section 56 of the Pollution Control Act (1981 no. 6), a permit does not rule out claims for compensation based on section 2 of the Neighbouring Properties Act (1961).[13] However, in some cases special rules apply, such as section 51 of the Minerals Act (2009 no. 101) which authorises authorities to require financial security for clean-up costs. In such cases, liability may be limited to the financial security required as part of the permit.

---

[11] Rt 2010, p. 443, para. 50.

[12] Ibid. para. 79.

[13] See section C. above.

L. Direct or Indirect Expropriation by EU Measures

As Norway is party to the Agreement on the European Economic Area and not a Member of the EU, EU legal acts are as a starting point to be regarded as public international law in the context of the Norwegian legal system. Section 2 of the Act Implementing the EEA Agreement (1992 no. 109) states that legislation or regulation to implement EU legal acts are to prevail over other laws and regulations to the extent of conflict. The rules that would apply regarding expropriation in such cases would be the same as if the expropriation was caused by ordinary legislation adopted by the Parliament or regulations adopted by the Government.[14]

[14] See sections F. and G. above.

Property and Environmental Protection in Poland

Barbara Iwanska & Mariusz Baran

A. Objects of Private Property; Property in Natural Resources

In broad terms, ownership is synonymous with the term 'property' defined as property and other property rights, i.e. the entirety of economic rights (Article 44 of the Polish Civil Code). In this sense 'ownership' is a comprehensive concept for all property rights, whose subject may be tangible objects which are things (lands), tangible objects which are not things (e.g. water, ores) or intangible goods (e.g. a literary work, an intellectual property work). In the literature on the subject, it is assumed that the property rights are[1] proprietary rights (ownership, perpetual usufruct [leasehold ownership], limited proprietary rights *[iura in re aliena]*) and other rights.

Natural resources can be the object of the right to property as a proprietary right or as another property right, both private or public (e.g. lands, forests, water).

Some natural resources, which due to their essence are not things, may constitute component parts of a thing/object which may not be a separated subject of ownership and of other proprietary rights.[2] Some component parts of the environment (like: the atmosphere, climate, flowing water, sea) are exclusively the object of public law provisions regulating their use. Special rules concern animals,[3] waters[4] and some ores (tangible objects which are not things).[5]

The boundaries of the content to and the exercise of a right to ownership have been defined in a large number of specific acts. They result from the provisions of the Civil Code concerning the so-called 'neighbours' law' serving to protect the rights and interests of third parties.[6] Most of the limitations to the

1 Cf. M. Bednarek, *A commentary to Article 44 of the Polish Civil Code*, LEX; and also W. J. Katner, *A commentary to Article 44 of the Polish Civil Code*, LEX.

2 E.g.: trees and other plants, from the date of having been planted or sown constitute component parts of the land (Article 48 of the Civil Code).

3 According to the Act on Protection of Animals, an animal as a living being, capable of suffering – is not a thing – however in matters not covered by the Act, the provisions related to things shall be used accordingly to animals. Cf also Article 2 of the Act of 13 October 1995 the Law on Hunting according to game animals in free state, as all-Poland (national) goods, are owned by the State Treasury.

4 Waters according to the provisions of the Water Law; waters constitute the ownership of the State Treasury, of other legal persons or of natural persons, cf. Section I Chapter II of the Water Law (*Right to the ownership of water*).

5 Ores, according to the provisions of the Geological and Mining Law Act determined deposits of ores, listed in the Act (e.g. crude oil, natural gas, hard bituminous coal and lignite (brown coal), treatment waters, thermal waters) are, regardless of where they may be found, the subject of mining ownership (cf. Article 10). The concept of mining ownership is a separate property right enjoyed solely by the State Treasury in separation from the ownership of a real property. A mining ownership right is an inalienable right including the possibility of making use of the object of the mining property in exclusion of others, as well as of disposal of the right of mining ownership exclusively by establishing the mining usufruct.

6 According to its Article 144 'When exercising his right, an owner of immovable property, shall refrain from actions which would interfere with the use of the neighbouring immovable property exceeding the

right of ownership have a public law nature stemming from administrative law, including *inter alia* from: (1) provisions of the Real Property Management Act, which enables expropriation of the property right due to the need to implement public aims, including to protect the environment; (2) provisions of the Spatial Planning and Land Development Act[7] as well as (3) provisions of environmental regulation. Here are some examples of restricting private property for protection of the environment with or without compensation stemming from the environmental regulation.[8]

1. *Restrictions by local area development plan*

Conditions for maintaining the balance of nature and the rational management of environmental resources are ensured in a local area development plan. The effect of the adoption of a local area development plan, or the changes thereto, may be qualified limitations in the use of a real property, for reasons connected with the protection of environment, which nevertheless grant the owners certain rights of compensation.[9] If the entitled person has not made use of the above-mentioned rights and he alienates the real property, he may demand compensation equal to a decrease in the real property's value from the commune. The owners cannot rely on their compensation claims when limitations in the use of a real property introduced to a spatial plan result from limitations following from others' acts, e.g. environmental ones.

2. *Restrictions based on the Environmental Protection Law Act*

One of the examples of limitation of ownership is the designation of quiet areas in an agglomeration and of quiet areas in open country (art. 118 of the Environmental Protection Law Act, hereinafter referred to as 'EPL Act'). The EPL Act introduces the right to demand a buy-out of a real property where, in relation to a limitation to making use of the real property by designating such

normal use, resulting from the social and economic purpose of the immovable property and from the local circumstances'.

7 According to the provision of art. 6 (1) of the Act : The findings of the local area development plan shall develop, along with other provisions, a manner to perform a right of real property ownership.

8 Cf. The following acts and measures provided therein as well as relevant case law affecting biodiversity and ecological connectivity in Polish law are wider presented in: B. Iwańska. L. Dubiński, Analysis of National Institutional Frameworks and Legislations Affecting Biodiversity and Ecological Connectivity in the Carpathian Countries – NATIONAL REPORT, POLAND, 2013, Legal analysis coordinated and supervised by Dr. Mariachiara Alberton (access on line).

9 According to Article 36 of the Spatial Planning and Land Development Act to which: If, in connection with the adoption of the local area development plan or with its alteration, use of the real property or a part thereof in the previous manner or in compliance with the previous purpose has become impossible or significantly reduced, an owner or a holder of perpetual usufruct [leasehold ownership] of the real property may demand from the commune compensation for actual damage [damnum emergens] incurred or that a real property or part thereof be bought out from him. The realization of these claims may also occur through the exchange of real properties.

area, the use of the real property in the previous manner has become impossible or significantly reduced, or a right to demand compensation for the damage incurred in connection with limiting the use of the real property; the damage includes also the decrease in the real property's value.[10]

3. Restrictions based on the Nature Conservation Act

Considerations of nature conservation may constitute a premise for expropriation of property (for example, in the case when a landowner does not agree with the establishment of a national park). Creating a protected area results in a range of restrictions on use of property within areas protected for nature conservation purposes, including the exclusion of a certain activity in a given area or the quest to adjust the current method of use so as to allow the completion of the above-mentioned nature conservation purposes. In the above-mentioned situation provisions of the EPL provide for the right to demand a buy-out of a real property or a right to demand compensation for the damage incurred in connection with limiting the manner to make use of the real property,[11] and the Nature Conservation Act provides for support measures in the form of support programs or in the form of indemnity.[12]

Another example of limiting the exercise of the ownership right in the Nature Conservation Act is controlling by prior authorization the removal of trees and shrubs from the area of the real property.[13]

4. Restrictions based on the Water Law Act

The Water Law Act defines a water ownership right and duties of water owners and of other real property owners, which could result in restrictions on the use of a real property. Restrictions on making use of a real property in connection with the creation of forms of water protection (protection zones of water intakes or protected areas of inland water reservoirs)[14] can constitute an example thereof. When it causes impossibility or a significant reduction in making use of the real property or a part thereof in the previous manner or in compliance with the previous purpose, an owner may demand compensation for the damage incurred or that a real property or a part thereof be bought out from him.[15]

---

10 Article 129 et seq. of the EPL Act.

11 Cf. Article 130 of the EPL Act .

12 According to Article 36 of the Nature Conservation Act if an economic activity requires adjusting to the requirements of the protection of Natura 2000 sites (areas), where support programs on account of reduction of profitability are not being applied, a regional director of environmental protection may enter into an agreement with an owner or with a holder of the site, which contains a schedule of necessary actions, methods and time limits for their implementation.

13 Cf. Articles from 83 to 90 of the Act of 16 April 2004 of the Nature Conservation Act.

14 Cf. Articles 51 and 60 of the Water Law Act. And also relative prohibitions concerning certain activities near flood banks to ensure the integrity and stability of the very flood banks (no compensation).

15 Cf. Articles 61 and 187 of the Water Law Act.

5. Restrictions based on the Act on Forests and the Act on the Protection of Agricultural and Forest Land

The Act on Forests applies to all forests, regardless of their form of ownership. The principles of forest management (like the continuity and the sustainable use of all forest functions), jointly with the provisions of the Act on the Protection of Agricultural and Forest Land set limits on the use of forests and forest land, including, for example by limiting the possibility of allocating forest land for purposes other than agricultural or forestry ones or limiting the admissibility of changing a forest into an agricultural use.[16]

6. Restrictions based on the Hunting Law

The provisions of the Hunting Law shape the content of a right of ownership due to the need to protect game animals (wild game) and the management of their resources in accordance with the principles of ecology and the principles of rational agriculture management, forestry and fishing management. Provisions of the Hunting Law constitute a basis for the creation of hunting districts regardless of the ownership of land, of which they are composed. The Hunting Law does not introduce indemnity for the mere introduction of hunting districts but it introduces a stricter discipline concerning the liability of hunters' associations and of the State Treasury for hunting damages, that is for damages caused while carrying out the hunting, and the damages caused by some of the game animals to cultivation as well as to agricultural produce.[17]

C. Private Property in Natural Resources

The common use of the environment is permitted *ex lege* to anyone and it extends to utilizing the environment, without using an installation, with a view to satisfying personal and household needs, including rest and the practice of sports, within the scope of releasing substances or energy into the environment.[18] However, the use of the environment beyond the framework

[16] In the judgment of 16 May 2006 the Constitutional Tribunal determined that forests are: 'something more than the subject of a right of ownership and of other proprietary rights. They represent a national [all-Poland] value of great public importance', which justifies inter alia the obligations imposed by the Act, burdening forest owners, which have been defined as 'the rational use of the forest in a manner that permanently ensures the optimal realization of its functions by acquiring timber within the limits not exceeding of the production capacity of the forest' (reference number P 32/05, OTK ZU 2006/5A/56).

[17] Cf. Chapter 9 of the Hunting Law. The Constitutional Tribunal determined that a provision of the Hunting Law which allowed the creation of a hunting district covering a privately-owned real property without providing an appropriate legal means of protecting the rights of the owner were contrary to the right of ownership because they infringed the essence of the ownership right – cf. the judgment of the Constitutional Tribunal of 10 July 2014, reference number P 19/13 (OTK ZU 2014/7A/71).

[18] Cf. Article 4(1) of the EPL Act.

of common use may, under an act of law, require a permit (such as an IPPC/IED permit) issued by the competent environmental protection authority that establishes the scope and conditions of said use.

Similarly, the common use of water is permitted to satisfy personal needs, household or agricultural ones, without the use of special technical equipment, as well as for recreation, hiking, water sports and, under the terms of separate provisions, for amateur fishing.[19] While the owner of the land is entitled to the normal use of water at its property and underground water contained in the soil, the Water Law Act does not provide for a right to erect water facilities without a permit.[20]

Under the Geological and Mining Law activities can be carried out after obtaining a concession (license) to exploit.[21]

According to the Hunting Law, hunting is conducted in the hunting districts by tenants or managers on the basis of annual plans and long-term hunting breeding plans.

1. *Private Property Used in Defense of Environmental Protection Remedies of legal protection at a public law level (inc. Case on Polluting Factory)*

The State is obliged to enforce the requirements specified in law concerning the use of the environment. In the event of a breach, administrative responsibility,[22] within the scope of the environmental protection law comes into being. It includes the power to suspend activities, revoke a permit or a license, impose financial sanctions. Apart from that criminal responsibility[23] may apply, such as of persons who pollute the surface of land with a substance in such quantities or in such a form that it may endanger human life or health or cause a significant decrease in the quality of water or of the land surface.

Within the scope of the administrative responsibility, the following could be applied:

a) The EPL Act or the Act on the Prevention and Remediation of Environmental Damage

Pursuant to Article 362 of the EPL Act *'If an entity using environment causes a negative impact on the environment, an environmental protection authority may, by way of a decision, impose an obligation to: 1) reduce the impact on the environment as well as risks it presents thereto; 2) restore the environment to the proper state (condition)'.*

19 Cf. Article 34 (2) of the Water Law Act; Everyone has the right to the common use of public inland surface waters, internal waters and internal waters of the Bay of Gdansk *[Zatoka Gda ska]*, and the waters of the territorial sea, unless otherwise specified in the Water Law Act.

20 Cf. Article 37 and also in detail Section VI Chapter 4 of the Water Law Act.

21 Cf. in detail Section III of the Geological and Mining Law.

22 Cf. in detail Title III Section IV, Title VI and Title VI Section III of the EPL Act.

23 Cf. in detail Title VI Section II of the EPL Act.

The provision also involves all (including the legal ones) conditions of the negative impact on the environment,[24] with the exception (since 2007) of a risk or of damages to environmental habitats / species or to waters or to surface of land, caused by the activity capable of creating the risk of damages to the environment. The latter are covered by the Act on the Prevention and Remediation of Environmental Damage (which is an implementation of the Directive 2004/35/EC to the Polish legal order).

Thus, in the present state of facts (the soil around the factory is poisoned) the Act on the Prevention and Remediation of Environmental Damage may apply, as well as the obligation of the perpetrator contained therein to undertake appropriate preventive or remedial actions, guaranteed by an obligation of public authorities to issue a decision requiring them to undertake it in the case of a failure to act by the perpetrator.

Alternatively Article 364 of the EPL, according to which *'if an activity carried out by an entity using environment (....) causes deterioration of the environment in large size or threatens the lives or health of people, a voivodship environmental protection inspector shall issue a decision to suspend the activity in which it is necessary to prevent the deterioration of the state of environment'.*

If the state wants to revoke the operation permit, could the factory claim any sort of property guarantee?

To revoke the operation permit the following could be applied:

- In the case of environmental permits (permits to introduce substances or energy into the environment), it is possible to withdraw such a permit or to limit it, *inter alia,* on the basis of Articles 195-196 of the EPL Act with compensation when reasons of environmental protection or the use of the permit (license) creates a risk to human life or health[25] or without compensation in the event of its infringement or of an infringement of the law or when environmental regulations have changed to the extent that the issue on the conditions specified in the permit is no longer possible,[26]
- In the case of the IPPC (IED) permit it is also possible to withdraw or amend it without compensation when, following the analysis of the very permit (at least once every 5 years or in the event of changes in BAT) a necessity to change the content of an integrated permit has been asserted (Article 215 -216 in conjunction with Article 195 of the EPL Act).

Additionally, the liability for damage made by the impact on the environment is not excluded by the circumstances that the activity being the reason for said damage is conducted under a decision and within its scope.[27]

---

[24] Cf. A. Lipiński (in:) *Ustawa – Prawo ochrony rodowiska. Komentarz,* J. Jendrośka (ed.), Wrocław 2001, at 867.

[25] Cf. Article 196 (1) of the EPL Act.

[26] Cf. according to Article 194 -195 of the EPL Act.

[27] Cf. Article 325 of the EPL Act.

2. *Remedies of legal protection under civil law:*

A preventive claim or a restitution claim would be possible on the basis of Article 323 of the EPL Act, and in addition a negatory action arising from neighbourly relationships (Article 144 in conjunction with Article 222 (2)[28] of the Polish Civil Code). These general civil rules are modified in some environmental regulations like in Article 323 of the EPL (*actio negatoria sui generis*) which is applicable to unlawful effects on the environment and modifies the legal conditions, the content and scope of the claims, as well as the *locus standi* to bring them.[29] The said modification is justified when one takes into account the object of the protection of this act (environment), the aim and principles of this protection.[30]

Liability for damages on account of torts (strict liability) of persons who run an enterprise or an establishment powered by the forces of nature or an establishment of an increased risk or of a great risk on their own account is envisaged (Article 435 (1) of the Polish Civil Code).

Establishment of liability for damages on account of torts (the strict liability) depends on the fulfilment of its conditions. There must be, therefore, an event *(an event causing the damage does not have to be a one-off one; it may be a period of activity of the establishment leading to a damage)*, which is also a cause of the damage (*to persons or to property*), as well as an adequate causal link between the event and the damage. In the indicated facts credible proofs are missing. It follows that it is rather a matter of expert witnesses' evidence and determining whether the activities of the plant in a given area for a specified period of time remain in the adequate causal associations with contamination of land or diseases the injured suffer from.

---

[28] A. Wasilewski indicates, that the possibility to file a *actio negatoria* depends on meeting the following conditions: 1) the existence of an infringement of property; 2) violations involving interference with property rights of others, but otherwise than by depriving the owner of the actual power to the thing; 3) the unlawful nature of the infringement, namely a non-support in the law or the subjective law of infringing party and 4) the alleged violation must take place when the claim is to be recognized in court – *Actio negatoria* jako instrument prawny ochrony środowiska (w świetle prawa polskiego), (w:) Vetera Vovis Augere. Studia i prace dedykowane Profesorowi Wacławowi Uruszczakowi, t. I-II, Kraków 2010 r., at 1139.

[29] It reads as follows: 'Everyone who through unlawful impact on the environment is directly exposed to hazard of an injury [damage] or upon whom the injury was inflicted may demand from a subject liable for this danger or violation that the lawful state be restored and that preventive measures be undertaken, especially through installing installations or equipment safeguarding against the danger or violation; in the case where it is impossible or excessively difficult, he may demand that the activity causing the danger or violation be discontinued (Sec. 1). If the danger or violation concerns the environment as a public good, the State Treasury, territorial self-governing unit as well as an ecological organization can file the above-mentioned claims (Sec.2)'.

[30] For the conclusion of the interpretation of Article 323 of the EPL Act cf. A. Wasilewski, *Actio negatoria...*, at 1145-1148.

This type of liability arises without regard to fault, as well as regardless of whether the damage occurred in the conditions of unlawful behaviour or not.[31]

In order to pursue claims using this mode, there is no need of a prior withdrawal of a permit.

D. Natural Resources as Public Property or Interest

1. The Constitution of the Republic of Poland and the ownership/right to property

According to Article 21 of the Constitution:
1. *The Republic of Poland shall protect ownership and the right of succession.*
2. *Expropriation may be allowed solely for public purposes and for just compensation.*

And in accordance with Article 64 of the Constitution:
1. *Everyone shall have the right to ownership, other property rights and the right of succession.*
2. *Everyone, on an equal basis, shall receive legal protection regarding ownership, other property rights and the right of succession.*
3. *The right of ownership may only be limited by means of a statute and only to the extent that it does not violate the substance of such right.*

Furthermore, in pursuance of Article 31 section 3 of the Constitution: *'any limitation upon the exercise of constitutional freedoms and rights may be imposed only by statute, and only when necessary in a democratic state for the protection of its security or public order, or to protect the natural environment, health or public morals, or the freedoms and rights of other persons. Such limitations shall not violate the essence of freedoms and rights'.*

2. *The Constitution and the environmental protection*[32]

Pursuant to the Constitution of the Republic of Poland, the state *'shall ensure the protection of the natural environment pursuant to the principles of sustainable development*[33]*'.*

This task is elaborated in further provisions of the Constitution that relate directly to the environment, in which the following was formulated.[34] (a) a constitutional duty of public authorities to protect the environment and to ensure the ecological safety to the current generation as well as to the future ones; (b) an everyone's duty of care of environment's quality as well as a prin-

---

[31] Such is an opinion of *inter alia* M. Safjan [in:] *Kodeks cywilny, tom I, Komentarz do artykułów 1-449[1]*, K. Pietrzykowski (ed.), Wyd. C.H. Beck, Warszawa 2008, at 1373 cf also note 27.

[32] Cf. B. Iwańska. L. Dubiński, Analysis of National..., op.cit.

[33] Cf. Article 5 of the Constitution.

[34] Cf. Articles 68 (4), 74, 86 and 31 (3) of the Constitution.

ciple of bearing responsibility for its degradation caused by themselves; (c)a universal subjective right to access to information on the quality of the environment and on its protection.

These solutions together with the possibility to interfere into property in favour of environmental protection (above cited Article 31 section 3 of the Constitution) refer to 'the constitutional and system tradition that treats 'the environment' as an objective asset constituting a 'common good' (...). Its use and protection should be widely available, i.e. for everyone, provided that the sustainable development principle and the requirements of inter-generation environmental ethics the same principle determines are respected'.[35]

The realization of the provisions which relate to the environment and its protection is carried out by virtue of laws in which the legislator in some cases expressly qualifies the environment as 'common good' although without giving that expression any further normative significance. Nevertheless, the common good within the meaning of environmental protection law may denote the environment itself, its individual components and the processes taking place within it, while taking at the same time into account those elements that are subject to or may be subject to 'an individual appropriation'[36] (e.g. lands, forests).

Expressing a concept of environment in terms of the common good constitutes a justification for creating determined rules governing the use of the goods in question as well as of effective legal instruments of their protection within the existing legal order.[37] This comes into being *inter alia* by shaping the content of ownership rights within the framework of provisions of law of environmental protection. In the case of private ownership it constitutes a manifestation of the individual's contribution[38] to protect the environment viewed as the common good and the realization of environmental protection and its elements regardless of who actually own them.[39]

---

35 A. Wasilewski, Dynamika zmian i kontynuacja we współczesnym prawie administracyjnym wyzwaniem dla doktryny prawa (na przykładzie prawa o ochronie środowiska) in: J. Supernat (ed.) Między tradycją a przyszłością w nauce prawa administracyjnego. Księga jubileuszowa dedykowana Profesorowi Janowi Bociowi, Wrocław 2009, at 771.

36 Cf. A. Wasilewski, Dynamika zmian..., at 771.

37 Cf. J. Boć, A. Błaś, Majątek publiczny, in: J. Boć (ed.) Prawo administracyjne, Kolonia Limited Wrocław 2004, at 293.

38 It is in such a way that the constutitional obligations are described by: J. Trzciński, Rzeczpospolita Polska dobrem wspólnym wszystkich obywateli in: J. Góral, R. Hauser, J. Trzciński (ed.), Sądownictwo administracyjne gwarantem wolności i praw obywatelskich 1980–2005, Naczelny Sąd Administracyjny, Warszawa 2005, at 46.

39 Cf. also A. Wasilewski, Obszar górniczy. Zagadnienia prawne, Warszawa 1969, at 109.. In one of its judgments, the Polish Constitutional Tribunal expressed the view that *'an environmental protection promise contained in article 31 section 3 of the Constitution emphasized not only the admissibility, but also the need to establish restrictions to freedoms and rights for giving consideration of the protection of the environment. Requirements in the field of environmental protection have primarily an effect on shaping the freedom to conduct business activities, but they also justify interference in the sphere of ownership rights while*

E. Property in Public Aids for Beneficial Use of Natural Resources

The Renewable Energy Sources Act provides such rights. The new act has just been issued and it is in force from 4 April 2015. It puts in place mechanisms and instruments to support the production of electricity from renewable energy sources, agricultural biogas and hot water (Chapter 4 of the project of Act). The Renewable Energy Sources Act transposes Renewable Energy Directive[40] into Polish law.

F. Expropriation

According to Article 21 of the Constitution *'expropriation may be allowed solely for public purposes and for just compensation'*. In the jurisprudence of the Constitutional Tribunal it is emphasized that the legislator has not formulated a legal definition of the term 'expropriation' in any provision of the Polish Constitution. It is defined broadly as 'any form of the state's interference in the ownership rights enjoyed by other entities'.[41]

The Real Property Management Act contains provisions relating to real properties' expropriation pursuant to which expropriation.[42]

- consists in deprivation of or in limiting rights to real property;
- comes into being solely to carry out a public purpose and involves fair compensation; the amount of *compensation* is determined in accordance with the conditions, destination and value of the expropriated real property; public purposes justifying the expropriation are set out in Article 6 of the Act and they include those relating to the protection of the environment or of environmental friendly investments,[43]
- may be carried out only if public purposes cannot be achieved in any other

maintaining proportionality of the interference and the essence of an ownership right. Environment constitutes a constitutional value of the particular importance' – Cf. the judgment of the Constitutional Tribunal of 15 May 2006, reference number P 32/05, OTK ZU 2006/5A/56.

40 Directive 2009/28/EC -Renewable Energy Directive.

41 Judgment of the Constitutional Tribunal of 16 October 2009, reference number K 28/06 OTK ZU 104/9/A/2007.

42 Cf. Section III Chapter 4 and 5 of the Real Property Management Act.

43 E.g.: (1) construction and maintenance of equipment (appliances) for the transmission or distribution of electric energy; (2) construction and maintenance of facilities and devices serving environmental protection, of reservoirs and of other water facilities serving to provide water supply, regulation of water flows and protection against flooding, as well as the regulation and maintenance of waters and of water management facilities owned by the State Treasury or local government entities; (3) protection of endangered species of animals or plants and natural habitats; other public purposes set out in separate acts (for instance, the Nature Conservation Act allows expropriation in the absence of an owner's consent to the establishment of a national park or nature reserve.

manner than by depriving of or by limiting rights to real properties, and these rights cannot be acquired by way of an agreement;
- is carried out within the administrative proceedings by means of the issue of a decision; the proceedings are preceded by negotiations concerning acquisition of rights by way of an agreement under which a replacement for the real property can be offered.

Expropriated property cannot be used for any other purpose than the one specified in the decision on expropriation, unless the owner fails to submit the application for the return of the very real property.

G. Indirect Expropriation by Environmental Regulation?

From a constitutional perspective, ownership is not of an absolute nature and it may be subject to a 'qualified' (expropriation)[44] or an 'ordinary' (restriction) interference from the State which must stand the test of proportionality and shall not violate the essence of freedoms and rights.[45] An intervention which violates the essence of a property right qualifies a legal intervention as expropriation which needs a fair compensation.[46]

Only in case of expropriation (qualified restriction) the compensation is a prerequisite of a legal restriction. It results from the Article 21 of the Constitution.

In case of limitations to use the property right for environmental protection reasons according to Article 31 section 3 of the Constitution (not related to expropriation) the legislator is free within the scope of shaping a right to claims having a compensatory (indemnity) nature consisting for example of offering a replacement for a real property or in payment of compensation on account of a need to tolerate certain activities on a person's land, or on account of a reduction in the real property's value.

However, this does not justify the shaping of the content of these rights in an arbitrary manner.[47] The legislator in this respect is bound by the principle of proportionality,[48] by the principle of equality before the law (Article 32 of the

---

44 Cf. section D and F above.

45 Cf. section D above.

46 The example can be the case in which the Constitutional Tribunal determined that 'with respect to a right of ownership, a violation of its essence (core, heart) would occur if the introduced restrictions regarded basic rights that make up the content of ownership, making it impossible in practice to exercise the very right. Restrictions may not lead to a "degeneration of ownership" or to imposing on the owner a burden which would be unbearable'(Judgment of 16 October 2009, reference number K 28/06 (OTK ZU 2007/9A/104)).

47 Cf. *inter alia alia* the judgment of the Constitutional Tribunal of 10 July 2014, reference number P 19/13 (OTK-A 2014/7/71).

48 This does not exclude private owners from participation in activities serving to protect the environment, but it does not allow a situation in which private owners bear the full costs of meeting the obligation of

Constitution) as well as by the principle of equal legal protection of ownership and of other property rights (Article 64 section 2 of the Constitution) and the need to preserve the balance of the values protected by the Constitution.[49]

In environmental provisions, both the general ones (EPL Act) and sector specific ones, there is no clear division between allowable restrictions and allowable restrictions with compensation (not related to expropriation) but one can distinguish:

- restriction of property rights for the protection of the environment with compensation (e.g.: a) in case of designating protected areas the right to demand a buy-out of a real property or a right to demand damages; b) the State Treasury's liability for damages inflicted by wild animals),[50]
- restriction of property rights caused by the economic activity of other parties with compensation (e.g. the right to demand a buy-out of a real property or to demand compensation in the case of limitation of making use of the environment as a result of establishing a restricted area around an airport),[51]
- restriction of property rights for the protection of the environment with 'compensation for the environment' (e.g. the obligation to obtain a permit to remove trees and shrubs and to pay a fee for their removal).[52]

Models of pursuing claims are varied – it may be carried out solely on the basis of the provisions of the Civil Code, or it may have a mixed character: the injured party is entitled to a recourse to the civil law only after an administrative decision was taken.[53]

---

public authorities to protect the environment.

49 Cf. *inter alia* judgments of the Constitutional Tribunal of: 13 February 2001, reference number K 19/99 (OTK ZU 2001/2/30), of 25 November 2003, reference number K 37/02 (OTK ZU 2003/9A/96). As for example in case number P 49/11, where the Constitutional Tribunal examined the compliance of Article 126 of the Nature Conservation Act setting forth liability of the State Treasury for damages caused by protected fauna species with the constitutional principle of equality before the law. The Constitutional Tribunal stated that:*"if the legislator granted on the basis of statutory solutions such right to one entities, he must also respect the constitutional principles, including the principle of equality before the law (Article 32 section 1 of the Constitution) and the principle of equal legal protection of real properties and of other property rights (Article 64 section 2 of the Constitution)".*

50 Cf. e.g.: Article 130 of the EPL Act and Article 126 of the Nature Conservation Act.

51 Cf. Title II Section IX Chapter 3 of the EPL Act concerning restricted use areas and Chapter 4 concerning industrial zones.

52 Cf. Chapter 4 of the Nature Conservation Act concerning protection of landscaping and of plantings.

53 E.g. with respect of the claims regulated by the EPL Act the injured party is entitled to a recourse to the civil law only after an administrative decision was taken (Article 131 EPL Act).

H. Dissolution of Property for Environmental Protection

The example can be a regulation concerning emission permits, aimed first and foremost at preventing pollution and restricting the direct or indirect anthropogenic discharge of substances or energy to the air, water, soil and the ground. According to the Environmental Protection Act the emission permit can be withdrawn or restricted without compensation when regulations concerning environmental protection have changed to the extent that the issuance of a new permit pursuant to the conditions specified in the old permit would be unlawful.[54]

I. State Liability for Environmental Damage to Private Property (incl. Case on Waste Disposal Site)

Around the landfill, a restricted use area should be established (Article 134 of the EPL Act). Its establishment may result in limitations concerning the use of that area. Then the owners of real properties located within the area of a limited use may file a claim for a buy-out of a real property or a part thereof or for compensation for the damage suffered, which was linked to a limitation of use of the real property, whereas the damage also includes a reduction in the value of a real property (Articles 135-136 in conjunction with Article 129 of the EPL Act).

The case provided raises the question concerning 'compensation', therefore a claim designed in particular on the basis of the provision of Article 435 (1) of the Civil Code[55] (in conjunction with Article 324 of the EPL Act[56]), constituting the basis of liability for damages for torts (a strict liability [a risk-related one]) could come into play. The occurrence of such liability depends on the fulfilment of its premises presented above[57] (event – damage – adequate causal link between them).

With respect to annual revenue within the Polish system, the damages do not have a sanction-related nature and may not result in damages being awarded in an amount greater than the damage which actually occurred (such a conclusion stems from Articles 361 and 363 of the Civil Code). Compensation should only be due within the limits of an adequate causal link.[58]

---

[54] Cf. Article 194 of the EPL Act.

[55] An operator who runs, on his own account, an enterprise or a plant that is operated by forces of nature (steam, gas, electricity, liquid fuels, etc.) is responsible for damage to a person or property that has been caused to anyone by the operation of the enterprise or plant, unless the damage was caused by force majeure, or exclusively through the fault of the injured party or a third party, for whom the operator does not take responsibility (art. 453 Civil Code).

[56] This provision broadens the scope of strict liability provided in art. 435 of Civil Code (as above) – it could also be used when the damage was caused also by so called 'establishment' of a higher or high risk, regardless of whether they are set in motion by natural forces.

[57] Cf. section C above.

[58] Cf. Article of 361 of the Civil Code: *'A person obliged to pay damages shall only be liable for ordinary effects of an action or omission which the damage resulted from (sec. 1). Within the above-mentioned limits, in the*

J. Proprietor's Liability for Environmental Damage

According to the Act on the Prevention and Remediation of Environmental Damage a holder of a real property shall be jointly and severally liable with the polluter for taking preventive and remedial actions, if a direct threat or damage to environment has been caused by his consent or even with his knowledge (unless after obtaining knowledge of a direct threat of damage to environment he files an appropriate notification).[59]

Pursuant to the EPL Act the holder of the soil where there is a history of contamination is obliged to carry out remediation.[60]

According to the Waste Act, a holder of the waste shall be obliged to immediately remove waste from places not intended for its storage or warehousing. The holder of waste is the waste producer or entity that is in their possession. It is presumed that a holder of a real property is the holder of waste on the real property. So, if the waste producer cannot be determined, the owner of the land is obliged to remove the waste.[61]

K. Permit Excuse in Environmental Liability

The general rules of the Civil Code, which concern traditional damage, are developed and modified in environmental regulations (e.g.: the EPL Act, the GMO Act, the Nuclear Law Act), which refer to situations in which damage occurs (not only traditional, but also environmental ones) due to defined environmental impacts, even the legal ones. According to Article 325 of the EPL Act: *The liability for the damage caused by the impact on the environment shall not be precluded by the circumstance that the activity which has been the reason for damages is carried out on the basis of a decision and within its boundaries.*

This provision applies to torts liability according to fault-based and risk-based liability.

L. Direct or Indirect Expropriation by EU Measures

Such measures are to be treated similarly to any other expropriation.

absence of a different statutory or contractual provision, the redress of damage shall involve losses which the injured party has suffered as well as profits which it could have obtained, if no damage were inflicted (sec. 2).'

59 Cf. Article 12 of the Act of 13 April 2007 on the Prevention and Remediation of Environmental Damage.

60 Cf. Article 101h of the EPL Act.

61 Cf. Article 26 in conjunction with Article 3 (19) of the Waste Act.

Property and Environmental Protection in Portugal

Alexandra Aragão

A. Introduction

Before analysing the potential and actual conflicts between the right to environment and property rights, we will briefly look at the constitutional norms protecting private property and the environment. Then, we will study ownership of natural resources and present the rules on natural resource management. Afterwards, we will describe the expropriation regime and restrictions to private property for environmental reasons in Portugal. Finally, we will analyse examples of cases where certain economic uses of property can be a threat to the environment and other cases where the environmental features of someone's property can be used as an argument against noxious activities.

B. The Right to Property and to Environmental Protection in the Constitution

In Portugal, the right to private property is a fundamental right but is not included in the core catalogue of constitutional rights and freedoms. Property right is the last of the economic rights and duties, after the workers' rights and the consumers' rights. When describing the content and extent of the right, the Constitution does not go beyond the right to transmit it and to be compensated when it is lost for reasons of public interest. The option not to repeat the classical Latin description of property as *ius utendi, fruendi et abutendi* in the wording of the constitutional text is usually considered as an indicator of low constitutional priority and reflects a social rather than liberal conception of property. In this context the Portuguese constitutional text is quite laconic:

> *Article 62 – Right to private property*
> 1. Everyone is guaranteed the right to private property and to the transmission thereof in life or upon death, in accordance with the Constitution.
> 2. Requisitions and expropriations in the public interest may only be undertaken on a legal basis and upon payment of just compensation.

On the other hand, the environment is also a fundamental right. It is one out of ten social rights and duties[1] in the Portuguese Constitution. But the environment is far more than a citizens' right. It is also a constitutional duty. Ever since it was laid down in the Constitution in 1976, the environment has been understood as a fundamental duty of the citizens. The description of its contents is quite detailed:

> *Article 66 – Environment and quality of life*
> 1. Everyone has the right to a healthy and ecologically balanced human living environment and the duty to defend it.

[1] Including social security, health, housing, family, parenthood, childhood, youth, disabled citizens and elderly rights.

2. To ensure the right to environment in the context of sustainable development, the State must, through appropriate bodies and with the involvement and participation of citizens:

a) prevent and control pollution and its effects, and all harmful forms of erosion;

b) organize and promote spatial planning, with a view to correct location of activities, balanced socio-economic development and enhancement of the landscape;

c) create and develop reserves and natural and recreation parks, classify and protect landscapes and sites, ensure the conservation of nature and the preservation of cultural assets of historical or artistic interest;

d) promote the rational use of natural resources, safeguarding their capacity for renewal and ecological stability, respecting the principle of solidarity between generations;

e) promote, in collaboration with local authorities, the environmental quality of villages and urban life, particularly in what concerns architecture and the protection of historic areas;

f) promote the integration of environmental objectives in various sectors of policy;

g) promote environmental education and respect for environmental values;

h) ensure that the fiscal policy renders development, environmental protection and quality of life compatible.

Besides, one of the constitutional tasks of the state is to protect and promote the cultural heritage of the Portuguese people, protect nature and the environment, conserve natural resources and ensure proper planning.[2]

C. Ownership of Natural Resources

Property law applies both to material things (be it real estate property or personal property), and to non-material things. Scientific, literary or artistic property is protected by the Constitution.[3] Certain rights having market value, such as author's rights, credit rights or company shares can also be the object of property rights.

In what concerns environmental resources, not all of them can be owned. For instance, air, light, climate or biodiversity,[4] are not appropriable. On the contrary, they are generally recognized as *res communis* (common goods) because no one can be excluded from their fruition.

---

2 Article 9 e) of the Constitution.

3 Article 42.

4 Considered as a whole and not individual species.

But most environmental resources can indeed be owned. Among these, some resources are privately owned by the citizens while others belong to the State.

Citizens (individuals, associations, corporations) are the usual owners of many environmental goods, like forests, quarries, green areas. The State or other territorial authorities can also be owners of private possessions submitted to a legal regime similar to the private property.

The public property of the State is called public domain. In this context, private property is a residual concept: what does not belong to the State can be owned by the citizens.

The Constitution establishes the core list of environmental resources[5] belonging to the public domain.[6]

a) The territorial waters, the adjacent seabed, lakes, ponds and water streams (navigable or floatable), including the water beds;

b) The atmosphere above the aerial limits of property;

c) Mineral deposits, mineral-water sources, natural underground cavities (other than rocks, common soil and other materials commonly used for construction);

Public ownership of water resources deserves special attention, because after decades of uncertainty, in 2005, the law finally clarified the ownership criteria for water.[7]

The Public maritime domain belongs exclusively to the State and comprises:[8]

a) Coastal and territorial waters;

b) The internal waters subject to tidal influence, rivers, lakes and ponds;

c) The bed of the coastal and territorial waters and internal waters subject to tidal influence;

d) The adjacent seabed of the continental shelf, covering the entire exclusive economic zone;

e) The margins of coastal waters and internal waters subject to tidal influence.

The public domain of lakes and rivers[9] comprises:

a) Streams and beds of navigable or floatable water, as well as the respective banks belonging to public entities;

b) Lakes and beds of navigable or floatable water, as well as the respective banks belonging to public entities;

---

[5] A general inventory of the public goods belonging to the state can be found, in general, in Decree-law 477/80 of the 15th October. Ordinance 671/2000 of the17th April identifies in detail the different species of mobile and immobile public domain goods.

[6] The list can be enlarged by law. Indeed, there are laws determining the public character of the goods such as military real estate and assets, or the electrical grid.

[7] Decree-law 54/2005 of the 15th November.

[8] Article 3 and 4 of Law 54/2005 of the 15th November, on ownership of water.

[9] *Idem*, article 5 and 6.

c) Streams of non-navigable and non-floatable water (including beds and margins), as long as they are located on public lands, or which are recognized by law as usable for public purposes such as the production of electricity, irrigation, or extraction for public consumption;

d) Canals and waterways of navigable or floatable water, or built by public entities;

e) Reservoirs created for public purposes, including electricity generation or irrigation, including the beds;

f) Lakes, beds and banks of navigable or floatable water, formed by nature on public lands;

g) Lakes and ponds surrounded by private property or existing within private property, whenever fed by public water;

h) Streams of non-navigable and non-floatable water emerging in private property, as long as it flows into the sea or other public waters.

The remaining public water comprises:[10]

a) Water born or existing groundwater on public land or buildings;

b) Water emerging in private property (including rainwater), after transposing the boundaries of private land, as long as it flows into the sea or into other public waters;

c) Rainwater falling on public lands or flowing into them;

e) Water from public fountains, public wells and public reservoirs, including those continually being used by the public or operated by public entities;

Besides, considering the geographic situation of Portugal – a narrow strip[11] of land facing the Atlantic – and also due to climate change effects (storm tides and coastal erosion[12]) two situations are becoming increasingly important: receding waters and advancement of waters.

In case of receding waters,[13] the public beds that are left dry do not add to surrounding private property but rather remain integrated in the public property. Exceptionally, in cases of huge recession, the water bed can be transformed into private property of the State.

In case of advancement of waters,[14] the soil covered by water becomes automatically integrated in the public property of the State and the owners of surrounding private property lose their property without any right to compensation.

---

10 *Idem*, article 7 and 8.

11 Continental Portugal is 560 km long and 220 km wide. The global territorial area is around 92 200 km2, the coastal line is 1230 km long in the continent, 667 km in the Azores, and 250 km in Madeira.

12 In the meantime, human intervention tries to control the erosion by building jetties and adding dredged sand to the beaches, causing significant fluctuations of the coastal line requiring detailed criteria for the delimitation of public domain and private property.

13 *Idem*, article 13.

14 *Idem*, article 14.

If the waters recede again without causing any corrosion of the land, the private owners retain their property right, but the State can nevertheless, expropriate these parcels. In this case there will be compensation.

In areas threatened by the sea (whenever it is technically proven that the sea level will rise and cover private land beyond the margins[15]), as well as threatened by floods,[16] the Government may declare the place as 'adjacent area'. The extension of the 'adjacent area' is defined by a Ministerial Decree and in the case of flood, the outer limit is the maximum height reached by the largest flood with a return period of 100 years. If there are no records for flooding, the outer limit is the maximum height reached by the largest flood which can be remembered, or at least 100 meters for each side of the river. As a consequence, the adjacent areas remain private property, but can be subject to public utility restrictions such as the prohibition of:

- cutting or destroying vegetation or changing the natural topography (except for traditional agricultural activities in farms);
- creating dumps, scrap yards or other deposits of materials;
- constructing buildings or works which might obstruct the free movement of water;
- dividing the property below the minimum areas admissible for agriculture.

Any authorization breaching the mentioned prohibitions is null and void.

Finally, a transitional regime for historical possession of land adjacent to public water was conceived to settle likely disputes caused by the new legal regime adopted in 2005. It is possible to recognize the private ownership of parcels of sea margins and river banks (streams of navigable or floatable water) which, according to the normal legal criteria, should be public. This possibility depends on bringing an action before a court, until January 1 2014,[17] for the recognition of continuous private ownership of land. For this purpose the citizens must prove, by means of written documents, that such land was obtained legally, for private or collective use, before a Royal Decree on public ownership,[18] or, in the case of steep cliffs, before the entry into force of the first Civil Code.[19]

D. Management of Natural Resources

Since the paradigm of liberal property was left behind, the recognition that there are limits to the use of natural resources, both by the citizens and by the State, for environmental reasons, is common ground.

[15] *Idem*, article 22.

[16] *Idem*, article 23.

[17] *Idem*, article 15.

[18] The Royal Decree on public ownership was adopted in December 31, 1864.

[19] The first Civil Code entered into force on the 22nd March 1868.

1. Limitations to certain private property rights

In May 2014 a substantial legal change introduced new rules and clearer criteria on the relation between property and environment in what concerns the soil. The recent Basic Law[20] ruling the public policy on soils, spatial planning and urbanism[21] regulates the rights and duties of both the private and public owners of the national territory.[22]

The legal framework is based on a large set of principles. The general principles are: intra- and intergenerational solidarity, responsibility, efficiency, coordination, subsidiarity, equity, participation, contracting and legal certainty. The environmental principles are: sustainable development, prevention, precaution, transversality, integration, polluter-pays, liability, recovery.

The mandatory balancing of conflicting values is also present throughout the Law. In the framework of the spatial planning and urbanism legal relations, the right to private property and other rights over the soil are weighted and shaped by constitutionally protected principles and values, particularly in the fields of national defence, environment, culture and cultural heritage, landscape, public health, education, housing, quality of life and economic and social development.[23]

For the first time, the law proclaims the duties of the citizens in relation to the soil, the public domain goods and the collective infrastructures, side by side with their rights to use and benefit from them.

Citizens' duties in general are:

- to use the territory and the natural resources in a sustainable and rational way,
- to respect the environment, cultural heritage and landscape,
- to use correctly the public domain goods, public infrastructures, urban services, equipment, green spaces or other spaces for collective use; and
- to refrain from performing any acts or from developing any activities which pose a danger to them.

There are also specific duties of the owners,[24] when they are granted urbanization rights:

- to give away parts of his property for the implementation of infrastructures,

---

20 Only the Parliament (and not the Government) can approve so-called *Basic Laws* that establish the normative framework and legal principles applicable to some major public policies. Besides the Basic Law on soils, spatial planning and urbanism, there are also Basic Laws on the environment, maritime planning, education, health, social security, sports, cultural heritage, and so on. The Government is allowed subsequently to adopt ordinary laws to implement the Basic Laws.

21 Law on the public policy for soils, setting the framework for land use planning and urbanism (Law no. 31/2014 of May 30).

22 Excluding the national maritime area.

23 Article 4, no. 2 of the Basic Law on soils, spatial planning and urbanism.

24 In the case of waste law, the property owner can be responsible for the environmental damage caused by waste because he is the holder of waste and should therefore take the necessary measures to manage it

facilities, green spaces and other spaces for collective use, as required by law,
- to create infrastructures, green spaces and other spaces for collective use,
- to support the costs of construction, maintenance, reinforcement or renovation of infrastructure, equipment and public spaces,
- to minimize the level of exposure to collective risks.

Of course, the sacrifices imposed on owners of the soil, which have an effect equivalent to expropriation, shall be indemnified.

But it is not only the citizens who have duties. The State also has duties, such as planning soil use, ensuring equality and transparency in the exercise of citizen's rights and duties namely through the rights of access to information and to participation, ensuring sustainable use and preventing soil degradation, creating and preserving public areas for infrastructure, equipment, green spaces and other spaces for collective use, ensuring the economic sustainability of public equipment and infrastructures and enforcing rules on use, occupation and transformation of soil.

2. *Limitations to certain uses of public domain*

While private property can be sold, rented, lent, exchanged, etc., public domain cannot be sold or in any way transferred and even less acquired by possession (*usucapio*).[25]

Unlike private property, public domain resources do not allow the exclusion of others from the fruits of the good. On the contrary, it implies the right of collective use in order to serve for community benefit.

According to the Law on public domain,[26] the administration has the duty to control and stop any abusive behaviour, non-authorized uses,[27] or, in general, any uses which may affect the public interest performed by the public domain and restore the previous situation. This administrative injunction can be coercively imposed, if necessary.

Nevertheless, the individuals have the right to use the public domain in two ways:[28] in common and non-exclusive use (free of charge or paying), or in private use.

---

even if it was illegally deposited by a third unknown person on his property (article Decree-law 73/2011, of 17th June).

25 Article 18-20 of the Law on Public Property (Decree-law 280/2007 of the 7th August). There are cases of actions brought against the court asking for ownership recognition after decades of good faith possession of coastal public property. The decision of the court nevertheless is undoubted refusal (Supreme Court of Justice decision of the 26th February 2013 on case 41/06.4TBCSC.L1.S2).

26 Article 21 of Decree-law 280/2007 of the 7th August.

27 Supreme Administrative Court Case 23/09 of the 28th September 2010 on illegal urban construction on the public domain.

28 Articles 25 to 27 of the public domain Law.

In fact, the individuals may acquire rights for private use, management or operation[29] of the public domain by means of a license or concession. This right is always limited in time and requires the payment of fees.

The termination of the concession before the expiring date, for reasons attributable to the grantor, gives the operator the right to compensation for damages.[30] The compensation shall correspond to the costs incurred that are not yet amortized and the investments in goods inseparable from the public domain or in goods that will be too deteriorated after removal. Most of the investments made in the public domain cannot be removed and therefore remain public. An example can be a concession to build and exploit a harbour. When the concession has expired, the harbour may not be destroyed. It is handed over to the State or municipality (the grantor of the concession).

The termination of the concession after reaching the contracted deadline does not give any right to compensation.

E. Expropriation

The Constitution declares that requisition of property or expropriation for public purposes is only possible in the cases prescribed in the law[31] and upon just compensation. Nevertheless Portugal has been condemned by the European Court of Human Rights several times in cases related to property and takings. Expropriations (nationalization) without compensation, insufficient compensation and late compensation, were the claims against the Portuguese State, accepted by the European Court of Human Rights.[32]

---

29 Idem, article 30.

30 Idem, article 29.

31 The legal regime is the same regardless of the fact that the expropriation is determined by an internal act or by a legal act implementing an EU directive.

32 Case 43359/07, decided on the 22nd August 2008;cases 17199/05, 24311/05, 24315/05, 24674/05, 24677/05, 25946/05, 26244/05, 28628/05, 30793/05, 30850/05, 31044/05, 31066/05, 31348/05, 31706/05, 31781/05, 31784/05, 31793/05, 31807/05, 31809/05, 32267/05, 32269/05, 32270/05 and 33221/05 decided on the 23rd December 2008; case 24668/05 decided on the 30th December 2008; case 44386/05 decided on the 15th March 2009; case 25025/05 of 16th March 2009; case 31720/05 05 decided on the 10th May 2009; cases 30808/05, 31702/05, 32264/05, 34167/05, 34706/05, 34883/05, 35265/05, 35531/05, 36176/05, 37279/05, 39334/05,39335/05, 39340/05, 40408/05, 41368/05, 42122/05, 42181/05, 42202/05, 42560/05, 44229/05, 44243/05, 44462/05, 44558/05 and 45602/05 decided on the 3rd June 2009;case 1408/06 decided on the 15th March 2010; Case 10143/07 decided on the 11th April 2011; cases 8851/07, 8854/07, 8856/07, 8865/07, 10142/07, 10144/07, 24622/07, 32733/07, 32744/07, 41645/07, 19150/08, 22885/08, 22887/08, 26612/08, 202/09 decided on the 18th April 2011; case 16153/09, decided on the 16th June 2013; cases 23321/11, 71007/11 and 71014/11 decided on the 9th December 2013.

But the Constitution does not set any criteria[33] on the amount of compensation to be granted in cases of expropriation.

In the Expropriation Code in force,[34] a just compensation shall be granted not only in cases of expropriation of full property[35] but also in cases of expropriation of limited rights (art. 32) like usufruct, surface right, lease (art. 30), etc. or even for the interruption of commercial, industrial, liberal or agricultural activity (art. 31).

The just compensation for loss of property is to be calculated on the basis of soil classification. For this purpose, there are two types of soil: soil suitable for construction and soil for other purposes (art. 25).

There are five alternative criteria to know if the soil is suitable for construction:

- having road access;
- being connected to the three networks of water, electricity and sanitation;
- being located in an urban area if it is connected only to one of the previous networks of water, electricity or sanitation;
- being classified as such in a land management plan;
- having a valid building permit;

Having at least one of the above mentioned features is enough to classify the soil as suitable for construction, and therefore restrictions excluding construction on such lands must be compensated.

In the calculation of the compensation it is important to know that the fair compensation does not aim at 'compensating the benefit achieved by the expropriating authority but rather offsetting the harm caused to the owner by the expropriation' (art. 23). The value to be paid corresponds to the actual and present value of the good, according to its actual or possible destination, considering a normal economic use, and taking into account the circumstances and conditions existing at the date of the declaration of public utility (art. 23).

If there are no other ways to infer the value, then the value of the soil amounts to 15 % of the value of the construction admissible plus some additional percentages (1 % if it is connected to water supply, 1,5 % if it is connected to the waste water collection system, 1 % to the gas supply, etc.).

The soil value for other purposes is an average of the prices for similar goods in the neighbourhood in the last 3 years, considering the parameters set out in the territorial plans applicable. Whenever it is not possible to apply this criterion, the calculation will be based on alternative criteria such as the nature of the soil

---

33 Criteria such as 'market value', 'declared value' or 'real value' were avoided by the Constitution.

34 Law 56/2008 of the 4th September.

35 A much debated case in Portugal which will probably arrive at the European Court of Human Rights is the case of the demolition, for esthetic reasons, of a huge apartment block in the middle of an old city (Viana do Castelo) where 300 people are living. Urban landscape was the argument which led to the approval of the decision to demolish. The Supreme Administrative Court decided the case (775/13) on the 15th May 2013.

and subsoil, the configuration of the terrain, the actual or possible productivity, the predominant culture and climate of the region, or other objective circumstances likely to influence the calculation (art. 27).

However, this Law is about to change. A new Expropriation Code is under preparation and the draft version of the Law already shows some important innovations.

- It defines the concept of 'sacrifice expropriation'. This concept was first identified and defined by the doctrine and later applied in the courts (also called 'planning expropriations') but had no legal definition. In the future, the 'sacrifice expropriation' will be the result of a legal act, an administrative regulation or an administrative act which, without declaring the public utility, precludes the current use of the good or precludes any kind of use of the property, in cases where this is not being used, or annuls its economic value (art. 1/3 and article 8).
- It regulates the regime for expropriation of concessions or privileges. When the concession contract is terminated by the initiative of the grantor, all the infrastructures essential to the proper functioning of the service may be expropriated.
- It regulates the regime of public servitudes. In some cases, instead of expropriation, a public servitude may be enough to fulfil the public needs. In that case the servitude will give rise to compensation when the value or productivity of the good is actually diminished.
- It regulates the regime of public utility restrictions. In some cases not even a public servitude is necessary and a public utility restriction may be enough to fulfil the public needs. There will be compensation in the same cases as the sacrifice expropriation (when the current use or any kind of possible use of the good is precluded or the economic value is annulled) or of the public servitudes (the value or productivity of the good is actually diminished).

F. Restriction to Private Property

Besides expropriation and forced sale, there are softer administrative means of intervention in the private property of the soil, such as preemptive rights and administrative easements.[36] Whenever administrative easements are permanent and have a territorial expression likely to prevent or restrict land use, they are necessarily translated into territorial plans. If they have an effect amounting to an expropriation, payment of fair compensation is due under the law.

---

[36] Restrictions consisting on withdrawing public subsidies for budgetary reasons can be considered legal and in accordance with the Constitution and the Law. Due to the economic crisis, in 2013 and 2014, the Constitutional Court accepted temporary but severe social regression (such as lowering of salaries and pensions). In this context, the Court will easily accept the withdrawal of subsidies for budgetary reasons.

The reservation of private property land for urban infrastructure, equipment, green spaces and other spaces for collective use, determines the compulsory acquisition by the Public Administration or the reservation will expire after five years.

Besides, the law authorizes the establishment of public utility restrictions to private property rights in order to fulfil the public interest objectives of the soil policy. The restrictions may only be imposed by law and shall be laid down in territorial plans of municipal or intermunicipal scope.

Additionally, the sacrifice of preexisting and legally consolidated rights (such as building rights deriving from territorial plans in force) can only take place in cases expressly provided for by law or territorial plans (namely, whenever the revision of a territorial plan withdraws building rights) upon compensation or payment of damages, including through equalization mechanisms.

Finally, the new basic law repeats the constitutional obligation: any sacrifices imposed on owners of the soil which have an effect equivalent to expropriation shall be indemnified.

As the Supreme Administrative Court said in 2009, 'the right to private property is not an absolute right, and nothing prevents the law from imposing constraints on its exercise (...), provided that those restrictions do not outrage the Constitution, and provided that the restrictions are limited to "the extent necessary to safeguard other rights or interests also constitutionally protected"'.[37] In fact, environmental law imposes obligations both on the owner and on the user of natural resources, be it public or private.

Limitations on the right to use and enjoy one's property, duties to perform activities and to tolerate third parties activities are becoming more frequent.

There is even the possibility of criminal sanctions against the owner in case of intentional destruction of important natural values present in the property. In 2013 and 2014 two separated actions (administrative and criminal) were brought against a real estate developer for the intentional destruction of vegetation in a wetland in the south of Portugal, where he intended to build a touristic resort. He was condemned in both cases and obliged to restore the vegetation.

Some examples of restrictions to property use or legal activities required for environmental purposes, are the prohibitions to develop agricultural activities using certain techniques like drainage of wetlands or aerial spraying of chemicals[38] (fertilizers or biocides), prohibitions to fish, hunt or cut down trees,[39] constraints to the installation of radio antennas (transmitters),[40] the duty to clean the forests (remove the underwood and excess vegetation to avoid forest fires), the duty to declare (waste production, substantial changes in an occupational activity), duty to register (GMO production), to notify (mandatory notifica-

37 Case 403/2008, decision of the 4th February 2009 on a partial overlap of a touristic resort and a nature conservation area, the Natural Park Sintra-Cascais.

38 Supreme Administrative court case 370 of 10 February 2004.

39 Supreme Administrative Court Case 371/10 of the 22nd November 2011 on the cutting of cork trees.

40 Supreme Administrative Court Case 719/09 of the 28th January 2010.

tion of plagues, like the wood nematode, hives of African bees, or infestations of palm beetles), to provide guarantees (such as insurance, securities or bank deposits for the purpose of ensuring future environmental liability), to pay administrative fees,[41] to cooperate during environmental inspections and audits to the productive infrastructures, to tolerate access to the margins and water of the reservoir of a dam.[42]

In some cases the restrictions derive from the classification of the soil (in administrative regulations or plans) for nature conservation and for other socio-ecological purposes. This is the case of:

- Natura 2000 sites, SPAs, or SACs, areas belonging to the national network of conservation areas (national park, natural park, natural monument, protected landscape) and
- national ecologic reserve (NER) areas.

In the areas classified for nature conservation, activities disturbing the species or affecting considerably the habitat are forbidden. Exceptionally, in accordance with EU law, some activities may be authorized provided that there are no alternatives and that there is a major public interest behind the activity.

In the national ecologic reserve there are some restrictions, too. The NER reserve includes all the areas submitted to a special protection regime, considering their high ecological value and sensitivity as well as their intense exposition to natural risks.[43]

The objectives of the national ecologic reserve are:

- to protect natural resources like water and soil as well as to safeguard biophysical coastal and terrestrial hydrologic cycle processes, ensuring environmental services, which are essential to the development of human activities;
- to protect the recharge of aquifers, the risks of sea and river flooding, of soil erosion and mass movements, contributing to the adaptation to climate change, preserving environmental sustainability and the safety of persons and property;
- to contribute to the ecological coherence and connectivity of the Fundamental Network of Nature Conservation Areas;
- to contribute to the implementation of the priorities of the EU Territorial Agenda in ecological areas and to the trans-European risk management.

---

[41] Supreme Administrative Court Case 1600/13 of the 3rd April 2014, on the payment of fees for the installation of advertising posters in private property, near the roads. The purpose of the Law, by establishing the fee, is to protect the environment and the landscape.

[42] This is the case 220/05 of the 30th September 2009 on an interdiction of building vertical barriers in a private property bordering with a public artificial water reservoir (dam). The vertical barriers (walls or fences) would hamper the access of tourists to the margins and to the water.

[43] Article 2 of the Decree-law 166/2008 of the 22nd August.

The national ecologic reserve includes three kinds of areas: areas of coastal protection, areas relevant for the sustainability of the terrestrial hydrological cycle and areas of natural hazards.

For the conciliation of property rights with the protection conferred by the NER there is a Decree which goes into the minimal detail to define with absolute precision[44] which activities are allowed and which are not allowed.

Some of the limitations imposed by nature conservation laws and by the ecologic reserve are so huge that they are tantamount to expropriation. In that case, the rules on compensation will be applied.

Others are so weak that they do not give rise to any compensation. For instance, when only certain limited activities are interdicted while several others are still admitted.

That is also the case of strong interdictions (no construction and no extractive activities are admitted) in sites whose natural features are such that it would not be likely to carry out any economic use. It is the case of areas having a geologic substrate or morphology which makes them unsuitable for most uses (agriculture, construction...), such as sloping areas, river banks or coastal areas.

Considering that the compensation depends on the normal use of the soil, there was a big doctrinal discussion two decades ago on whether the owner's right automatically includes the right to build (*ius aedificandi*) or not. In several decisions the Supreme Administrative Court denied the recognition of an abstract *ius aedificandi* as a natural right of the owner regardless of the concrete *de facto* conditions of the soil.[45] According to the Supreme Court it is important to consider the natural features of the soil: there are soils with certain characteristics – instable, wet, sloping, and fluid – which are not suited for construction. In these cases the fact that construction is not admissible does not involve any compensation rights for the owner, considering what the authors call the 'situational binding of the soil'.[46] This means that it is the owner who has to bear the burden of a 'bad' location.

Still, the territorial administrative authorities (municipalities), where these areas are located, can be compensated for the 'ecological burden' *via* the distribution of the revenue of certain taxes (mostly VAT and income tax). According to the law on local finances[47] there are financial transfers from the State to the municipalities to provide them with the financial conditions necessary to the accomplishment of their duties. This transfer is proportional to the population

44 This legislative technique was the consequence of allegations of corruption in the application of the previous national ecologic reserve Law, dating back to the nineties.

45 For instance case 621/07 (decision of 04.12.08), case 390/06 (decision of 22.3.07); case 883/03 (decision of 14.12.2005); case 663/03 (decision of 18.2.2004); case 48.179 (decision of 7.3.2002), case 443/02 (decision of 9.10.2002), case 47.859 (decision of 3.12.2002); case 33 857 (decision of the 5.12.96).

46 In the words of the Supreme Administrative Court there will only be compensation rights if there are significant constraints equivalent to an expropriation of preexisting and legally consolidated rights to use the soil (case 996/06 of 20 June 2013 case 412/10 of 28 September 2010).

47 Article 28.

of the municipality but also to the municipal area consecrated to nature conservation.[48]

G. Environmental Protection *Against* Private Property

The most emblematic cases were raised before the Constitutional Court in 2001.

The first case[49] was raised by the owner of a quarry who was condemned to pay a fine for having proceeded extracting stone from the quarry after a dinosaur track was discovered and classified by law as natural monument.

He went on to the Constitutional Court claiming that his property right had been offended without compensation and thus he was entitled to go on with the activity he usually developed on his land. The Court declared that the fact of not having received any compensation does not allow him to go on with the extraction works in the quarry. The law on natural monuments established a total prohibition of activities consisting on changing the morphology of the soil or removing the vegetation cover. Furthermore, he had been warned by the National Institute for Nature Conservation to stop the illegal activity.

The second case[50] was raised by the owner of a dwelling built after a procedure of dubious legality in a natural park. The claimant, land owner in the park, argued that his property right allowed him to build on his land and therefore his right to housing was at stake due to the administrative order to demolish.

The Constitutional Court very clearly said that the demolition was not a disproportionate restriction to property. Building rights are not inherent to property rights but are rather granted by an administrative act in accordance with the territorial planning in force. In this case there was no administrative act so the building had to be torn down.

For the sake of comparability we will address two fictional cases of environmental damage caused by noxious activities where the right to property is likely to be used as an argument to maintain business as usual despite of the nuisance caused to the neighbours. Both cases represent typical situations, quite likely to occur anywhere. We will describe the possible solution in the Portuguese context.

---

48 Article 32 goes further into the details of the transfer: 5 % equally is distributed for all cities; 65 % in proportion to the population, 25 % in proportion to the area weighted considering the altimetry and 5 % in direct proportion of the area affected to the Natura 2000 network and other protected areas. For municipalities with more than 70 % of the territory dedicated to Natura 2000 network and other protected areas, the values are 20 % considering the altimetry and 10 % in direct proportion of the Natura 2000 and conservation area.

49 Case 57/01 of the Constitutional Court (decision of 23 October 2001).

50 Case 457/01 of the Constitutional Court (decision of 23 October 2001).

Solution to the case of Question 3:

The obligations of the State in such a case would be analysed in the context of environmental licensing. The national laws transposing the IPPC directive and more recently, the industrial emissions directive[51] make no provision for a category of gradual dissolution of vested rights without requirement of compensation for reasons of environmental protection. Nevertheless, the old industrial permits issued without a fixed term have been replaced by new environmental permits with a maximum time limit up to 10 years.

If, by the time the contamination is revealed, the end of the validity deadline would be close, the permit should not be renewed and, as a consequence, the installation would have to be shut down. If the end of the permit validity is not so close, the operating conditions can be reconsidered and updated or changed. In this case, an environmental inspection should be carried out with the mandatory cooperation of the operator. If a direct or indirect relation between the activity and the local pollution is revealed then the emission limit values set out in the permit should be revised and lowered (without prejudice to the liability actions to be brought against the operator if the breach of the license and the causal link between the industrial activities and the environmental damage became clear). If the environmental inspection reveals that the activity cannot fulfil the new conditions then the industrial installation should be closed down. Finally, the cessation of the activities and closure of the site should be followed by the necessary measures, taken by the operator, to return the site to an acceptable state.

In the described conditions, the factory owner could not claim any sort of property guarantee. Besides, the existence of a State permit does not exclude the holder from liability towards third persons in case of damage caused by undertakings although hopefully there will be an insurance contract to pay the damages.

Solution to the case of Question 9:

The law on landfills does not establish straight forward criteria for the location of waste disposal sites but leaves it to the administration to decide whether a certain location can pose a danger to residential, recreational, agricultural, urban areas or to waterways, water bodies, nature conservation areas, or natural and cultural heritage.[52] In a case such as the one described the neighbours would have to request the withdrawal of the operation permit, before claiming damages or compensation. Concerning state liability, there will only be compensation for government based environmental deteriorations of private property caused by unlawful measures in two cases: fault of the public officer or defective functioning of the public service.[53] In the case of a waste disposal site for danger-

[51] Decree-law 127/2013 of 30th August.

[52] Annex I 1 of Decree-law 183/2009, of 10th August.

[53] Article 7 of the Law 67/2007 of 31st December, modified by the Law 31/2008 of the 17th July, the Law on State liability.

ous waste, there could be State liability based on risk provided that the waste disposal site would be considered a 'particularly dangerous administrative service' except in case of *force majeur* or contribution of the victim to the damage.[54]

H. Environmental Protection *Through* Private Property

Finally, we will describe the cases in which noxious property uses can be labelled as abusive and limited on grounds of property rights of the neighbours.

Even some 'environmental uses' of property can be restricted when impairing the neighbours' property and also personality rights. Some examples are:

The noise and blinking shadow of windmills[55] was recognized as an offence both to absolute personality rights (the rights to enjoy one's property) and to property rights.[56]

The right to enjoy the landscape was declared to be a personality right and not an *in rem* right. It does not integrate the content of property right. The right to enjoy the landscape is everyone's right. Every citizen, regardless of being property owner or not, has the right to enjoy the landscape.[57]

The right to develop an industrial activity (pig farming, for instance) in one's property is not inherent to a property right. A property right is not an absolute right, but it is not an abusive use of property as well.[58] The use of one's property for goat breading is not a normal use of property in an urban area.[59]

The right to develop a certain economic activity (noise produced to keep sparrows away from a vineyard)[60] does not prevail over personality rights, such as the right to live in a quiet environment. These are absolute rights which prevail over property rights.

Depreciation of property, aesthetic damages, and health risk are arguments also raised against projects like poles of high electricity voltage.[61]

I. Conclusion

The relation between property and the environment is getting more and more complex as an ever growing block of legal restrictions limit the right to private use of property and the possible uses of public domain.

---

54 Article 11 of the Law on State liability.

55 Supreme Court of Justice decision of 30 May 2013 on case 2209/08.0TBTVD.L1.S1.

56 The windmill was next to a bullfighter's knight farm.

57 Supreme Court of Justice decision of 6 September 2011 on case 111/09.7TBMRA.E1.S1.

58 Supreme Court of Justice decision of 27 March 2007 on case 07A400.

59 Supreme Court of Justice decision of 28 June 2004 on case 04B4781.

60 Supreme Court of Justice decision of 15 March 2007 on case 07B585.

61 Supreme Court decision of 961/09 of 11 February 2010.

After the denial of *ius abutendi*, now it's the *ius utendi et fruendi* which are at stake under the influence of sustainable development, both at the European and at the national level.

References:

- Canotilho, José Joaquim Gomes – 'O Caso da Quinta do Taipal: protecção do ambiente e direito de propriedade', *Revista de Legislação e Jurisprudência*, ano 128, nº3850-3851, Maio 1995.
- Canotilho, José Joaquim Gomes; Moreira, Vital – *Constituição da República Portuguesa Anotada*, vol I, Coimbra Editora, 2007.
- Capitão, Gonçalo – *Expropriação e ambiente*, Editora Lusíada, Lisboa, 2004.
- Correia, Fernando Alves – *Manual de Direito do Urbanismo*, vol. I, II e III, Almedina, Coimbra, 2008-2010.
- Fernandez, Maria Elisabeth – *Direito ao Ambiente e Propriedade Privada*, Coimbra Editora, Coimbra, 2001.
- Moniz, Ana Raquel Gonçalves – *Domínio Público. O Critério e o Regime Jurídico da Dominialidade*, Almedina, Coimbra, 2005.
- Pâques, Michel (ed.) – *Natura 2000 and Property Rights. International and National Reports*, Bruylant, Brussels, 2005.
- Passinhas, Sandra – 'Portuguese Property Law', Boletim da Faculdade de Direito, vol. LXXXI, Coimbra, 2005.
- Silva, Vasco Pereira da – *Verde Cor de Direito. Lições de Direito do Ambiente*, Almedina, Coimbra, 2003.

Property and Environmental Protection in Slovenia

Rajko Knez

A. Objects of Private Property

The regulatory regime of property is defined, in general, in the Constitution of the RS.[1] The approach used is not self-sufficient: Art. 67 foresees that it is the legislator that defines what exactly the property is, how it is described, how the property can be obtained and what the benefits, i.e. *implied* rights, of the property are. At the same time, the mentioned provision defines that property is *limited by its commercial, social and ecological function.*[2] It is therefore for the legislator to define the actual content of 'property' and this is not done by the Constitution itself.

According to private law rules, property can be obtained not only on real objects but also on rights, especially private law rights. On the other hand, there are objects that are excluded from property. This is especially true for objects that are defined as *public goods*, which might be *natural public goods* or *constructed public goods*. Natural resources, generally speaking, are not objects of public rights; they are public goods, belonging to all, to the community, the State being entrusted to manage them.[3] But from the constitutional point of view, property comprehends also rights, market shares, etc. It is not only real things that are objects of property, although real things, especially immovable, are having some special rules (for instance that limitation in the use or ownership of the immovable is subject to compensation; Art. 69).

However, it is common that legal language refers only to rights, not to property in the above sense. For instance, certain official documents awarding an allowance to a person (like an environmental permit), will be treated as an *acquired* or *vested* right, although not as a property right. If somebody has a permit to build a certain construction, that right cannot be used as a property that would outweigh environmental protection measures.

B. Private Property in Natural Resources

Rights to use natural resources are primarily given to the State alone, because, as noted above, natural resources are public goods.[4] However,

---

1 Ustava RS, Official Journal of the RS, Nr. 33-1409/1991I, RS 42-2341/1997, RS 66-3052/2000, RS 24-899/2003, RS 69-3092/2004, RS 69-3090/2004, RS 69-3088/2004, RS 68-2951/2006.

2 Article 67, (Property): 'The manner in which property is acquired and enjoyed shall be established by law, so as to ensure its economic, social, and environmental function.
The manner and conditions of inheritance shall be established by law.'

3 Therefore, if natural resources are part of certain spot, which is in private property, the owner is not entitled to use that natural resource without a permission i.e. the concession, and this is part of the constitutional limitation of the property rights due to the ecological reasons.

4 According to the Environmental Protection Act (EPA), a natural resource shall mean any component of the environment which is subjected to economic exploitation / commercially exploited. This is a definition in Art. 3 of the EPA, Official Journal of the RS, 41-1694/2004, RS 17-629/2006, RS 20-745/2006,

the State authorities (and also local authorities) can award rights to exploit natural resources. Under Art 164 of the Environmental Protection Act (EPA) the state, or a municipality, may award, against payment, concessions to use or to exploit natural assets to a legal or natural person when that person is qualified to exercise that concession. Concessions are awarded for a certain period of time but not more than 30 years. This is for instance true for concessions to exploit forests in Slovenia.

It was, until recently, a general trend to award concessions, also in cases where the state or municipality owned (public) company could have exploited the natural resource. This practice was followed also by the *Statute on Private-Public Partnerships*,[5] which makes obligatory, under Art 141, for all public companies to reorganize in two ways: they can be 100% owned by the state/municipalities or they can be organized as private companies. A substantive number of former public companies became private and they asked for concessions. This way the state/municipalities lost certain control embodied in the public companies, but most importantly, the public interest was replaced for the private one.

Private interests in using the natural resources are, as we are evidencing now in Slovenian practice, not welcomed; the Court of Auditors of the RS is also very critical in its assessment to the concession's approach. The Court of Auditors estimates that approximately 16 mil EUR is lost every year due to the inefficiency of the system.[6] The system of concessions is therefore not found appropriate by the Court of Auditors. The concessions will end on 2016 and the court proposes to the legislator to adopt a new approach, i.e. a new, more efficient system that would enable more sustainable treatment of natural resources.

C. Private Property Used in Defense of Environmental Protection

There are, legally speaking, several possibilities to invoke private property for or also against environmental protection. In private law enforcement, an individual can rely on property as a defence against activities of other persons, who might be neighbours or any third persons (like companies, i.e. factories, investors, also perhaps against activities of an army (like military exercises), also against actions of hunters; i.e. against everybody that is not included in the notion of the State. Actions can be legally based on a provision of so called 'neighbouring law' (like nuisance), or in *actio popularis*. The latter is well framed in the Civil Code (Article 133). It reads:

RS 49-2089/2006, RS 66-2856/2006, RS 33-1761/2007, RS 57-2416/2008, RS 70-3026/2008, RS 108-4888/2009, RS 48-2011/2012, RS 57-2415/2012, RS 92-3337/2013.

5 Official Journal of the RS, No 127/2006.

6 Report of the Court of Auditors of the RS, of 18 May 2012, Directing forests in Slovenia, Nr. 321-2/2010/93, available http://www.rs-rs.si/rsrs/rsrs.nsf/I/K38B07CAD3EAF5421C1257A000030F18C/$file/Gozd_SP09.pdf.

> (1) Any person may request that another person dispose of a source of danger that threatens major damage to the former or an indeterminate number of persons and refrain from the activities from which the alarm or risk of damage derives, if the occurrence of alarm or damage cannot be prevented by appropriate measures.
>
> (2) At the request of an interested person the court shall order appropriate measures to prevent the occurrence of damage or alarm or to dispose of a source of danger to be taken at the expense of the possessor thereof should the latter fail to do so.
>
> (3) If damage arises during the performance of generally beneficial activities for which permission has been given by the relevant authority it shall only be possible to demand the reimbursement of damage that exceeds the customary (usual) boundaries.
>
> (4) Nevertheless, appropriate measures to prevent the occurrence of damage or to reduce damage may also be demanded in such a case.

This action can be used also in cases where the State issues permission for activities that are harmful to the environment and private property; in these cases, only measures that can prevent or reduce the damage are possible.[7] However, the action cannot be brought towards the state (administrative authorities) to change or to annul permissions, but only to private parties. Procedures against the State can be brought in different procedures. An owner, that can prove his property being affected by activities, harmful to the environment, and whereby the permission was issued, can claim, first in the administrative procedure and later on with a lawsuit at the administrative court to change or to annul the permission. It is not so rare that environmental NGOs are filing such actions, helping at the same time an individual owner who is usually *one-shot player,* i.e. mostly not being in position to search for legal protection against the State measures at courts. NGOs are, on the other side, often parties (plaintiffs) seeking state's measures to be changed. On the other side, it is a different approach against private investors, relying only on civil law measures. Namely, state measures, general and individual, like permissions, are still those that, in the first place, allow activities; no private action to stop activities would be successful, if the State authorities allow certain activities. It is therefore, first, necessary to change the state's rules or measures.

Another, rather important feature in private law actions is also a standard of '*usual boundaries*'; only if damages exceed that boundary, the legal defense is possible. This 'case-by-case' approach brings certain legal uncertainty and it can be a difficult task for the court to define it in particular cases. For instance, is it bad odour because of the farm, something that is within the limits of usual boundaries in rural areas.

---

7 Burden of proof is in Slovene law, in case of dangerous activities, where the strict liability applies, on the defendant. In case of the strict liability, Slovene law foresees the burden of proof in the sphere of the party being engaged in the dangerous activities. Taking together *actio popularis* and the reverse burden of proof, Slovene law makes for the plaintiff rather acceptable procedural position.

How would the following case be treated in Slovenia?

A factory, situated near a town, has been operating for decades. People are slowly realizing that statistically the inhabitants in the city and in the vicinity do not live average age and the cancer is more frequently present among them, also the frequent cause of the deaths. They have no direct proofs that the factory could be responsible, although it is rather clear that the soil around the factory is poisoned and that the heavy metals found in the vegetable could be linked to the factory. However, credible proofs are missing. What could be the obligation of the state? Could the inhabitants rely on the public remedies procedure? If the state wants to revoke the operation permit, could the factory claim any sort of property guarantee?

The State shall check the procedure and the best available techniques (BAT) in the factory. There are possibilities for state authorities (inspectors) to investigate and to search for proofs. In case they find necessary proofs, they can impose measures (*restitutio integrum*, ban the production, change of the production techniques). However, the state inspector will not demand the factory to compensate damages to individuals. That has to be claimed by individuals alone (private law remedies). The public remedies procedure will be essential for inhabitants (sufferers), since it will be unlikely for them to obtain necessary proofs themselves. Although the courts under private law remedies procedures are not bound by decisions and findings of executive authorities, but usually they follow them or take them into account.

If the State revokes the operation permit for reasons of noncompliance, there is no right for the operator arising out of the property guaranty. As explained above, a permit cannot be used against mandatory provisions on environmental protection. From this point of view, the permit will not be seen as a guaranteed property. The sole goal of the permit is to allow the factory to operate. However, even though the factory is in line with the permit, damage might be caused. The state, although it issued the permit, is not responsible and the factory cannot rely on the permit and exclude itself from the obligation to compensate for damage. However, if the operation permit is revoked for any ground which is in the sphere of the State and whereby the operator is not liable for the revocation, then the operator is entitled for compensation.

D. Natural Resources as Public Property or Interest

According to Arts. 5, 70 and 73 of the Constitution the State is responsible to safeguard and administrate natural resources. Natural resources are public goods; there is no private ownership. While this is not explicitly expressed either in the Constitution of the RS or in the statutes, the Constitution Court has clearly ruled to that effect, interpreting that land can be public good if, either so defined in the law or if it is obvious that land aims to be used by anybody under the same conditions.[8/9] It is the duty of the State to adopt rules for proper safeguard of natural resources, to supervise and also, importantly, to act in cases of pollution, environmental strain, (possible) environmental damage, taking preventive and curative actions in case of inactivity of the polluter or in case the polluter is not known (which is called subsidiary duty). Most of these duties are defined in the EPA.

E. Property in Public Aids for Beneficial Use of Natural Resources

Subsidization itself is a subject of a decision of the State (Agency for Energy in case of feed-in-tariff). Subsidization is usually possible only in the transparent procedure and therefore it is open to competition. Once awarded, it can also be changed. In case of green energy the approach is different. The government is entitled to adopt rules – who, which facility is entitled to the subsidy and how much subsidy is given.[10] This is exactly so in case of feed in tariffs. The *Energy Act*[11] determines that executive authorities are entitled to regulate, on annual basis, the level of subsidization. It is also up to the Government to increase/decrease not only the level of the subsidization, but also change tendering criteria for subsidization, etc. It cannot, therefore, be said that subsidization is construed as a property right in the Slovenian legal system in absolute terms. It is true that the facility, which fulfils the legal requirements, has a right to apply for a subsidy, but the Government can easily change the requirements (with no retroactive effect).

F. Expropriation

Expropriation is, among others, regulated in the *Spatial Management Act*.[12] The part of the act that regulates expropriation is based on the Constitutional provision on expropriation; Art. 69 of the *Constitution* defines that '*Ownership rights to real estate may be revoked or limited in the public interest with the provision of compensation in kind or monetary compensation under conditions established by law.*' On that basis, it is possible, according to Art. 93 of the *Spatial Management Act*, to expropriate the owner also in cases of public commercial infrastructure. That means that, for instance, in the case of renewable

8 Decision of the Constitutional Court of teh RS, No U-I-176/94-16, of 5.10.1995.

9 Par. 11 of the above Constitutional Court judgment. Also civil courts are following this decision. See also Order of the Supreme Court Sklep II Ips 347/2005 of 16.3.2006.

10 Regulation on supports for the electricity generated from renewable energy sources, Official Journal of the RS, No 37/09, 53/09, 68/09, 76/09, 17/10, 94/10, 43/11, 105/11, 43/12, 90/12 and 17/14 – EZ-1).

11 Official Journal of the RS, No 17/2014, of 7. 3. 2014.

12 Official Journal of the RS, Nr. 110/02, 8/03 – popr., 58/03 – ZZK-1, 33/07 – ZPNačrt, 108/09 – ZGO-1C and 80/10 – ZUPUDPP).

energy infrastructure, such a condition would be fulfilled. It suffices that there are official plans for the public infrastructure, at the level of the State or local spatial plans. Once such plans are adopted, the public interest is to be presumed. There is also a special act for the infrastructure of national importance.[13] This act is even stricter for the owner and favours the investments in infrastructures. It determines in Art. 47: '*When, within 30 days following upon the service of the offer for the sale of real estate or for the acquisition of rights over real estate, an investor does not manage to conclude an agreement, upon the proposal of an investor the State shall immediately file a proposal for expropriation or for the restriction of the rights of ownership.*' This rule is applicable for different infrastructure: roads, railways, transport terminals, air transport terminals, border crossings, water infrastructure etc. It is only necessary that the project is part of infrastructure and that is included in the spatial acts at the State level.

The procedure for expropriation can be initiated by the State or by the local communities (municipalities). The authority, competent to decide in the expropriation matters, is the Ministry for the Environment. The decision of the Ministry is final but can be a subject of a court's supervision, i.e. in a dispute at the administrative court.

The Slovene legal system formerly had a different approach, where courts were competent to decide on expropriations. It has now been several years since this was not in the competence of courts but of executive authorities. Courts are only competent in cases where either party would like to annul the final decision taken by executive authorities.

G. Indirect Expropriation by Environmental Regulation?

Regulatory restrictions to use property are possible. The general rule is that restrictions, even those in the public interests, are to be compensated. This derives from Art. 69 of the Constitution, which determines that compensation (in kind or monetary compensation) shall be assured in cases of expropriation. However, in practice, in such cases the State would rather buy certain land for purposes of State interest (like for instance roads, motorways, etc.). Expropriation is an option of the last resort. In cases where infrastructure is needed and buying-off the land or the expropriation are not proportional solutions, the State or municipalities can agree with the owner to use the property (they conclude contracts on use). It is also possible that courts define necessary restrictions of the property like inevitably allowance to use private property (for instance, if somebody needs access to his plot of land and that is only possible by using the (neighbouring) plot of other owner. The latter, if there is no other possibility of the access; have to allow crossings of his plot). The *Property Act*[14] also

[13] The Act Regarding the Siting of Spatial Arrangements of National Significance in Physical Space (ZUPUDPP), Official Journal of the RS, No.

[14] Official Journal of the RS, Nr. 87-4360/2002, RS 91-3303/2013, RS 17-540/2014.

defines that appropriate reimbursement shall be paid to the owner of the land, which serves for the crossing (or also other purposes).

On the other hand, certain valuable natural resources can be specially protected. Notably, the *Law on Nature Conservation*[15] defines specially protected areas (SPA), besides Natura 2000 protected areas, which are subject to a special regime, whereby the use of private property can be restricted. In these cases the owners are not entitled to the compensation, but the whole area would usually gain public economic help for different purposes. That way regulatory restrictions would be outweighed by the State financial investment in these areas.

H. Dissolution of Property for Environmental Protection

According to the law, vested rights need to be respected; the *Constitution* prohibits retroactive effects.[16] It is also determined in the *Constitution*, that ownership rights of real estate may be revoked or limited only in the public interest and with the provision of compensation in kind or monetary compensation under conditions established by law.[17] This is, however, only a special provision in case of immovables. Generally speaking, this is not the approach for other rights. For instance the Slovene Constitutional Court adopted a different solution in the case of social rights. Because Slovenia was faced with the financial crises, the Slovenian government decided to balance public expenses with the public revenue. A special statute, the *Fiscal Balance Act* was adopted for this reason[18] and its rules touch upon quite a number of social rights, like optional in stead of mandatory retirement, social financial transfers, subsidization for social housing, subsidization of students nourishment; etc. The *Fiscal Balance Act* therefore limits and restricts different rights that are financed by the State. Some parts of the act were challenged at the Constitutional Court. Annulments were sought maintaining that vested rights were not respected. However, for the first time, the Constitutional Court decided that severe economic financial circumstances in the country justify restrictions of vested rights.[19] The Court added that restrictions shall be proportional and that there should be a certain time limit for the introduction of restrictions of vested rights.

---

15 Official Journal of the RS, Nr. 56-2655/1999, RS 31-1/2000, RS 119-5832/2002, RS 41-1693/2004, RS 61-2567/2006, RS 32-1223/2008, RS 8-254/2010.

16 Art. 155.

17 Art. 69.

18 Fiscal Balance Act, Official Journal of the RS, Nr. 40/12, 96/12 – ZPIZ-2, 104/12 – ZIPRS1314, 105/12, 25/13 – odl. US, 46/13 – ZIPRS1314-A, 56/13 – ZŠtip-1, 63/13 – ZOsn-I, 63/13 – ZJAKRS-A, 99/13 – ZUPJS-C, 99/13 – ZSVarPre-C, 101/13 – ZIPRS1415 in 101/13 – ZDavNepr).

19 U-I-13/13, of 14.11.2013.

The same is also true for subsidising green electricity. In 2014, the new *Energy Act*[20] was adopted and that law empowers the Government to change the level for subsidies for green electricity in accordance with the circumstances on the market, public, finances, etc. This is not done in a clear way, but rather only with the fact that subsidization is subject of the rules adopted by the Government, not by the legislator.

In the field of the environment, things are no different. It is necessary to outweigh the right which is at stake with other rights (principle of proportionality). A decision of the Constitutional Court[21] is one such an example: 'A measure adopted by a municipality and regulating the navigation on the waterways within the territory of this municipality on the basis of the law and comprising certain local and other limitations of the usage of water as an asset in common use is not in conflict with the law. In regulating the navigation, a municipality is authorized to prescribe, apart from the conditions stipulated by the law, also other conditions which safeguard human life and the environment.' This clearly indicates that limitation of rights due to the environmental reasons are possible, but it is necessary to take into account the nature of the right that is reason for limitation of the property and other rights and also that the principle of proportionality is respected.

I. State Liability for Environmental Damage to Private Property

An exemplary case: A communal waste disposal site is located not far away from a place with appr. 150 individual houses. Inhabitants assert that they smell bad odour and they would like to sell their property, but, of course, there are no potential buyers. Their property is almost worthless. The waste disposal site is equipped with the necessary permits. Are the inhabitants in the neighbourhood entitled to compensation (perhaps to annual revenue)? Do they have to search for withdrawal of the operation permit first?

There are legal remedies under public and private law. In case of harm caused to inhabitants, they can, within private law remedies, use *actio popularis*[22] to require the operator to improve a waste disposal site with necessary measures to reduce the bad odour. *Actio popularis* can be invoked by anybody that suffers damage and it makes possible to start a procedure against the person (operator) responsible for the danger. It is further on up to the rules of the civil liability, if the inhabitants will have to prove cause and produce evidence; if the activity can be regarded as dangerous, a strict liability system will apply and it will be up to the operator to exclude himself from the liability, meaning that he, not the plaintiffs (inhabitants), will have to produce evidence. In case of fault-based liability

---

20 Official journal of the RS, Nr. 17/14.

21 U-I-3/92 of 17/9-1992.

22 Art. 133 of the Slovene Obligation Code.

this will be, on the contrary, the burden of the plaintiffs. Most likely, due to the nature of the activity of the dumping site, the strict based liability will be applied in the case.

If the State issued a permit for the disposal site and the odour is inappropriate (there are no odour limits set in Slovenian legal order; but the case can be regarded as 'a-normal'[23]), the inhabitants can claim measures that will reduce the odour. But they cannot claim to close the site down. The fact that property loses its value is also a reason for compensation. The withdrawal of the permit is not a precondition for compensation, but it is of substantial help, since one of the conditions for the compensation is also a proof of violation of the law. If the permit remains valid it is necessary to prove its violation or noncompliance.

With respect to legal remedies in the public interest, inhabitants can give notice of the problem at stake to the state inspectorate. This body is under a duty to start the procedure if a public health issue is at stake (i.e. if there is no pure private relationship). The inspector can order the facility to close or to remedy, i.e. reduce the odour. Inhabitants are not parties to this procedure, but are witnesses. If they want to claim compensation they have to initiate a parallel procedure or wait until the administrative procedure is closed and then use the decision of this procedure to prove liability of the operator.

Constitutional remedies are possible once the regular courts procedures (administrative or private) have been exhausted.

J. Proprietor's Liability for Environmental Damage

The answer here is positive. One can be responsible for (environmental) damage only because one owns the property. According to Art. 157.a of the *Environmental Protection Act* the owner of the property shall bear the costs for the restitution (*restitutio integrum*) of the land in question, in case the polluter cannot be find or cannot be identified. So far, the courts did not find this solution contrary to the Constitution of the RS or to Art. 1, Protocol 1 of the ECHR or to the EU rules or even to the principle of proportionality. There are, however, different views present on that legal framework among the scholars.

K. Permit Excuse in Environmental Liability

The permits issued by the State, in general, do not exclude a holder of such a permit from the liability toward third persons. A permit is understood only as permission by the State for the holder of a permit to perform certain activities, use dangerous substances, etc. However, any kind of damage

[23] This is a question of a standard of 'usual boundaries' – in another words, what is normally accepted and what is not. As noted above this is not an easy task of the court. Due to the difficulties to foresee the reaction of the court (legal foreseeability), plaintiffs are not always keen to bring an action.

caused by the holder to third persons is not covered by the permit, neither the permit derogates the responsibility of the holder. This is also seen from the implementation of the Directive 2004/35/EC of the European Parliament and of the Council of 21 April 2004 on environmental liability with regard to the prevention and remedying of environmental damage. This directive makes possible, under Art. 8, that Member States may allow the operators who are not at fault or negligent not to bear the cost of remedial measures, in situations where the damage in question is the result of emissions or events explicitly authorised. This is the option given to the Member States to exclude the holder of a permit from the liability toward third persons. This option was not adopted in Slovenia. The Directive is implemented in the EPA, however without the option mentioned.

Even more, in certain cases (construction) investors are not allowed to start with construction, if the building permit is not final. That means that no court remedies are possible any more. The finality obtained in the administrative procedure (within executive authorities) is not enough. If the investor would like to start with the construction despite that, he will have to bear the consequences in case the court annuls such state permit (Art. 3 of Construction Act).[24]

L. Direct or Indirect Expropriation by EU Measures

I am not aware of any such cases. I presume the approach would be the same. The EU rules enter the national legal order also due to Slovene Constitution (Art. 3a): 'Legal acts and decisions adopted within international organisations to which Slovenia has transferred the exercise of part of its sovereign rights shall be applied in Slovenia in accordance with the legal regulation of these organisations.' The EU has no rule in this respect. It is true that the EU can be responsible for the damage caused, but EU does not demand expropriations. It might be that the EU rules have an effect to property rights and their limitation, but this does not mean that the EU is responsible. If the MS adopts rules that limits property rights, the case will be dealt with as noted above, according to Art. 15 of the Slovene Constitution, i.e. *the principle of proportionality* and weighing of the interest of the two rights that collide.

[24] Construction Act (Zakon o graditvi objektov), Uradni list RS, št. 102/04 – uradno prečiščeno besedilo, 14/05 – popr., 92/05 – ZJC-B, 93/05 – ZVMS, 111/05 – odl. US, 126/07, 108/09, 61/10 – ZRud-1, 20/11 – odl. US, 57/12, 101/13 – ZDavNepr in 110/13.

Property and Environmental Protection in Spain

Agustin Garcia-Ureta

A. Objects of Private Property

The Spanish Civil Code of 1889 defines property in wide terms ('Ownership is the right to enjoy and dispose of a thing, without greater limitations than those set forth in the laws').[1] However, the Civil Code also acknowledges the existence of limitations. Article 33.1 of the 1978 Constitution admits the right *to* property but it does not provide a definition. Article 33 reads: '1. The right to private property and inheritance is recognised. 2. The social function of these rights shall determine the limits of their content in accordance with the law. 3. No one may be deprived of his or her property and rights, except on justified grounds of public utility or social interest and with a proper compensation in accordance with the law'. The Spanish Constitution neither guarantees ownership rights on any types of goods nor designates their material scope.[2] In fact, Article 128.1 sets out that the entire wealth of the country in its different forms, irrespective of ownership, shall be subordinated to the general interest. This aspect is also clearly stated in the 1954 Expropriation Law, which refers to any form of singular dispossession of private property or of legitimate interests without establishing any classification as to the range of properties that may be affected by such powers. Therefore, the Constitutional Court has indicated that expropriation powers extend to all kinds of rights and patrimonial interests justified by a diversity of public and social purposes. Despite the variety of properties, the Constitution provides a notion that affects all possible types [i.e., its 'core content' (*contenido esencial*) (Article 53.1)] and that must be respected by the legislator unless an expropriation (with compensation) takes place.[3] The core content refers to the essential characteristics of a fundamental right without which it could no longer be conceived as such,[4] i.e., the rights of use, enjoyment and disposal parallel to Article 17 of the EU Charter of Fundamental Rights.

No properties are protected from environmental laws, including those under military rules. However, certain pieces of legislation (as interpreted by the courts) grant much more significance to certain goods in cases requiring a balance of interests between, on the one hand, the environment and, on the other hand, development. Four cases may illustrate this state of affairs.

1) The exploitation of mining resources has traditionally taken priority over natural areas, the rationale being the need to guarantee the supply of those resources. However, it should be noted that this ruling from the Constitutional Court was adopted in 1982 before Spain's accession to the EU.[5]

2) Nonetheless, in 2014 the Constitutional Court held that the Autonomous Communities are not entitled to resort to more protective environmental measures under Article 149.1.23 of the Constitution to ban the use of hydraulic frac-

1 Article 348.

2 Constitutional Court Judgment (CCJ) 37/1987.

3 CCJ 204/2004.

4 CCJ 11/81.

5 CCJ 64/1982.

ture (*fracking*) because this contradicts the competence of the State on energy matters.[6]

3) The authorisation of energy installations, i.e., windmills, and the supply of electricity have been conceived as 'essential to the functioning of society' albeit the production of electricity must be reconciled with the protection of the environment. In the Supreme Court's view wind power is one of the most advanced technologies and its implementation constitutes a legal and social priority. This standpoint has been held to reject appeals against authorisations for the execution of those installations in spite of their environmental effects on wildlife.[7]

4) Coastal protection legislation exemplifies the limits of the myth of the public domain as a tool for environmental protection. Neglecting some of the acute current problems deficiently tackled by Law 29/1988,[8] the 2013 reform (Law 2/2013) allows concessions on the maritime public domain for a period that has been extended to 75 years (a majority of existing concessions were to expire by 2019).

B. Private Property in Natural Resources

A concession is conceived in Spanish law as a transfer to an individual of a function or a good originally attributed to a public authority (e.g., the authorization for the extraction of water, to build a public work, to exploit mineral resources; to storage CO2 or for the occupation of the marine-terrestrial public domain among others). In this sense concessions can be conceived as property titles. This legal nature is reinforced by the fact that a concession limits the number of possible beneficiaries. By contrast, authorisations do not normally attribute rights on goods. They rather allow for the carrying out of an activity previously prohibited, e.g., the management of a waste disposal site. However, the differences between concessions and authorisations have been blurred in recent years. In general terms, the case law has pointed out that neither concessions nor authorisations have a homogenous treatment. Their content and scope will largely depend on the applicable legal regime.

6 CCJ 106/2014; CCJ 134/2014.

7 Agustín García-Ureta, 'Evaluación de impacto ambiental y proyectos de parques eólicos: balance de intereses, Red Natura 2000 y aspectos procedimentales' (2014) Actualidad Jurídica Ambiental <www.actualidadjuridicaambiental.com/wp-content/uploads/2014/07/2014_07_01_Garcia_Ureta_EIA.pdf>.

8 Approximately more than fifty per cent of beaches and seventy per cent of dunes on the Spanish coast are degraded or profoundly altered; more than sixty per cent of the immediate surroundings of the beaches of the Southern Mediterranean, Atlantic coasts and archipelagos are urbanized. With the rhythms of occupation followed in the last sixty years, including the three periods of economic recession, by 2030 the entirety of the Spanish coast will be affected by human activities; Miguel Angel Losada, 'La destrucción de las playas españolas', El País (20 August 2010) at 21.

C. Private Property Used in Defense of Environmental Protection

An exemplary case: A factory, situated near a town, has been operating for decades. People are slowly realizing that statistically the inhabitants in the city and in the vicinity do not live to an average age and the cancer is more frequently present among them, also the frequent cause of the deaths. They have no direct proofs that the factory could be responsible, although it is rather clear that the soil around the factory is poisoned and that the heavy metals found in the vegetable could be linked to the factory. However, credible proofs are missing. What could be the obligation of the state? Could the inhabitants rely on the public remedies procedure? If the state wants to revoke the operation permit, could the factory claim any sort of property guarantee?

The employment of private property for the defence of the environment depends *inter alia* on town and country planning legislation. State Land Law (Royal Legislative Decree 2/2008) defines rural lands as those preserved from urban sprawl by territorial and town plans. This category embraces at least lands excluded from such transformation by legislation concerning the public domain, nature protection, cultural patrimony; or lands that must be protected owing to their values, e.g., ecological, agricultural, cattle, forestry, or landscaping. Owners of rural lands have to protect terrains and vegetation to avoid risks of erosion, fire, flood, risks for public security or health, damage to third parties or to the general interest, including the environment. They also have to prevent soil, water or air pollution and maintain the operation of services derived from uses and activities developed on those terrains. The aforementioned obligations (largely enshrined in previous urban Laws and regulations) have not however avoided the continuous degradation of the environment in the last decades. Further restrictions on property rights are also included in Law 42/2007, on the natural patrimony and biodiversity. In the case of nature protected areas management plans prevail over the instruments concerning spatial, urban, and in general physical planning. The latter can only contradict or not integrate the content of natural resources management plans for compelling reasons of public interest, in which case the decision must be motivated and published. Management plans divide protected areas into different zones subject to a varying degree of restrictions. In addition, according to Law 42/2007, fencing and enclosures of lands, the installation of which is subject to administrative authorisation, must be built in such way that in the whole perimeter the passage of protected wildlife is not hampered, and in the case of species subject to hunting the risks of inbreeding is avoided.[9] Forestry exploitations have sustainably been managed by municipalities (a practice that remains) through the figure of communal forests helping to preserve local economies but also soils and water resources. Private individuals may agree on the imposition of limitations on their own properties either with another private individual or with the public authorities. Law 42/2007, on the natural patrimony and biodiversity, includes

[9] Article 62.3.f).

rules on 'land stewardship' whereby the public authorities promote agreements between stewardship organisations and proprietors of private or public lands. The public authorities enjoy other powers affecting property rights to maintain the integrity of protected areas. This is the case of the right of first refusal (*derecho de tanteo*) and the right to repurchase (*derecho de retracto*) in respect of businesses concluded for good and valuable consideration celebrated *inter vivos* and creating, modifying, transmitting or extinguishing property rights on real estate located within a protected area.[10]

As regards the case, the authorities could declare the installation as a nonconforming activity with planning regulations (a nonconforming activity is an activity that met the applicable zoning requirements in effect at the time it was established, but it is no longer allowed in the corresponding area under current urban regulations). This means that works of modernization, consolidation, increased volume or improvement can no longer be authorized, save works deemed necessary for the maintenance of the building in minimum conditions of habitability and health and those directed to avoid damage to third parties. In other words, such declaration would represent the announced closure of the activity. However, the closure does not grant any right to compensation to the holder of the installation. If the authorities are not able to file a case against the factory they would be forced to compensate for the closure. Alternatively, if there is a breach of the conditions under which the installation operates the revocation of the authorisation would be feasible without compensation (with the prior guarantee of the right to be heard). Likewise, the closure would be feasible if a decision imposing a fine is taken owing to the breach of the conditions of the authorisation. Private individuals could certainly initiate civil law proceedings claiming compensation but they could not force the public authorities to close the installation unless they prove that it was illegally granted. Spanish law provides a venue to challenge at any time administrative decisions provided they are null and void.[11] The provisions of the Law on environmental liability, contaminated sites and integrated pollution prevention and control would be applicable requesting the holder of the authorisation to carry out the decontamination of the site.

D. Natural Resources as Public Property or Interest

There are certain goods that are conceived as *res communis omnium*, e.g., wind,[12] and consequently no property rights can initially be asserted, e.g., wild species.[13] The Civil Code indicates that '[p]roperty capable of appropriation without an owner, such as game or wild fish, hidden treasure

[10] These powers do not apply to Natura 2000 sites.

[11] Article 102 of Law 30/1992, on the common administrative procedure.

[12] Supreme Court Judgment (SCJ) of 28 March 2006, appeal 5527/2003.

[13] According to CCJ 69/2013, Law 42/2007 conceives the natural heritage biodiversity as goods of public interest public. This category includes those whose legal regime, regardless of their public or private

and abandoned movable things, are acquired by occupancy'.[14] Other goods are also subject to a special regime, i.e., the public domain, particularly applicable to water resources and coasts (according to the conditions set out in the Constitution and the corresponding laws). Hence, they are regarded as *res extra commercium*. In this respect, Article 132.2 of the Constitution declares that '[a]ssets under the State's public property shall be those established by law and shall, in any case, include the foreshore, beaches, territorial waters and the natural resources of the exclusive economic zone and the continental shelf'. Other goods are also defined as public domain, i.e., mining resources or communal forests. Therefore the Roman maxim according to which one who owns land owns it '*ad inferno usque ad coelum*' does not apply. Public domain goods remain inalienable and imprescriptible and cannot be subject to attachment or encumbrance.[15] Nature protected areas under Law 42/2007 are not regarded as public domain albeit they may certainly encompass zones subject to this legal category, e.g., watercourses or communal forests. In the case of nature stewardship worthy lands from an environmental viewpoint are put in the hands of non-profit custody organisations so that environmentally suitable management measures are adopted to reach conservation objectives. They act as intermediaries between, on the one hand, the public authorities that provide economic means for appropriate environmental management of the land, e.g., through fiscal measures, aids or economic benefits derived from a contract and, on the other hand, the individual owners who are committed to carry out a type of management transferring the running of the land to the organisation in exchange for a determined economic benefit granted by the Administration.[16]

E. Property in Public Aids for Beneficial Use of Natural Resources

This matter has been exemplified by the reduction of feed in tariffs in the case of solar power installations. The Spanish Supreme Court held in a judgment of January 13, 2014 (appeal 357/2012) that even though a limitation in profits was well documented, that did not mean that the special legal framework to which they were subject had substantially been altered thus requiring compensation. The Supreme Court based its findings on the following assertions: (1) the principle of reasonable profitability had to apply to the whole life of the installations. (2) The holders of solar power installations did not enjoy a right to maintain the current (at that time) legal framework unaltered. Since

ownership, or even its nature as *res nullius*, is linked to the general interest, in order to ensure their restoration and conservation, and the right of everyone to enjoy them.

[14] Article 610.

[15] Article 132(1) of the Spanish Constitution.

[16] There are approximately 130 organisations. By the end of 2010 1,300 agreements had been concluded covering a total surface of 292,746,96 ha.

they were protected from competition they were also subject to legal changes. In other words, the elimination of entrepreneurial risks owing to the existence of feed in tariffs was in effect an advantage in comparison with other operators who were subject to open competition. Therefore, they should have known that the existing (at that time) legal framework could be modified to adapt it to future changes. (3) According to the Supreme Court, the principle of legal certainty (as deterrence from possible legal changes) was particularly ill-suited in the case of renewables owing to their continuous evolution. Hence, economic and technological changes justified a review of initial rules by the public authorities. A limitation of the regulated rate or, in general, of the initial regime that favoured the renewable energy sector was foreseeable in view of the evolution of subsequent economic and technical circumstances, especially after 2007 (the beginning of the economic downturn). In the Court's opinion, that was enough to dismiss the claim regarding the breach of the principle of legitimate expectations. (4) In the light of Article 1 of Protocol 1 to ECHR, the Supreme Court held that it was necessary to examine, in the circumstances of the case, whether the interference by the public authorities had respected the right balance to be achieved between the interests of individual operators and those of society as a whole. In this particular case, the Court concluded that there was not a breach of the right to property ownership insofar as the regulatory measures put into question were not unreasonable and aimed at preserving the sustainability of the electricity network.

F. Expropriation

Expropriation is defined in the 1954 Law as any imperatively imposed deprivation of private property (or of rights or legitimate economic interests) be it a sale, swap, census, lease, temporary occupancy or mere cessation of exercise. Since the Constitution does not guarantee a right to private ownership on any goods, nor determines its material scope, the 1954 Expropriation Law refers to 'any deprivation' of goods and rights owing to all kind of public and social purposes. It should be observed that any individual or institution (save those protected under international or UE law)[17] may be subject to expropriation. However, expropriation powers may only affect certain elements of property rights, i.e., those required to achieve the public interests that are pursued. Expropriation powers require a previous *causa expropiandi* justifying the compulsory purchase of private ownership rights. The *causa expropiandi* may basically be specified following three different paths: (i) By a law of Parliament stating, in general terms, a *causa exproprinandi* (albeit the public authorities have to subsequently specify it in a particular case, e.g., the designation of strict protected areas); (ii) by a law in a particular case; and (iii) implicitly in plans regarding the construction of public works (a common feature in Spain).

[17] Protocol 36 to EU Treaties.

Expropriation procedures essentially consist of different intermediate steps: (1) A declaration on the need to occupy the goods (*declaración de necesidad de la ocupación*). This declaration specifies such goods, controls the legality of the *causa expropiandi* and serves to determine the location of the works or installations benefiting from the expropriation of private property. According to the 1954 Law, the declaration can only affect the essential properties for the carrying out of works or installations. Therefore, expropriation powers are subject to the proportionality principle.[18] When the expropriation involves only a section of a property in such a way that the non expropriated area has no further economic use, the owner is allowed to request the expropriation of the entire estate. (2) The Constitutional Court has interpreted the expression 'and with a proper compensation' in Article 33.3 of the Constitution as not requiring the prior payment of reparation. Therefore, it is not unconstitutional to delay the payment of compensation to the last phase of the expropriation procedure. The calculation of reparations may be initially agreed upon by the owner and the public authority. Both parties are entitled to value the property. If this first venue is not successful then it is determined by a special administrative body (*jurado provincial de expropiación*) within the limits of the respective calculations done by the owner and the public authority. Its decisions enjoy the presumption of accuracy and veracity of administrative acts. However, they may be challenged before administrative law courts. According to the case-law, the value of a property is its faculty to obtain another property in exchange for it. Hence, the true value of an asset is the price the market is willing to pay for it. (3) Once the reimbursement is determined the public authorities carrying out the expropriation (or the beneficiary of the expropriated goods) have to pay it within 6 months. If there is a dispute between the owner and the authorities as to the amount of compensation, or the former party is opposed to receive the payment a compensation up to the limit at which there is an initial agreement between both parties will be deposited in a bank.

G. Indirect Expropriation by Environmental Regulation?

In constitutional terms an essential distinction is that of 'expropriation' and 'delimitation' (or 'regulation'). The former category involves the duty to compensate any deprivation imperatively imposed to by the public authorities. In other words, compensation must be paid because a public authority aims to directly deprive ('mutilate') a property right. In the case of the latter notion (delimitation or regulation) there is no such duty to compensate since, in principle, the measures adopted by the public authorities do not restrict the core content of property ownership. In other words, delimitation fixes abstract and general powers and duties on the property without affecting its core content. Legal measures of delimitation or general regulation of property rights, albeit constituting restrictive limitations of some of their powers are therefore

[18] CCJ 48/2005.

not prohibited by the Constitution. The dividing line between expropriation and regulation is not always easy to draw up, the question being the degree of 'regulation' that can be reached without becoming, in fact, a 'deprivation' of property rights (e.g., how many daisy petals should be taken off to conclude that a deprivation has taken place?). In more accurate terms, it seems apparent that a prohibition concerning the rearing of livestock in a protected area (an activity previously carried out) would represent a deprivation whereas a limitation on the number of cattle would be a regulation (without compensation). Similarly, the impossibility to graze on a protected area *versus* a change from irrigated to dry land farming use would explain the difference between expropriation and regulation. Accordingly, the separating line between delimitation (regulation) and expropriation (mutilation giving rise to compensation) is the respect of the essential content of property rights. In other words, the legal delimitation of economic rights or the introduction of new limitations cannot ignore their essential content (mentioned above); otherwise in such cases there would not be a general regulation of property rights, but a deprivation of such rights. In this sense, the courts consider that a dispossession of hunting or forestry exploitations (e.g., cork; or of the right to cut dry trees in a natural park for self-consumption); or the restrictions imposed by measures for the recovery of a species are not mere limitations imposed on property rights but a deprivation (e.g., prohibition of use of machinery) thus requiring compensation.[19] However, a reduction in the number of species that may be hunted does not represent an expropriation but a delimitation.[20] In certain cases, e.g., designation of protected areas, the dividing line between expropriation and delimitation has taken as a reference the respect for traditional and consolidated uses before the imposition of the corresponding restrictions.[21] As long as those traditional rights or activities are respected, the regulations affecting them will not be conceived as expropriation.[22] However, the case law consistently requires owners to ascertain that (i) the uses did previously exist,[23] and (ii) were effectively carried out before the applicable restrictions (in other words they were in effect incorporated into the patrimony of the affected owners).[24] Likewise, mere expectations cannot be upheld, e.g., an alleged reduction in the value of an estate owing to the impossibility to exploit

19 SCJ of 20 September 2012, appeal 7089/2010; SCJ of 24 June 2009, appeal 1182/2005; SCJ of October 21, 2003, appeal 10867/1998; SCJ of April 30, 2009, appeal 1949/2005.

20 Jugment of the High Court of Castilla-La Mancha of November 4, 2005, appeal 1026/2001.

21 CCJ 170/1989.

22 SCJ of December 10, 2009, appeal 4384/2005.

23 Judgment of Audiencia Nacional of September 14, 2001, appeal 54/2001 (alleged ecoturism activities in Doñana national Park); Judgment of the High Court of Catalonia of March 9, 2011, appeal 217/2010 (alleged use of intensive agriculture with pastics or irrigation).

24 SCJ of 24 May 2013, appeal 2134/2010; Judgment of the High Court of the Autonomous Community of Castilla-La Mancha of 20 May 2002, appeal 279/2002; Judgment of the High Court of the Autonomous Community of Valencia of January 13, 2005, appeal 1138/2003.

plots as irrigated lands.[25] Private ownership rights are not incompatible with legal obligations requiring prior authorisation.[26]

Spanish environmental laws conceive industrial activities as continuous installations (*tracto continuo*) and logically subject to changes (output, emissions or scope). Therefore, their authorisations may also be subject to amendments regarding the conditions under which they operate. It is for this reason that, in principle, any modifications of the initial (or subsequent) conditions are not subject to compensation. In other words, they are not regarded as expropriation owing to the changeable nature of the activity. This is clearly reflected in Law 16/2002, which transposes Directive 96/61 (currently Directive 2010/75). Following the requirements of the Directive, Law 16/2002 enumerates certain cases requiring an amendment of the conditions to which an installation may be subject. None of those cases allows for compensation as expressly mentioned in the Law.[27]

Different laws contain rules affecting private properties without compensation. Law 42/2007 on the natural patrimony and biodiversity allows the public authorities to completely or partially suspend hunting rights if the management of a farm negatively affects the sustainability or renewal of resources. Owing to the nature of this measure no compensation is foreseen. Forests Law 43/2003 provides that the Autonomous Communities shall ensure the restoration of forest land previously burned. For the attainment of this purpose, the Law prohibits (1) the change of forest uses for at least 30 years; and (2) any activity incompatible with the regeneration of the vegetation cover during the period determined by the Autonomous Communities.[28]

H. Dissolution of Property for Environmental Protection

As the Constitutional Court has observed, the Constitution does not include the term of 'vested (or acquired) right'. According to the Court, '[f]rom the point of view of the Constitution, it must be avoided any attempt to apprehend the elusive theory of acquired rights, because the Constitution does not employ the term 'acquired rights' and presumably the constituents avoided it because the defence at all costs of acquired rights does not fit with the philosophy of the Constitution; it does not respond to the requirements of the rule of law proclaimed in the first article of the Constitution; and basically because the theory of acquired rights, forcing the Administration and the courts when examining the legality of the acts of public authorities, does not concern the legislative branch, nor the Constitutional Court when interpreting the Constitution'.[29]

[25] Judgment of the High Court of Castilla-La Mancha of July 26, 2010, appeal 400/2007.

[26] SCJ of 24 April 2012, appeal 1630/2009.

[27] Article 25.5 of Law 16/2002.

[28] This is likely to change with a future amendment to law 43/2003.

[29] CCJ 27/1981.

Holders of legal titles, e.g., authorisations or concessions, enjoy rights derived from those enabling titles. Therefore, in principle, the public authorities cannot annul or revoke such titles without (i) proper reasons (set out in the law) and (ii) following a procedure. Third, the annulment of a legal title does not *per se* grant a right to compensation.[30] However, Spanish law does foresee the grant of compensation in certain cases, e.g., the cancellation of an authorization owing to the adoption of new criteria (e.g., the closure of a petrol station in urban areas) or the annulment of an authorization if it was wrongly granted.

The transformation of private property into concessions (as a way to grant the corresponding compensation required by the Constitution) is well exemplified in the case of the 1988 Spanish coasts Law (amended by Law 2/2013).[31] According to this Law, private ownership rights on lands declared as maritime-terrestrial public domain (hereinafter MTPD) by judgments prior to 1988 turned (*ope legis*) into rights of use (concessions) for a period not exceeding thirty years of duration that could be extended to other thirty years. These concessions had to respect existing uses (including any constructions) but were not subject to taxation. The same solution was adopted in the case of owners that, according to the demarcation carried out under the 1988 Law, enjoyed property rights not regarded as MTPD before 1988 but had been included into the MTPD by reason of this Law. Any buildings and facilities on the MTPD but already illegal under the regulations prior to 1988 were demolished unless the State legalised them for reasons of public interest. The buildings and legalised constructions and those that had been erected in accordance with the previous regulation had to be knocked down but only after the expiry of the concession into which the property title had been transformed. In its judgment regarding the 1988 Law, the Constitutional Court examined may aspects of the Law, *inter alia*, the decision to transform private ownership rights into temporary administrative authorisations or concessions. The debate was mainly focused on whether that decision was in effect a compulsory expropriation without compensation breaching the mandate of Article 33.3 of the Constitution. In the Court's view the elimination of private ownership on lands included into the MTPD could not be considered as an arbitrary decision or devoid of justification, because it was the simplest arrangement to put in practice a decision already made by the Constitution. According to the Court, it was apparent that the 1988 Law had foreseen the grant of compensation. The expropriation had occurred owing to the transformation of private properties into concessions and the Law itself was the instrument that had fixed the compensation. Besides, nothing prevented those affected by the expropriation from challenging the corresponding decision transforming their rights into concessions. The solution designed by the Spanish Parliament in 1988 was, to a great extent, endorsed by European Court of Human Rights (ECHR) in two decisions (*Brosset-Triboulet v France and Depalle v France*) that in

30 Article 102.4 of Law 30/1992, common administrative procedure.

31 See Iñigo Lazkano and Agustín García-Ureta, 'The 2013 reform of Spanish coastal legislation: a further step towards diminishing environmental protection' (2014) *Environmental Liability* 1.

spite of being concerned with the demolition of facilities located in the French MTPD, mentioned the provisions of the 1988 Spanish Law without finding any relevant objection; rather they were mainly employed to reinforce the ECHR's conclusions in those two cases.

Water resources are also categorized as public domain in the Spanish Constitution. Water Law 29/1985 fixed a maximum term of seventy-five years for the enjoyment of preexisting water rights on public waters. In certain cases those rights had been gained for a longer term and even had the status of perpetual rights in accordance with previous water legislation. As regards that seventy-five year time lapse, the Constitutional Court held that it could not be conceived as an expropriation but as a new regulation of the essential content of those rights.[32] Unlike private ownership (not subject to any time constraints) private rights on goods belonging to the public domain could not be conceived as permanent rights. In other words, the enjoyment of perpetual water rights was not compatible with the principles of inalienability and imprescriptibility of the public domain as set out in the Constitution. For that reason, the temporary limitation of such rights was not a deprivation, but a new regulation that did not affect their essential content.

I. State Liability for Environmental Damage to Private Property

An exemplary case: A communal waste disposal site is located not far away from a place with approximately 150 individual houses. Inhabitants assert that they smell bad odours and they would like to sell their property, but, of course, there are no potential buyers. Their property is almost worthless. The waste disposal site is equipped with the necessary permits.

Private individuals are, under the terms laid down by law, entitled to compensation for any harm they may suffer in any of their properties and rights, except in cases of *force majeure*, whenever such harm is the result of the operation of public services.[33] This strict liability regime applies to any acts and omissions causing damages private individuals should not have the legal duty to bear. As regards State's (legislator) liability a distinction must be drawn between expropriation laws that unavoidably require the payment of compensation (as required by the Constitution) and any other laws causing harm to citizens without there being a legal to duty to bear such harm. In this latter case it is for the legislator to foresee any applicable compensation; otherwise the citizens do not enjoy a right to claim damages.[34]

In the light of the abovementioned case, a legal action claiming State liability for the existence of a harmful activity would be available. However, as said

---

[32] CCJ 227/1988.

[33] Article 106 of the Spanish Constitution.

[34] Article 139.3 of Law 30/1992, on the common administrative procedure.

before, the plaintiffs must demonstrate that (1) the public authorities caused the damage by granting the authorisation or by maintaining a harmful activity (provided it did not comply with corresponding standards); (2) that they were not under any obligation to bear the damage (in other words, there was no legal duty to tolerate the harmful effects derived from the activity); and (3) there was a causal link between the grant of the authorisation (and the lack of control) and the damages. It should be verified whether the inhabitants already lived nearby the installation or arrived once it was operating. In the former case, the chances of obtaining compensation owing to the loss of value would be greater than in the latter case.

J. Proprietor's Liability for Environmental Damage

This matter is expressly foreseen in the case of contaminated lands. According to Law 22/2011, on waste and contaminated land, those responsible for the pollution are forced to carry out decontamination and recovery operations. If there are several persons responsible they will be jointly answerable. Owners of polluted soils and the holders thereof will subsidiarily respond. In the case of concessions on public domain lands, the persons responsible are (1) the possessors and (2) the holders of the concession. The recovery of decontamination costs must not be done above the levels of contamination associated with the use of the land at the time when the pollution was caused. If decontamination and recovery operations are to be done with public financing, it may only be granted provided any possible capital gains revert to the public authority granting the aids. The decontamination of the soil for any intended use may be carried out through a voluntary reclamation project approved by the competent Autonomous Community. Owners of lands where potentially polluting activities may have been carried out must state this fact in the corresponding public deed should they transfer them to a third party. This fact must appear in the Property Registry. Law 16/2002 (as amended) includes the requirements of Directive 2010/75 concerning the cessation of the activities and the measures necessary to address the pollution that may have been caused to return the site to the state prior to the commencement of the IPPC activity.

K. Permit Excuse in Environmental Liability

This matter is regulated by Law 26/2007, on environmental liability. According to this law, the operator of an installation is not obliged to bear the cost of remedial actions where (1) he demonstrates that he was not at fault or negligent and that the emission or the fact directly causing environmental damage constituted the express and specific purpose of an administrative authorisation issued in accordance with the rules applicable to the installations subject to the law.[35] (2) The operator has to prove that the environmental damage was caused by an activity, an emission, or the use of a product that, at the time of its use, was not considered as potentially harmful to the environment (according to the state of scientific and technical knowledge existing at that time). However, these provisions may not impede civil liability claims based on fault or negligence. Notwithstanding the aforesaid Law 26/2007 indicates that the liability set forth in this law is compatible with penalties or administrative sanctions for the same acts causing environmental liability.

L. Direct or Indirect Expropriation by EU Measures

First, it should be observed that it would be a matter for EU law to determine whether an indirect or direct expropriation has taken place owing to the application of an EU rule, e.g., the *Hauer* case.[36] Indirect expropriations would be included within the concept of regulation which, as seen above, would not require prior compensation. The question whether there is an expropriation owing to the application of EU law would initially be subject to Spanish law, albeit it is likely that the courts would submit a preliminary ruling to the European Court of Justice.

[35] Additionally, it will be necessary that the operator strictly adjusted in the development of the activity to determinations or conditions laid down for that purpose in the authorisation and with the rules applicable at the time of the causal event of environmental damage.

[36] Case 44/79 *Hauer v Land Rheinland-Pfalz* [1979] ECR 3727.

Property and Environmental Protection in the United Kingdom

Eloise Scotford

Overall Comments

The focus of this chapter will be on English law, which to a large extent reflects UK law generally. However, the environmental law of the UK is increasingly devolved to the different UK administrations (England, Scotland, Wales and Northern Ireland), and so there is no longer a single picture of 'UK' environmental law.

The UK has no written constitution, and there is no explicit 'constitutional' property guarantee in UK law. UK law contains a number of legal principles and doctrines that serve directly or indirectly to protect property interests, ranging from tort and public law doctrines to principles of statutory interpretation and legislative prescriptions for the protection of property in certain regulatory contexts. All these legal avenues are examined below but overall they present a fragmented legal picture. Notably, there are no explicit or unifying constitutional principles for the protection of property in UK law, beyond the UK's obligations to implement the property guarantee in Article 1 Protocol 1, which it does through the Human Rights Act 1998 and (increasingly) through associated case law.

A. Objects of Private Property

Objects of 'property' in UK law are wide-ranging. They include real estate (including immovable property, such as buildings and fixtures, attached to the land), rights associated with land (such as mining rights or rights to fish), moveable tangible objects (machines, animals, furniture, and other tangible chattels), and intangible property (intellectual property, private law causes of action, debts, shares in companies, financial instruments, business goodwill). Contested or uncertain forms of property include those in body parts and confidential information. However, whether something can be classified as 'property' essentially depends on the legal protection or implications that might apply.[1] Equivalent legal protections might not attach to different objects that might broadly be considered to be property. For example, while we can say that, at its broadest, property in UK law includes a legitimate expectation of being able to develop land on the basis of existing planning permission (*Pine Valley Investments v Ireland* (1992) 14 EHRR 319), there are no general property law protections that necessarily flow from this classification in UK law (other than protection under the Human Rights Act). In fact, one of the interesting questions in UK property law is, at what point, newly created rights (such as rights to feed-in-tariffs for generating renewable energy, or 'allowances' in the

1 For example, some English law torts that protect property protect 'personal property' only (detinue, conversion, trespass to goods), whilst the UK tax regime considers that business goodwill to be a taxable asset.

EU emissions trading scheme) turn into 'property' because of the legal consequences or protections that flow from or attach to them.

Objects that are *not* objects of property rights – in that there are no property-type controls or protections that automatically apply to them – include rights to economic opportunity, rights to bring public law cases (which are subject to the permission of the court) and rights to access the market (beyond those that exist in EU law).

In relation to which potential objects of property might be used as a defence *against* environmental protection regulation, there is currently an awkward legal interaction between property rights and environmental regulation in UK law. In short, there is no settled legal doctrine about how to resolve the tension that can exist between the protections that are claimed to attach to property rights and the operation of environmental regulation that can affect those rights, and interesting cases continue to appear in the UK courts in relation to this question, many of which turn on their facts (see section K below). Notably, this issue of when property rights might be asserted against environmental regulation has mainly arisen in the context of *rights to land*, which have been asserted to resist the impact of planning law, nature conservation regulation or pollution control permitting in particular.[2] As for asserting other forms of property rights against environmental regulation, there have been no notable cases so far in UK law where this kind of argument has succeeded. However, the form of property right protection that would most likely apply to other novel forms of property – such as planning permissions or allowances under the EU ETS – in the face of environmental regulation would be that flowing from Article 1 Protocol 1 (A1 P1) of the European Convention on Human Rights (ECHR), in light of the expansive interpretation given to the notion of 'possessions' by the European Court of Human Rights.[3]

B. Private Property in Natural Resources

Rights to use natural resources are framed as property where they are ordinary incidents of the ownership of land, including rights in relation to adjoining watercourses ('riparian rights').[4] Animals are also natural resources that are capable of being owned, although wild animals need to be tamed,

[2] Not all legal interactions between property rights in land and environmental regulation are problematic. Many forms of environmental control are simply accepted by landowners as social incidents of land ownership, and other interactions are resolved by statute, as where compensation is provided for landowners whose property is entered in order to lay pipes for electricity or sewerage works (see n 32 below).

[3] *Pine Valley Developments v Ireland* (1992) 14 EHRR 319. But note the limited impact of A1 P1 in UK case law to date, even where it is prima facie applicable eg *R (Trailer & Marina (Leven)) v SS for Environment, Food and Rural Affairs* [2004] EWCA Civ 1580 (see n 33).

[4] Riparian rights are common law rights that landowners have to use bodies of water that flow adjacent to their property. These include rights to access the water for boating and fishing, to use the water for

captured or killed before they are recognised as belonging to the owner of the property on which the animal is present. Furthermore, planning permission, once granted, attaches to the land and is treated essentially as a property right.[5] It cannot be later revoked or be subject to new conditions without compensation being paid (including compensation for lost profits).[6]

However, most rights to use natural resources now require environmental permits or legislative concessions in the UK – ownership of land is not enough. These include rights to discharge into watercourses, rights to emit polluting substances into the air, rights to extract underground resources, rights to operate a landfill site, and so on. Such permissions are *personal* to the individual or company who has successfully applied for them, rather than proprietary. In relation to environmental permits in particular, the legislative scheme for their grant and continuing oversight contemplates that permits are subject to ongoing review (and possible adjustment by the regulator) and even revocation without compensation.[7] Where a regulator exercises its power to change or revoke a permit, it must notify the regulated entity and provide relevant reasons, as allowed under legislation.

In relation to concessions granted by government to exploit state-owned natural resources, such as mining sites or deep-sea petroleum resources, these are contractual and usually long-term arrangements, such that the owner of a concession would have legal recourse if the government sought to terminate this kind of legal arrangement prematurely. Property law does not have a strong role in any of these arrangements, although again interesting A1 P1 arguments could likely be made in relation to the deprivation of permits or concessions in unreasonable circumstances.

C. Private Property Used in Defence of Environmental Protection

The case law examples where private individuals have used property rights in defence of environmental protection have been largely strategic. In general, private property owners are under no obligation to act in the public interest. However, private individuals may sue in tort law (in private nuisance) in relation to activities of other property owners that are causing 'unreasonable' inference with their individual rights to use land, and such actions may coincide with a wider public interest in environmental protection.[8] Historically, such actions were brought when there was a failure of state regulation to control

domestic irrigation purposes (so long as downstream right-holders are not unreasonably affected), and the right to protect land from flooding.

5 Town and Country Planning Act 1990, s 75(1).

6 ibid, s 107.

7 Environmental Permitting (England and Wales) Regulations 2010 SI 2010/675, regs 13-25.

8 *Attorney-General v Birmingham Corporation* (1858) 70 ER 220.

environmentally harmful activities.[9] However, this legal avenue essentially concerns obligations in respect of neighbouring private property interests, rather than those owed in the broader public interest.[10]

How would the following case be treated in the UK?

> A factory, situated near a town, has been operating for decades. People are slowly realizing that statistically the inhabitants in the city and in the vicinity do not live average age and the cancer is more frequently present among them, also the frequent cause of the deaths. They have no direct proofs that the factory could be responsible, although it is rather clear that the soil around the factory is poisoned and that the heavy metals found in the vegetable could be linked to the factory. However, credible proofs are missing. What could be the obligation of the state? Could the inhabitants rely on the public remedies procedure? If the state wants to revoke the operation permit, could the factory claim any sort of property guarantee?

The best avenue of legal recourse in this situation is the contaminated land regime in Part IIA EPA (see further, section J below). The implementation of this regime is based firmly on risk assessment procedures where information about contaminants causing harm to health or to the environment cannot be proved conclusively – risk assessment is important in determining whether a 'significant risk' of harm exists in order for the regime to apply. If such a risk is found, there would be an obligation on the state to begin the Part IIA process, and on the factory to remedy the contaminated land as an 'appropriate person' under the regime.

In relation to deaths caused, it is harder to pin liability for this on the factory, without evidence showing a definite causal link between its activities and the deaths. The negligence claim in *Corby Group Litigation* is not dissimilar to this case,[11] and shows that a negligence claim against the factory is probably the best legal avenue for any individual suffering cancer (or surviving relatives) and

9 See also *St Helen's Smelting Co v Tipping* (1865) 11 HLC 642.

10 Cf Ben Pontin, *Nuisance Law and Environmental Protection: A Study of Nuisance Injunctions in Practice* (2013, Lawtext Publishing Ltd).

11 [2009] EWHC 1944 (TCC). In this case, the local council was decontaminating a former steelworks site and a cluster of birth defects occurred in the vicinity whilst the works were being carried out, or soon after. The court held that the council owed a duty of care to pregnant mothers (and their children) in the area to take reasonable care in the execution of the reclamation works to avoid injury to the mothers and unborn children. To establish a claim in negligence (which requires proof of damage and its causation by the defendant), the court relied on epidemiological and toxicological evidence, as well as evidence of foetal medicine and the relevant state of scientific knowledge at the time, to show that a causal link existed between the breaches of duty by the council (such as transporting toxic material in uncovered trucks through the local neighbourhood) and the kinds of birth defects that formed the basis of the claim.

that causation challenges in such cases can be overcome with sufficient expert evidence.

In any case, there is no case for the factory to claim any loss if its permit is revoked (as set out above, the English environmental permitting regime allow permits to be reviewed regularly). In the case that the factory's permit is not revoked, citizens could seek judicial review against the relevant Agency on the grounds that they are legally obliged to revoke the relevant permission. However, a court would have to be convinced that the Agency has acted wholly unreasonably in not revoking the permit. If the evidence is not clear, the prospect of such an action being successful is low.

D Private Property Used in Defence of Environmental Protection

In English and UK law, there is no doctrine of public trust or public domain. Rather, we have a number of regulatory mechanisms by which certain areas of land, with significant natural features, are protected and maintained in the public interest. To this end, there are various 'enclave' techniques that are employed to further nature conservation – through the designation of Areas of Outstanding Natural Beauty, national parks, national/local nature reserves, sites of special scientific interest (SSSIs), and European protected areas (SACs, SPAs, SCIs). In such areas, there is a range of restrictions on use of property.[12] Notably, much of this land is privately owned, even in the case of national parks. However, charities or trusts also play an important role in owning or managing protected areas. The English nature conservation regulator, Natural England, also owns and manages about 30% of the national nature reserves. Furthermore, in general, no compensation is available for owners whose land is subject to nature conservation obligations, except in some cases where owners have given up existing uses of land.[13]

E. Property in Public Aids for Beneficial Use of Natural Resources

In short, subsidisation of a 'beneficial use of natural resources' is not currently construed of as property in UK law. There has been one con-

[12] Restrictions on the rights of landowners include controlling all development within the area through dedicated governing authorities (national parks), preventing any potentially 'damaging operations' without consent of the nature conservation regulator (SSSIs), and preventing any development that may adversely affect the integrity of the site (SACs).

[13] See n 35 and Wildlife and Countryside Act 1981, s 28M. Note that there was a change in regulatory policy in 2000, when a more limited regime for granting compensation was introduced to bolster the effectiveness of the SSSI regime.

tentious case when a subsidy for renewable energy was withdrawn quickly for reasons of economic affordability of subsidy schemes, which have led economic operators to mount legal challenges in relation to their defeated financial expectations. In *Secretary of State for Energy & Climate Change v Friends of the Earth*,[14] the Court of Appeal found that the government had acted unlawfully in altering the guaranteed rate of return on solar energy generation by small-scale suppliers after capital expenditure had been incurred. The Court's reasoning was based on a proper statutory construction of the Energy Act 2008, which allowed the relevant 'feed-in-tariff' scheme for solar energy, rather than any questions of property law. The court found that the government had no power to take away an existing entitlement without statutory authority, interpreting the relevant legislation in line with the presumption against retrospective operation.

Whilst *SS for Energy v FOE* was resolved as a matter of statutory construction, it is worth noting that another relevant avenue of legal challenge in such cases might be the administrative law ground of challenge based on 'legitimate expectations'. On this basis, individuals might bring a judicial review action against a public body if the body has made a representation/promise, or generated an expectation based on a course of conduct, where the expectation is sufficiently clear and unambiguous and such that the individual can expect the body to be bound by it.[15] Whether a body will be held to a promise or expected course of conduct will depend, amongst other things, on: whether the expectation is procedural or substantive; the unfairness to the claimant individual in departing from the expectation; whether the damage can be made good by financial compensation; and whether there is an overriding public interest in allowing the public body to resile from the promised or expected position.[16] There is no guarantee that a public body will be bound by the representations it makes, or the expectations it generates – substantive expectations are hardest to enforce legally and much will depend on the circumstances of the case.

F. Expropriation

There are two main legal protections in UK law in relation to expropriation of property. First, there is a common law principle of statutory construction that requires judges to presume that the legislature does not intend to *take* private property rights without compensation, unless a contrary intention is clear, and further to interpret legislation on the basis of that presumption.[17] Some takings are explicitly compensated under statute, such as when title to

---

[14] [2012] EWCA Civ 28.

[15] *R (Bancoult) v Secretary of State for Foreign and Commonwealth Affairs* [2009] 1 AC 453.

[16] *R v North and East Devon Health Authority; ex p Coughlan* [2001] QB 213.

[17] See eg *London and North Western Ry Co v Evans* [1893] 1 Ch 16, 28; *Inglewood Pulp and Paper Company v New Brunswick Electric Power Commission* [1928] AC 492, 498–499; *R (Lord Chancellor) v Chief Land Registrar* [2005] EWHC 1706 (Admin) at [35]; [2006] QB 795, 805.

land is expropriated for projects in the national or public interest,[18] although there can be arguments about how many properties are 'blighted' by large-scale projects (including those driven partly by environmental imperatives) and thus should be compensated by the government.[19]

Beyond cases of straightforward compulsory purchase or expropriation of property through deprivation of title, there can be more contentious cases in determining whether or not property is 'taken'. As section G below indicates, regulatory *restrictions on use* of property do not ordinarily require compensation, but some restrictions, or combinations of restrictions, on use of property can be so detrimental to a property owner's rights as to deprive them of all usefulness. Viscount Simonds held in the leading case of *Belfast v OD Cars* (see further below) that '*a measure which is ex facie regulatory may in substance be confiscatory... [T]he question is one of degree and the dividing line is difficult to draw.*'[20] It would usually be an extreme case where such a line was crossed. Pollution control legislation would not be such an extreme case, even pollution control legislation that required a licence holder to update technology to continue exploiting land (as under the IPPC regime).[21] However, environmental controls that go so far as to render a property owner's rights 'useless' could amount to a de facto expropriation of property that requires compensation. *London & North Western Railway Co v Evans* suggested that legislation that effectively deprived an owner of coal reserves of the right to mine them (by requiring the land containing coal to support a canal) required compensation.[22] There are in fact many environmental controls that can have harsh impacts on rights to exploit land.[23] The key issue seems to be whether they render the property useless. Overall, determining the precise point at which regulatory restrictions, or a number of restrictions, add up to an effective taking or expropriation of property is difficult to ascertain from the case law.[24]

[18] Under the Acquisition of Land Act 1981, with compensation assessed under the Land Compensation Act 1961.

[19] Town and Country Planning Act 1990, pt VI, ch 2 and sch 13. See eg contentious blight compensation for property owners who live in the vicinity of the proposed UK HS2 ('High Speed 2') rail line: http://www.bbc.co.uk/news/uk-england-stoke-staffordshire-26951860 (accessed 29 April 2014).

[20] [1960] AC 490 at 520.

[21] Updating conditions attached to an environmental licence could be considered an appropriation of property, but nearly all regulatory regimes give the licence holder in such circumstances the right to appeal the merits of the decision, either to a government inspector or a specialist tribunal – in essence allowing a second look at the decision.

[22] [1893] 1 Ch 16.

[23] The EU emissions trading scheme has caused serious financial difficulties for some UK businesses (arguably as it is intended to do). See eg http://news.bbc.co.uk/1/hi/wales/6214332.stm (accessed 18 September 2014). A year later Alphasteel went into receivership.

[24] Kevin Gray, 'Can Environmental Regulation Constitute a Taking of Property at Common Law?' (2007) 24 *Environmental and Planning Law Journal* 161–181.

Second, there is the Convention right in A1 P1 ECHR that guarantees every natural or legal person the peaceful enjoyment of his possessions, of which he shall not be deprived 'except in the public interest and subject to the conditions provided for by law and by the general principles of international law'. In UK law, this is implemented by the Human Rights Act 1998 (HRA), which requires: the Government to introduce legislation that is compatible with the Convention;[25] judges to interpret legislation in a Convention-compatible manner; and public bodies, including courts, to exercise their powers in a manner consistent with the Convention.[26] Notably, we do not have any UK/English case law examples of A1 P1 being infringed but justified in the public interest on environmental grounds.

G. Indirect Expropriation by Environmental Regulation?

In UK common law, the starting presumption is that regulatory restrictions on rights to use land are lawful and do not require compensation.[27] If it were otherwise, 'the costs of social and economic organisation would become prohibitive'.[28] The leading case on this issue is *Belfast Corporation v OD Cars*.[29] In this case, the House of Lords held that a refusal of planning consent to develop land did not amount to a 'taking' of property that required compensation (under the relevant provisions of general Irish legislation at the time, which required compensation for takings of property). The House of Lords noted that restrictions on the use of property through the planning system were in the public interest and an acceptable, not uncommon incident of ownership. Notably, Viscount Simonds and Lord Radcliffe both accepted that there might be cases where the *administrative implementation* of regulation, such as planning control, might amount to an excessive restriction on use and constitute a 'taking' of property. However, any such situation should be decided by courts on a case-by-case basis and that possibility was no reason to impugn planning legislation as unlawful when in most cases it would operate in a manner that did not 'take' property but merely regulated its use. But, as set out above, once planning permission is granted, this is regarded as equivalent to a property right. Thus if the planning authorities subsequently change their mind and revoke the permission, they must pay compensation.[30]

---

25 The Human Rights Act permits the Government to expressly state that proposed primary legislation is contrary to the Convention, and seek Parliamentary endorsement of that measure.

26 Human Rights Act 1998, ss 3, 6, 19. Only where primary legislation makes it impossible for the body to follow the Convention may they do so.

27 *Grape Bay Ltd v A-G of Bermuda* [2000] 1 WLR 574 (Privy Council).

28 Kevin Gray (n 24) 6.

29 [1960] AC 490.

30 Above n 6. Obviously if the planning permission was subsequently found to be unlawful following court action there would be no compensation. But sometimes authorities wish to change their planning

This tendency to defer to the administrative sphere to make reasonable 'regulatory' land use determinations that do not require compensation has continued,[31] particularly in the context of Human Rights Act arguments. In *Lough v First Secretary of State*, a proposed residential development near the Tate Modern Gallery in central London was challenged for alleged breaches of Article 8 and A1 P1 ECHR. The claimant resident association was concerned that the development would lead to a loss of privacy, overlooking, loss of light, loss of a view and interference with television reception (breaching Article 8), and general diminution in the value of the claimant's properties (constituting a partial taking of property in breach of A1 P1). Finding that there was no breach of the HRA, Lord Justice Pill emphasised that Convention rights should 'normally be considered as an *integral part* of the decision maker's approach to material considerations [which are required to be weighed up by the planning authority in deciding a development application] and not... in effect as a footnote'.[32] Since the planning inspector's decision-making process in approving the development was well within the margin of appreciation in this case, taking into account and weighing all relevant considerations (including those raised by the claimants), there was no reason to find any infringement of the Convention, particularly since the 'concept of proportionality is inherent in the approach to decision making in planning law'.[33]

However, there are some exceptional cases where restrictions are considered to require compensation due to their impact on owners' rights to use property, and land in particular. First, legislation may give powers to bodies such as electricity or sewerage undertakers to enter land, to lay pipes etc. Legislation will normally provide for compensation for landowners in such cases.[34] Second, there seems to be a distinction between the impacts of regulatory restrictions on owners whose rights to use land are directly affected and those of neighbours who are affected. Thus, whilst it has been accepted that the state can increasingly restrict landowners' rights to use land without compensation for nature

policy, and revoke a legally valid permission before development starts. Revocation, however, is very rare because of the heavy costs of compensation involved. A 1993 example of planning permission granted for a supermarket, followed by a strong local campaign, led to the permission being revoked after the supermarket chain secured some £2 million in compensation: source House of Commons Library. Note also that withdrawal of consents to use land in nature conservation protected areas in particular ways will also general rights to compensation: Wildlife and Countryside Act 1981, s 28M.

31 See Rachael Walsh, '*Belfast Corporation v OD Cars* – Setting Parameters for Restricting Use' in *Landmark Cases in Property Law* (Hart Publishing, 2015).

32 *Lough v First Secretary of State* [2004] EWCA Civ 905[48] (emphasis added).

33 ibid [49].

34 eg Electricity Act 1989, sch 4, para 7; Highways Act 1980, s 28. But note that not all such intrusions into land permitted under statute are accompanied by a right to compensation: compare Water Industry Act 1991, s 159, sch 12, para 2, and *Manchester Ship Canal Company Limited v United Utilities* [2014] UKSC 40 (where an implied right to discharge waters from sewerage works onto the claimant's land was found not to require compensation in some cases).

conservation purposes,[35] the impact of planning or environmental permitting decisions on the property rights of *neighbouring landowners* is a different matter. The impact on neighbours' rights in the latter case may give rise to compensation via a private law claim against the owner who is subject to the relevant planning permission or environmental permit, where there is unreasonable interference with neighbours' property rights and thus liability in private nuisance, rather than compensation being owed by the state.[36] This state of affairs indicates a complex interplay between environmental regulation and property rights when more than one set of property rights is affected.

H. Dissolution of Property for Environmental Protection Reasons

There is no such category or legal precedent in UK law. In the regular case, rights to run a nuclear power station or other forms of large-scale infrastructure are contractual (rather than proprietary), often with the government as the other contracting party. Any withdrawal of rights to operate a nuclear facility or similar may amount to a compensable breach of contract, depending on the relevant terms. In some cases, such arrangements may be based on a subsidy set for a period of years.

I. State Liability for Environmental Damage by Government Action to Private Property

Compensation might be provided for the deterioration of private property due to government actions or decisions in three cases. First, private owners of land might apply for compensation where their properties are 'blighted' by planning decisions, which is where property values decrease in light of permitted development or development restrictions.[37] In extreme cases, the Town and Country Planning Act 1990 provides for rights of compulsory purchase and compensation for property owners whose land has become 'incapable of reasonably beneficial use in its existing state' due to planning decisions.[38] These forms of compensation under the planning system are not necessarily triggered by 'environmental' deteriorations of property, but they would apply where such deteriorations affect the economic value of land or render it incapable of 'beneficial use'. Second, the government might be liable to pay compensation for any breach of A1 P1, where their actions cause the environmental deterioration of private property in such a way as to breach that Conven-

35 *R (Trailer & Marina (Leven)) v SS for Environment, Food and Rural Affairs* [2004] EWCA Civ 1580.

36 *Coventry v Lawrence* [2013] UKSC 13; *Barr v Biffa Waste* [2012] EWCA Civ 312.

37 See n 19.

38 Town and Country Planning Act 1990, pt VI, ch 1.

tion right. Such deterioration would have to be significant and not justified in the public interest.

Third, compensation might be available, not from government, but from neighbouring private landowners in relation to land that has been adversely affected by government regulation that allows damaging activity on the neighbouring land. Such private compensation would be sought by a private nuisance claim, as explained in section G above.

How would the following case be treated in the UK?

A communal waste disposal site is located not far away from a place with appr. 150 individual houses. Inhabitants assert that they smell bad odour and they would like to sell their property, but, of course, there are no potential buyers. Their property is almost worthless. The waste disposal site is equipped with the necessary permits.

Are the inhabitants in the neighbourhood entitled to compensation (perhaps to annual revenue)? Do they have to search for withdrawal of the operation permit first?

This scenario is similar to that dealt with by the Court of Appeal in *Barr v Biffa Waste* (discussed in section K below). As in that case, the residents should sue the waste disposal site in private nuisance for compensation that reflects the diminution in the value of their properties. The success of such an action depends on the court finding that there is an 'unreasonable' interference with the amenity of the houses on the facts, and is subject to Carnwath JSC's subsequent comments in *Coventry v Lawrence* that his position on property rights trumping environmental regulation in *Barr* might have been too stark.[39] There is no requirement for the inhabitants to seek to have the waste permit removed before bringing an action in private nuisance. However, any nuisance action would likely trigger the regulator to review the terms of the site's waste disposal permit, which the regulator might then amend if it does not provide adequate conditions to protect neighbours from adverse amenity impacts.

J. Proprietor's Liability for Environmental Damage

The best example of this is the contaminated land regime in Part IIA Environmental Protection Act 1990 ('EPA'). This regime relates to land that is identified as causing significant harm due to historical pollution (or as generating a significant risk of causing such harm). In such cases, the obligations to remediate the land fall primarily on those who 'caused or knowingly permitted' the contaminating substances to be in, on or under the land. However, if such persons cannot be found, perhaps because they are companies that

39 [2014] UKSC 13 [197].

no longer exist, then liability to remediate the land falls on current owners or occupiers (EPA, s 78F(4)).[40]

In the case where waste is illegally deposited on land by a third party, the owner of the land has an obligation to ensure that it is collected or treated. This might cause considerable expense to an owner of land in the case of 'fly-tipping' of waste onto their land by waste offenders, but there is a provision for such costs to be recovered from the waste offender, assuming they can be found and that they are solvent (EPA, s 33B).

K. Permit Excuse in Environmental Liability

Generally, no 'permit defence' is provided in environmental permitting legislation. However, in recent years the courts have had to deal with and acknowledge the growing complexity and demands of modern environmental regulation, and have explored the relationship between regulatory and liability systems in more detail. It is a complex and evolving area of law, as indicated in section G above.

In *Barr v Biffa Waste*,[41] the Court of Appeal held that holding and complying with an environmental permit (to operate a landfill site) was no legal protection from a nuisance claim brought by neighbouring residents in relation to unreasonable interference with their property rights due to unpleasant odours coming from the landfill site. According to Lord Justice Carnwath, 'there is no basis, in principle or authority, [short of express or implied statutory authority to commit a nuisance] for using such a statutory scheme to cut down private law rights'. More recently, in *Coventry v Lawrence*,[42] the UK Supreme Court was faced with a similar issue of alleged noise nuisance in relation to a motor sports track that was operating (just) within the terms of its planning permission. Again, the Supreme Court found that the motor sports track owners could be liable in private nuisance to neighbouring property owners for unreasonable noise emanating from their property. However, the judgment also acknowledges that the terms of the relevant planning permission (including conditions setting out when the track can be operated for different kinds of motor racing) might be relevant in determining whether there is an 'unreasonable' interference with the neighbouring property rights (and thus an actionable nuisance) in the first place.

40 The legislation provides that where the authority considers that placing this responsibility on current owners may cause undue financial hardship (such as in the case of a poor household), the costs of decontamination may be picked up by the public authority.

41 [2012] EWCA Civ 312.

42 [2014] UKSC 13.

L. Direct or Indirect Expropriation by EU Measures

There are no UK cases to date in which EU acts have led to 'expropriation' or takings of property. This is likely due to the fact that extensive regulatory restrictions on property are permitted without amounting to de facto expropriation and requiring compensation (see section G above). This is not to say it could not happen.

PART IV

Comparative Studies

In the Name of "Common Interest": Framing Environmental Goods as Common Goods

Massimiliano Montini & Mery Ciacci

A. Introduction

Whom do natural resources belong to? Are States the only entitled subjects to own and steward natural resources? If so, is the current regime of public ownership appropriate enough to protect natural resources in the common interests of all citizens? In a world increasingly showing the limits of the human governance on natural resources and in which natural resources are often scarce or not adequately protected from pollution and over-exploitation, the answer to these questions becomes a crucial one.

In the various European jurisdictions, the ownership of natural resources has traditionally been conceived as a prerogative of the State. To different extents, European States hold the property of most of the natural resources existing in their territory. Natural resources are usually inscribed in constitutional provisions listing them among those goods belonging to the public domain, thus keeping their possession aside from citizens' private property and limiting their use through specific provisions. States act as a sort of trustees for natural resources, by exercising their power to limit and control the use and management of environmental goods both in the public and private sphere. From this point of view, it could be stated that the State holds the property or the control over natural resources in the name of public interest. Indeed, some limits and restrictions to regular private property rights are set by the law in order to protect the quality of the environment, to halt biodiversity's losses and land's degradation, to mitigate climate change, and so on.

In spite of this assumption, the current state of natural resources' degradation and the increasing number of polluting phenomena and accidents in Europe highlight the limits deriving from the traditional regime of public and private ownership. Environmental damages and ecological disasters are often a consequence of the incautious governance of States which do not manage to sufficiently regulate the exercise of certain economic activities nor to take adequate measures preventing and controlling pollution. An example in this sense is given by the case of the steel factory ILVA in Southern Italy.[1] We may wonder, then, to what extent the current property regime of natural resources is appropriate to protect the common interest of citizens, or – using the language of international law – the 'common interest of mankind'.

Would the qualification of natural resources (or environmental goods) as 'common goods' empower citizens – and not only States – to act for the protection and conservation of environmental goods? Possibilities for citizens to act through legal remedies for the protection of common interests, such as those connected to a clean and safe environment, are currently available *via* the enforcement of human rights: for instance, the ECHR case law shows that the protection of common interests is very often connected to the enforceability of private property-related rights and the right to live in a clean environment.[2]

1 See M. Montini, Chapter Italy.

2 See the well-known cases Lopez Ostra v. Spain (ECtHR Series A N. 303C.) and Guerra and others v. Italy (EctHR Rep (1998-I) 210), in which the Court of Strasbourg found a breach of protected rights (namely

As scholars have pointed out, such an approach by human rights courts, and in particular the European Court of Human Rights, contributed to the jurisprudential development of certain environmental obligations impinging upon States' parties, thus marking an undeniable progress toward the protection of the environment.[3] Yet, it is not always possible to connect the protection of environmental concerns to someone's private property or to the enforceability of individual human rights. Therefore, one may question to what extent human rights may be considered an efficient and adequate legal remedy for environmental common interests. Instead, would the recognition of environmental goods as common goods in the interest of humankind be a step forward for a more efficient protection of the environment?

In the present chapter we will try to answer these questions. In order to do so, after a brief introduction to the topic, we will provide a sketch of the private and public property regimes concerning natural resources currently existing in various European countries. This first part will draw on the answers of the national surveys contained in this volume and will be useful to outline which limits may derive from the traditional understanding of environmental goods as belonging to the State's property. Following this analysis, we will explore what remedies a citizen can rely on to protect common environmental interests according to the current classification of environmental goods as public or private goods, in order to assess whether a citizen is empowered to act in the name of a 'common interest'.

On this basis, in the last section, we will advance the proposal to consider environmental goods as 'common goods' or 'public goods in the common interests of mankind', as a possible solution to promote a better protection of the environmental goods. In such a context, relying on the research findings of Nobel prize winner Elinor Ostrom, we will argue that environmental resources should be classified as 'commons', a concept that calls for common management and responsibility, in the light of the 'common interest of mankind' which is embedded in those goods. In so doing, we will refer, in particular, to the work of the Italian Commission on Public Goods (so named *Commissione Rodotà* by the name of its chairman), which was set up in 2007 by the Italian Government with the aim to reconsider the traditional distinction between public and private goods. Finally, we will argue that the recognition of the new category of 'common goods' should hopefully influence and should eventually be integrated into the several European national jurisdictions, in order to pursue a truly sustainable use and management of the environmental goods.

---

the right to private and family life (Article 8 ECHR) and the right to life (Article 2 ECHR)) as a consequence of industrial installations' activities affecting the quality of the environment around the private properties of the applicants.

3 F Francioni, 'International Human Rights in an Environmental Horizon', 2010, 21:1 EJIL, 41, at 49-50.

B. Public Ownership and Private Ownership of Environmental Goods in the European Jurisdictions: an Overview

The majority of European countries list environmental goods among those whose ownership can only be attributed to the State (or other territorial public authorities), which should act as a trustee for their citizens. Environmental goods (or natural resources) – such as the air, rivers, forests, seashores, beaches, lakes, mountains, superficial and groundwater – are usually included into the public domain by Constitutional or Civil Codes' provisions in civil law systems.[4] For instance, in Italy, the Constitution distinguishes between public and private property (article 42) and the Civil Code places natural resources among those objects belonging to the public property of the State or other territorial public authorities. State's public property in Italy is named '*demanio*' (public domain) and is characterized by the fact that the goods falling under this category are unalienable, which means that they cannot be sold or transferred. A similar regime is foreseen by the Portuguese Constitution, which establishes a core list of environmental resources belonging to the public domain, which are, therefore, unalienable.[5] Spain has a similar definition of public domain, but also foresees the possibility to consider certain goods – such as wind[6] and wild species[7] – as *res communis omnium*, and consequently no property rights can initially be asserted on them; hence, they are regarded as *res extra commercium*.

When an object pertains to the public domain, the State holds rights and duties on it. As a consequence, the State decides about the allowed uses and must take care of the management, protection and conservation of natural resources on behalf of the community. From this point of view, the State acts as a trustee. The State may also grant private persons the right to use and manage environmental goods, under certain limits and conditions, through specific legal instruments, such as concessions or authorisations. Normally, concessions and authorizations confer private persons (natural or legal persons) the right to use natural resources: these rights are usually limited in time and subjected to the payment of fee, but they can never be considered as equivalent to property rights.[8]

4 See for instance article 822 of the Italian Civil Code. Such a provision, with regard to waters, was supplemented by Law 36/1994, which determines that all superficial and underground waters are to be considered public goods and belong to the State.

5 See A. Aragao, Chapter Portugal.

6 See the Spanish Supreme Court Judgment of 28 March 2006, appeal 5527/2003.

7 According to Spanish CCJ 69/2013, Law 42/2007 conceives the natural heritage biodiversity as goods of public interest public. This category includes those whose legal regime, regardless of their public or private ownership, or even its nature as *res nullius*, is linked to the general interest, in order to ensure their restoration and conservation, and the right of everyone to enjoy them.

8 See M. Montini, Chapter Italy, A. Aragao, Chapter Portugal, R. Knez, Chapter Slovenia, A. García Ureta, Chapter Spain.

Why are environmental goods mostly excluded from the sphere of private property and the enjoyment of regular private rights? From the analysis of the information provided in the national surveys, it emerges that what normally leads to classify natural environmental goods as public goods is the underlying acknowledgment of the fact that they are goods of a 'common interest'.[9] In other words, as in the case of historical and archaeological goods, cultural heritage and environmental goods, it is acknowledged that such goods serve the collective interest of the society. This recognition determines the need to grant environmental goods a special regime of protection – namely the one stemming from the State's public property – so as to ensure that the whole community can enjoy their use, while protecting them from the risks of over-exploitation or deterioration that may derive from a private ownership.[10]

The need to safeguard natural resources through a special regime for the common interest of all citizens is acknowledged also in those jurisdictions where a similar concept of public domain is not present, such as in English and UK law,[11] or where the ownership of natural resources is not fully excluded from the private sphere, as in Germany, Croatia and Portugal.[12] Indeed, in some European States there may be cases where citizens can own environmental goods. However, in such cases, their relevant private property rights must be exercised within the limits set by the law and the administrative regulations which may be enacted by public authorities. Boundaries and restrictions to the use of environmental goods falling under private property are envisaged by the law, so as to ensure a certain level of protection of the relevant natural resources, as well as to guarantee the protection of archaeological, artistic and landscape values that may be connected to such resources.

The rationale behind this kind of restrictions rests upon the evidence of the common interest involved. In Germany, for instance, '*the protection of natural resources is considered as a public interest justifying the adoption of appropriate measures.*' According to German law, natural resources are not conceived as a public trust, common property or common good. Nevertheless, the traditional concept of public things ('*öffentliche Sachen*') is partially applicable to natural resources because of the recognition of the public interest embedded in such objects. This concept frames publicly usable assets (such as streets, squares, railways, but also parks, dikes, sewage purification plants, forests, mineral resources, etc.) as items that are subject to a special public regime determining the obligation of the State (or the other relevant territorial public authority) to ensure the rights of community to their free common use (*Gemeingebrauch*), as well as the allocation of and payment for special uses by private persons (*Sondernutzung*). This

9 See M. Montini, Chapter Italy, Lana Ofak, Chapter Croatia, A. Aragao, Chapter Portugal, M. Galey, Chapter France.

10 A. Farì, Beni e Funzioni Ambientali. Contributo allo studio della dimensione giuridica dell'ecosistema, (Jovene Ed., 2013), 37.

11 See E. Scotford, Chapter UK.

12 See G. Winter, Chapter Germany, Lana Ofak, Chapter Croatia, A. Aragao, Chapter Portugal.

specific regime for natural resources is sometimes used as a means of protection for the environmental integrity of the concerned goods: this is, for instance, the case of protected areas like forests or parks, which aim to preserve these natural areas against their over-exploitation.[13]

Similarly, the Croatian Constitution foresees a 'special' property regime for those goods that are considered of a certain interest for the State and therefore need a special protection.[14] Furthermore, the Croatian Act on Ownership and Other Real Rights (AOORR),[15] states that those components of nature which by reason of their characteristics cannot be under the control of any natural person or legal entity individually, but are used by all – such as the air and water in rivers, lakes and the sea, as well as the seashore – cannot be the object of the right of ownership and other real rights (Art. 3/2 of the AOORR).

English and UK law provide another example of lawful boundaries impinging on the private property of environmental goods. While no doctrine of public trust or public domain exists in English and UK law, there are a certain number of regulatory mechanisms protecting and maintaining certain areas of land, with significant natural features, in the *public interest*. To this end, there are various 'enclave' techniques that are used to promote nature conservation – for instance through the designation of Areas of Outstanding Natural Beauty, national parks, national/local nature reserves, sites of special scientific interest (SSSIs), and European protected areas (SACs, SPAs, SCIs). In such areas, although much of this land may be privately owned (even in the case of national parks), there is a range of restrictions on use of property.[16] In general terms, no compensation is available for owners whose land is subject to nature conservation obligations, except in some cases where owners have been forced to give up existing uses of land.[17]

---

13 See G. Winter, Chapter Germany.

14 Art. 52 of the Croatian Constitution stipulates: 'The sea, seashore, islands, waters, air space, mineral resources, and other natural goods, as well as land, forests, flora and fauna, other components of the natural environment, real estate and goods of particular cultural, historical, economic or ecological significance which are specified by law to be of interest to the Republic of Croatia shall enjoy its special protection. The way in which goods of interest to the Republic of Croatia may be used and exploited by holders of rights thereto and by their owners, as well as compensation for the restrictions imposed on them, shall be regulated by law.' (L. Ofak, Chapter Croatia).

15 Art. 3/2, Croatian Act on Ownership and Other Real Rights (AOORR), NN no. 91/96, 68/98, 137/99, 22/00, 73/00, 114/01, 79/06, 141/06, 146/08, 38/09, 153/09, 90/10 and 143/12.

16 Restrictions on the rights of landowners include controlling all development within the area through dedicated governing authorities (national parks), preventing any potentially 'damaging operations' without consent of the nature conservation regulator (SSSIs), and preventing any development that may adversely affect the integrity of the site (SACs). (E. Scotford, Chapter UK).

17 See R (Trailer & Marina (Leven)) v SS for Environment, Food and Rural Affairs [2004] EWCA Civ 1580and Wildlife and Countryside Act 1981, s 28M. Note that there was a change in regulatory policy in 2000, when a more limited regime for granting compensation was introduced to bolster the effectiveness of the SSSI regime. (E. Scotford, Chapter UK).

A further and different example is given by the Danish legislation on nature protection and use of natural resources, which is not based on the concept of public trusteeship, public property or land stewardship, but on the regulatory power of the State (namely the Parliament) to decide what part of and to what extent nature shall be protected. Danish Law does not foresee the same legal status for all natural resources and the right of using natural resources on private land is considered a property right to the extent its exercise is lawful. For instance, raw materials (such as sand and clay) are part of the property of the private land and the mining right belongs to the owner, provided that mining is permitted on a certain land. Conversely, oil and gas and other minerals placed in the deep underground are defined, by the Underground Act, as property of the State. Anyway, when natural resources are not defined as public property, they are considered private property and the private rights connected to them can be limited or restrained only if justified by public interest.[18]

C. Ownership in Whose Interest?

From the analysis of the national surveys, it emerges that natural resources can fall under public or private ownership, according to the different legal and normative traditions of the European countries. However, both in cases when they are considered as public domain, or as the object of private property, the recognition of the special nature of environmental goods as goods embedding a common interest is relevant in all the European legal systems. This recognition determines the need to limit and condition the ownership and the use of environmental goods, in order to ensure that the whole society may enjoy these goods. The public property or the restrained private property regimes applying to environmental goods should then safeguard the interest of all the members of the community – citizens and States – and strike a balance between the different interests that may be at stake. But how is the concept of 'common interest' shaped and understood in Europe? Is the common interest connected to the notion of 'common concern'? To say it in legal terms, does the concept of 'common interest' turn into common rights and duties, so as to empower both public authorities and private persons as environmental goods' trustees? It would be logical enough to assume that when a common interest is officially acknowledged, rights and duties connected to the management, preservation and stewardship of that interest should be commonly shared. Yet, such understanding does not seem to be reflected in the classic notion of 'public good', under which most European Constitutions or national legislations place environmental goods; nor can it find its place under the notion of private goods which are traditionally conceived as belonging to one's exclusive property.

As the above presented examples show, when environmental goods are classified as public goods, they belong to the State, which (together with other

---

18 Section 73(1) of the Constitution of Denmark.

territorial public authorities) is the only subject entitled to have rights over national resources. Indeed, in such cases, it is only the State (or another competent territorial public authority) that can grant private persons the right to use or manage natural resources, through concessions or authorizations. In such a context, it is noteworthy to recall that, although, in most cases, such concessions and authorisations are granted under specific conditions,[19] and do not affect the existing property rights, they are notwithstanding likely to generate some paradoxical situations. For instance, in Italy concessions create an exclusive right of use with respect to a certain land or resource, which gives the concession holder (*'concessionario'*) the right to exclude all others from using such a resource, without foreseeing any duty of compensation for the rest of the community that is excluded from its use.[20] Furthermore, in spite of the fact that there is not a general right of trust or legitimate expectation in the perseverance of the authorisation/concession, until recently a sort of 'right of preference' in the perseverance of a concession existed in the domain of concessions, for instance with regard to the use of beaches, which awarded exclusive rights of exploitation for the provision of touristic services in a given beach or part of the beach. In such a case, the concession was periodically reviewed, but the owner of the concession enjoyed a 'right of preference' (*diritto di insistenza*) over other possible interested parties, which *de facto* rendered the concession almost permanent. Considering that the collective use of the natural resources seems to be left aside and no benefits are shared among the members of the community, one may wonder, then, whether the State (or another competent territorial public authority) is properly coping with the common interest embedded in the public environmental good by creating such a situation. It is not surprising that the European Commission challenged this type of concession, which existed in Italy, by starting an infringement procedure. This prompted Italy to modify the relevant regulatory regime of concessions, thus abolishing such a right of preference for the concession holder in relation to the exclusive right of use of beaches.[21]

A similar situation occurs in France, where public authorities can issue long term leases or occupation permits, providing the permit holder with a right *in rem* upon them.[22] In this case, there is no protection for the environmental interest of lands against the discretionary power of public authorities to change their use or to favour their economic development, since environmental protection is not an explicit purpose of such public domain regime.[23]

19 E.g.: they are limited in time and subjected to the payment of fees.

20 A similar situation is present in Portugal, Spain and Slovenia.

21 European Commission, Infringement procedure No. 2008/4908. See M. Montini, Chapter Italy.

22 V. Inserguet-Brisset, *Droit de l'environnement*, Rennes: PUR, 2005, 292 p., pp. 164-165. See M. Galey, Report France.

23 S. Caudal-Sizaret, 'La domanialité public comme instrument de protection de l'environnement', *AJDA* 2009.2329, pp. 2332-2334; M. Deffairi, *La patrimonialisation en droit de l'environnement*, Thèse, 2013, Université Paris I (Panthéon-Sorbonne), p. 861. See M. Galey, Report France.

Another shortcoming emerging from the national legislation analysed in the surveys is the absence of provisions establishing duties of conservation, preservation or restoration of the environmental resource either upon the concession holder,[24] or upon national and local authorities.[25] On this issue, the EU secondary legislation has given a positive contribution by introducing Directive 2004/35/EC on environmental liability with regard to the prevention and remedying of environmental damage (ELD) caused by operators carrying out occupational activities (namely, economic activities).[26] The Directive defines three categories of environmental damages: the first one deals with 'damage to protected species and natural habitats', which is any damage that has significant adverse effects on reaching or maintaining the favourable conservation status of such habitats or species;[27] the second one refers to 'water damage', which is any damage that significantly adversely affects the ecological, chemical and/or quantitative status and/or ecological potential, as defined in the Water Framework Directive 2000/60, of the waters concerned; the third category considers 'land damage', which is any land contamination that creates a significant risk of human health being adversely affected as a result of the direct or indirect introduction, in, or under land, of substances, preparations, organisms or micro-organisms.[28] The ELD directive establishes a framework based on the polluter pays principle[29] and the duty to both prevent and remedy such environmental damages upon the economic operator.[30] Two innovations are, then, brought by the ELD directive into those national legal orders which did not foresee specific duties upon authorized operators: the first one is the duty to take all appropriate measures to prevent and remedy environmental damages; the second one is the duty to pay for the remediation costs related to harm caused

[24] See M. Montini, Report Italy, and A. García Ureta, Report Spain.

[25] For instance, Danish legislation does not contain legal binding duties for the national or local environmental authorities to protect the natural resources or and wild life in any specific way subject to legal review, except when such duties follow from EU legislation on nature protection.

[26] Directive 2004/35/CE of the European Parliament and of the Council of 21 April 2004 on environmental liability with regard to the prevention and remedying of environmental damage, OJ L 143 , 30/04/2004, p. 0056 – 0075.

[27] The habitats and species concerned are defined by reference to species and types of natural habitats identified in the relevant parts of the Directive 2009/147/EC of the European Parliament and of the Council of 30 November 2009 on the conservation of wild birds (so called Birds Directive) and the Habitats Directive 92/43/EEC (Habitats Directive).

[28] Article 2 of Directive 2004/35/CE.

[29] The polluter pays-principle is set out in Article 191(2) of the Treaty on the Functioning of the European Union.

[30] Article 2(6) of the ELD defines the 'operator' as 'any natural or legal, private or public person who operates or controls the damaging occupational activity or, where this is provided for in national legislation, to whom decisive economic power over the technical functioning of such an activity has been delegated, including the holder of a permit or authorisation for such an activity or the person registering or notifying such an activity.'

to the environment. This second feature is particularly relevant, since, according to the ELD directive, the liable operator must bear the cost of the necessary remedial measures. Therefore, where environmental damage occurs, the operator shall promptly inform the competent authority and take all steps to immediately control, contain and remove the relevant contaminants in order to limit or prevent further environmental damage. Following this, the operator must take the necessary remedial measures, and pay the related costs, in accordance with the relevant provisions of the ELD (its Annex II in particular).

It should be recalled here that, under the ELD directive, third parties – natural or legal persons, including NGOs – can submit to the competent authority any observation relating to instances of environmental damage or an imminent threat of such damage of which they are aware and shall be entitled to request the competent authority to take action under the Directive's provisions.[31]Third parties can also request the judicial review of the competent authority's decisions, acts or failure to act.[32] However, they need to prove that they are affected or likely to be affected by environmental damage, or they have a sufficient interest, or are among those whose rights have been impaired. Considering that the national law of the Member States shall determine what constitutes a 'sufficient interest' and 'impairment of a right', the effective judicial empowerment of citizens may be limited by narrow and rigid national definitions of these concepts at national level; or by the fact that most national legislations do not define nor establish thresholds concerning the concept of environmental risk. Moreover, although the ELD does not apply to cases of personal injury, to damage to private property or to any economic loss,[33] the application of the ELD directive is limited only to the three categories of environmental damages as specified in the Directive.[34] For instance, in the case of land damages, the financial responsibility of the operator can be challenged only in case of land's contamination, but not in case of land's erosion or degradation. Nor can the hydrogeological risk be considered to fall under the ELD directive's definition of land damage. As a consequence of the limits of the ELD Directive shown above, it may be argued that such a piece of legislation may certainly give a positive contribution to the protection of the environment in Europe, although it seems

31 Article 12 of the ELD Directive.

32 Article 13 of the ELD Directive.

33 Anyway, the ELD Directive does not affect any right regarding these types of damages (see Recital 14 of the Directive).

34 It is worth recalling that the ELD was amended three times through Directive 2006/21/EC on the management of waste from extractive industries, through Directive 2009/31/EC on the geological storage of carbon dioxide and amending several directives, and through Directive 2013/30/EU on safety of offshore oil and gas operations and amending Directive 2004/35/EC. The amendments broadened the scope of strict liability by adding the 'management of extractive waste' and the 'operation of storage sites pursuant to Directive 2009/31/EC' to the list of dangerous occupational activities in Annex III of the ELD. The Offshore Safety Directive, containing an amendment to the ELD (extension of the scope of damage to marine waters), was adopted in June 2013.

neither to fully cover all the possible situations in which a common interest may be at stake, nor to take into proper account the collective dimension of natural resources as common goods.

A further problem is represented by the difficulty which may be encountered by citizens to claim for a State's (or another territorial public authority) intervention in a case where the protection of the common interest related to a certain environmental good is at risk. In other words, the relevant issue which arises here is related to the following question: how to empower citizens to act as environmental trustees or to enable them to ask the State's (or another territorial public authority) intervention for the protection of the common interest in such a similar situation?

In this sense, a starting point may be represented by the approach taken by art. 3(1) of the EU Directive on access to information,[35] as well as by art. 4(1) of the Aarhus Convention,[36] which guarantee a broad right of access to environmental information (and a related access to justice) held by or for public authorities, without the need for the applicant to prove any particular interest or any damage suffered. Instead, it is well known that neither the Aarhus Convention, nor the European Union legislation, have so far extended the same approach to a generalized right of public participation to all administrative procedures leading to decisions which may affect environmental goods as well as to a generalized access to justice for every citizen and organization with a view to improve the protection of the environmental goods, without the need to prove a specific interest. This is a very serious limitation to the full empowerment of citizens to act as environmental trustees, which should be overcome with a view to provide a more effective protection of environmental goods.

D. In the Name of 'Common Interest': Environmental Goods as Common Goods

The analysis carried out above shows that the current classification of environmental goods as public or (conditioned) private goods is not adequate to ensure the effective protection of the common interest embedded in natural resources. As also some scholars have pointed out, in spite of the improvements with regard to the access to environmental justice brought by the recent judicial practice in human rights adjudication, progress in the field of environmental law remains limited.[37] This may be due *inter alia* to the predominance of the 'individualistic' perspective through which human rights courts address the environmental dimension and raises the question of

35 Directive 2003/4/EC of the European Parliament and of the Council of 28 January 2003 on public access to environmental information and repealing Council Directive90/313/EEC.

36 Aarhus Convention (Convention On Access To Information, Public Participation In Decision-Making And Access To Justice In Environmental Matters), done at Aarhus, Denmark, on 25 June 1998.

37 F Francioni, 'International Human Rights in an Environmental Horizon', above footnote No. 3, 41-55.

whether the legal instruments for human rights protection are the proper legal tools for dealing with the increasing challenges affecting environmental goods. Such a reductionist approach, indeed, does not cope with the inner nature of the environmental goods as public goods '*indispensable for the life and welfare of society as a whole*'.[38] A different approach to the understanding, classification and treatment of the environmental goods is therefore needed. To this end, it may be useful to have a look at some multilateral environmental agreements (MEAs), as well as at some other international conventions dealing with the protection of environmental and cultural heritage as goods in the common interest of the mankind.

Under international law, indeed, the collective dimension of goods of environmental and cultural value is brought to the forefront since they are often defined as '*part of the world heritage of mankind as a whole*' and, in reason of this, '*it is incumbent on the international community as a whole to participate in the protection of the cultural and natural heritage of outstanding universal value, by the granting of collective assistance which, although not taking the place of action by the State concerned, will serve as an efficient complement thereto*'.[39] On the same line, several MEAs explicitly link the conservation, preservation and sustainable management of natural resources – such as wild fauna and flora, water, etc. – to the *interests of all mankind as a whole*.[40] More recently, this concept has been widened by the alternative definition of '*common concern of humankind*', which encompasses not only rights but also duties, and overcomes the idea that only the State is entitled to act.[41] In fact, as some authors noted, '*common concern of humankind*' focuses on the multitude of individuals who are part of the humanity as a whole.[42] Such recognition, should, by consequence, provide the basis for stronger demands from civil society for legal, political, economic and institutional action to properly address the management and conservation of environmental goods.[43]

The shift from 'common heritage' to 'common concern' under international law can be seen as a step forward toward the recognition of common responsibilities and shared duties for environmental goods. Some authors argue that while the notion of 'common areas' or 'common heritage' are limited to certain geographic areas and resources, the 'common concern' is a broader concept

38 F Francioni, *ibidem*, at 41 and 44.

39 Preamble of the UNESCO Convention on the Conservation of World Cultural and Natural Heritage (1972).

40 1959 Antarctic Treaty (Preamble) and its 1991 Madrid Protocol on Environmental Protection (Preamble); 1973 Convention on International Trade in Endangered Species of Wild Fauna and Flora".

41 1992 UN Framework Convention on Climate Change, 1992 Convention on Biological Diversity, 1994 Convention to Combat Desertification.

42 D Shelton, 'The Common Concern of Humanity', (2009), *Iustum Aequum Salutare*, at 35.

43 B Boer, Land Degradation as a Common Concern of Humankind, in F Lenzerini and A F Vrdoljak, *International Law for Common Goods Normative Perspectives on Human Rights, Culture and Nature*, (2014, Hart Publishing), 289, at 307.

because it refers to unlimited areas and calls for a spirit of global partnership.[44] This idea seems to be reflected in the Article 3 of the Draft Covenant on Environment and Development, titled the Common Concern of Humanity, which states that '*the global environment is a common concern of humanity and under the protection of the principles of international law, the dictates of the public conscience and the fundamental values of humanity*'.[45] The acknowledgement of the 'public conscience' as one of the founding elements of the global environmental governance emphasizes the fact that citizens, as members of humanity, are not only the users of the environmental resources, but also their guardians and can thus contribute to the sustainable stewardship of the collective natural resources.

On this argument, it is worth recalling Elinor Ostrom's theory of commons, as presented in her work '*Governing the Commons*', which proposes a way to solve the well-known problem of the 'tragedy of commons'.[46] Ostrom, indeed, highlights that a third way to own and manage common goods, such as natural resources, is possible. This should be promoted by involving local communities, whose members become trustees of such common resources, also named as 'commons', which are classified neither as public nor as private properties.[47] The author bases her theory on the identification of a number of factors conducive to successful resource management by observing how some real-world communities manage communal resources – such as fisheries, land irrigation systems, farmlands and pastoral lands.[48] She identifies eight principles for managing commons in a durable and sustainable way.[49] Among those, she lists the presence of a community governing the use of common goods through rules based

44 J Brunné, 'Common Areas, Common Heritage and Common Concern' in D Bodansky, J Brunné and E Hey (eds), *The Oxford Handbook of International Environmental Law* (Oxford, 2007), at 564.

45 Article 3, Draft Covenant on Environment and Development, Fourth edition conveyed to the UN Member States on occasion of the High-level Event on Biodiversity on 22 September 2010 during the 65th UN/GA.

46 G Hardin, 'The tragedy of Commons', (1968), *Science* 162 (3859): 1243–1248. doi:10.1126/science.162.3859.1243.

47 It should be noted that the term 'commons' has come to identify things such as the atmosphere, oceans, rivers, fish stocks, energy or any other shared resources which are not formally regulated. We could also define them as *res communis omnium*.

48 E Ostrom and her co-workers studied local communities and villages in Switzerland, Kenya, Guatemala, Nepal, Turkey, and Los Angeles.

49 The eight principles identified and proposed by Elinor Ostrom are the following ones:
1. Define clear group boundaries. 2. Rules governing use of common goods to local needs and conditions. 3. Ensure that those affected by the rules can participate in modifying the rules. 4. Make sure the rule-making rights of community members are respected by outside authorities. 5. Develop a system, carried out by community members, for monitoring members' behavior. 6. Use graduated sanctions for rule violators. 7. Provide accessible, low-cost means for dispute resolution. 8. Build responsibility for governing the common resource in nested tiers from the lowest level up to the entire interconnected system. Source: http://www.onthecommons.org/magazine/elinor-ostroms-8-principles-managing-commmons.

on local needs and conditions and sharing the burden of common responsibilities. It is fundamental then to have appropriate community-based rules and procedures in place together with built-in incentives for responsible use and punishments for overuse. Other crucial principles are the following ones: to ensure that those affected by the rules can participate in modifying the rules; make sure that the rule-making rights of community members are respected by 'outside authorities' (e.g. public administrative authorities), and develop a system, carried out by community members, for monitoring members' behaviour.

Ostrom's analysis builds around an integrated and multidisciplinary approach, which mixes concepts and notions of economics, anthropology, social and political sciences, environmental science, and law. According to Ostrom's theory, this third way of managing natural resources as 'commons' can strike an appropriate balance between collective and individual interests. Moreover, it may turn the meaning of the concept of *public conscience* into concrete rules, duties and rights commonly shared among the member of the community.

In recent times, an attempt to introduce the theory of 'commons' into the broader framework of a national legal order has been developed in Italy, where a challenging debate on the opportunity to revise the traditional distinction between public and private property contained in the Italian Civil Code has widely spread in the last years. In 2007, the Italian Government set up the so-called *Commission on Public Goods*, also called *Rodotà Commission*, by the name of its chairman. The Commission prompted and steered a very broad discussion on the revision of public and private property concepts in the Italian legal system and proposed the institution of a third category of goods, which ought to be identified as 'common goods'. The common goods should include all the goods that aim at satisfying common general interests and are functional to the exercise of fundamental rights, for the benefit of present and future generations. Common goods may be subject to public or private property, but their common and collective use must be guaranteed. The new category of common goods should include most natural resources, such as rivers, lakes and their sources; all waters; the air; parks, forests and other woods, high mountains, glaciers, environmentally protected coasts and seashores, wild fauna and protected flora; and, more generally, all archaeological, cultural and environmental heritage as well as landscape protected areas.

The reason for the quest to establish the new category of 'common goods' lies in the fact that the State or the other local territorial public authorities, which currently exercise property rights or regulate the management of those goods, are often not able to provide them adequate protection, insofar as such institutions often find themselves in a position of conflict of interest. For instance, while on the one side the State (or another local territorial public authority) might have an interest to protect parks and other cultural, environmental or landscape protected areas, on the other hand such a conservationist interest may compete and be in conflict with the parallel interest to gain profits from their commercial exploitation. For this reason, the proposal of the *Rodotà Commission* aims at reinforcing the protection of those goods, while enhancing their collective use, in the interests of the present and future generations. In order to achieve this objective, in line with Ostrom's findings on the most successful management of commons, the preferred governance system for common goods should be based on local community's management. Such a type of common management should imply a greater involvement of civil society, stakeholders and all citizens in decision-making processes, through a greater transparency, a better information flow and an increased use of public consultation as an appropriate management tool.

Along this line of reasoning, according to the proposal of the *Rodotà Commission*, when the community's management of common goods is not feasible, the possibility to give a concession to private parties for the exclusive exploitation of the common goods should still be possible, but ought to be subject to more severe constraints and controls, as compared to the current concession regime granted, for instance, under the Italian Civil Code's regulation on public goods.

The ultimate aim of the proposal of the *Rodotà Commission* is to lead to an amendment to the relevant provisions on property law of the Italian Civil Code. So far, despite a broad support gained by the proposal, this has not happened yet; however, since its publication, the work of the *Commission* has given rise to an intense scholarly and public debate, which may eventually exercise a certain influence not only on the Italian legal order, but possibly extend its reach also to other jurisdictions.

E. Conclusion

The analysis conducted in the present chapter has shown that in the majority of the European jurisdictions the ownership of environmental goods is normally attributed to the State (or other territorial public authorities), which should act as trustees on behalf of their citizens. However, the State and the other relevant territorial public authorities may also grant private persons the right to use and manage environmental goods through concessions or authorisations, which normally confer private persons the right to use natural resources, subject to some limitations.

Moreover, in some European countries there may be cases where citizens can have the ownership of environmental goods; however, in such cases, their relevant private property's rights must be exercised within the limits set by the law and the administrative regulations which may be enacted by public authorities.

In both cases, whether the environmental goods are falling within the public domain, or are the object of private property, the recognition of their special nature as goods embedding a common interest is relevant in all the European legal systems. This recognition determines the need to limit and condition the ownership and use of environmental goods, in order to ensure that the common interest of the whole society related to such goods is satisfied. To this respect, we have seen that the main question to be addressed is the following one: in whose interest is ownership of environmental goods exercised? Is there a guarantee that the common interest is effectively pursued by the owners or managers of environmental goods?

In such a context, we have tried in particular to determine whether the concept of 'common interest' turns into common rights and duties, so as to empower both public authorities and private persons as environmental goods' trustees. In this sense, the research conducted has shown that citizens may sometimes encounter some difficulty in claiming a State's (or another territorial public authority) intervention in a case where the protection of the common interest related to a certain environmental good is at risk. Therefore, we have argued that the approach taken by the EU Directive on access to information (Directive 2003/4/CE) as well by the Aarhus Convention, which guarantee a broad right of access to environmental information held by or for public authorities (and a related access to justice), without the need for the applicant to show any particular interest or any damage suffered, should be further extended. In particular, we held that such an approach should promote the recognition of a generalized right of public participation to all administrative procedures leading to decisions which may affect environmental goods as well as to a generalized access to justice for every citizen and organization with a view to improve the protection of the environmental goods, following the spirit and the requirements of the Aarhus Convention.

In the final paragraph of the chapter, we have claimed that the current classification of environmental goods as public or (conditioned) private goods is often not adequate to ensure an effective protection of the common interest embedded in natural resources. Therefore, environmental goods should be re-classified and re-framed on the basis of the concept of *'common concern of humankind'*. Such a move should be seen as a step forward towards the recognition of common responsibilities and shared duties for environmental goods and should provide the basis for stronger demands from the civil society for legal, political, economic and institutional action to properly address the management and conservation of environmental goods.

This reasoning is inspired by Elinor Ostrom's theory on commons, which proposed a third way of managing natural resources, notably as 'commons'. In particular, we have seen how this approach can strike an appropriate balance between collective and individual interests and may turn the meaning of the concept of *public conscience* into concrete rules, duties and rights commonly shared among the member of the community.

Moreover, we have presented a brief account of the work of the *Rodotà Commission*, which proposed a revision of public and private property concepts in the Italian legal system and the institution of a third category of goods, which ought to be identified as 'common goods'. In such a context, the common goods should include all the goods, either subject to public or to private property, that aim at satisfying common general interests and which are functional to the exercise of fundamental rights, for the benefit of present and future generations. To this respect, the collective use of the common goods should be properly guaranteed. Such a proposal is obviously based on the assumption that the State and the other local territorial public authorities, which currently exercise property rights or regulate the management of those goods, are often not able to provide them an adequate protection, insofar as they often find themselves in a position of conflict of interest.

As we mentioned above, despite the yet uncertain outcome of the *Rodotà Commission* proposal, which aims at leading to an amendment to the relevant provisions on property law of the Italian Civil Code, it should be underlined that, in any case, such a proposal may eventually exercise a certain influence not only on the Italian legal order, but also to other jurisdictions, for the management of environmental goods as 'common goods', in the true name of common interest.

Private Property in Request for Environmental Protection

Rajko Knez

A. Introduction

The meaning of property differs not only between national legal systems, but it is also not the same under constitutional law, civil or administrative law. Under constitutional law, it is much broader. In addition, one has to take into account also the international concept of property, especially Art. 1 of the Protocol 1 of the ECHR.[1] On the other hand, environmental law, a broad area of law, has close links with all mentioned areas of law, including international and EU law. That means that the notion of property in the field of environmental law must reflect many different interrelations with environmental issues. By reading the national reports in this book, one can learn different approaches of the Member States of the EU to this matter.

In principle, property can be used as a reason against environmental protection measures of the state or, *vice versa*, as a reason to request more or additional environmental protection measures from the state. On the one hand, property is invoked as bulwark against state measures of environmental protection (*for instance, an industrial operator defending his property and his factory against measures restricting air pollution, a farmer defending his farm property against nature protection measures*), and on the other hand, property is invoked to trigger state based environmental protection measures (*for instance a resident asking the competent authorities to protect him from pollution from a neighbouring factory or any other industrial operator*).[2]

This chapter will focus on the second aspect.[3] In order to do so, one has to distinguish, which area of law is applicable, whether constitutional, administra-

1 Despite the absence in the ECHR of any explicit regulatory framework to condemn violations of environmental protection thresholds or the failure to implement court orders requiring the cessation of harmful or hazardous activities, the ECtHR has nevertheless ended up indirectly guaranteeing a minimum level of environmental protection. In fact, a constructive and dynamic interpretation of the ECHR has permitted these concerns of a novel nature gradually to filter into the interpretation of first generation human rights. As a result, a right to basic environmental protection can be based on existing human rights, such as the right to life (Art. 2), the right to the fair trial (Art. 6), the right to private and family life and the home (Art. 8), the freedom of expression and information (Art. 10), as well as the freedom of assembly and association (Art. 11). However, with respect to property, Art. 1 of the Protocol 1 of the ECHR remains the basic rule. See, more in this respect, Nicolas de Sadeleer, EU environmental law and the internal market, Oxford university press, 2014, p. 113.

2 A case that illustrates such approach is included in the national reports: A factory, situated near a town, has been operating for decades. People are slowly realizing that statistically the inhabitants in the city and in the vicinity do not live average age and the cancer is more frequently present among them, also the frequent cause of the deaths. They have no direct proofs that the factory could be responsible, although it is rather clear that the soil around the factory is poisoned and that the heavy metals found in the vegetable could be linked to the factory. However, credible proofs are missing. Readers can find varieties of answers given by different authors, from the viewpoint of administrative, private, constitutional, EU law, etc.

3 The first aspect is dealt with in G. Winter, Chapter Private property versus environmental protection.

tive or private law. The answer to this question mainly depends on the nature of the legal relationship; whether the case is about the legal relationship between individuals, hence private law rules being applicable, or between individuals and the state, meaning that administrative law is applicable. Nevertheless, one has to take into account that constitutional law might be applicable in both cases, and this is true also for international rules and international commitments which rather oblige the state, but can, indirectly, also be applicable in cases involving only individuals.

And there is another feature, in case of environmental law; namely, one has to distinguish between damage in the traditional sense of affecting private property, and environmental damage which is damage caused to the environment as such and where ownership is not important. In the latter case, the rights of non-governmental environmental associations (NGOs) are extremely important; namely, in case state measures are ineffective or insufficient, NGOs can be in a position to force competent state authorities to act differently, more effectively, for the sake and in the interest of the environment.[4] Although, this is not the thrust of analysis of this chapter, it is hereby mentioned in order to distinguish between the property and notion of traditional damage in the one hand, and on the other hand the environmental damage where property does not play a decisive role.[5]

B. Property Based Remedies Asking for Environmental Protection

As mentioned above, legal remedies are different in private and in administrative law. Also, procedures are rather different. In administrative law, decisions taken by state authorities are of the *'de iure imperii'* nature, that is they are binding, state authorities acting on entrusted powers and therefore parties (on the one hand state authorities and on the other hand individuals) not being on equal footing. This means that individuals are usually not in a position to negotiate in administrative procedures. Only as a second step, when the individual brings the case to court, is there equality of rights in the court proceedings.

Contrastingly, in the private law sphere parties are usually on equal footing; they can negotiate having the same rights and duties; their acts are *'de iure gestionis'*. If a dispute arises, they can apply to a court (or alternative dispute resolution) as a third body, which can resolve the dispute as an independent and objective institution just as in the case of court proceedings on administrative matters.

---

4 In this respect, see in particular J.H. Jans & A. Outhuijse, Chapter The Netherlands, which focuses also to this issue.

5 See more in this respect G. Winter, Chapter Germany.

These differences are reflected in two different kinds of legal remedies: the first one, within administrative law, is usually called *public law remedies*, and the second one within the private law relationships, *private law remedies*.

1. Private Law Remedies

Under private law different remedies are available in order to defend property rights for environmental reasons. They include: *tort claims* to recover damages to an individual (but not the environmental damage as such), *actions to prevent damage* (like to prevent exploitation of natural resources),[6] *nuisance claims* within neighbourhood law aiming at damage compensation and prevention, and *actio popularis*.

There is an important difference concerning possible defendants in civil law and common law systems as can be shown in nuisance claims. In both systems an action for nuisance can be brought against private individuals. The systems diverge when it comes to harmful activities of public authorities like if a local authority runs a communal waste landfill as supposed in the questionnaire, question 9. In civil law systems nuisance claims would then only be applicable if the local authority acts in a private (or 'fiscal', as it is sometimes called) capacity, such as if it has entrusted a private company with operating the landfill. Other remedies would apply if the activity is categorised as public, such as compensation for 'damage from public works' (*dommage de travaux publics*) in French law or for 'expropriation-like interference' (*enteignender Eingriff*) in German law.[7] In contrast, in common law systems no difference is made between private and public capacities of public authorities. Nuisance is applicable in any case.[8]

In substance, however, the nuisance concepts do not differ much between the two systems. Crucial is to determine what the acceptable level of environmental adverse effect is. In the Slovene, French and German legal systems it is necessary to establish that the damage is 'unusual' in the relevant neighbourhood.[9] In the Netherlands and the UK the applicant must show that burden is an 'unreasonable' interference with neighbouring property.[10] These are legal standards that have to be assessed on a case-by-case basis so that case law is a primary tool, together with scholarly debate, to give answers in each particular case. It appears from the cases discussed in the national reports that the differences in practice are not significant. As a matter of fact, in every case-by-case assessment there is a certain risk, and the parties, especially applicants,

6 According to the EU Court of Justice, one has to take into account the precautionary principle, even in cases where damage is still uncertain. Therefore, actions are possible also in cases where it is 'likely' that certain activity will affect a site, a property, etc. See, case C-127/02, *Waddenzee* [2004], ECR I-7405, para. 44.

7 See M. Galey, Chapter France, Question 9; G. Winter, Chapter Germany, Question 9.

8 J.H. Jans & A. Outhuijse, Chapter The Netherlands; E. Scotford, UK Chapter, Question 9.

9 R. Knez, Chapter Slovenia; M. Galey, Report France; G. Winter, Chapter Germany, all on Question 9.

10 E. Scotford, Chapter UK, Question 9.

cannot be sure what will be the outcome of the case. This is a certain handicap, but it does not appear that it substantially reduces the number of environmental claims.

Often there is administrative regulation which defines the thresholds of tolerable environmental effects. In that case it must be determined if such regulation is also binding in the private law sphere, or if that sphere is autonomous. The national reports show that the legal systems answer differently to this question.[11]

The French report draws attention to a further criterion for solving nuisance situations – the question of time. According to the so-called *'pre-occupation principle'* a private landowner cannot resort to a private law action in nuisance against polluting activities on neighbouring lands in order to get an injunctive relief or even compensation for environmental damage, if these activities, whether agricultural, industrial, commercial or traditional, took place before the landowner settled, and if they comply with public regulations and statutes.[12] Nevertheless, the landowner's legal position in France regarding environmental liabilities has been strengthened in the wake of the passing of the environmental charter and the constitutional value it gives to the prevention principle.[13] Indeed, the mere risk of harm is now recognized by civil case law as a valid ground for suing neighbours in an action for private nuisance.[14]

Apart from nuisance claims tort liability is a possible remedy in cases of environmental adverse effects on property. It is in the first place fault based, but in case of dangerous activities or dangerous substances, strict liability applies (e.g. toxic waste, exploitation of groundwater, nuclear energy, soil contamination).[15]

In Slovenia is the *actio popularis* the widest legal base for actions against individuals in environmental matters[16] and also against the State in case where state authorities are allowed to undertake certain activities, but additional preventive measures are requested. *Actio popularis* is not only a very important

---

11 See for a comparative analysis E. Scotford, Permit Excuse.

12 This principle was passed in statute law through some planning act in 1976 (Code de la construction et de l'habitation, art. L.112-16), on the demand of farming organisations grumbling against abusive (or deemed to be so) litigation introduced by residential owners. The French constitutional council has recently held that the pre-occupation rule did comply with the requirements of the environmental charter – Constitutional Court decision N° 2011-116 QPC of 8 April 2011. See in this respect *M. Galey*, Chapter France.

13 B. Parance, 'Le sort du propriétaire dans la responsabilité environnementale', in C. Cans (dir.), *La responsabilité environnementale: prévention, imputation, réparation*, Paris: Dalloz, 2009, 421 p., p. 319 à 322.

14 For example: Civ. 2è, 10 juin 2004, req. n° 03-10.434; Civ. 1è, 28 nov. 2007, req. n° 06-19.405; Civ. 2è, 15 mai 2008, *Billy v. Valmory*, req. n° 07-13.453.

15 L. Lavrysen, Chapter Belgium.

16 M. Juhart, Okoljska odgovornost – med javnim in zasebnim pravom, v: Zbornik znanstvenih razprav Pravne fakultete v Ljubljani. LXVIII/2008, str. 107–127.

legal instrument in the field of the environment; usually, it is also applicable in different private relationship cases, where an individual would like to abate certain dangerous activities, *ex post* and *ex ante*. However, in the case of the environment such an action can also have an important indirect effect. If an action is brought by one individual against another for the sake of its property and environmental harm, the effect will also affect the area of environmental damage as such.[17] The *actio popularis* is regulated in Slovene *Obligation code* in a very wide manner; according to paragraph 1 of Art. 133 *any person* may request that another person, liable for danger, which might cause major damage, refrains from activities that might cause damage and to take preventive actions. A question, who is eligible to ask the court to prevent threats or possible future damage, remains to some extent open in the Slovenian legal order. Among scholars this question is not uniformly represented. Some authors, warns that too wide interpretation might not be proper.[18] Case law, on the other hand, is not directly dealing with it.[19] Most of cases refer to neighbourhood relations where the court has now difficulties dealing with definition of *locus standi* for 'any person'. Namely, it is rather evident, that a neighbour, whose immovable is affected by other neighbour, has a legal interest to claim legal protection. However, in cases, which refer to the environment, courts uses also additional legal bases to support *locus standi* for *actio popularis;* Art. 72 of Slovenian Constitution, which assures a right to a healthy living environment; and to Art. 15 of the Law on the Environmental Protection, which offers *locus standi* to citizens and their associations against anybody that threatens the environment.[20] In environmental matters, therefore, courts use a broad approach. However, it is necessary to emphasize that *actio popularis* can be used only when substantive damage or a substantive danger is at stake; it is therefore limited in this respect. Nevertheless, *actio popularis* is rather uniquely regulated in the Slovenian legal

17 *Actio popularis* is primarily about *locus standi*. Certain national legal orders are having restrictive standing requirements. But, one has to take into account that the national courts and the tribunals of the Member States are, as well as the EU Court of Justice, guardians of the EU legal order and the judicial system of the EU. It is therefore up to the national courts to ensure judicial protection of individual rights under EU law. However, as said, national procedure laws have shown an amazing variety of approaches, ranging from wide interpretation of *actio popularis* to very restrictive standing requirements, such as the impairment of the individual legal right. As a result, standing requirements remain a major procedural hurdle that many litigants are unable to overcome. See also, N. de Sadeleer, EU environmental law and the internal market, Oxford University Press, 2014, p. 97.

18 B. Strohsack, Odškodninsko pravo in druge neposlovne obveznosti (II), Časopisni zavod, Uradni list RS, Ljubljana 1996, p. 54.

19 B. Zuljan, Civilnopravna odgovornost povzročitelja za obremenjevanje okolja, Pravna praksa, 2009, št. 27, p. 22.

20 Preventive actions are always interpreted by the court in connection with Art. 15 of the Environmental Protection Act, which assures preventive actions to any Slovene citizens against any other person of private law, like an industrial operator, as well as Art. 72 of the Slovene Constitution, assuring a personal right to a healthy environment.

order, but still not widely used by individuals who are not directly affected by somebody else's activity. The reason is that possible failure in the court procedure may result in substantive costs, that would need to be reimburse to the defender by the plaintiff.

In practice, plaintiffs under *actio popularis* rule are mostly individuals, who can also prove damages. They are directly affected. Only affected individuals might bring a claim for damages (par. 3), whereby preventive action (par. 1) can be brought by any person. In practice, as a rule, claims based on *actio popularis* provision are usually used by individuals who suffer damages.[21]

2. Public Law Remedies

By *public law remedies*, property holders can challenge administrative acts permitting damaging activities (and also omissions by administrative authorities; i.e. action for inactivity). Such remedies are available both in civil and common law systems. Usually, individuals need to prove that they are individually concerned. As noted above, this will usually not be the case if the environmental damage as such is at stake (usually state authorities act *de iure imperii)*. NGOs may bring actions in such cases within the realm of Art. 9 Aarhus Convention on access to justice as transformed by Directive 2003/35/EC and interpreted by the ECJ in *Lesoochranarske*.[22] An individual can also claim interests in an action, if his/her property is at stake. For instance, a farmer, whose land will be or was polluted, can challenge the responsible administrative body to take measures, so that the usability of the land is restored, not however that rare species shall be resettled or the ground water to be cleaned up.

Within public law, the main legal remedy is a possibility to challenge administrative acts, which usually are different kinds of environmental permits, in order to obtain the annulment of the whole act or part of it. Sometimes the removal of a certain permit will be searched for a subsequent action of private nuisance (compensation). The plaintiff may also sue the administrative authority for compensation of damage caused by the unlawful permit.[23]

Private law remedies are in many respects closely connected with public law. Especially, as mentioned above, in cases where activities, dangerous to the environment and to the individuals, are to be, or already are, allowed by permit or another administrative act. Several approaches are possible: The first question is whether an existing permit can prevent any kind of private law action or legal

[21] Comp. a judgment of Supreme court of the RS, II Ips 204/2014.

[22] ECJ Case C-240/09. In addition, the German report explains also a trick where environmental NGOs can, outside the reach of the said directive and court opinion, file an action as a property holder. The trick is to buy a piece of land in the neighbourhood of a contested development just for the purposes of seeking legal protection as a land owner. In that case the land is called stopping estate (Sperrgrundstueck). See G. Winter, Chapter Germany.

[23] See, for instance, Latvia, where such compensation is provided even without the negligence of the authority being required. See Z. Mikosa, Chapter Latvia.

remedies (for instance for nuisance, compensation, preventive actions, etc.). A second question asks whether such permit can be annulled, or changed. Thirdly, it is important whether a mandamus action is admissible, i.e. if the court can be asked to order the competent administrative authority to intervene and take appropriate measures against the offender. Fourthly, it may be that the administrative authority is liable under private or public law to pay compensation when it has unlawfully failed to take measures preventing environmental damage to private property.

This wide range of questions are differently answered in the reports. Some reports explain that in case of a permit, the state cannot be held liable (neither the operator), while others explain that an administrative permit does not hinder the compensation claim. But, in all cases, it is clear that private law remedies depend much on the public law rules; especially it is worth challenging first the administrative act, or to ask for its change (like the possibility to invoke article 13 (5) and (7) of the Industrial Emissions Directive 2010/75/EU).[24] Revising permit conditions can be triggered on the request of the inhabitants or *ex-officio* by the administration itself. If the operator (factory) causes serious negative effects for the environment and a change of permit does not provide a reasonable solution, the administrative authorities may be required to close the factory. This, however, as explained in the Dutch report, is rarely the case.[25]

Challenges of public acts (permits) will usually take a lot of time; first, parties have to prove *locus standi*, the possibility to be a party, and that the industrial operator causes damages which is not an easy task if damages are not clearly visible (like damages to the health of the individuals,[26] damages to nature which takes time, even decades, to become visible). Also, it is sometimes difficult to establish a causal link between the damage and the operator.[27] Moreover, court proceedings take time and might also be very expensive. This is why the said remedies are not very effective, and individuals think twice before commencing them, especially in legal systems where the costs of the procedures are high and where the losing party has to repay all the costs to another (i.e. winning) party.

If procedures last too long, then justice is delayed instead of being served. Interim measures are correct answers in this respect, including also measures

---

24 OJ L 334, 17.12.2010, p. 17.

25 J.H Jans & A. Outhuijse, Chapter The Netherlands.

26 It seems, from the landmark judgment of *Janecek*, C-237/07, that the EU Court of Justice is keen to offer more protection (*locus standi* and assessment on direct effect of directive's rules), in cases where individuals or public health is at stake. L. Krämer, Environmental justice in the European court of justice, in J. Ebbesson and P. Okowa (Eds., Environmental Law and Justice in Context, Cambridge, 2009, p. 209).

27 See in this respect case Tatar v. Romania (application no. 67021/01) and dissenting opinions of judges Župančič and Gyulumyan, explaining that the causal link in environmental matters is not properly regulated. Judges, inter alia, wrote *'Le respect de la vie privée est une valeur primordiale, dont la défense, par le juge européen, ne saurait être limitée par l'absence d'une certitude absolue, surtout dans le contexte des maladies modernes'*.

by competent inspections. Inspections are usually obliged to take actions if public interests are at stake (but not for the sake of private interests); since the environmental issues are of public interest, this condition is usually fulfilled.

In addition to public remedies as explained above, there is legal protection of property for environmental reasons also through criminal proceedings. This is not part of the national reports, although some reports mention also this possibility.[28] In most cases, criminal actions for violation of environmental protection rules are in the competence of state authorities (prosecutors). Individuals are not competent to file such actions. Nevertheless, they can induce prosecutors to start procedures.

Criminal environmental law has also been introduced by EU law. One can see this as a pilot project of the EU. Although there are very limited competences of the EU in the field of criminal law, the EU adopted Directive 2008/99/EC on the protection of the environment through criminal law, which imposes obligations on the Member States to regulate criminal offences against the environment.[29] Criminal law is of extreme importance in the field of the environment, because it focuses on the persons responsible rather than on the companies. Since the environment is often destroyed or deteriorated by industrial operators, i.e. commercial companies, where the liability is limited to the assets of the companies, the responsibility usually does not reach the person in charge. If they can 'hide' behind the company and behind the rules of a 'corporate veil', then individuals truly responsible for improper orders and measures remain unpunished. In this respect, criminal law serves as additional pressure for proper corporative decision-making and measures in the field of the environment. Still, one huge problem remains: that criminal offences according to the Directive 2008/99/EC are only those, which are defined as offences in administrative environmental law. However, environmental regulation cannot foresee all possible actions that need to be forbidden and therefore often administrative prohibitions are lacking that may trigger criminal prosecution.[30]

C. Conclusion

Based on the above, one can make certain analyses and conclusions. Going back to the beginning of this chapter, the question was posed whether there are differences between, on the one hand, where property is invoked as a bulwark against state measures of the environmental protection,

[28] See in particular the national chapters on Belgium, Spain, Portugal, Italy in this volume.

[29] Directive 2008/99/EC on the protection of the environment through criminal law, OJ L 328, 6.12.2008, p. 28-37.

[30] See, in this respect, case 96/2000 of the Supreme Court of the RS, where a truck polluted the environment with some oil and since the offence made was not an environmental one, but rather the offence of the administrative traffic rules. The court was therefore of the opinion that there was no criminal offence against the environment or nature.

and on the other hand, where property is invoked to trigger more state based environmental protection measures. To rephrase the question, what are the differences of using property rights *for* or *against* environmental measures.

Claiming additional environmental measures would usually result in a better environmental situation. Opposing environmental measures would usually reflect in a worse environmental situation. In most cases, measures will be claimed from the state authorities or against state authorities. This is true in both cases, *for* and *against* state measures.

In the first case, an activity of state authorities will be claimed and in the second case both, an activity and an inactivity of the state authorities can be requested. In all cases, we can apply a *unity principle*; i.e. in both cases a question arises of who is entitled to claim activity/inactivity. This is a procedural question. However, from a substantive point of view, it will be decisive how the administrative law system (*command & control*) regulates environmental standards (planning standards, emission standards, etc.). This is a question, which is to a certain, rather substantial, extent regulated by the EU rules. It is *ius cogens* corpus of the environmental law rules (on international[31] or EU level, on national level – administrative law) that defines, how one may use one's own property and affect the property of another person.

In both cases, whether property is used for new environmental measures, or against them, the situation is quite alike. First, limitations and rights of the property are subject to the public interests and further on it is necessary to balance between the property rights and the interests of the environment (public interests). Since the national legal orders remain to a large extent free in making this balance, the differences remain. The differences are nevertheless minimised in the sphere of EU environmental rules, especially if there are standards of the *command and control* approach.

[31] See for instance investment treaties; rules of international law protecting the property rights of foreigners are well established. Customary international law grants states a broad measure of discretion in relation to the treatment they accord to the property of aliens on their territory, including foreign investment. Measures intended to protect the environment are part of the rules, which could have the effect of limiting the economic benefits of the investment, or of bringing such benefits to an end altogether. It is accepted, however, that the state's discretion is not unlimited, and customary law requires a state to observe certain minimum international standards in respect to the property of aliens. See more in this respect, P. Sands, J. Peel, A. Farba, R. MacKenzie, Principles of International Environmental Law, 3rd edition, Cambridge, 2012, p. 870-871.

Private Rights and Public Regulation

Civil Liability and the 'Permit Defence'

Eloise Scotford

This short chapter concerns a deceptively simple issue – if a state authorizes an activity, does that authority absolve the operator of legal liability for any damage that his authorized activity might cause? On one view, it seems contrary to find that a lawful activity is unlawful. But the issue is not so simple. What the state might authorize as lawful for a regulatory purpose might still have effects on third parties and impact on their legal rights. The issue above is deceptive, simple because it concerns different layers of law within a legal system, regulating different things – industrial or other environmentally impactful activity, on the one hand, and individual rights not to suffer harm, on the other. Reconciling these layers can be understood in different ways: as an accommodation of public law and private law rights; as concerning the scope of regulatory authority; as a constitutional balancing of administrative and judicial controls; as a competition between community-based activity and individual property rights; as a means of seeking environmental protection through private rights; or as a conflict of legal priorities and norms in an era of increasing regulation and control over land use. This chapter addresses this multi-faceted issue by focusing on the regulation of polluting activities and the rights of neighbouring (or otherwise affected) third parties to enjoy their land. It shows that, on a comparative analysis amongst EU Member States, there is no simple answer to the issue above. In some cases, individual rights to enjoy property can still be asserted against operators who are carrying on lawfully sanctioned activities. In other cases, operational permits seem to close down any rights of neighbouring property right holders to complain about damage caused to their land. In all cases, however, there is a difficult legal issue that reflects a fundamental challenge to individual property rights posed by the modern administrative state and the extensive state environmental controls that now exist across the EU. The different legal approaches adopted by Member States to this challenge reflect not only divergent legal choices over whether public law or private rights take priority, but also different understandings about the nature and role of property rights in an era of extensive land use regulation.

A. No Permit Defence to Third Party Liability of Regulated Entities

To illustrate the legal question at issue, consider the following problem. A communal waste disposal site is located not far away from individual residential houses. Inhabitants claim that they smell bad odour due to the operation of the landfill and that the enjoyment of their land has been seriously compromised. Some would like to sell their property, but there are no potential buyers and their property is almost worthless. The waste disposal site is equipped with the necessary permits and is operating within the permitted odour limits. In most, if not all, EU member states, there is a legal cause of action available to individual property right holders for an actionable 'nuisance' caused by a neighbouring property that is impacting on the enjoyment of their land, including through foul smells.[1] The question here is whether this cause of action might be defended successfully by a defendant, such as the landfill operator in this example, who has a permit to carry on the activities that are causing the bad odour experienced in neighbouring properties. In some EU Member States, the answer is 'no'. There is no 'permit defence' available to regulated operators who are causing a civil law nuisance, which impacts on the amenity and value of neighbouring properties. Whilst this approach seems to give priority to individual property rights over environmental regulation, a closer look at some of the legal positions in Member States shows that this position is not so clear cut.

In at least the following Member States, an individual landowner can bring a civil law action in relation to an alleged nuisance that is otherwise allowed by a regulatory permit: Belgium, Croatia, Czech Republic, Denmark, France, Norway, Slovenia and the United Kingdom. A strong statement defending private law rights in this situation can be found in English case law, in the judgment of Lord Justice Carnwath (as he then was) in *Barr v Biffa Waste.*[2] This was a case with very similar facts to the above scenario, involving a waste processing operation that caused odour problems for neighbouring residences, and the English Court of Appeal found that the neighbouring properties were entitled to bring a claim in nuisance. Carnwath LJ stated:[3]

> The common law of nuisance has co-existed with statutory controls, albeit less sophisticated, since the 19th century. There is no principle that the common law should 'march with' a statutory scheme covering similar subject-matter. Short of express or implied statutory authority to commit a nuisance..., there is no basis, in principle or authority, for using such a statutory scheme to cut down private law rights.

Even more explicitly, Belgian regional legislation concerning environmental permits provides that a regulatory permit has no influence on the rights of third parties.[4] Civil liability can thus arise even when an operator is acting completely in conformity with the conditions of its environmental permit.[5] In Denmark, the position is so protective of neighbours' rights that some scholars argue that the creation of nuisance should be considered an expropriation of their property rights.[6]

1 This is a form of civil or tort law liability in most EU Member States applying nuisance law, a duty of care or other 'neighbouring law principles'; or statutory liability in others (such as under the Norwegian Neighbouring Properties Act (1961)).

2 *Barr v Biffa Waste Services Ltd* [2012] EWCA Civ 312; [2013] QB 455.

3 Ibid [46].

4 E.g. Art 8 Decree of the Flemish Region of 28 June 1985 concerning the environmental permit; Art 49 of the Decree of the Walloon Region of 11 March 1999 concerning the environmental permit.

5 A. Van Oevelen, 'Civielrechtelijke aansprakelijkheid voor milieuschade', in Centrum voor Beroepsvervolmaking in de Rechten – UIA, *Rechtspraktijk en milieubescherming. Antwerps Juristencongres 1991* (Kluwer rechtswetenschappen 1991) 139.

6 See P. Pagh, Chapter Denmark.

However, the picture is not so simple as finding that no permit defence exists in most Member States. There is often not a clear priority given to private rights over public regulation. There are at least two ways in which a defendant's compliance with a regulatory permit may still affect any civil liability owed to third parties. First, the conditions of the permit might impact on a finding of liability in the first place. Second, compliance with a permit might affect the remedy available in any third party claim.

These two qualifications can be seen in the recent UK Supreme Court decision in *Coventry v Lawrence*,[7] which concerned an alleged noise nuisance caused by a motor racing track in a rural neighbourhood. As in *Barr v Biffa Waste*, the outcome of the case supported the right of the neighbouring residential property to bring a claim in nuisance. However, the reasoning of the Supreme Court grappled with the interplay of private law rights and public law regulation in more depth, and found that the planning permission for the motor track to operate (with certain consequential noise in the vicinity) could be relevant to the nuisance claim in the two ways indicated above. First, the lead judgment of Lord Neuberger suggested that the conditions of the regulatory permit concerning acceptable noise levels might be relevant 'evidence' as to what was an unacceptable level of noise in the area and thus an actionable nuisance in the first place.[8] The reasoning here is intricate but it shows that the existence of a permit to operate complicates, and in some cases might undermine, any finding that the use of land by the defendant is 'unreasonable'.[9] Nuisance liability can also be affected by compliance with a regulatory permit where the regulated operations were established before the aggrieved neighbour moved into the area and became affected by the polluting activities of the permit holder. This is the position in French law, where the principle of 'pre-occupation' means that a private landowner cannot resort to a private law nuisance action in order to get injunctive relief or even compensation for environmental damage, if polluting activities on neighbouring lands took place in the area before the landowner settled there and were in compliance with relevant permits.[10]

Second, the majority of the court in *Coventry v Lawrence* supported the view that remedies available to the claimant would be influenced by the track's permit to operate.[11] Rather than an injunction being available to stop the noise nuisance (as is the common remedy for actionable nuisances in English law), some members of the Court suggested that compensation should be the proper remedy in this case, in light of the defendant's permit to operate.[12] This is a

7 [2014] UKSC 13 ('*Coventry*').

8 Ibid [96]. See also Lord Carnwath's separate judgment at [218].

9 As is required to establish nuisance liability in English law.

10 See M. Galey, Chapter France. Cf English law where 'coming to the nuisance' has not been a valid defence in nuisance law, although there might be some scope to challenge this position after *Coventry v Lawrence:* n (7)[53].

11 *Coventry* (n 7) [125] (Lord Neuberger), [161] (Lord Sumption), [169] (Lord Clarke), [246] (Lord Carnwath).

12 Ibid. See the judgments of Lords Neuberger and Sumption in particular (cf Lords Carnwath and Clarke). For further analysis on these points in the Supreme Court's judgment, see Maria Lee, 'Private Nuisance

common position in other Member States. In Croatian law, for example, if damage to third parties results from a defendant performing an activity in the public interest for which an approval has been obtained from a competent authority, only compensation for the damage may be required. The position is similar in Denmark, Norway and Slovenia.[13] The existence of liability to a third party thus does not necessarily stop the permitted activities of a regulated operator. Rather, through civil law obligations leading only to a compensatory remedy, there is a legal accounting for the externalities caused by a regulated entity's operations. This adds a legal obligation and cost for their business, but does not undermine or negate their lawful permission to operate.

This more nuanced reasoning shows that private law property rights, whilst they might be asserted against regulated entities, still exist within a regulatory context of land use control and are affected by that context. They are not absolute rights to the enjoyment of land that trump regulatory permissions. Findings of civil liability may be partly determined by how regulatory decisions have accommodated and balanced the interests of neighbouring properties within a particular area.[14] Having said that, rights to bring claims in nuisance or other civil law obligations remain significant legal rights where they can be asserted against operators that are subject to regulatory control. The subsistence of these rights can be seen as a continuation of strong historical protection for individual property owners, in that individual rights are not simply subjugated to the community interest as this is taken into account in setting permit conditions to control the polluting impacts of a regulated installation. However, private rights do not need to be set against public entitlements. Civil law rights of individual property owners can also be seen as complementing public control – a form of regulatory back up that acts as a second line of defence for environmental protection when regulatory controls do not control polluting impacts adequately. In this way, property rights can be exploited to pursue environmental protection, rather than being restricted or controlled by environmental regulation. By the same token,

in the Supreme Court: *Coventry v Lawrence*' (2014) 7 *Journal of Planning and Environmental Law* 705.

13 Although in Slovenian law, measures to limit adverse impacts can be required as well as compensation. Notably this position has changed in Belgian law. Whilst previously a court could only order an operator causing damage to compensate a third party financially, this approach has been abandoned since a judgment of the Supreme Court of 26 June 1980, in which the Court held that ordering the reparation in kind was not incompatible with the separation of powers: Van Oevelen (n 5) 151-154; H. Bocken, 'Aansprakelijkheid voor schade veroorzaakt door milieuverontreiniging naar Belgisch recht' in H. Bocken and D. Ryckbost (eds), *Verzekering van Milieuschade/ L'assurance des dommages causés par la pollution/Insurance of Environmental Damage* (E Story-Scientia 1991) 63; H. Bocken, D. Ryckbost and S. Delodddere, "Deel 8. Herstel van schade door milieuverontreiniging . Titel 1. Aansprakelijkheid en financiële zekerheden', Interuniversitaire Commissie tot Herziening van het Milieurecht in het Vlaamse Gewest, *Voorontwerp Decreet Milieubeleid* (die Keure, 1995) , 866-867.

14 Eloise Scotford & Rachael Walsh, 'The Symbiosis of Property and English Environmental Law – Property Rights in a Public Law Context' (2013) 76 (6) *Modern Law Review* 1010. See also Maria Lee, 'Tort Law and Regulation: Planning and Nuisance' [2011] *Journal of Planning Law* 986.

in cases where there is strong regulatory control limiting the polluting impacts of an installation, the motivation of neighbouring property owners to pursue a liability claim is likely to be minimal, and a finding of liability equally unlikely. The interplay between private and public control of land is thus complex and 'there is no simple hierarchy between [civil law remedies] and different forms of regulation'.[15] Much will depend on the facts of an individual case in determining if and how civil liability will arise in the context of regulatory control.

B. Permit Defence to Third Party Liability of Regulated Entities

By contrast with the position set out in the previous section, in some Member States, a 'permit defence' does exist for civil liability claims brought against a regulated entity that is operating within the terms of its permit. This position is found in at least Germany, Italy, Portugal, Spain and Latvia. This legal situation might seem more straightforward than cases where civil liability persists – public controls here simply override private rights. However, again, that characterisation is too crude. This is because most Member States limit the extent of any permit defence and, in some cases, allow third parties to challenge the content of any permit or to claim compensation in certain circumstances if there are adverse impacts on neighbouring properties. The common legal theme, where a permit defence against civil liability exists, is that the administrative law sphere is the primary legal sphere for controlling polluting emissions from land use, including their impacts on the amenity of neighbouring properties.

In those Member States where a permit defence applies, the basic concept is that a claim in nuisance (or some other form of civil liability between neighbours) will fail if the defendant is a regulated entity that is operating in accordance with the conditions of its permit in causing the alleged polluting harm. This is usually quite a strict defence. The Spanish position is representative – the defence will operate if the emissions that directly caused the relevant environmental damage fall within the express and specific purpose of an administrative authorisation. However, the defence will not operate where the emissions are due to actions that fall outside the terms of any permit; where there is some legal fault on the part of the defendant;[16] where there has been a criminal violation of public health or environmental law;[17] or, in Latvia at least, where the damage results from a 'high risk source'.[18]

[15] Maria Lee 'Safety, Regulation and Tort: Fault in Context' (2011) 74(4) MLR 555, 556. For more on the complex interplay of regulation and individual rights protected through private law in the UK, see Lee, ibid.

[16] Presumably this would be some form of negligence or intentional fault on the part of a defendant, even if the relevant polluting emissions do not strictly contravene permit limits.

[17] See M. Montini, Chapter Italy.

[18] See Z. Mikosa, Chapter Latvia.

The main concern of the permit defence that applies in these Member States is the robust regulation and control of any polluting emissions, rather than prioritising the interests of affected individuals (whether through the payment of compensation or injunctive relief to require cessation of regulated operations). In this way, a permit defence does not act as a shield to protect the emission of pollutants where these are excessive and not being properly regulated. The key difference from those Member States where civil liability persists is that any legal action brought by neighbouring properties in relation to offending pollution would be through administrative law or the regulatory system, not civil law. German law provides a good example of this model. In Germany, an affected neighbour might ask for technical improvements to the operations of an excessively polluting installation in line with 'best available techniques' where this is economically feasible.[19] The neighbour might also, under administrative law, ask the competent regulatory body to modify the permit and order the operator to improve the installation if it causes emissions having adverse effects on his/her health.[20] In other Member States, the position is similar – as a matter of legal doctrine, any permit allowing the offending emissions would need to be amended in the first instance, or lifted before a civil claim for damages could be brought. In addition, there might be other regulatory controls that require the operator of a polluting facility (even if operating within the terms of its permit) to remedy any damage caused by its operations.[21]

This state of affairs shows that the existence of a permit defence is not a blanket defence that insulates regulated entities from the consequences of their polluting activities once and for all after they have been granted a permit for their activities. Rather, in these Member States, the dominant sphere of legal control is different. It is the regulatory system and public law that aggrieved property owners affected by the polluting emissions of a regulated installation must rely on. Again, as in the case of civil liability claims, there is no absolute right of property owners to be protected from pollution or environmental damage, however any excessive harm or actual damage is likely to result in regulatory action (either to amend or withdraw the operational permit of a regulated entity).

---

19 BImSchG, art 14. Similarly, in Latvian law, a regulated entity could under obligations to act to prevent ongoing environmental damage to neighbouring properties, even though not civilly liable to pay the owners any compensation: see Chapter Latvia.

20 See G. Winter, Chapter Germany. Notably, compensation might still be payable in cases where an adverse interference with the rights of neighbouring properties is significant and sufficiently serious (that is, it is more serious than what is customary in the location). In this case, compensation will only be payable where preventive measures to deal with the adverse impact are too costly.

21 This is the position in Spain, where regulated entities are obliged at all times to adopt the measures of prevention, avoidance and remediation of environmental damage. However operators can recover the costs of such measures where they were complying with a permit and the damage was caused by an activity that at the time it was being carried out was not regarded as potentially harmful according to the state of scientific and technical knowledge: Article 14 of Law 26/2007 on environmental liability.

C. Conclusion

There are two overall conclusions that can be drawn from the comparative legal analysis of this chapter. First, careful characterisation of the applicable law in different Member States in relation to properties adversely affected by the emissions of a regulated installation shows that the position is more complex than there simply being two divergent approaches, one allowing a claim under civil law and the other not. In both cases, there are avenues of legal recourse for affected individual property owners. However, these avenues are different. In some Member States, private law remedies are important for vindicating individual property rights, whilst in others the public law sphere is the appropriate realm for regulating polluting installations and controlling their impacts. Whether or not this legal situation is by deliberate design in these different legal systems, it reflects varying legal cultures in which overlapping public law and private law rights are differently accommodated. In those states where there is a 'permit defence', the scope of regulatory authority as a source of norms and decision-making in relation to polluting installations is wider and takes priority. As a result, ex ante administrative controls of polluting activities (taking into account their impacts on neighbouring properties) take precedence over ex post judicial decisions concerning the infringement of private rights. In those states where no permit defence applies, individual property rights are protected by strong legal norms against a backdrop of increased regulatory decision-making at a community level. In this latter case, the private and public law layers of control remain distinct, so that individual property rights might be seen as an additional and supporting form of legal control and environmental protection when private properties are subject to environmental damage. This position reflects a different constitutional balance in relation to the rights of individual property owners, where judicial decision-making remains an important site of legal control.

Second, and as this concluding analysis already suggests, the proper characterisation of legal approaches in these cases is not mere legal semantics. There are doctrinal and practical consequences, and even constitutional dimensions. The predominance of the regulatory system in Member States such as Germany, Italy and Spain reflects a legal culture in which property rights have less priority and are more directly affected and effectively constituted by regulatory decisions over land use. In one sense, this is doctrinally cleaner – the public law sphere is primarily responsible for decision-making and control in relation to land use, which inevitably involves the accommodation of a wide range of interests (including private property interests) in a world of finite land-based resources. At the same time, in these Member States, the responsibility on regulatory authorities to protect the interests of individual property owners in their decision-making is significant, and the risk of regulatory capture or the poor resourcing of regulatory agencies could have serious consequences for individual property owners.

By contrast, in those Member State where civil liability persists irrespective of any regulatory permit possessed by the defendant – such as Belgium, Croatia, France and the United Kingdom – there is a more symbiotic relationship between private rights and public controls in relation to land. Both forms of control over land use respond to one another and arguably keep each other in check.[22] Individual property rights are an important legal line of defence where regulatory systems might be weak or compromised or too focused on expediency.

In the result, the comparative legal picture of the existence of a 'permit defence' in different EU Member State states shows that this deceptively simple legal question exposes an interesting, and perhaps inevitable, flashpoint in modern regulatory systems where property rights are subject to and affected by environmental controls. Public law and private law systems interact and doctrinally purity is difficult to sustain. The legal resolution of individual claims of civil liability against regulated entities reflects doctrinal choices that do not necessarily limit avenues of legal challenge and appeal for property owners, but which reflect different priorities given to regulatory systems, different constitutional approaches, and different conceptualisations of property rights.

[22] Scotford and Walsh (n 14).

Questionnaire

A. Objects of private property

What are, according to your country's legal system, potential objects of „property" (such as real things, private law rights, public law rights, a business, a market share etc) the use of which is being defended against environmental protection regulation?

B. Private property in natural resources

Are rights of using natural resources framed as property, such as a concession to exploit a resource or an authorisation/allowance to emit noxious substances? If not, is there nevertheless some kind of protection of trust in the perseverance of the authorisation?(Possible overlap with question 7))

C. Private property used in defense of environmental protection

Has private property been used in defence of environmental protection? How would the following case be treated in your country?

A factory, situated near a town, has been operating for decades. People are slowly realizing that statistically the inhabitants in the city and in the vicinity do not live average age and the cancer is more frequently present among them, also the frequent cause of the deaths. They have no direct proofs that the factory could be responsible, although it is rather clear that the soil around the factory is poisoned and that the heavy metals found in the vegetable could be linked to the factory. However, credible proofs are missing. What could be the obligation of the state? Could the inhabitants rely on the public remedies procedure? If the state wants to revoke the operation permit, could the factory claim any sort of property guarantee?

D. Natural resources as public property or interest

How is public management of natural resources legally framed (public domain, public trust, public property, land stewardship etc)? What specific legal duties and rights are attached to such construction?

E. Property in public aids for beneficial use of natural resources

Is the subsidisation of a beneficial use of natural resources (such as a guaranteed feed-in tariff for renewables) conceived as property? Is the legislator free to withdraw subsidies for budgetary or other reasons?

F. Expropriation

How does your legal system construe (direct) expropriation (definition, preconditions, and legal effects)?

G. Indirect expropriation by environmental regulation?

Concerning regulatory restrictions to use property: does your legal system distinguish between allowable restrictions and allowable restrictions with compensation? What are the criteria of distinction between the two kinds (weight of public interest, proportionality, etc)? Are these criteria sector-specific enriched, such as in nature protection from intensive agriculture, land-use planning, prevention of pollution from industrial installations, removal of water extraction rights, prevention of climate gas emissions etc?

H. Dissolution of property for environmental protection

Is there a category of (possibly: gradual) dissolution of vested rights without requirement of compensation for reasons of environmental protection (example of stepping out of nuclear power)?

I. State liability for environmental damage to private property

Concerning state liability: Is compensation provided for government based environmental deteriorations of private property (side effects of lawful measures, unlawful measures), including primary and secondary legal protection? How would the following case be treated in your country?

A communal waste disposal site is located not far away from a place with appr. 150 individual houses. Inhabitants assert that they smell bad odour and they would like to sell their property, but, of course, there are no potential buyers. Their property is almost worthless. The waste disposal site is equipped with the necessary permits.

Are the inhabitants in the neighbourhood entitled to compensation (perhaps to annual revenue)? Do they have to search for withdrawal of the operation permit first?

J. Proprietor's liability for environmental damage

Can one be responsible for the environmental damage only (solely) due to the fact of ownership of the property (i.e. for instance, the owner of the land where the waste is illegally deposited by the third (unknown) person)?

K. Permit excuse in environmental liability

Does the state permit (like IPPC permit, operation permit etc) exclude the holder from the liability towards third persons (in case of damage cause by undertakings)?

L. Direct or indirect expropriation by EU measures

How does your national legal system deal with situations where indirect or direct expropriation may be caused by EU legal acts or their implementation?